1

JOHN F. HALL

THE PENNSYLVANIA STATE UNIVERSITY

THE LIPPINCOTT COLLEGE
PSYCHOLOGY SERIES
UNDER THE EDITORSHIP OF

CARL P. DUNCAN, NORTHWESTERN UNIVERSITY
AND

JULIUS WISHNER, UNIVERSITY OF PENNSYLVANIA

PSYCHOLOGY

OF

MOTIVATION

J. B. LIPPINCOTT COMPANY
CHICAGO . PHILADELPHIA . NEW YORK

COPYRIGHT © 1961 BY J. B. LIPPINCOTT COMPANY
LIBRARY OF CONGRESS CATALOG CARD NUMBER: 61–10947
PRINTED IN THE UNITED STATES OF AMERICA

PREFACE

Since 1954 I have had the task of teaching a course in motivation for advanced undergraduate and graduate students, and for most of these years the only available text in the field was twenty years old. This lack of an up-to-date text was sufficiently annoying that within a few years, I decided to try to remedy this deficiency. The present text represents the culmination of these efforts.

In examining that which has been frequently described as motivational material, one cannot help but be impressed at the breadth of the subject matter and appalled at the confusion and lack of organization. As a result, a *primary objective* in writing has been to provide an *organization* which can incorporate much of the material traditionally found in this area. Although there may be some quarrel with this structure, the specific chapters represent topics which are familiar to most students working in the field, and, within limits, their order of presentation may be varied to suit the convenience of the instructor.

The breadth of the subject matter has necessitated my narrowing it to manageable proportions. Thus, much of the material frequently found in clinical and personality texts has been omitted, and I have been content to examine primarily the literature which may be loosely defined as *experimental*. It will be readily apparent to readers that in many areas this review has been selective rather than exhaustive. I hope that my selection, however, has not been biased by my own theoretical predilections. My object has been to present as representative a picture as possible of the current state of affairs and draw conclusions of a scope which can be borne by the weight of the evidence presented.

I have felt it important to discuss methodological problems from time to time, because it seems to me that many of our current motivational controversies cannot be settled until our methodological house is in order. And finally, I have tried to provide the reader with some historical perspective of many of our motivational concepts since in many instances investigators have been seemingly unaware of their historical antecedents.

Few texts are a product of a single individual, and this is no exception. My debts are many. Winfred F. Hill, Howard S. Hoffman, Douglas N. Jackson, William M. Lepley, Lorraine Low, Donald R. Meyer, and Delos D. Wickens were kind enough to read and comment upon various portions of the manuscript, while William F. Prokasy's review and detailed criticisms of the complete manuscript were most helpful. I am also grateful to Carl P. Duncan and Julius Wishner, co-editors of the LIPPINCOTT COLLEGE PSYCHOLOGY SERIES. Both of these men made suggestions which resulted in a number of important changes. I should like also to acknowledge the editorial work of Mrs. Ross Lehman who helped to make the text a more readable one. Finally, I am most grateful to my wife, Jean, whose help commenced with the transcribing of my original notes and continued with the typing of a number of rough drafts of the manuscript as well as the final one. It is to her that this book is affectionately dedicated.

I should like to express my thanks to the following individuals and organizations who very kindly gave me their permission to use figures or quotations obtained from their publications: J. R. Brobeck; H. F. Harlow; J. Mayer; N. E. Miller; C. Pfaffman; J. P. Quigley; J. B. Titchener; F. R. Treichler; *The American Journal of Clinical Nutrition; The American Journal of Psychology;* The American Psychological Association for its several journals; Annual Reviews, Inc.; Appleton-Century-Crofts, Inc.; Columbia University Press; Holt, Rinehart, and Winston, Inc.; The Journal Press; The Macmillan Company; The University of Nebraska Press; The New York Academy of Sciences; D. W. Norton and Company, Inc.;

Ronald Press; Charles Scribner's Sons; George Wahmann Manufacturing Company; John Wiley and Sons, Inc.; Williams and Wilkins Company; and Yale University Press.

University Park, Penna. · JOHN F. HALL
February, 1961

CONTENTS

ix

INTRODUCTION

1 • INTRODUCTION

Motivation is concerned with why individuals behave as they do. For as long as individuals have lived together, the importance of motivation has been profoundly appreciated by the individual operating as an individual or as a part of a larger social organization. The behavioral interaction that usually takes place among people in a society makes it important for the individual to constantly assess the motives of others as well as his own. Such an assessment begins early in life and continues until death.

Why does one child work hard in school, while another does not? Why does a student choose to attend one university rather than another, or select a given vocational goal? These are the questions that are answered only by analyzing the motives of the individuals concerned. It has been just as important for individuals, operating as members of a larger social group, to recognize the importance of motivation. Our law enforcement officers must usually determine the motive for a crime before going on to a successful solution. And neither judge nor jury look upon a premeditated killing in the same way as they look upon a killing in self defense. The motive becomes an important consideration before passing sentence. Our school systems have passed from a period when motivation for the child to learn was accomplished by frequent threats of punishment to a time when the child's interests play an ever increasing role in achieving learning. And our industrial organizations have become increasingly aware of the needs of their customers as well as their employees.

Only recently has motivation been of primary importance to the psychologist; nonetheless, its importance in psychological thought at the present time is challenged only by that of learning.

Although motivational constructs of some type have been in use for a long time, it is appropriate to discuss whether or not such constructs are necessary or useful for the scientists working in the area of behavior; for in recent years some have felt that motivational concepts have contributed little to the understanding of behavior, and have advocated their abandonment. The introduction of any concept in science, however, appears to be justified if it will aid in a better understanding of the subject matter. In psychology the need for a motivational construct is determined by whether or not it will help the psychologist in making better predictions about behavior. The question that must be raised is what are some of the conditions which have led to the inclusion of motivation as an important variable in most psychological systems?

When psychologists recognized that their primary objective was the prediction of behavior, the question of "why" made an immediate appearance. Why does an individual behave as he does? Perhaps even more basic was, "Why are organisms active at all?" The search for the origins of activity led to a consideration of the external stimulation that the organism received; quite frequently such stimulation was not correlated with the organism's activity. Richter (1922), an early behaviorist, set himself the task of determining what factors were responsible for "driving" the organism about in its environment. His experimental work led him to conclude that stomach contractions were one of the important internal factors upon which behavior is dependent.

The determination of the origins of activity, however, falls far short of predicting why one kind of response occurs rather than another. And such prediction has been difficult because of the tremendous variability that we find not only among living organisms, but within the same organism. Such variability of behavior, in spite of apparent constant external conditions, again leads one to look for some construct which can help in accounting for it. Let us examine the operation of this notion on a relatively simple level. A group of hungry rats is placed in Skinner boxes and given the same amount of training in the learning to press a bar for food. If the animals are then returned to the box forty-eight hours later, with some animals being satiated while others have not been fed for twelve or twenty-four hours, we find considerable variability among the groups with respect to the number of bar depressions. Our satiated group depresses the bar only a few times; the twelve-hour deprived group makes many more bar depressions, but our twenty-four hour group makes even more. It is obvious that such variability of behavior cannot be accounted for in terms of differences in the animal's external environment, nor in terms of previous learning. The differences in behavior must be accounted for by reference to some construct which is related to the internal state of the organism.

Or in the area of human behavior, the reason why one individual stops in front of a drinking fountain but another does not cannot usually be found in analyzing whether or not each knows the location of the fountain, or in the number of times each individual has stopped there in the past, but in knowing whether or not either is thirsty. Furthermore, a knowledge of how thirsty the individual is will enable us to make a prediction not only about whether the individual will drink, but also how much water will be ingested.

Although the presence of internal conditions or physiological states of the organism is important in a better understanding of the variability of behavior, the relationship they bear to the presence of goal objects or incentives is likewise important. A hungry rat running a simple T maze finds food in the left alley and an empty goal box in the right. Examining the animal's behavior over the course of a number of trials, we find he turns to the left with greater and greater frequency, until finally a left-turning response almost always occurs when he is placed in that situation. In this instance, it is to be noted that a knowledge of the internal state of the organism *as well as its relationship to some goal object* enables us to predict something about the animal's response with an accuracy that is considerably greater than chance.

The role of internal states in the human, in contrast to organisms lower on the phylogenetic scale, is somewhat more obscure in the determination of behavior. As a result, more emphasis is placed upon the motivational constructs of goals and incentives when dealing with humans.

A boy who seeks attention from his classmates may first try to obtain it by being a good student. If he is not successful, he may attempt to gain attention by becoming proficient in some athletic endeavor. Again failing, he may find that the only way to get attention would be to engage in some anti-social behavior. The understanding of such variable behavior is possible, not through the knowledge of some internal state of the organism, but through an understanding of the goal which the individual seeks.

Finally, analysis of behavior frequently reveals that some organisms, in contrast to others, exert more energy and do so for longer periods of time in their attempt to obtain some particular goal object. The cat which is hungry when placed in a puzzle box with a piece of food on the outside will persist in its attempt to get out for a much longer time than will the satiated animal. So it is with humans. Again, in an attempt to account for differences in the persistence of the organism, recourse is made to a construct which is related to (a) certain internal conditions of the organism as well as (b) certain goal objects.

Note that we have not, as yet, defined motivation. In fact, we will find that it is probably impossible to state a definition of motivation which all psychologists would accept. Nonetheless, we have pointed out that certain conditions are important in helping us make a better prediction about an organism's behavior.

In summary then, it appears that the use of motivational constructs can be justified in order to predict something about (1) the activity level of the organism, (2) the direction of such activity, and, finally, (3) the organism's persistence in attempting to reach an appropriate goal object.

2 • INSTINCT

In man's long history of persistent effort to account for his own as well as the behavior of other organisms, a number of motivational constructs have been posited. Probably the most frequently used has been the concept of instinct. Wiln (1925) has credited the Stoic philosophers of the first century A.D. with its early beginnings; discussion could begin almost any time thereafter, inasmuch as it has proven to be a hardy concept. Since we are concerned primarily with psychological thought, the treatment of instinct by William James (1890) is an appropriate starting place.———

James defined psychology as the science of mental life—the sensations and feelings, desires and cognitions of the organism. These manifest themselves, however, in movement or behavior, and such behavior could be classified into (1) voluntary and (2) automatic.⇐ It was voluntary behavior under which James subsumed instincts. James' discussion of instinct is important because he provided a presentation from which many subsequently borrowed. First, he recognized the importance of a careful definition of the term, and he believed the older writings on the topic were ineffectual wastes of words. In contrast to these older writings, he defined an ⇐ instinct as the faculty of acting in such a way as to produce a certain end, without foresight of that end, and without the individual's having previous education in the performance. Looked at from a slightly different point of view, instincts were the functional correlates of structure.

It was James' contention, contrary to popular belief at the time, that man had more instincts than any other animal. In fact, he contended that man had so many that they frequently tended to obscure one another. A partial list of them included sucking, clasping, crying, sitting up, standing, locomotion, vocalization, imitation, rivalry, pugnacity, sympathy, acquisitiveness, play, curiosity, and jealousy.

These instincts were not blind and invariable, however, for experience combined with them to produce behavior that frequently differed from the original act. ". . . *every instinctive act, in an animal with memory, must cease to be 'blind' after being once repeated,* and must be accompanied with foresight of its 'end' just so far as that end may have fallen under the animal's cognizance" (James, 1890). In contrast to more mechanistic definitions of instinct, James' conception contained experiential, perceptual, as well as cognitive aspects.

Structuralism

Paralleling James during this era was the psychology of Wundt and Titchener. For these men and their students, the subject matter of psychology was the science of "consciousness" or of the mind, and the method of analysis was that of introspection. With the primary task of the psychologist to analyze consciousness into its elements or component parts, the problem of why man acted as he did was not a question to be answered within the framework of their definition of psychology.

Titchener did acknowledge the instinctive aspects of behavior, but for him, it was only the conscious content of the instinctive act, and not the instinct itself that could be properly studied by the psychologist:

. . . the plan and programme of a psychology of instinct seems clear enough. The term is common to two distinct sciences, psychology and biology; and the result of this community has been that the psychologists are tempted to write a speculative biology, and the biologists to manufacture a psychology of instinct. The mutual recrimination that has ensued is a doubtful gain to science. What we have to do is to leave biology to formulate its own problem, and to accept its solution of that problem, while we ourselves, as psychologists, describe and explain the instinctive consciousness (Titchener, 1913).

Functionalism

Although the Functionalists recognized that the study of behavior could be included in their definition of psychology, the question of "why" continued to be ascribed to instinct. Although no single volume or article represented Functionalism as Titchener's *A Text-Book of Psychology* represented Structuralism, Angell's *Psychology* (1908) may be viewed as representative of the early thinking of one of its founders. For Angell, psychology continued to be the science of consciousness; however, conscious content had its ultimate significance and final outcome in motor activities. And in the analysis of such motor activities, Angell posited the importance of instinct in accounting for them. Angell's list of instincts included fear, anger, shyness, curiosity, affection, sexual love, jealousy and envy, rivalry, sociability, sympathy, modesty, play, imitation, constructiveness, secretiveness, and acquisitiveness.

Behaviorism

Watson's early Behaviorism continued in the same vein. Although he recognized inherent difficulties in using the term instinct (i.e., the widely different meanings attached to it), nonetheless, its usefulness and convenience led him to accept it as part of his early system. In his work, *Behavior, An Introduction to Comparative Psychology* published in 1914, he conceived of instinct as being a series of innate reflexes which unfold under appropriate stimulation. Although Watson felt that it was impossible, with the survey of animal activity that had been made up to that time, to provide a complete inventory of the various classes of instinct, the following general classes were posited: action systems, obtaining food, shelter, rest, sleep, play, sex, defense and attack, and vocalization.

Five years later Watson's point of view, expressed in his *Psychology from the Standpoint of a Behaviorist* (1919), had not changed. Broadly conceived, instinct was a hereditary mode of response; examined more analytically, it was a system of chained reflexes. Watson pointed out that no one had succeeded in making even a helpful classification of instincts, and it was far more difficult to devise such a classification for the human than for the infrahuman organism. Fairly serviceable classifications in the animal world were food-getting; home-building; attack and defense; and migration. He indicated that most of the instincts attributed to man (acquisition and possession, hunting, collecting, hoarding, migration, gregariousness, manipulation, imitation, etc.) were really consolidations of both habit and instinct.

William McDougall

American psychology was dominated by Structuralism and Functionalism at the time that McDougall brought into focus the problem which psychologists up until that time had considered only as a peripheral area of inquiry—the problem of *why* man behaves rather than merely how. In a series of publications, beginning with his *Primer of Physiological Psychology* (1908), McDougall defined psychology as the science of conduct or behavior. He felt that a somewhat similar definition adopted by the Behaviorists a few years later was carried to an extreme by their rejection of introspection as a method, by their lack of concern over the problem of experience and consciousness, by their rejection of 'mind' [1] and by their emphasis upon the fact that human conduct was determined wholly and strictly by the mechanical action of the body.

It was in his *Introduction to Social Psychology* (1926), that McDougall advanced his basic thesis. The fundamental tenet of all behavior, animal or human, was its purposiveness. Behavior was directed toward a goal or an end, and it was this end that was clearly anticipated or foreseen by the organism. The key to the understanding of such behavior lay in the knowledge that the human mind has certain innate tendencies which are essentially springs or motive powers of all thought and action. These tendencies were classified as instincts. More specifically, an instinct was responsible

---

[1] McDougall writes, "The mechanistic psychologist will say: What you call 'the mind' is just what I call 'the brain.' Why go out of your way to set up this vague, mysterious, purely hypothetical *something* which, as you admit, no one has ever seen or handled or can hope to see or handle, while all the time you have the brain, as solid and as real as a lump of cheese, which we positively know to be concerned in all experience and in all behavior, and about which the labor of thousands of expert workers has built up an immense mass of knowledge? To this I would reply: I do not underrate the value of this physiological knowledge and research; but I assert that, in the present state of science, it is not profitable to substitute the brain for the mind. To do so limits unduly our freedom of thought; it ties us down to one kind of explanation, leads us to absurd consequences . . . and worst of all, is apt to blind us to facts of observation, and biases our interpretation of other facts" (McDougall, 1923).

for (1) the organism's perceiving one class of objects rather than another, (2) its experiencing in their presence a certain emotional excitement, and (3) either a specific act toward the object or an impulse to such action. Each instinct involved, then, a perceptual, an emotional, and a motivational aspect. Instinctive responses became capable of being initiated not only by the perception of objects of the kind which directly excited the innate disposition, but also by ideas of such objects and by perceptions and ideas of objects of other kinds.

Instinctive behavior did not necessarily reflect itself in stereotype of movement, but was indicated by a change in the organism's situation which its actions, regardless of type, tended to bring about and which, once achieved, brought the behavior to an end. In his *Outline of Psychology*, published in 1923, McDougall posited fourteen such instincts—escape, combat, repulsion, parental, appearance, mating, curiosity, submission, assertion, social or gregariousness, food seeking, acquisition, construction, and laughter.

Sigmund Freud

The psychoanalytic movement was not in the experimental tradition, but it must be given consideration in our discussion of instinct, for it lent support to the growing movement in psychology which placed emphasis upon the motivational aspects of human behavior.

The central thesis of Freud's system was that all behavior was a reflection of the operation of some motive, conscious or unconscious, operating within the individual. The forgetting of a familiar name, the slip of the tongue, or an apparent blunder all reflected a real but unacknowledged motive. The basis of such motivation was reflected in the instinctive capacity of the individual.[2]

The development of a theory of instincts was regarded by Freud as one of the most basic problems in psychology. In his volume, *An Autobiographical Study* (1927), he stated that the need was urgent for psychologists to build a securely founded theory of in-

[2] Most historians agree that instinct as postulated by Freud had little in common with traditional definitions. In fact, it has frequently been pointed out that its use in American psychology came about as a result of an inexact translation of the German word *Trieb*, which has connotation closer to drive than to instinct. From a historical point of view, it seems appropriate to discuss his contributions at this point.

stincts. He regretted that nothing of the sort existed, however, and that psychoanalysis was driven toward making tentative efforts toward some such theory.

Freud's definition of instinct varied, depending upon the time that he wrote. Most frequently, he wrote of instincts as being forces or energies which were directed toward some object. In his *Three Essays on the Theory of Sexuality,* published in 1905, instinct was conceived of as ". . . the psychical representative of an endosomatic, continuously flowing source of stimulation, as contrasted with a 'stimulus,' which is set by single excitations coming from without." Thus instinct was a pressure which produced the need for a response and impelled its execution. The goal of an instinct was defined as "the act toward which the instinct tends," i.e., a consummatory act. Inasmuch as not all instinctual energy was expended in the same type of behavior, Freud classified different instincts in terms of their aims.

The Decline of Instinct

With the opportunity to explain the motivational aspects of behavior by instinct, it is not surprising that the lists of instincts posited by writers working in the field continued to expand. A survey made by Bernard (1924) indicated that in approximately 500 books and periodicals, representing over 400 authors who employed the concept of instinct, no fewer than 849 separate types or variations were put forth. Of these, 504 were sufficiently distinct to warrant their classification as separate and distinct, and from these it was possible to construct 325 separate or irreducible classes.

The concept was used principally in one or two ways, and the distinction between them was not always recognized or made explicit. First, the concept was frequently used in a *descriptive* sense. Thus it was used to indicate or denote that the behavior under consideration was innate or unlearned. In this sense, when an investigator wrote about a kind of behavior which was instinctive he meant that such a behavior pattern was unlearned. Secondly, many authors used the term as an *explanation* for certain kinds of behavior. That is, instinct was a motivator or an impeller of action. Under the circumstances, if an author wrote of the fighting instinct, he meant that the reason *why* an organism engaged in such behavior was because of an instinct to do so.

The attack upon the use of the concept was signalled by Dunlap's article "Are there any Instincts?" (1919–1920) and was followed by many others, notably Kuo (1921, 1922, 1924), Bernard (1921), Ayres (1921), and Faris (1921, 1922). In 1924 Bernard's classic text on instinct appeared. Bernard continued the attack on the concept by summarizing much of what had been written previously as well as providing basic arguments of his own.

In general, the arguments against the use of the concept were as follows: first, it was obvious to many that behavior patterns which had been labeled as instinctive, and thus presumed to be innate or unlearned actually had large amounts of learned components within them. The positing of an "instinct for parliamentary government" or an "instinct for salmon fishing" illustrates such a point of view. When instinct was defined as an impeller of action or as a motivator, it was recognized that such a definition was not an explanation. Holt (1931) in criticizing the concept wrote, "For instance; man is impelled to action, it is said, by his instincts. If he goes with his fellows, it is the 'herd instinct' which actuates him; if he walks alone, it is the 'anti-social instinct'; if he fights, it is the instinct of 'pugnacity'; if he defers to another, it is the instinct of 'self-abasement'; . . . Thus everything is explained with the facility of magic—word magic." Finally, it was further recognized that instinct used as an explanation prevented further inquiry into more basic explanations for the behavior under consideration.

The net result was that there was an attempt on the part of many writers to divorce the concept from psychological thinking and writing. In 1925 instinct was completely divorced from Watsonian behaviorism. Watson (1925) indicated that there was no longer any need for the term, that everything the psychologist had been in the habit of calling instinct belonged to man's learned behavior. In the score of years that followed most psychologists agreed that the term had no place in psychology.[3]

The Return of Instinct

Lashley's American Psychological Association presidential address in 1938, *An Experimental Analysis of Instinctive Behavior,* was a

[3] The need for the use of such a concept as instinct was not eliminated by merely abandoning the term. It was apparent to a number of investigators that many types of behavior too complex to be considered as reflex action appeared although the organism did not have the opportunity to learn such behavior. The terms "unlearned" or "innate" rather than "instinctive" were applied to such behavior. Allport's (1924) maturation hypothesis was an example of this approach. This hypothesis posited that some behavior came about entirely as a result of a maturing or ripening of physiological or neural components.

prime indicator that instinct would again return to the vocabulary of the psychologist. Lashley believed that the study of instinct involved two problems. The first was investigating the responses of the organism to definite objects. Thus the primiparous female rat gathers paper to build a nest or cleans her young of foetal membranes. With this type of problem, it was necessary to analyze the properties of the stimulus which were actually effective in arousing behavior. Accumulated observations, Lashley noted, suggested that instinctive behavior was sometimes dependent upon a complex of stimuli, while at other times such behavior seemed to be aroused by only single elements within the complex.

The second problem that Lashley delineated was the investigation of responses to a stimulus deficit. A mother rat deprived of her young responds by running restlessly—a chick deprived of companions inhibits its feeding responses. Lashley noted that when theories of drive were first conceptualized, there was no evidence that activity could be sustained or continued within the central nervous system, hence the need to look for peripheral stimulation which would arouse and sustain activity. Since the discovery of recurrent nervous system circuits, it was no longer necessary to depend upon a somatic sensory facilitation base for motivational theory. Activity measured by the obstruction apparatus, for example, did not represent continuous peripheral stimulation but was an expression of central nervous system activity. All cases of motivation were not disturbances of organic equilibrium but merely the excitation of a specific sensory motor mechanism irradiating to affect other reaction systems.

Contemporary Points of View

Although some psychologists feel that the concept of instinct should be abandoned, a more prevalent position is best exemplified by the experimental work of Stone, Beach, and others. These investigators have been less interested in the classification of behavior than in assessing those factors that are responsible for its development and organization. From their point of view, the experimental analysis of those activities which have been frequently labeled "instinctive" is essentially no different from the analysis of "learned behavior," although the choice of variables to investigate may differ, depending upon whether or not the investigator believes the response to be studied is innate or acquired.

Beach's (1951) analysis of reproductive activities, a type of behavior which has been frequently classified as instinctive, is illustrative of the method employed as well as the type of information obtained. Beach has analyzed such behavior in terms of (a) the contribution of external stimulation, (b) the contribution of internal factors, and (c) its development and modification by experience.

In examining external stimulation factors, one finds that stimulation which plays a part in the sexual response may be of such a nature as to change the physiological readiness of the organism. These experimental factors do not evoke the sexual response but rather prepare the organism for a response to more specific types of sensory cues. The experimental work of a number of investigators has shown that by manipulating either lighting or temperature conditions a number of small mammals can be brought into full breeding conditions during those months in which this typically would not occur. Dawson (1941), for example, has demonstrated that although the normal oestrus season in cats seems to be from February to June, it is possible to produce oestrus in November and December by subjecting them to increased daily artificial illumination.

Other external stimuli may actually elicit the sexual response itself. Aronson (1948) has shown that the female African mouth-breeder fish seldom digs a nest, lays eggs, or shows other sexual activity if she is visually isolated. If another mouth-breeder can be seen, however, such activity is periodically elicited. Tinbergen (1951) in his work with the stickleback fish has found that visual cues provided only by the female arouse sexual behavior. Females that contain eggs have swollen abdomens. Nest-guarding males display courtship behavior when the visual stimulation in the form of a model which has the abdominal region enlarged is presented. Sexual responses on the part of the male are not evoked if the abdominal area on the model is slim.

In the analysis of stimuli which were adequate in eliciting mating behavior in the rat, Beach (1942) found that neither olfactory, visual, nor cutaneous sensitivity was necessary for the arousal of copulatory behavior in the inexperienced male rat. The elimination of one of these modalities did result in a reduction of the excitability of the male. The probability of copulatory behavior was further reduced if more than one modality was eliminated.

The second area of investigation has centered around the internal correlates of sexual behavior. It has been found, for example, that alterations in parts of the nervous system or in the organism's blood chemistry may seriously affect sexual activity. Beach (1940), found a significant relationship between the amount of cortex removed from the male rat and (1) its sexual responsiveness as well as (2) its frequency of copulation. Animals with less than 20 per cent of their cortex removed continued to copulate normally; as cortex removal was increased from 20 per cent to 60 per cent, the frequency of copulation systematically decreased.

The last area to be considered concerns how sexual responses develop as a result of experience. As an example of such research Stone (1922) has reported that sexually mature rats, although reared in isolation, display essentially the same type of mating pattern as experienced animals. The importance of an organism's position on the phylogenetic scale for such behavior is indicated by the work of Bingham (1928), and Yerkes and Elder (1936) who have reported that the coital responses of sexually inexperienced monkeys and apes are usually not successful.

The experimental work indicates, then, that sexual behavior as an example of a so-called instinct develops in various ways and may be controlled by manipulating internal as well as external conditions. Beach (1951) points out that such experimental evidence would seem to contraindicate the classification of sexual behavior as instinctive or unlearned. Discarding the concept of instinct, however, should not force individuals into making the error of classifying all behavior as learned, for the present conceptualization of learning seems too confused to be very useful in understanding much of the variable and complex behavior that occurs under natural conditions. Beach believes that the most fruitful approach would be to discard the unlearned-learned dichotomy of classifying behavior and simply study a greater number of responses so that they can profitably be compared and contrasted. Thus, when several kinds of responses in a number of species have been analyzed, it is then possible to compare the same pattern in different species or different patterns in the same species. It is by these means that we can hope to understand how an animal's "instinctive" behavior resembles and differs from its performance in a maze or a puzzle box, and only after such an analysis will differences and similarities in any given type of activity be understood.

Ethology and the Concept of Instinct

A few years before Lashley made his presidential address, which, it will be recalled, touched upon the topic of instinct, an approach to behavior which also emphasized instinct, and which is now described as the ethological movement, had its primary impetus from the work of Konrad Lorenz (1937). This approach stressed the examination of behavior which was typical of animals living in their natural environment in contrast to that which was controlled or limited by experimental surroundings. Lorenz posited that basic in the analysis of such behavior were the animals' innate behavior patterns or instinctive acts. His position was that such behavior patterns were something that animals of a given species *had* in the sense that they had claws or teeth or a definite morphological structure. In a sense, such a point of view provided an approach to the taxonomic analysis of behavior.

In 1951, Tinbergen published *The Study of Instinct*. At that time, this text was one of the best sources for American investigators to become acquainted with the ethological approach to instinct. The theoretical model as proposed by Tinbergen and in its barest outline was that the instinctive act was a rigidly stereotyped, innate movement based upon the activity of a specific co-ordinating center localized in the nervous system of the organism. In this center, there was a continuous accumulation of energy which was specific for the instinctive act itself. When the organism contacted an appropriate external situation for the performance of the act, the stimuli provided by the situation released the energy, the instinctive act was performed and the excitation was dissipated. The center specific for the act was thus able to co-ordinate the instinctive act completely independently of the receptors. Once the act was released, the performance occurred in complete form, co-ordinated by impulses from the center and without chain reflex characteristics.

The model as outlined by Tinbergen (1951) had a number of provocative hypotheses. One of these had to do with the accumulation of specific energy for a given action. Basically, it was postulated that some sort of energy specific to one definite activity accumulates; as it accumulates, it results in lowering the threshold to certain kinds of stimulation. The threshold for such stimulation is not constant, however, but undergoes a continuous process of lowering which goes on throughout the time during which the reaction does not come about. This gradual lowering of threshold may presumably reach the theoretically possible limit of zero, when the activity in question would go off in a vacuum without the appropriate stimulation.

The consequences of the damming up of certain innate activities were not confined to lowering the threshold of the mechanism which released the activity, but there was also an active and particular excitation which influenced the whole organism whenever it found its outlet for the stimulation blocked. The undischarged activity resulted in a kind of generalized tension state which produced random activity until the appropriate stimuli were encountered, at which time the instinctive act was performed with the dissipation of the energy which had been accumulated.

A second hypothesis concerned the action of an innate releasing mechanism or IRM. Although there is a presumed accumulation of energy specific for a given behavior pattern, it is obvious that the behavior is not continuously performed. It is not performed because of the postulation of an inhibitory center—an innate releasing mechanism. The effect of appropriate external stimulation is to release the instinctive center from this inhibition. We may then liken the accumulation of action-specific energy to the conception of a wound-up spring. Such a conception implies the existence of some trigger mechanism—a mechanism which holds the action of the spring back until the right moment, at which time it is set off. The observational facts are suggestive of a mechanism something like that of a filter letting through only certain or particular stimuli while excluding others.

The theoretical system of Lorenz and Tinbergen, although enthusiastically supported by many workers in the field, has not gone unchallenged. One specific criticism of their point of view has centered around their postulation that particular stimuli have the capacity to elicit specific behavior patterns. Tinbergen (1951) postulated that "shape in relation to direction of movement" acts as a sign stimulus for young gallinaceous birds, ducks, and geese, independently of any previous experience with these configurations—thus, the same shape moving in different directions serves as a sign to release different responses. Tinbergen has reported that a cardboard model designed to look like a hawk when flown in one direction resulted in escape reactions, whereas this same model when flown in the opposite direction looks like a goose and elicited only superficial interest on the part of the subjects. Recent experimental findings by Hirsch, Lindley, and Tolman (1955) and Rockett (1955), two of the few American studies investigating the Lorenz-Tinbergen approach, have not confirmed the Tinbergen hypothesis. In the first study, "hawk" and "goose" models were presented to eight-week-old leghorn chickens, and an analysis of the animals' fear responses did not reveal differences between the two models.[4]

The most basic criticism of this approach, however, has been provided in the articles of Lehrman (1953), Hebb (1953), and Verplanck (1955) and has been directed at the classification of behavior as "innate" or "instinctive," as contrasted to behavior which is learned. Lehrman (1953) has pointed out that by classifying behavior as "innate," Lorenz and Tinbergen have led investigators away from rather than toward the specific origins of behavior patterns. In essence, such criticism is in keeping with the general approach taken by Beach (1951, 1955) and presented earlier; that is, the labeling of a given pattern of behavior as "innate" precludes further analysis of it. Or as Verplanck (1955) has written:

As we list the criteria proposed for distinguishing the innate from the learned, many examples of learned behavior can be found that satisfy one or more—or most—of the criteria for the innate. Stereotypy, universality of appearance, orderliness, adaptivity, resistance to modification—all of these fail, and only one criterion remains: execution of the behavior on its first opportunity to occur, *without* the possibility of previous learning. *How* does one rule this out?

We are forced into the position of acknowledging that the only criterion for distinguishing between innate and acquired behavior is one that requires us to accept the null hypothesis as proven.

We are forced into the position that no meaningful distinction can be drawn between learned and innate behavior, that is, between the stereotyped and highly predictable behavior studied in inframammalians by the ethologists, and the more variable behavior studied in the T maze and Skinner box. We can no more distinguish between behavior that is innate and behavior that is learned than physicists can distinguish between light that is made up of corpuscles and light that is made up of transverse vibrations.

The result has been as Verplanck (1958) has written, " . . . most ethologists have radically changed their viewpoint on the interrelationships between genetic structure and behavior: instinct is once again dead." [5]

[4] In reply to the work of Hirsch, Lindley, and Tolman (1955), Tinbergen (1957) has pointed out that a large number of factors could account for the divergent findings. In general, he pointed out that: "Facts found in one species, or hypothesis formed about one species, simply cannot be disproved by testing another species . . ." Hirsch (1957) has replied that inasmuch as chickens are gallinaceous birds Tinbergen's original postulation should be modified.

[5] It should not be assumed that the elimination of the concept of instinct has resulted in any lessening of the importance of what may be conceived as the ethological point of view. For a description of the work that is carried on in this area, the reader is referred to articles by Verplanck (1958) and Hinde (1959).

3 . DRIVE AND MOTIVE—
NATURE AND FUNCTION

As we have noted, the period of the early twenties was a time when psychologists placed greater emphasis upon the dynamic aspects of behavior. Concomitantly, the concept of instinct which had played such an important role in the movement was in the process of being discarded. The result, as Harlow states (1953), was that the motivational theory of the Behaviorists was left with an aching void. Biologists of this time, however, were also interested in the problems of motivation, and it would appear that psychologists of this era were much indebted to them for their contributions to this area.

BIOLOGICAL ANTECEDENTS OF DRIVE AND MOTIVE

One of the contemporary biological theories of behavior during that era was the tropism, conceived by Jacques Loeb (1918), who believed that behavior could be explained in terms of forced orientation of the organism, based upon the symmetrical structure of the body. Loeb postulated that the processes which produced movement in the organism were equal in both halves of the central nervous system, and this resulted in the organism's locomoting in a straight line. If external stimuli resulted in an increase in velocity of chemical reactions on just one side of the body, however, the physiological symmetry of both sides of the central nervous system was upset. The muscles connected to the side which had the increased velocity of chemical processes contracted more strongly, and, as a result, the muscles turned the organism toward the source of stimulation. This adjustment continued until central nervous system activity was again symmetrical, which then resulted in a straight-line movement. Thus the conduct of the animal consisted of movements which were essentially dictated or forced by the external stimulation.

In contrast to Loeb's emphasis upon external stimulation and essentially stereotyped movement, Jennings (1906) emphasized the importance of internal states and trial-and-error behavior. Jennings posited that the physiological state of the organism was the sum total of all of the physiological factors which determine the excito-motor integration pattern at any given moment. When interferences with such processes occurred, the organism's behavior changed inasmuch as motility was a fundamental aspect of the action system of the organism. Although the organism's movements were random, and thus not necessarily directed toward a relief of the disturbance of the physiological state, some movements might provide relief, resulting in cessation of such activity. Trial and error behavior was fundamental to any behavior analysis, as was the process of adjustment or regulation. In fact, from Jennings' point of view, behavior was adjustment or regulation.

Early Psychological Points of View

The biological point of view of Jennings is evident in Richter's *A Behavioristic Study of the Activity of the Rat* (1922), which represented an early attempt to handle motivation of the organism without recourse to instinct. Richter noted that psychologists were becoming more interested in the problems of learning, or as he termed it, general adaptation, and that the problem of *why* the organism works dealt with the more dynamic aspects of behavior. This required the determination of the origin of the organism's activity—that is, what it was that drove it about in its environment.

For Richter, the origin or source of the activity was contained within the organism, and his search for the source led him to study the stomach. Cannon and Washburn (1912) had found that contractions in the empty stomach seemed to coincide with rate of spontaneous activity; Richter used such evidence to conclude that stomach activity was the cause of gross bodily activity.

Richter's analysis of the interrelationship between learning and motivation has a surprisingly contemporary ring. At birth, he noted, members of the mammalian species have stomach contractions almost continuously. The contractions furnish the drive for continuous activity. When the random activity does result in the animal's mouth contacting the teats of the mother, sucking movements are elicited; the subsequent flow of milk relieves the stomach contractions, and a period of quiescence follows. When the contractions commence again, the whole process is repeated. As this trial-and-error process goes on, the onset of the stomach contractions becomes more and more associated with the motor movements associated with the relief of the contractions, while other responses fall into disuse.

Richter incorporated such an analysis within the concept of equilibrium. He felt that there was a tendency in all living organisms to maintain a metabolic balance or equilibrium. In the case of hunger, the stomach was empty and the balance was destroyed. The physiological conditions produced by the lack of food were looked upon as agents which set up the process of re-establishing equilibrium.

An examination of Richter's paper reveals two major hypotheses: (1) disturbances in the internal state of the organism drive the organism about in its environment and (2) such disturbances result in disequilibrium, so that the organism's activity is directed toward the re-establishment of equilibrium.

It was the first hypothesis which resulted in considerable experimental interest. Wang (1923), working under Richter, demonstrated that increasing periods of activity in the female rat coincided with its oestrus cycle, while Hoskins (1925), a short time later, found decreasing activity in male rats which had been castrated. About this time, Moss published his famous study of *Animal Drives* (1924). Continuing in the same vein as Richter, it was Moss's basic thesis that the behavior of any animal was dependent upon its drive state, as well as the "opposing resistances." By drive Moss meant "the impelling forces in the situation that stimulate the animal toward certain positive behavior." For example, if an animal is kept without food for a certain length of time, certain organic stimulation of the nerve endings in the stomach provoke in the animal restless and seeking behavior until food is found and the "drive" is stopped for the time being. A series of eleven experiments was performed in an effort to develop a method for quantifying drives and resistances. Work by Tsai (1925) and Warden and his students, summarized in Warden's *Animal Motivation Studies* (1931), continued on this same problem.

In 1927, Richter published *Animal Behavior and Internal Drives*. This paper was a continuation of his early study and investigated the relationship between spontaneous activity and a number of physiological states. As in his earlier work, Richter attempted to show that the spontaneous activity of the rat was periodic and dependent upon periodically functioning organs. Notable was his attempt to use a "balloon in the stomach" technique with the rat, bullfrog, pigeon, human infant, and the adult human in order to relate stomach contractions to gross bodily activity.

Carr, in an introductory text (1925), was one of the first to incorporate and to elaborate on the then current thinking about motivation. A motive was defined as a relatively persistent stimulus that dominated the behavior of an organism until it responded in such a manner that it was no longer affected by it. Hunger, thirst, sex, pain, and extremes of temperature were some of the more important and fundamental human motives. These fundamental motives were often called "organic needs" because their satisfaction was essential to the continued welfare and existence of the organism or the species. Although such motives were also referred to at times as drives, Carr believed that the drive concept should not imply that an individual would cease to act without its presence. Motives were not essential to activity, but they were to be regarded as forces which determined the direction of behavior. Thus Carr placed emphasis upon what he called the directive function of a motive, in contrast to Richter (1922), who emphasized its energizing function.

The place of a drive state in animal behavior was obvious—Carr felt that drive had an important applicability to human behavior as well. He reasoned that the hunger drive was responsible for all of the activities involved in the production, distribution, and preparation of food, while the need for equable temperature resulted in all of the activities involved in production of clothing, heat, and shelter. The sex motive also had wide ramifications, for it exerted an influence upon dress, social custom, art, literature, and law, and was indirectly responsible for the family organization of society and the various agencies concerned with the education and care of the young.

Tolman (1925–1926) posited the existence of second-order drives as well as primary ones in order to encompass human behavior within the drive system. First-order drives, broken down into appetites and aversions, had direct and immediate physiological implications; second-order drives did not. An appetite such as hunger evoked an internal physiological disturbance which drove the organism to "seek" a given type of situation.

Interestingly enough, Tolman focused attention on an area which has continued to interest motivational theorists—that of incentive motivation. In certain instances it seemed as if the presence of an appropriate goal object "aroused" the appetite which then led to the consummatory response. The example used was that of a pretty girl who aroused the sex drive which up to that time was apparently not present. Tolman's solution was that a true understanding of the case would indicate that the drive was already somewhat aroused, and the presence of the goal object merely hastened the process. Although second-order drives had no physiological basis, they were built upon and causally determined by first-order ones. Candidates for such second-order drives were curiosity, gregariousness, self-assertion, self-abasement, and imitativeness. Precisely how these drives were built upon first-order ones was not indicated, although there is some indication that Tolman believed that these second-order drives were present in varying degrees along with primary ones. His method for the investigation of the second-order drives was to control the strengths of the first-order ones, and then to seek to discover what correlated variations would appear in the strengths of the various second-order ones.

In 1928, Dashiell's introductory text appeared, and motivation was given a prominent place in its organization. Dashiell's discussion of motivation was similar to Carr's, except that the physiological aspects of motivation were given more prominence. Dashiell's contention was that the basis from which man's elaborate motives originate was found in the tissue conditions—the primary drives which gave rise to stimulation and excited the organism to overt activity. The functions of the motive were two: (1) an energizing function—"to get a man into action" and (2) a directive one.

With regard to the energizing function, Dashiell, like Carr, did not assume that without a motive there would be a "motionless" organism, for he recognized that spontaneous activity could be primarily an expression of the metabolic functioning of the individual. The tendency of the healthy, adult man was to be doing something rather than to be lying motionless.

It was the directive function, however, to which Dashiell paid primary attention. He noted that the general hypertonicity and activity seen in infancy and aroused by the organic needs was eventually directed to highly differentiated and elaborate objectives. This was the problem that Tolman solved by positing the existence of second-order drives. Although Dashiell felt that the knowledge of how the native sources of energy develop divisions into definite lines of activity was incomplete, he emphasized learning principles as one solution. The most important principle, based upon stimulus substitution, was that external stimuli achieve increasing importance in arousing activity. More specifically, Dashiell felt that when an external stimulus occurred frequently with the drive stimulus, the external stimulus became a substitute for the drive. Thus he established the early beginnings of the concept of acquired motives.

The Concept of Adjustment

It will be recalled that an important contribution of Richter's *A Behavioristic Study of the Activity of the Rat* (1922) was the suggestion of a regulatory or adjustment process found in the behavior of the organism. This process was accepted by most biologists and although applied by them to physiological functioning was also extended to behavior. Child (1924) stated that in studying the functional activities of organisms, particularly the higher animals and man, one could not proceed very far without becoming aware of the existence of various mechanisms and processes which serve to control and adjust the various activities to varying conditions in such a manner that the physiological unity and harmony of the organism in an ever-changing environment was maintained. Through such mechanisms and processes, the activity of organisms were regulated within certain limits. Physiologists accordingly called them regulatory mechanisms and processes.

Such processes had important implications, for Child believed that even simpler organisms behaved in ways that favored their maintenance. Thus organisms when placed in a region of insufficient oxygen attempted to escape; those living in darkness or weak light tended to move away from strong light; those needing light moved from darkness or weak light into stronger light, etc. All such responses were not only, physiologically speaking, equilibrations, but were also regulations in the stricter sense that they were useful. This point of view, which provided a general principle upon which to base a motivational system, seemed to have considerable appeal for the psychologist.

The concept of equilibrium was expressed by Rignano (1923), and then by Raup in his small but interesting book on *Complacency* (1925). Rignano wrote that every organism was a physiological system in a stationary condition and attempted to preserve this condition or to restore it as soon as it was disturbed by any variation occurring within or without the organism. This property constituted the foundation and essence of all "needs," of all "desires," and of all of the most important appetites. For Raup, the adjustment tendency was the central factor in human behavior, and the primary function of living matter was to relate itself to other forms of matter so as to maintain itself relatively constant while taking on their energy, utilizing it, and giving it off. This principle of complacency or equilibrium was the most basic principle, not only of behavior, but of all life processes.

In the early thirties, Cannon published *The Wisdom of the Body* (1932), a text which had a profound effect upon psychological thinking, and which continued to emphasize physiological regulation and equilibrium. The highly constant internal state, Cannon chose to call homeostasis. Thus he wrote:

The constant conditions which are maintained in the body might be termed *equilibria*. That word, however, has come to have fairly exact meaning as applied to relatively simple physico-chemical states, in closed systems, where known forces are balanced. The co-ordinated physiological processes which maintain most of the steady states in the organism are so complex and so peculiar to living beings—involving, as they may, the brain and nerves, the heart, lungs, kidneys, and spleen, all working cooperatively—that I have suggested a special designation for these states, *homeostasis*. The word does not imply something set and immobile, a stagnation. It means a condition—a condition which may vary, but which is relatively constant.

As examples of homeostasis, Cannon provided illustrative data showing that the blood tends to maintain a constant percentage of water, sugar, protein, fat and calcium; that the body tends to maintain a constant temperature, etc. The relationship between these constant states and behavior was illustrated with deprivation conditions which animal psychologists had long used as primary sources of motivation. In this regard Cannon wrote:

The ways in which appetites for food and drink and sensations of hunger and thirst act to maintain the bodily supplies of nutriment and water may be regarded as typical of other arrangements in the organism which operate for the welfare of the individual or the race. Behavior may be directed either by movements to get rid of disturbing, annoying stimulation, or by movements to prolong or renew agreeable stimulation. Hunger and thirst belong to the first category. Each of these states is associated with an impulsive factor; each one more or less vigorously spurs or drives to action; each may be so disturbing as to force the person who is afflicted to seek relief from intolerable annoyance or distress. . . . If the requirements of the body are not met, however, in this mild and incidental manner, hunger pangs and thirst arise as powerful, persistent and tormenting stimuli which imperiously demand the ingestion of food and water before they will cease their goading. By these automatic mechanisms the necessary supplies for storage of food and water are made certain.

The influence of physiology, not only in the area of motivation but on psychology *in toto,* was never more apparent than in Holt's *Animal Drive and the Learning Process* (1931). Holt's picture of the living, growing, and learning organism was based upon physiological foundations, with drive playing a central role. The energizing function of drive was fundamental to life itself. The chemical energy of food taken into the body and released resulted in a living organism. It was this release of stored energy that Holt spoke of as "drive" but it was the directive function of the drive that primarily concerned him.

The steering mechanism was conceived of as the organism's responding in one of two ways: either *adiently,* a term Holt had used to indicate that the response was a type which gave the organism more of the stimulus, or *abiently,* a response which carried the organism out of the range of the stimulus.

Adient steering was basically conceived of in terms of Bok's reflex circle and Pavlov's law of the conditioned reflex. The "reflex circle" commenced with an aimless, chance innervation of muscle and ended with the establishment of a reflex which was always a response that was not only correlated with a stimulus, but one that was often distinctly "purposive." Most frequently, the reflex-circle principle equipped the organism from an early period of its life with an overwhelming number of reflexes which approached stimuli, obtained more of them, and repeated the stimulation. Without this underlying positive responsiveness of the organism, Holt postulated that the "instincts" of imitativeness, curiosity, acquisitiveness, and the character of general initiative of the organism could never arise.[1]

The physiological basis of the abient response was as follows: although every organism at first responds positively toward any stimulus, if the stimulation is too intense, a state of random activity ensues. One of the random movements invariably carries the organism away from the stimulus, and with the termination of the stimulation, cessation of the individual's movements results. This was the process of trial-and-error learning.

Holt's ambitious attempt to provide the physiological foundations on which the integrated behavior of the individual was built was only partially successful. There was little dissent with his conception of the importance or function of motives; it was his physiologizing of the steering process that provoked the criticism.

Motivation in the 1930's

The importance of drives as primary factors, incorporated into the larger motivational framework of equilibrium or self-regulation, continued to be a fundamental tenet in most psychologists' treatment of motivation. In the revision of his introductory text, Dashiell (1937) indicated that the essence of animal and human behavior was to seek and to maintain optimal conditions for one's self so that the interorganic processes were adequately furthered. The basis for the persistent forms of animal and human behavior was found in the tissue conditions within the organism which gave rise to stimulation which excited the organism to overt activity. A man's interests and desires could be exceedingly refined, socialized, sublimated, or idealistic, but the basis from which they were developed was found in the phenomena of living matter.

From the early thirties to the present, drive and motive were more and more frequently encountered when accounting for the why of behavior. It was apparent to most, however, that there was no universal agreement as to how each term should be defined. Granich (1932), writing early in this period, pointed to more than six different definitions for "drive," and twice that many for "motive."

A few years later, Lashley (1938), in his presidential address, called attention to the fact that the concepts of drive and motive

[1] By instinct, Holt meant nothing more than a behavior pattern.

were being used as explanations for behavior in much the same way that instinct had some years previously. Lashley's warning, sound as it was, went unheeded, and the terms continued to be used.

CONTEMPORARY POINTS OF VIEW

The Nature of Needs, Drives, and Motives

A contemporary and frequently encountered approach to the problem of motivation commences with a discussion of the organic or physiological needs of the organism. A need is defined as some deficiency or excess found within the organism, which, if not corrected, would result in (1) the impairment of the general health and well-being of the organism or (2) the elimination of the species. The lack of water or food is an example of a fundamental need which must be met for the organism's health to be maintained, while the satisfaction of sexual deprivation is necessary for the survival of the species. Although most needs are included in the deficiency category, stimulation in the form of shock or other noxious stimuli which would result in tissue irritation or injury comprise the excess category. A listing of the various physiological needs includes a general hunger as well as specific hungers: thirst, sex, pain, temperature regulation, and the need for excretion, oxygen, and sleep.

Such needs are believed to produce one of two general types of behavior: (1) activity, usually thought to be undirected or spontaneous, or (2) if a goal object is present, consummatory activity. The antecedent-consequent relationship, consisting of needs on the one hand and activity on the other, has been the basis of what many investigators have meant by the term drive. An important consideration in such a definition is that it excludes learning or associative factors. Thus the activity that is found is presumed to be unlearned or spontaneous—a reflection of metabolic processes in the organism. Similarly, it is assumed that the consummatory behavior which arises is essentially independent of learning factors.

If the activity which arises from a need is directed to some goal object which results in the elimination of the organism's need, then a number of writers have posited the presence of a motive. In other words, when the organism *learns* to make appropriate responses to obtain the goal object or reward which satisfies its needs, the organism is said to be motivated. Although needs continue to be appropriate antecedent conditions, it is instrumental activity on the consequent end which ties down a motive's definition. Associative factors thus become an integral aspect of the definition. We have, then, a motive conceived of as an intervening variable tied to need states on the antecedent side and anchored on the consequent side by behavior which is directed toward the satisfaction of such needs.

It would be misleading to give the impression that the definitions of drive and motive which we have presented here were the only ones, for as we have pointed out earlier, general agreement has not been reached, and there is considerable diversity of opinion. Some individuals have described drive by referring only to the antecedent conditions. Thus some psychologists have defined drives simply in terms of needs, or the deprivation operations required to produce them. An animal deprived of food for 22 hours has a "22-hour hunger drive." In other instances, a drive is conceived as being a goad—a stimulus which arises from need states and drives the organism to activity. One difficulty with this latter conceptualization has been in identifying the specific drive stimuli which are associated with the varying need states. Which stimuli are associated with the need for food or water? Although needs provide characteristic stimuli to which responses can be attached, a given need state should not necessarily be equated with the internal stimuli produced by the need. Sometimes the need framework is omitted and drives are defined as "strong stimuli which impel action" (Dollard and Miller, 1950). Drives have also been defined in terms of the organism's behavior. Spontaneous or consummatory activity has been frequently used to infer the presence of a drive.

Finally, drive has been defined in terms of what are believed to be its functional properties. Young (1946) and Morgan (1957) as well as many others have defined drive as the energy or the impetus of behavior. Lindsley (1957) has defined a drive as an organic state which not only initiates activity, but which also predisposes the organism toward making differential responses that presumably aid in obtaining a satisfaction of its needs.

The definitions of motive have been as diverse as those of drive. Motives have been thought to be synonymous with drives or like drives have been defined in terms of specific antecedent conditions, i.e., 22 hours of food deprivation. Instrumental activity has been used as the behavioral measure from which motives have been inferred. Finally, motives have also been defined in terms of their functions. For example, McClelland (1951) defines a motive as the anticipation of affective changes, while Lindsley (1957) has defined motivation "as the combination of forces which initiate, direct and sustain behavior toward a goal." For Schreier (1957) the definition of motivation is the "explanation of psychological phenomena by reference to psychological phenomena."

It appears that with regard to some reasonable acceptance of a definition of drive and motive we are in no better position than we were in 1932.

Functions of Drive and Motive

Although it appears to be difficult to come to any general agreement with regard to a definition of drive and motive, there does seem to be more agreement with respect to their functions.

First, because needs apparently cause activity, such evidence has been used to indicate that drives and motives have an energizing function. That is, the presence of the need state presumably results in increased activity of the organism. It should be noted, however, that the energizing function has been questioned on a number of counts. If there are difficulties with the need-activity relationship, then the generality of the influence of the energizing function can be similarly questioned. It appears more appropriate to discuss this, however, after we have examined the experimental evidence which has been used to support this function.

If a need is accompanied by an appropriate goal object, consummatory activity takes place. This merely states that the hungry organism, when provided with food, will eat; the thirsty, provided with water, will drink. A consummatory function appears to be a second functional characteristic of drives and motives, and one from which drives have been inferred.

A third function of a motive is related to its directive or cue characteristics, for it is frequently assumed that the motive directs the activity of the organism as well as energizes it. In his discussion of a motive's directive function, Melton (1950) has stated that in a "new" situation all responses that might be made by the organism are not equally probable. Some are more likely to occur than others, and direction as reflected in an increased probability for a given class of responses to occur is partly a function of a motive. That is, if a stimulus is conceived to be a concomitant aspect of the presence of a drive or motive, that stimulus becomes a part of the stimulus complex which is subsequently followed by appropriate responses. When the motive occurs in a new situation, there is some tendency for it to result in behavior which resulted in its satisfaction in the earlier situation. Experimental support for this function can be found in the studies of a number of investigators. Hull (1933), for example, found that a rat could learn to make a right turn in a maze when it was hungry and a left turn when it was thirsty.

The directive function of a motive has been vigorously criticized by Brown (1953), who has pointed out that *"every case of directed behavior is to be ascribed, not to drives or motives, but to the capacities of stimulus cues, whether innate or acquired, to elicit reactions."* Here, of course, Brown is making a distinction between a drive state and a drive stimulus. The antecedent conditions which produce a drive state may also produce characteristic stimuli that have directive properties. For Brown, this directive property is a characteristic of the stimulus, not of the drive per se.

The last function has been called the selective function. An examination of the empirical law of effect states that responses which lead to consequences that satisfy a motivating condition are selected and strengthened, while those leading to consequences which do not satisfy a motivating condition are eliminated. In other words, those which lead to a goal object are selected and fixated, while those which do not lead to a goal object are eliminated. Although such selection and fixation is frequently thought to be a function of the goal object, it will be noted that it is the organism's need which determines the appropriateness of the incentive. Thus, it is apparent that the selection of appropriate behavior in the learning situation is determined not only by the presence (or absence) of the incentive, but by the need of the organism as well. Melton (1950) has pointed to this relationship as an appropriate function of a motive.

Brown (1953) has also classified this relationship between need and reward or punishment as having a motivational function. Thus, he points out that (1)

. . . a reduction in drive following a response will function under special conditions to increase the probability that the response will occur again in the same situation and (2) an abrupt increase in drive following a response will function under special conditions to reduce the probability that the response will occur again in the same situation.

Other Points of View

As we have noted, the primary needs of the organism have been generally regarded as an important component in considering the definition and function of drive and motive. Secondary or acquired needs have been posited to be derived from the primary ones.

Ryan (1958) has argued that an account of motivation does not need to start with postulated variables like drive, and that the freezing upon a primary-secondary need conceptualization of motivation has resulted in a dearth of working hypotheses against which to examine most types of human behavior. Useful and meaningful research, he suggests, can be done without reference to such concepts.

The approach which Ryan suggests is one which places emphasis upon the task confronting the individual. A large proportion of behavior is initiated by tasks, and a large proportion of tasks lead to the kind of behavior specified by the task. The task is considered to be the causal factor or necessary condition for most kinds of action and must be considered as a functional term in the experience of the individual.

The relationship existing between the type of task and the kind of behavior, Ryan posits, can be examined from a number of different explanatory levels, with specific motivational concepts being more appropriate for one level of explanation than another. The first level proposed concerns the specific behavior pattern which is related to a specific task. Once the task is known, the individual's behavior makes sense. For example, the behavior of an individual wandering around a field is understood when we find that he is looking for a lost wallet.

A second level of explanation relates the individual's behavior to the characteristics or properties of the task. The experimental work in the area of ego involvement, for example, illustrates the type of research that is appropriate to this level. The third level of explanation is concerned with the examination of those variables which determine whether or not the task is accepted by the individual. The fourth level appraises the functional properties of interests, while the fifth is related to the developmental history of interests as well as other motivational concepts. As Ryan points out, much current theorizing has concerned itself with this level and it has been generally assumed that conceptualization begins at this point. His program for the investigation of motivation proposes working hypotheses and empirical studies to be made on each level.

The general confusion that has permeated the motivational area has led Irwin (1958) to consider the study of motivation as primarily the investigation of preference behavior. Irwin believes that to state that an individual has a certain "motive" is to state that, if tested, the individual will indicate a preference for members of some particular class of objects over objects which are not members of this class. The establishment of preferences and the proper classification of their objects represents the key to the diagnosis of motivation.

The concept of preference is intimately related to discrimination. If an organism exhibits a discrimination, it also exhibits a preference. The objects of preference, however, are never identical with the objects of discrimination, for the objects of a preference are related to act outcomes, while the objects of a discrimination are features of the situation present before the organism acts.

Irwin makes an important distinction between biases and preferences. To illustrate, if an individual is asked to indicate which of the two colors he prefers, red or green, the experimental findings may indicate that over a series of trials he most frequently points to red. Although it is often assumed that the individual's behavior indicates a preference, such an interpretation is not in keeping with Irwin's point of view. The differential response exhibited by the individual in the situation exhibits only a bias inasmuch as differential outcomes are not contingent upon the kind of response that the individual makes. The outcome associated with the response of pointing to red does not differ from the outcome obtained when the individual points to green. For a situation to provide an indication of preference behavior, the occurrence of preferred and nonpreferred outcomes must be differentially contingent upon the subject's behavior.

An Organizational Model

As valuable as new approaches to motivation may be, the fact is that most of the experimental literature in the area has been related to traditional points of view. Accordingly, we shall continue the tradition and consider drives and motives as intervening variables anchored to needs on the one hand and to behavior on the other. This organization provides a pragmatic model for which we have organized most of the remaining chapters. The antecedent conditions must be broadened from the limited number of need states to include those stimulus conditions which individuals working in the area have assumed to be related to a motive's functions. This would mean that rewards also represent typical motivational antecedents. And in recent years, there has been considerable emphasis upon varying types of external stimulation which are also believed to have motivational functions. The diversity of these motivational antecedents precludes, at the present time, positing a definition of motivation or general theoretical schema that will organize all of these conditions into a meaningful as well as defensible whole.

An examination of the literature reveals that, with regard to consequent conditions, almost all types of responses have been used to (a) examine the influence of motivational antecedents as well as to (b) infer something about their functional properties. For convenience, we shall classify such behavior as (1) spontaneous, (2) consummatory, and (3) instrumental.[2]

[2] The classifying of behavior as instrumental does not have any implication for the classical-instrumental dichotomy of conditioning. Responses learned in either type of situation would be classified as instrumental.

MOTIVATIONAL ANTECEDENTS

4 . PRIMARY AND ACQUIRED NEEDS

Primary Needs

The biological requirements or primary needs of the organism, frequently produced by deprivation operations, have been conceived of as the appropriate antecedent conditions necessary for the establishment of a drive or of a motive. Any survey of the experimental literature would reveal many specific instances in which an animal's need for food and water has been so used. Unfortunately, the ease with which these food and water needs can be manipulated, as well as the way they support contemporary motivational theorizing, has obscured certain difficulties with the use of need states as a general condition upon which to anchor the concept of drive or motive.[1]

One difficulty with using need states as a base upon which to build a motivational system lies in their specific determination. That is, how do we determine what a need is? Many individuals have assumed that an organism's primary needs are essentially unvarying and that their satisfaction results in an optimally healthy organism. The criterion of optimal health, however, is difficult to ascertain. Lack of illness or freedom from disease, optimal growth, and longevity are three such criteria, with perhaps the first being

[1] It is really not surprising that food and water needs provide such support inasmuch as a motive's functions were derived from them in the first place.

the most frequently used. If a diet adequate to maintain health represents a primary need of the organism, these criteria are certainly appropriate. As Snapper (1955) has written, however, one difficulty arises in evaluating the criteria which are correlated with the diet. A standard diet in the Western world consists of carbohydrates supplying 55 per cent of the total caloric intake, fats supplying 30 per cent, and protein supplying 14 per cent. In the Orient, 80 per cent to 85 per cent and sometimes even 90 per cent of all calories are obtained from carbohydrates, with 5 per cent to 10 per cent being obtained from protein and 7 per cent to 8 per cent obtained from fats. The intake of calcium and of certain vitamins is also small, as is the number of calories. For example, the Filipino averages only 2,180 calories in contrast to the 2,500 which is indicated as minimum. Now it appears to be true that the low protein, low-caloric diet of the Oriental increases the spread of tuberculosis and decreases resistance against many communicable diseases. On the other hand, the Western diet seems to result in gout, serious diabetes, gall and renal stones, and premature sclerosis. The support of the Western diet in contrast to the Oriental depends upon a value judgment made by the observer as to the seriousness of the illness associated with the diet. The inability to define optimal health results in an inability to define need. The criterion of a need, then, is not invariant.

A second difficulty is related to the behavior which is presumed to arise from need states. Some experimental work has indicated that a behavioral product or characteristic of a need state is activity— hence, the need-activity relationship referred to in Chapter 3. Experimental evidence can be obtained to support such a relationship when the organism has a need for food or water. But what of other needs? A need for oxygen does not appear to result in increased activity as attested by the behavior of an individual who inhales carbon monoxide. A deficiency in thyroxin, certainly a primary need of a human organism, results in mental and physical sluggishness—in general, inactivity rather than activity. Here then, the use of need states as a general condition upon which to anchor drives or motives has obvious difficulties.

ACQUIRED DRIVES OR NEEDS

Anecdotal evidence suggests that seldom do the primary drives or needs play an important role in the motivation of the adolescent or the adult human being. Rather, behavior appears to be related to the needs of a psychological variety—achievement, security, recognition, affiliation, etc. As a result, varying mechanisms have been posited to "explain" or account for the development of these other motivational determinants.

Even when instinct was postulated to be an important motivational antecedent, Woodworth (1918) was aware that the positing of a limited number of them could not account for all of man's behavior. His answer to this problem was to divide behavior into two component parts: mechanism and drive.[2]

The mechanism was concerned with *how* we do a thing; the drive was concerned with *why* we do it. The example that Woodworth used to make this distinction was the classic case of the pitcher in a baseball game. "The problem of mechanism is the problem of how he aims, gauges distance and amount of curve, and coordinates his movements to produce the desired end. The problem of drive includes such questions as to why he is engaged in the exercise at all, why he pitches better on one day than on another, why he rouses himself more against one than against another batter, and many similar questions" (Woodworth, 1918).

If the distinction between a mechanism and a drive is made with respect to the action of a machine, the drive is the power which makes the machine go, while the machine itself is the mechanism. The distinction between the two was never absolute, for Woodworth believed that every drive was itself a mechanism.

The crux of the problem was whether the many activities which the individual had the capacity to perform were themselves only mechanisms, each requiring the drive of an instinct, or whether each mechanism could be directly aroused and continued in action without such assistance. Woodworth believed that any mechanism except perhaps the simple reflexes was capable not only of furnishing its own drive, but also of lending drive to other mechanisms. Therefore, although many activities could have drives furnished from a particular instinct (i.e., food getting, exploration, etc.), it

[2] Woodworth was probably responsible for introducing the word "drive" into the language of motivation. In a personal communication to P. T. Young (1936) he has written, "I believe you are right in supposing that the current use of 'drive' in animal psychology and other psychology springs from my use of the word in 'Dynamic Psychology,' 1918. I am sure I did not derive the word from any previous psychologist. I got it from mechanics. A machine has a mechanism, such that if it is put in motion it operates in a certain way; but it must be driven in order to move. The 'drive' of a machine is the supply of energy that puts it in motion."

was Woodworth's contention that such instincts were only the initiator and that the mechanisms themselves furnished the drive for the activity to continue. Such mechanisms became the motivational antecedents for subsequent behavior.

Functional Autonomy

A position similar to Woodworth's and one which has attracted considerable attention was taken by Allport (1937) in his text, *Personality: A Psychological Interpretation.* Rejecting the belief that much of man's behavior was governed by physiological needs, Allport emphasized the concept of functional autonomy. The principle can best be explained by quoting Allport himself: "The dynamic psychology proposed here regards adult motives as infinitely varied, and as self-sustaining, contemporary systems, growing out of antecedent systems, but functionally independent of them" (Allport, 1937).

Allport supported his principle only by anecdotal evidence. A workman originally does "clean-cut" jobs in order to gain security and the praise of others. Long after security has been achieved, as well as an enviable reputation for good workmanship, the workman continues to maintain his high standards. Although a need for the security and the praise of others was responsible originally for the superior workmanship, the behavior has become a motive in itself, functionally independent of the original motives which were responsible for the behavior. Other types of behavior used by Allport to buttress his position were the circular reflex which, after so many repetitions of an act, a child repeats for its own sake; the presence of conditioned responses which do not require reinforcement; and the neurotic behavior which persists long after the original motivation has disappeared.

Attractive as such a concept might be in accounting for the complex motivational structure of man, mounting criticism has been leveled against it. Bertocci (1940), McClelland (1942), Rethlingshafer (1943), and Oppenheimer (1947) have all provided a thorough and searching analysis of its operation.

McClelland (1942) has proposed that functional autonomy was only a special case of extinction which was delayed longer than the observer expected because of unusual factors which were present. Such factors might be:

(1) An inadequate criterion for the absence of the motive. It is easier to state that the instigation has been removed than to actu-

ally prove it. The experimental work of Bayer (cited by Anderson, 1941) who found that animals will eat after having been judged as satiated was cited as a case in point.

(2) Anticipatory instigations. In certain instances the instigation may be an anticipation or an expectancy. The removal of the instigator does not necessarily remove the anticipation.

(3) Improper identification of the instigation. In complex behavior there may be many instigators, and the removal of one does not remove all of them.

(4) Conditioned instigators. Here the removal of the instigation does not guarantee that stimuli conditioned to the instrumental act will not remain in sufficient strength for some time.

(5) The final basis for expecting an instrumental act to drop out is the most common of all—the removal of reward. This is, obviously, the extinction process. A number of conditions (i.e., partial reinforcement) may contribute to delay extinction with the result being that such behavior might then be classified as functionally autonomous.

Since Allport did not specify the conditions under which an act becomes functionally autonomous, in contrast to those acts which do not, the experimental validation of the concept has not been possible. A number of investigators, however, have reported observations which have appeared to provide some support for the principle. In contrast to Allport's designation of the concept as one which had primary relevance to human behavior, these studies have utilized animals as subjects.

In 1929, Olson reported that an artificially induced ear scratching response maintained itself even after the primary tissue irritation had vanished. Since Olson observed only four rats in all, Datel and Seward (1952) have replicated the study. Collodion was applied to the ears of eight rats on five successive days, while eight other subjects served as a control. Observations were confined to one ten-minute period each day with each period divided into fifty twelve-second sub-periods. Animals were credited with one scratching response regardless of whether they touched their ear only momentarily or scratched constantly during each sub-period. The results substantiated Olson's findings in direction, if not in degree. For at least sixteen days after cessation of treatment the mean scratching score for the experimental animals was significantly higher than that of the controls. Figure 4.1 shows the ear scratching responses for the two groups as a function of days of observation. Unfortu-

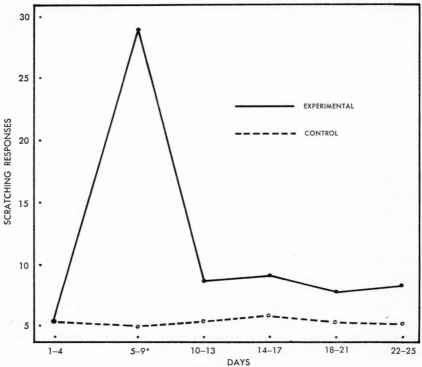

* Days on which collodion was applied to Group E.

FIG. 4–1. MEAN NUMBER OF SCRATCHING RESPONSES PER DAY PER RAT. (Adapted from Date and Seward, 1952)

nately, the authors do not report any microscopic examination for possible continued irritation after the collodion was removed. They have pointed out, however, that since there was no relationship between the number of scratches and the length of time since the collodion had been removed, this was evidence that the collodion did not continue to be a source of irritation.

A number of other investigators have also reported behavior patterns which appear to be autonomous. Ross, Smith, and Nienstedt (1950); Licklider and Licklider (1950); and Stellar, Hunt, Schlosberg, and Solomon (1952), have all reported some tendency for hoarding behavior to continue after the stimulus conditions which were originally responsible for the behavior had been removed. The problem is that hoarding is a complex type of behavior and is influenced by a large number of variables; consequently, it is difficult to be sure that the stimulus conditions which the investigator relates to be such behavior are the basic ones operating in the situation. As McClelland (1942) has indicated, there may be many instigators for this type of behavior and the removal of one does not insure that others do not remain.

A somewhat better example is found in the study of Earl (1957), who trained two groups of mice to dig sand under 20 hours of food deprivation. Both groups soon reached a stable performance level. One group was then satiated, while the other group was placed under 16 hours of deprivation. Both groups were then permitted to dig. At the end of fifteen days under these conditions, the satiated animals were digging at approximately 80 per cent of their asymptotic output with no trend toward extinction. As the author states: "Viewed empirically, it was as if the very act of digging had become demanding or had developed 'invitational character.' " The crux of the problem of functional autonomy is contained in the author's last discussion statement, "There is no way at present to specify the conditions that would or would not give rise to invitational character. . . ." Until it becomes possible to explicitly state the conditions under which a behavior pattern may continue to be elicited independently of its motivational antecedents, the concept of functional autonomy will be of little value.

The Role of Learning

Another position having considerable prominence in the area of acquired drives, and one of the first to emphasize the role of learning, was proposed by Dashiell (1937). It will be recalled, as we have noted in Chapter 3, that Dashiell hypothesized that when an external stimulus occurred frequently with the drive stimulus, the external stimulus became a substitute for the drive. Dashiell felt that this principle was an important one in bridging the gap between the basic organic needs which aroused only a general activity in the infant and the complex behavior of the adult.

Anderson (1941) attempted to demonstrate this type of operation experimentally, and he termed this *externalization of the drive*. Although he felt that this concept was related to Allport's functional autonomy, it seems to be more closely associated with Dashiell's position of stimulus substitution. Regardless of its antecedents, Anderson argued that the association and satisfaction of a drive in a constant stimulus situation should result in its externalization. He states:

For the present purposes, it will be assumed that the hunger drive is originally aroused by physiological conditions within the organism, that is to say, it is an internally aroused drive. If this internally aroused drive is satisfied over a long period of time in a relatively constant external situation, then the drive mechanism will become aroused by this external situation. We may now say that the originally internally aroused drive has been externalized. It is also assumed that the process of externalization gradually spreads from one external stimulus constellation to another so that, in time, practically any stimulus object that has been associated in any way with the drive may come to arouse that drive and should lead to the type of persistent behavior characteristic of motivated actions.

Twenty-nine specific hypotheses were generated from this general position. Most of them were concerned with changes in the animal's behavior that would be expected to occur either early or late in the learning process as a result of disruption of internal or external factors.

As an example, Anderson (1941a) posited that disrupting the animal's drive state by satiation early in the learning trials would produce more disturbance in the animal's error score than satiation provided late in the learning trials. This would follow because satiation, which disrupts internal factors, should show most influence on the animal's behavior at the time when the internal factors played their most dominant role. Late in the learning trials when the drive has become externalized, a disruption in the external aspects of the learning situation should be expected to produce a greater increment in error scores than if such a disruption had been produced early.

Finally, a basic hypothesis, and one which has important implications for a theory of acquired motives, was that rats which have had prolonged training on one maze under hunger-reward conditions which produced externalization may be expected to learn a new and different maze in the absence of the normal hunger and reward conditions (Anderson 1941b). An experiment designed to test this hypothesis produced results which were in the predicted direction, although the findings were difficult to evaluate as statistical tests of significance were not reported.

Hull (1951) offered a corollary, as a part of his theoretical system, which bore a marked similarity to the position which Anderson had proposed some years earlier. Hull hypothesized that when neutral stimuli were associated with the evocation of a primary or secondary drive and this drive stimulus underwent an abrupt diminution, the neutral stimuli acquired the capacity to elicit the drive stimulus. Studies by Anderson (1941b) and Miller (1948) were cited to provide experimental support, while Hull speculated that the conversion of the sex drive to the status of secondary motivation embodied similar principles.

Studies by Teel and Webb (1951), Danziger (1951), and Calvin, Bicknell and Sperling (1953), have supported both Anderson and Hull's position. In the Teel and Webb study (1951), hungry rats were given training in a T maze with food designating the correct side. They were given four training trials daily; following each day's training trials, they were fed and then given two additional trials. Results indicated that the satiation of the relevant drive had little or no detrimental effect upon the continued performance of the learned response. The authors have interpreted their findings as confirming Anderson's hypothesis of an "externalization of drive" but have favored an interpretation which was oriented toward the role of habit as the mediating mechanism.

Danziger (1951) had hungry rats run down a runway to a food reward. The animals were then satiated in their home cages and placed in the starting box. These animals continued to run down the runway and eat food in small amounts. Control animals without previous eating experience in the goal box, on the other hand, ran more slowly and did not eat. Again these results support the Anderson-Hull hypothesis, although the author has preferred an explanation emphasizing the making of a consummatory response. Danziger states ". . . only situations associated with the consummatory act require a capacity to rearouse the drive in the satiated animals."

In the Calvin, Bicknell, and Sperling study (1953), two groups of rats were placed in striped boxes 30 minutes a day for 24 consecutive days. One group received this daily experience under 22 hours of deprivation; the other group received it under a one-hour deprivation period. Following this, the food consumption of each group in the striped box was measured under 11½ hours of deprivation. The results indicated that the 22-hour group ate more food than the one-hour group.

On the other hand, studies by Siegel (1943), Koch and Daniel (1945), Siegel and MacDonnell (1954), and Greenberg (1954) as well as those by Myers and Miller (1954), Low (1958), and Dyal (1958) have not supported any of the acquired-drive hypotheses. Siegel's essential replication of Anderson's study (1941b), and Siegel and MacDonnell's replication of the Calvin, Bicknell and Sperling (1953) experiment have failed to confirm their findings.

Koch and Daniel (1945) attempted to measure the strength of a bar-pressing response which was mediated by maximum habit strength when the motivation of the original learning was reduced to zero. Hungry rats, following 70 or 90 reinforcements of a bar-pressing response, were satiated and returned to the apparatus. Results indicated that bar-pressing behavior was strikingly close to zero.

One problem in attempting to promote learning between a stimulus and some need such as hunger or thirst is that the latter physiological states arise in a gradual fashion. An animal under 22 hours of food deprivation has been exposed to a multitude of stimuli during the total deprivation period. It would be unusual if an association should take place between the need state and a specific neutral stimulus which occupies only a small portion of the total stimulation occurring over the entire deprivation period. Greenberg (1954) has examined the relationship between neutral stimuli and abruptly produced needs. By injecting rats with a saline solution, he was able to produce an almost immediate need for water. A blinking light was then paired with the presence of the need state. Measures of the amount, frequency, and incidence of drinking during a test period in which the light was present without the prior injection, however, indicated no acquired drive.

Although not performed in an acquired drive context, a study by Andersson and Larsson (1956) appears to be relevant in this area. These investigators attempted to condition the drinking behavior of goats by pairing a light or tone with electrical stimulation to the hypothalamus which evoked the drinking response. Results indicated, in spite of a large number of pairings of the CS and UCS, that the response could not be conditioned.

Myers and Miller (1954) were interested in finding out if a neutral stimulus, after having been paired with a primary need, could motivate a new response. In their study, four groups of rats placed under 23 hours of food deprivation were given 0, 10, 30, or 70 trials in associating a white compartment with their need for food. The subjects were started in a white compartment and learned to touch a door to open it and run into a black compartment containing food. In a subsequent test for the acquisition of an acquired motive, these four groups, now satiated and not rewarded, were required to learn a new response of pressing a bar to open the door to the goal compartment. Although all groups learned to press the bar there were no significant differences among them. Myers and Miller have rejected an explanation in terms of an acquired motive, and have posited an exploratory motive to account for the learning that took place. Low's (1958) study, although done in a different experimental context, has confirmed the Myers and Miller experimental finding.

The evidence that external stimuli may acquire some motivational function by association with primary needs is controversial. Perhaps such stimuli, under conditions which have yet to be adequately defined, may acquire an energizing function—the activation of a response which was learned under a motivated state. If a more stringent criterion for the presence of an acquired drive is demanded (i.e., the need for the organism to learn some new response), much more evidence is needed before acquired motives based upon appetitional needs can be postulated to exist.

FEAR AND ANXIETY [3]

A second group of studies must be considered before concluding the topic of learned motives. These studies are concerned with fear or anxiety. Although these concepts have had divergent usages, a number of writers have used the terms synonymously.

One of the first experimentalists to assign motivational properties to anxiety was Mowrer (1939), who defined anxiety as a learned response occurring to signals or conditioned stimuli which were followed by pain. Anxiety was the conditioned form of the pain reaction and was basically anticipatory in nature. More recently, Schoenfeld (1950) has taken a similar position.

It was Miller (1948) and May (1948), however, who simultaneously published experimental studies investigating fear as an acquired source of motivation. In May's study, rats were first trained to cross a barrier in a shuttle box in order to escape shock. An animal was placed in one part of the box and without warning

---

[3] The discussion of fear and/or anxiety is limited to a consideration of those experimental studies which have placed these concepts within an acquired-drive context. In Chapter 6, they shall be considered in a somewhat different manner.

was shocked until it escaped by jumping over the barrier to the other side. The second phase of the study was to pair the buzzer with shock under conditions which prevented the escape response. Here, the animal was placed in a small box, and a buzzer sounded for ten seconds. During the last five seconds the buzzer sounded concurrently with shock. The last phase of the experiment consisted of placing the animals in the shuttle box and sounding the buzzer for ten seconds. Responses for experimental groups given such training were significantly greater than for control groups trained and tested in the same way except that the buzzer was never paired with shock.

Miller's experimental design (1948) was somewhat different from that of May's. His apparatus consisted of two compartments, one white, which contained a grid, and the other black. Figure 4.2 shows this apparatus. Animals were given a series of trials in which they were shocked in the white compartment and allowed to escape into the black one. When they were given a series of nonshock trials, the animals persisted in their behavior of running to the black box. Miller felt that an adequate test of whether there was a learned motive would be one in which the animals would have to learn a new response. In order to demonstrate this, the door between the compartments was closed, but the animals could open it by moving a wheel for a fraction of a turn. Figure 4.3 indicates how the speed of operating the wheel increased as a function of trials.[4]

Miller has explained his findings by stating that fear is associated with the shock given in the training series—fear being a learned response to a painful situation. Neutral stimuli, in this instance the white box, which were closely associated with the painful experience should come to elicit the fear response. The fear response also elicits strong stimuli which have motivational functions. The organism should learn a new response which will result in the reduction of this motivating state. Fear becomes a learned "drive"—learned in that it is a response to previously neutral cues, and a drive because it is a stimulus which can motivate the learning and performance of new responses in the same way as thirst, hunger, or other drives.

Brown and Jacobs (1949) believed that Miller's experimental findings might be attributed to the frustration engendered by the blocking of the running response. They reasoned that the new re-

[4] Miller (1941) orally reported this experiment some years earlier.

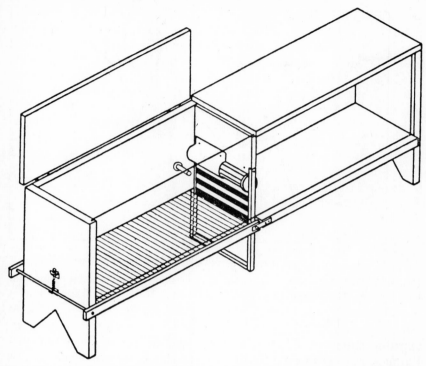

FIG. 4–2. ACQUIRED DRIVE APPARATUS. The left compartment is painted white, the right one black. A shock may be administered through the grid which is the floor of the compartment. When the animal is placed on the grid which is pivoted at the inside end, the grid moves down slightly, making a contact that starts an electric timer. When the animal performs the correct response, turning the wheel or pressing the bar as the case may be, he stops the clock and actuates a solenoid which allows the door, painted with horizontal black and white stripes, to drop. (Adapted from Miller, 1948)

sponse (wheel turning, etc.) would reduce frustration by permitting the resumption of the running response. In their experiment, rats were locked in one of two identical compartments and given trials during which a light and tone were paired with shock. Following this, nonshock trials were given in which the compartments were separated by only a small barrier. With each trial, the light and tone were presented until the animal made his way into the other compartment. Results indicated that the speed of crossing the barrier increased as one would normally expect to find in a

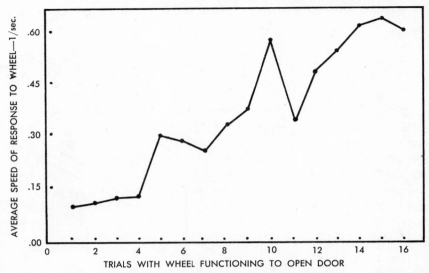

FIG. 4–3. THE LEARNING OF A NEW RESPONSE BASED ON AN ACQUIRED DRIVE OF FEAR. (Adapted from Miller, 1948)

learning situation. Control animals who were not given the preliminary pairing of light and tone with shock did not learn.

The situation which has been used to demonstrate the acquisition of a learned motive based upon pain is quite dissimilar to those experimental situations designed to show acquired motives based upon appetitional states, i.e., food or water deprivation. In this latter type of study, there has been no postulation of a response which the neutral stimulus elicits and which in turn has stimulus characteristics to which some instrumental response can be attached. A diagram will perhaps make this distinction somewhat clearer.

A learned motive based upon pain:

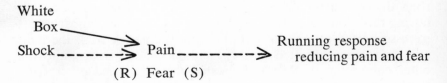

A learned motive based upon food deprivation:

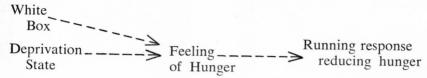

If the fear paradigm represents the prototype for the acquisition of all learned motives, food and water deprivation states must produce some response within the organism which can be elicited by the neutral stimulus. The response elicited must have stimulus (and motivating) functions. The difficulty may be that neutral stimuli cannot elicit an actual feeling (response) of hunger or thirst, or that the response which is elicited does not have a stimulus (and/or motivating) function to which an instrumental response can be attached.[5]

[5] Seward (1953) has also been aware of the difficulty of subsuming under a single heading acquired drives based upon both pain (aversion) and upon appetite. He has suggested that acquired drives fall into two classes, secondary or tertiary, depending upon how they have been acquired. Secondary drives arise from the conditioning of aversive stimulation and are illustrated by Miller's (1948) operations. Tertiary drives arise from the blocking of learned responses—responses which have previously resulted in reinforcement—and their appearance would be primarily related to appetitional states. In essence, he is considering frustration as an acquired drive, a topic we will discuss in Chapter 6.

5 • THE NATURE OF REWARDS

In the confusion that surrounds the definitions of drive and motive, reward is often conceived to be an adjunct to the concept of motivation. One frequently comes across the phrase "motivation *and* reward"—the implication being that what is meant by motivation is something apart and distinct from that of reward. Presumably in such a phrase, motivation is defined in terms of the organism's needs with a concomitant energizing function, while rewards are defined as stimulus objects which follow certain responses and have reinforcing or selective functions.

Such a dichotomy ignores the fact that, in many instances, the energizing and selective functions are products of the joint action of needs and rewards. There is some experimental evidence to support the belief that the energizing function cannot be assigned to needs acting alone and without ever having had any relationship to rewards. When an organism obtains a reward in a given situation, an expectation or cognition of reward combines with the accompanying need state to provide a need-reward relationship which on subsequent occasions assumes the burden of energizing or eliciting certain kinds of responses. Experimental evidence relating to such a position will be postponed until Chapter 7, where we shall discuss the energizing function in greater detail.

A similar argument may be advanced with regard to the action of rewards. Food, for example, is a reward only to the hungry animal. The assigning of a selective function to food without reference to the animal's needs ignores the fact that rewards are basically determined by the needs of the organism.

We believe that the dichotomy of motivation and reward only compounds the confusion that is present in this area, and with the organizational model that we have provided earlier, rewards must be considered only as another motivational antecedent.

Two individuals in American psychology have been primarily responsible for emphasizing the role of reward in the learning situation—Edward L. Thorndike with his law of effect, and Clark Hull with his law of primary reinforcement; it is to these laws that we will direct our attention.

The Law of Effect

The historical antecedents of Thorndike's law of effect may be found primarily in the work of Spencer (1872). Spencer believed that the relationship between the unpleasant or painful and the injurious were primarily established by natural selection. Behavior which proved pleasant to the organism was also beneficial, and as a result it became a part of the organism's mode of responding, and thus led to survival. Behavior which was unpleasant was also injurious and if not discontinued led to the elimination of the organism. Bain (1868), James (1890), and Baldwin (1906), as well as others, also emphasized a similar hedonistic point of view.

Thorndike's law of effect continued in the same tradition. In his *Animal Intelligence* (1911), the law was defined as follows:

Of several responses made to the same situation, those which are accompanied or closely followed by satisfaction to the animal will, other things being equal, be more firmly connected with the situation, so that, when it recurs, they will be more likely to recur; those which are accompanied or closely followed by discomfort to the animal will, other things being equal, have their connections with that situation weakened, so that, when it recurs, they will be less likely to occur. The greater the satisfaction or discomfort, the greater the strengthening or weakening of the bond.

Thorndike's law was one of effect, not affect. In contrast to his predecessors who made pleasure and pain the variables responsible for fixation or elimination, Thorndike emphasized satisfaction.

Satisfaction, however, was defined as that "which the animal does nothing to avoid, often doing such things as attain and preserve it." By a discomforting state of affairs he meant one which the animal avoids and abandons. As a result of later experimental evidence, Thorndike eventually revised the law to eliminate the "stamping out" action of punishment.

From the time of Thorndike's original formulation of the law of effect until early in 1940, the experimental work as well as the theoretical discussion related to it was voluminous, and it is not within the scope of this text to examine and analyze it. The interested reader, however, may find much of the material summarized in Postman's excellent review (1947).

The Law of Primary Reinforcement

A derivative of the law of effect is found in Hull's law of primary reinforcement, a basic postulate found in his *Principles of Behavior* (1943). Here, reward is defined not in terms of Thorndike's conception of satisfaction, but as the reduction of a primary need. Hull, in his early formulation of the law of primary reinforcement, stated that if a stimulus-response relationship was followed by a reduction in need, the probability was increased that on subsequent occasions the stimulus would evoke the response. Such a principle seemed to be clearly demonstrated in the rat's learning to escape from a charged grid. Of the many responses made by the animal in the situation, the response that removed the animal from the situation was the one which was learned. It was learned because the animal's need to escape injury (a primary need) was reduced by such a response. Later, Hull (1951) revised his law of primary reinforcement so that a reduction in the drive stimulus (rather than the drive) became the critical factor in reinforcement.

Hull (1943) was cognizant of the frequency with which learning took place in the absence of need reduction and so offered a corollary to his law of primary reinforcement—the law of secondary reinforcement. ". . . the power of reinforcement may be transmitted to any stimulus situation by the consistent and repeated association of such stimulus situation with the primary reinforcement which is characteristic of need reduction."

Hull's reinforcement position has been much like that of Thorndike in generating a large amount of experimental work and theoretical discussion. Much of it has centered around (1) the general problem of whether learning can take place without primary (or secondary) reinforcement as well as (2) an examination of the operation and parameters of secondary reinforcement.

Hull's Need or Drive Reduction Hypothesis

Hull's drive reduction hypothesis, occupying an important role in his theoretical system, has stimulated considerable research and controversy. And any reasonably complete survey of related material would not only lead us far from the primary purpose of this chapter but would require more time and space than we have available. Under the circumstances, we shall limit our discussion to what we believe are some of the more critical aspects of reinforcement theory.

The large number of experiments which have shown learning to occur as a result of supplying food to a hungry rat or water to a thirsty one demonstrate that need reduction may serve as a *sufficient* condition for learning. Whether such need reduction is a *necessary* condition for learning, however, has been attacked from a number of vantage points.

Early arguments against the reinforcement position utilized the experimental evidence from some of the latent learning experiments. We shall not attempt to present nor evaluate the host of studies in this area, although the interested reader may refer to Thistlethwaite's review (1951) for a good summary of the research. Two findings related to those latent-learning studies which have used multiple T mazes, however, are generally accepted: (1) nonreinforced animals gradually eliminate errors as a function of trials, and (2) there is an abrupt decrease in errors when a nonreinforced animal is given reinforcement.

Although the abrupt decrease in the number of errors following the presentation of reinforcement provided some difficulty for the early Hullian system to handle, Hull's later revision (1951) did take care of this problem nicely. On the other hand, the gradual decline of maze errors, which reflects learning without reinforcement, has provided Hull's reinforcement position with some difficulty.[1]

---

[1] Osgood (1953) does not believe that maze learning in the absence of primary reinforcement poses any special problem for Hull inasmuch as there is no guarantee that all forms of reinforcement were eliminated in these studies. He states, "it is quite conceivable that motives were present and *were* being reduced during unrewarded trials or casual meandering." The question immediately arising from Osgood's statement must be: "What motives were present?" The burden of proving that a need was present and reduced during the unrewarded trials falls upon the reinforcement theorist.

A second line of attack upon a need-reduction point of view has been to use incentives to which the organism would respond, but which would not satisfy any need. In the first of a series of studies by Sheffield and his collaborators, Sheffield and Roby (1950) demonstrated that the nonnutritive sweet taste of saccharin could serve as a reward for a rat learning a position habit in a T maze. A second study by Sheffield, Wulff, and Backer (1951) indicated that naive male rats with no previous history of ejaculation would learn to run and climb hurdles with the only reward being the opportunity to copulate with a receptive female. Need reduction in the form of ejaculation, however, was not permitted. In both experiments, Sheffield pointed out that learning had taken place without need or drive reduction. Furthermore, since the reward value of saccharin did not extinguish over a long period of time, an explanation based upon secondary reinforcement was untenable.

These experiments, along with another by Sheffield, Roby, and Campbell (1954) which indicated that the vigor of a consummatory response appeared to be the determining factor in the reinforcing function of a reward, have led Sheffield to propose what he has called a "drive induction" theory of reward. The theory states that a reward stimulus at the onset of an instrumental learning situation is an "unconditioned" stimulus for the consummatory response. That is, it will regularly elicit such a response. This response then becomes conditioned to immediate neutral cues, particularly those which precede the onset of the reward. On subsequent trials, these cues arouse a part of the consummatory response, and this arousal of a portion of the consummatory response works its way from the goal backward over the instrumental response sequence. As Sheffield has written, this theory of rewards depends upon arousal rather than reduction of excitement and treats rewards as incentives rather than satisfiers.

A related attack has used evidence similar to that obtained by Sheffield, although neglecting his theoretical explanation. In general, these studies have called attention to the role of (a) affective states and (b) sensory stimulation. Young and Shuford (1955), emphasizing the former, found it possible to train satiated rats to learn a response on the basis of the palatability of food rather than its reinforcing characteristics. In a similar vein, Smith and his associates have stressed the role of sensory satisfaction which they believe operates in addition to need reduction. Smith and Kinney (1956), using a Skinner box, found no significant differences between performances of hungry and satiated rats when sucrose was used as a reward. Furthermore, they pointed out that their animals received a total of less than 1 cc. of sucrose solution over a 46-minute period; thus, it was argued that taste rather than need reduction must have been the important attribute of reinforcement. Subsequent studies by Smith and Duffy (1957a), Schulz and Lawrence (1958), and Wetzel (1959) have also demonstrated that satiated rats are capable of learning not only relatively simple but complex discrimination problems as well, with their only reward being a taste of a sucrose solution.

Another group of studies has demonstrated that certain stimuli will act as reinforcement although they also appear to bear little relation to need reduction, affective states, or sensory satisfaction. Studies by Marx, Henderson, and Roberts (1955), Kish (1955), Kling, Horowitz, and Delhagen (1956), Butler (1957a), Hurwitz and De (1958), Roberts, Marx, and Collier (1958), Clayton (1958), and Davis (1958), to mention only a few, have demonstrated a reinforcing function of stimuli apparently unrelated to need reduction. Most of these studies have shown that the onset of a weak light which follows a response may act to increase the probability of the occurrence of that response.[2, 3]

In the Marx, Henderson, and Roberts study (1955), rats had the opportunity to make nonreinforced operant responses in the dark for varying numbers of 30-minute pretest periods. This was followed by a number of 30-minute test periods during which a relatively weak light accompanied each bar press. Statistically significant increments in bar pressing were obtained as a function of the presentation of light. Kish (1955) has also noted this effect with mice.

Kling, Horowitz, and Delhagen (1956) found that for an eleven-day experimental period, decreased responding was noted not only within each 20-minute daily session, but between daily

[2] An exception is that of Butler (1957a) who has shown that rhesus monkeys will learn a position discrimination problem when the correct response was rewarded by just 15 seconds of sound emitted from a monkey colony.

[3] Although some investigators have considered the specific characteristics of the stimulus to be reinforcing, others have interpreted the findings to mean that the reinforcing state of affairs is simply one of sensory change. Thus, Moon and Lodahl (1956) have found that increased responding in monkeys could be obtained if the response was followed by either an increase or a decrease in illumination. As the authors have stated, the effective factor seemed to be change *per se* rather than the direction of such change. Forgays and Levin (1958) have taken a similar position.

sessions as well. Davis (1958) has also reported decrements in response over a three-day test period, and, in contrast to most other investigators, has suggested that the reinforcing power of light onset may be more closely related to the phenomenon of secondary reinforcement than is generally believed.

A last difficulty with the reinforcing position relates to its handling of instrumental learning situations based upon fear. As we indicated in Chapter 4, Miller hypothesized that the learning of the fear response to neutral stimuli as well as the learning of the instrumental responses to fear which acts as a stimulus may be accounted for by a reinforcement position. In contrast, Mowrer (1947) has posited a two-factor theory of learning in which the two types of processes in learning were (1) conditioning and (2) problem solving. Problem solving, Mowrer has pointed out, operates on the principle of reinforcement and is a process which has to do with the acquisition of overt instrumental responses. Conditioning, on the other hand, was a learning situation which emphasized the role of contiguity and was a process whereby emotions, meanings, attitudes, and cognitions were acquired through stimulus substitution.

In Miller's explanation of fear as an acquired drive, the reduction of fear reinforces the instrumental response which removes the organism from the fear-producing situation. The same reinforcing situation is also responsible for strengthening the relationship existing between the fear-producing stimulus, such as the white box, and the response of fear itself. In contrast, Mowrer believes that the fear-producing stimulus (white box) and the fear response is learned as a result of mere contiguity of stimulus and response. The learning of the instrumental response which results in removing the organism from the fear-producing situation, however, comes about as a result of reinforcement. The differing theoretical approaches to this aspect of the fear learning situation have resulted in considerable controversy.

Mowrer and Suter (1950) used a blinking light as a CS and paired it with shock as the UCS. The CS was begun five seconds before the shock, which lasted for a fixed duration of ten seconds. For one group, the CS overlapped and terminated with the UCS. In the other group, the CS ended with the onset of shock. Mowrer and Suter believed that a reinforcement position would predict that the shorter the interval between the CS and the termination of shock, the greater should be the learning of the fear response. Under the circumstances, the group in which the CS coincided with the termination of the UCS should show better learning of the avoidance response. Results, however, indicated no significant difference between the groups in the learning of a running response to avoid shock.

Mowrer and Aiken's study (1954) also has relevance to this problem. Five groups of rats, all of which had been deprived of food, were placed in the left side of a two-compartment box and remained there until they had depressed a bar and obtained food 20 times. The subjects were then placed in the right side of the box. After five minutes they were given a blinking light associated with shock. The relationship between the onset and the termination of the light is schematically represented in Figure 5.1. Following such training, each subject was again placed in the left side of the apparatus and permitted to press the bar and obtain food for five minutes. This procedure established the subject's operant response level. For an additional period of 25 minutes, every subject after pressing the bar experienced the blinking light for three seconds. Presumably the number of bar presses during the 25-minute period provided an index of the amount of fear learning which occurred in the training situation. The results indicated that Group 1 (those subjects in which the CS terminated with the onset of the shock) inhibited their bar pressing responses most strikingly. Figure 5.2 reveals the varying number of responses made by each group.

A slightly different experimental design, but one in which there was also an attempt to test the Miller vs. Mowrer approach, was the study by Mowrer and Solomon (1954). Hull (1943) had indicated that learning occurred most rapidly when the reinforcing state of affairs which was provided by drive reduction was short rather than long, and abrupt rather than gradual. Mowrer and Solomon (1954) used the same type of experimental situation as found in the Mowrer and Aiken study (1954), except that the relationship between the CS and the length and abruptness of the UCS was changed. These relationships are indicated in Figure 5.3. Results indicated that the differences among the varying groups were not statistically significant.[4]

[4] One major difficulty with any conclusion drawn from nonsignificant findings is that it is assumed that the animals were capable of discriminating among the varying combinations of stimuli which were used. In this sense, the Mowrer and Suter (1950) and Mowrer and Solomon (1954) studies are inconclusive.

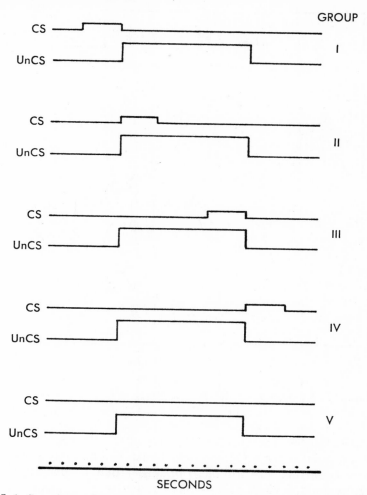

FIG. 5–1. SCHEMATIC REPRESENTATION OF THE FIVE DIFFERENT ARRANGE-MENTS OF CONDITIONED (*CS*) AND UNCONDITIONED (*UnCS*) STIMULUS. The conditioned stimulus (a blinking light) in Group V was not immediately associated with the unconditioned stimulus (electric shock) in any way, but was presented alone, two minutes after the *UnCS* had terminated. (Adapted from Mowrer and Aiken, 1954)

Studies by Bitterman, Reed, and Krauskopf (1952) and also by Coppock (1950) using the human GSR have also confirmed Mowrer's position that the important determinant of such conditioning has been shock onset rather than shock termination.

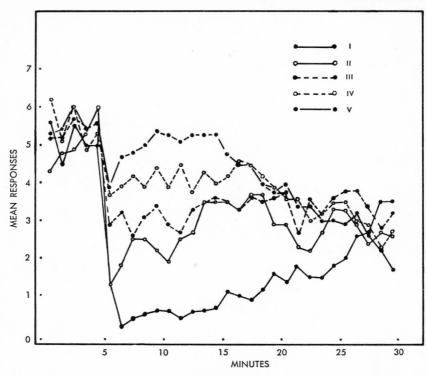

FIG. 5–2. CURVES SHOWING THE INHIBITION OF THE HUNGER-MOTIVATED RESPONSE. (Adapted from Mowrer and Aiken, 1954)

Although these studies provide difficulty for a need-or drive-re-duction point of view, Miller (1951) has pointed out how such a theory could account for these findings—that is, that fear is apparently conditioned by shock onset rather than by shock termination. The first possible explanation that he has suggested is based upon the findings of Adrian that the onset of a stimulus at first produces a strong burst of impulses which is followed by a rapid reduction in the rate of firing. Such an adaptation factor, or reduction in the rate of transmission of neural impulses, constitutes partial drive reduction. A second possibility is that temporary drive reduction occurs when the animal leaps into the air when the grid is first charged. Davitz's study (1955) was designed to control these factors. To minimize the possibility of temporary escape, a small inverted box was placed over the animals to prevent them from

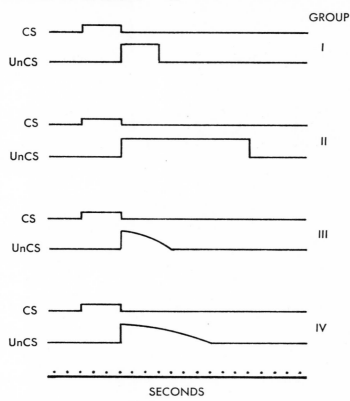

FIG. 5–3. SCHEMATIC REPRESENTATION OF THE DIFFERENT FORMS OF UN-CONDITIONED STIMULUS (SHOCK). The signal, or conditioned stimulus, was a blinking light of three seconds duration, which was followed in each of the four groups of Ss by a shock of the duration and form shown. (Adapted from Mowrer and Solomon, 1954)

jumping from the grid. To offset the effects of adaptation, shock was gradually increased throughout the period of shock presentation. Using activity as the behavioral index, and making the assumption that fear reduced such activity, Davitz's results indicated that shock onset seems to be of greater importance than shock termination.

Finally, two studies by Zeaman and Wegner (1954, 1957) are pertinent. In their first study, which supported a reinforcement position, they found that whichever phase of the unconditioned heart beat (acceleration or deceleration) that was occurring when

their unconditioned stimulus (shock) was terminated, was the phase which was conditioned. They have pointed out that what the heart is doing at the time the shock is terminated seems to make the difference. In their second study, they hypothesized that if a very long shock were used (15 seconds), the heart should have returned to its normal functioning by the end of the shock, and thus no conditioning should occur. Similarly, if a very short shock was used (.1 second)—it should be over before the heart had time to change its rate, and again no conditioning should occur. Their results indicated, however, that conditioning did take place and they have concluded that the mechanism for conditioning autonomic responses is not drive reduction.

SECONDARY REINFORCEMENT

Hull, in his *Principles of Behavior* (1943), recognized that although experimental evidence indicated that reinforcement had to follow a stimulus-response relationship within 30 seconds if it were to have any effect, a great deal of behavior took place in prolonged sequences in which primary reinforcement occurred only after the final response. As indicated earlier, in order to handle this difficulty, he formulated the principle of secondary reinforcement. Briefly, he postulated that the power of reinforcement could be transmitted to any stimulus situation by consistent and repeated association of the stimulus situation with primary reinforcement. When such an association took place, the stimulus was said to be a secondary reinforcer. An early experiment by Cowles (1937) was one of a number which he used to illustrate its operation.

Hungry chimpanzees were first trained to insert poker chips into a slot machine which delivered a raisin for each poker chip that was inserted. In this manner, an association was built up between the primary reward of raisins and a secondary one, poker chips. Following such training and as a way of further establishing reward values for the poker chips, the investigator required the chimpanzee to work for the chip by pulling a weighted handle; the animal being permitted to exchange the chip for a raisin as soon as it was received. Little by little, however, the animals were required to accumulate chips before they could make the exchange. In subsequent learning tasks, poker chips proved to be adequate rewards.

A lack of experimental studies prevented Hull from spelling out in greater detail exactly how secondary reinforcement operates; his general formulation of the concept, however, has resulted in a large number of studies, investigating not only its parameters but also the basic principles underlying its operation.

The Role of Need States

One of the basic questions in this area is concerned with whether or not secondary reinforcement can actually reduce a primary need. Studies by Simon, Wickens, Brown, and Pennock (1951) as well as Calvin, Bicknell, and Sperling (1953a) have demonstrated that secondary reinforcing stimuli do not reduce primary needs. In the Simon, et al. study, the investigators compared the quantity of water consumed by thirsty rats whose bar-pressing responses had been previously accompanied by secondary reinforcement with the amount consumed by equally thirsty rats whose bar-pressing responses had not been so accompanied. Results indicated no significant differences between the groups.

A second problem is concerned with the influence of need states or deprivation levels (1) on the establishment of secondary reinforcing stimuli or (2) on their subsequent operation. In the investigation of the influence of the need state upon the establishment of secondary reinforcing stimuli, the need is varied during the period in which the neutral stimulus is being associated with primary reinforcement, and then held constant during its subsequent testing. In the second situation, the reverse is true; the need is held constant during the period in which the neutral stimulus is being associated with primary reinforcement, but is then varied during its subsequent testing.

With regard to examining the role of level of need during the establishment of secondary reinforcing stimuli, Hall (1951a) provided a training period for rats in which a black or white goal box was associated with water, with the animals being under either 6 or 22 hours of water deprivation. Following such a training period, all animals were placed under 22 hours of water deprivation and given a learning series on a T maze in which the previously reinforced goal box was used on one arm and a neutral goal box on the other. The number of responses to the previously reinforced goal box during the learning series was not significantly different for animals under either 6 or 22 hours of deprivation.

Miles (1956) examined the effect of need level on the *operation* of secondary reinforcing stimuli. To establish a secondary reinforcing stimulus, he gave 240 rats 80 reinforcements under 24 hours of food deprivation. Associated with each reinforcement was a light and click of the food delivering mechanism. Following the conditioning period, the animals were randomly assigned to six deprivation groups, and underwent extinction under either 0, 2.5, 5, 10, 20 or 40 hours of deprivation. Half of the subjects in each group extinguished with the secondary reinforcers present and the other half extinguished with them absent. Results indicated a positive relationship between the amount of deprivation and resistance to extinction. Figure 5.4 presents this relationship.

Brown's study (1956) has confirmed the findings of both Hall and Miles. It is apparent that the level of the organism's need is not an important variable in the establishment of a secondary reinforcing stimulus, but its role is significant during its subsequent operation.

Continuing with the influence of needs, Estes (1949) was interested in whether or not a secondary reinforcing stimulus would be effective in strengthening new responses when a new need was substituted for the original one. In the initial phase of the Estes study, rats were placed under water deprivation and received an auditory click with a reward of water. The subjects were then divided into two groups with half remaining on water deprivation while the other half was placed on food deprivation. The animals then received training in the bar-pressing task in which, associated with the bar depression, was the auditory click associated previously with water. Estes found no significant differences in the number of bar-pressing responses between the two groups, even though the only reinforcement was that mediated by the auditory stimulus. He concluded that the effect of the secondary reinforcement had generalized from thirst to hunger, and had thus reinforced the acquisition of the bar-pressing response.[5]

Estes' experimental findings have been confirmed, at least in part, by D'Amato (1955), whose technique was to associate a goal box with reinforcement in a runway situation, and then give his ani-

[5] These findings have not been confirmed by Reid and Slivinske (1954), who, although using a Skinner box and a click as a secondary reinforcing stimulus, used resistance to extinction as their response measure. Not only did they find a significantly greater number of extinction responses for those subjects continuing under the same need during extinction in contrast to a group of animals whose need was changed, but that the number of responses made by this changed need group was not significantly different from a group of animals which was not presented with the secondary reinforcing stimulus during the extinction series.

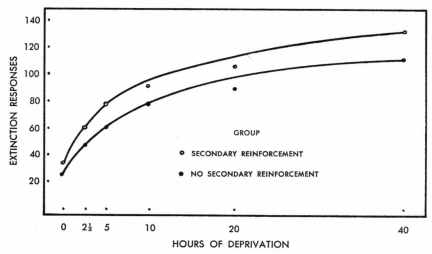

FIG. 5–4. MEDIAN NUMBER OF EXTINCTION RESPONSES THROUGHOUT THE DEPRIVATION PARAMETER. Secondary reinforcement groups received light-click stimulation during extinction. (Adapted from Miles, 1956)

mals a learning series in a T maze in which the previously rein-forced goal box was used on one arm. In his first experiment, ani-mals were trained under approximately 22 hours of water depriva-tion, with the learning series being run under 22 hours of food deprivation. In his second experiment, the deprivation conditions were reversed. Results of both studies indicated significantly more choices to the previously reinforced goal box than would be indi-cated by chance; lack of a group which learned the new response under deprivation conditions similar to that found in training, how-ever, prevented confirmation of Estes' findings of no difference be-tween the original and changed need.

Estes' (1949a) second study was designed not only to verify the findings of his first study, but also to determine whether the pres-ence of a strong need during the new learning situation was a nec-essary condition for the transfer of secondary reinforcement. Essen-tially the same experimental procedure was utilized as in his first experiment, although the animals were first pretested for rate of un-conditioned bar pressing. They were then placed under 23 hours of water deprivation and learned to associate a click with receipt of water. During the test period, one group was deprived of food for 23 hours and satiated on water while a second group was deprived of food for just six hours and satiated on water. A control group which did not have the pairing of the water with the click was also placed under 23 hours of food deprivation. Bar-pressing responses during the test period produced only the auditory stimulus. Results indicated that the number of bar-pressing responses during this test period for the 23-hour food-deprived group increased significantly over that of the pretest period; but this was not true for the other two groups. Estes concluded that a secondary reinforcing stimulus will be effective in strengthening new responses when the original need has been eliminated by satiation, provided that some other source of motivation is present in sufficient intensity to produce activity.[6]

Amount of Primary Reinforcement

The studies of Lawson (1953) and Hopkins (1955) provided no evidence that the effectiveness of a secondary reinforcing stimulus would vary as a function of the amount of primary reinforcement with which it had been paired. Hopkins used six groups of rats and trained them on a black-white discrimination with food reinforcement in the amounts of .05, .20, .60, 1.20, and 2.40 grams. Animals in the sixth group received .20 grams of food with a .33 per cent saccharin concentration. Following discrimination training, all subjects were given 20 trials on a T maze. A white box similar to the one in which the animals received food during discrimination training was placed at the end of the nonpreferred arm of the T maze for each subject. Food reinforcement was not given during the T maze training. Although the results showed that the white box acquired secondary reinforcing properties, the effectiveness of the secondary reinforcing stimuli did not vary as a function of the quantity or quality of the food reinforcement with which it had been paired.

However, studies by D'Amato (1955a), Powell and Perkins (1957), Lawson (1957), Butter and Thomas (1958), and Stebbins (1959) have revealed positive findings. The general technique which these first three studies have utilized has been one in which

[6] The conclusions from all of the studies in this general area (Estes 1949, 1949a; Reid and Slivinske 1954; D'Amato 1955) are difficult to interpret because food and water deprivation states are not independent. Animals which are thirsty have some need for food even though food may be available, and vice versa. See the discussion in Chapter 9 under irrelevant motivational antecedents.

the experimental animals have been given an opportunity to learn about both rewards—a type of differential training, in contrast to those earlier studies in which the experimental animals could learn about only one magnitude of reward. D'Amato's (1955a) study illustrates the method used. Animals first learned to associate five pellets with a goal box of one color and just one pellet with a goal box of another color. The test period consisted of then giving the animals non-rewarded trials on a T maze with the high-reward goal box placed on one arm of the T and the low-reward box on the other. In this type of study, the stimuli whose secondary reinforcing strengths were to be compared were placed in direct competition. Results indicated that the mean number of responses to the high-reward side were significantly greater than chance; in fact, 18 of the 20 animals tested had eight or more responses (of 15 given) to the high-reward side.

The securing of positive findings with the differential training method contrasted with the negative findings found with the single-reward technique, suggests that the type of training is an important variable in determining whether or not the strength of a secondary reinforcing stimulus will vary as a function of the amount of primary reinforcement with which it has been associated. In fact, Lawson's (1957) utilization of both training techniques within the same experimental study has appeared to confirm such a conclusion.

Butter and Thomas (1958), however, have objected to such an interpretation. They have pointed out that in Lawson's study (1957) (part of which employed a single reward technique) the magnitude of the large and small rewards was such that there was no difference between his single-reward groups even in the training situation which utilized primary rewards.[7] Thus, they point out that it is not surprising that stimuli associated with reward amounts which were functionally equivalent as primary reinforcers did not differ in effectiveness as secondary reinforcers. In their study, in which their absolute reinforcement groups (24 per cent sucrose

---

[7] The lack of effect in varying amount of reward has been found not only with Lawson's (1957) study, but with most other studies in which the absolute training technique has been used. In Hopkin's (1955) study, in which the amount of food reinforcement was varied from .05 to 2.40 grms.; he reports that none of the response differences found among the groups during training was significant. On the other hand, differential training invariably results in the learning which takes place under conditions of high reinforcement being superior to that of low.

solution vs. 8 per cent) did differ in their original training (approach to a magazine click) significant differences were obtained in the subsequent test situations.[8]

Butter and Thomas' point of view is well taken. If differences in primary reinforcement do not result in producing differences in the original training, how can one expect secondary reinforcing stimuli to produce such an effect in the test situation? On the other hand, when differences in training do appear and are presumably related to the amount of primary reinforcement, the test situation is nothing more than a positive transfer situation which continues to reflect those differences which were previously present in the original training.

Number of Primary Reinforcements

The experimental studies of Bersh (1951), Hall (1951), and Miles (1956) are unequivocal in indicating that the strength of a secondary reinforcing stimulus is a function of the number of times it has been paired with primary reinforcement. Thus, in the Bersh study (1951), five groups of rats were given 10, 20, 40, 80, or 120 food reinforcements for bar pressing. Each response produced a three-second light with reinforcement occurring after the light had been present for one second. A control group was given 120 regular reinforcements without the accompanying light. The strength of bar pressing was then reduced to the same level for all groups by a period of extinction in the dark. When this had been achieved, each bar depression was permitted to produce a training light for one second. A negatively decelerated curve of low initial slope was obtained for the number of bar-pressing responses made during an hour and a half of testing. Figure 5.5 shows this relationship.

Partial Reinforcement

Since a common finding in many learning studies has been one in which partial reinforcement has resulted in greater resistance to extinction than continuous reinforcement, the strength of secondary reinforcing stimuli has been investigated as a function of this variable. In one study, Mason (1957) trained animals to learn two

[8] Stebbins' (1959) finding has confirmed the Butter and Thomas' (1958) results. A different group for each sucrose solution (5.0, 8.0, 12.7, 20.1, 32.0, and 50.0 per cent) was used. Each concentration was associated with a light and sound which acted as secondary reinforcers. Subsequent secondary-reinforcement tests revealed that the rate of response was a function of the per cent concentration.

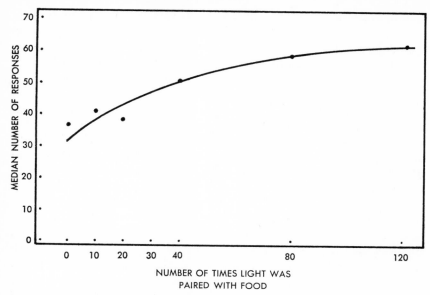

FIG. 5–5. MEDIAN NUMBER OF RESPONSES AS A FUNCTION OF THE NUMBER OF PRIMARY REINFORCEMENTS. (Adapted from Bersh, 1951)

discriminations: (1) black-grey with black positive and (2) white-grey with white positive. The positive stimulus in one discrimination task was reinforced 50 per cent of the trials, while in the other discrimination task, the positive stimulus was reinforced 100 per cent. Two groups of animals were given the same number of trials (thus, number of reinforcements varied), while two other groups were given the same number of reinforcements (number of trials varied). Following acquisition trials, the two positive stimuli of the previously learned discriminations were paired and the animals given ten nonrewarded trials. Results indicated that 17 of the 20 animals trained under the conditions of either equal numbers of trials or equal numbers of reinforcements made six or more choices to the stimulus alley in which they had received continuous reinforcement.

The Mason study (1957) was confirmed by D'Amato, Lachman, and Kivy (1958). These latter investigators indicated, however, that if an absolute training method was used, namely, one group trained under partial and a second group trained under continuous reinforcement, Mason's generalization would not hold. When continuous reinforcement was provided to one group, and partial to another, results indicated that the secondary reinforcing stimulus was significantly stronger when established under conditions of partial rather than continuous reinforcement.

Temporal Relationships

It has been shown that an important variable in the learning situation is the time interval existing between the making of the response and the securing of the reward. Such a gradient should also be important in the determination of the efficiency of a secondary reinforcing stimulus. Jenkins (1950) first trained rats to approach a pan and take a pellet of food at the sound of the food-delivering mechanism. A preliminary buzzer signal was presented at various intervals (1, 3, 9, 27, or 81 seconds) before the pellet was delivered, and the rats were thereby conditioned to approach the food pan at the sound of the buzzer. Next, a bar was introduced which when pressed sounded a buzzer but gave no food. When compared with a control group which had not learned the buzzer-food sequence, the experimental group showed a higher rate of bar pressing. More important was that the shorter the time interval between the sound of the buzzer and the food, the greater the rate of bar pressing. Thus, the time interval between the presentation of the secondary reinforcing stimulus and the receiving of the primary reinforcement was shown to be related to the strength of the secondary reinforcer.

In a somewhat similar experiment, Bersh (1951) has also found that the temporal relation between the neutral stimulus (which later acquired secondary reinforcing strength) and the primary reinforcement with which it is paired is an important variable in the determination of secondary reinforcing strength. Interestingly enough, time intervals of less than one second between the onset of a light and the dropping of the pellet into a food tray were less efficient in strengthening a bar-pressing response than was a one-second interval, the period of time which appeared to be optimal of the varying times used (0, ½, 1, 2, 4, and 10 seconds).

GENERAL AND THEORETICAL ISSUES RELATED TO SECONDARY REINFORCEMENT

Durability

Although, as we have noted, many studies have shown that stimuli can acquire secondary reinforcing characteristics, there has been little evidence to indicate that secondary reinforcing stimuli can operate effectively over a long period of time. It has been the lack of such evidence that has resulted in a number of individuals' being skeptical of its ability to "explain" the protracted behavior sequences which have been divorced from primary reinforcement and which are so typical of man's behavior. The experimental demonstration of secondary reinforcement acting over a long period of time and without opportunity to be even occasionally associated with primary reinforcement is a fundamental requirement if the concept is to assume the heavy burden that reinforcement theorists have placed upon it.

One step in this direction has been taken by Zimmerman (1957, 1959) who has found it possible to provide secondary reinforcing stimuli with much more durability than previous studies have indicated. Briefly, he has utilized an intermittent reinforcement schedule in the establishment as well as in the administration of the secondary reinforcer. A concrete example will illustrate this technique. During the training period, a buzzer is at first always associated with water reinforcement. The training is then changed to that of a fixed-or variable-ratio schedule, with a number of presentations of the buzzer being associated with a single reinforcement. During such training, Zimmerman (1957) reports that the vigor with which the animal responds to the water-delivery mechanism following the buzz does not lessen, although the frequency with which the animal finds water is progressively decreasing. Following such training, the buzzer is tested for its secondary reinforcing properties by presenting it as a consequence of the animal's pressing a bar which is made available to it. Instead of having the buzzer invariably follow bar pressing, which is fairly typical of most secondary reinforcement studies, the procedure again involves intermittent reinforcement. Here the animal may be required to make a large number of bar presses, with the buzzer occurring only a small percentage of the time. Utilizing such a technique, Zimmerman points out, a large number of bar presses can be obtained, and a highly stable response can be maintained through the action of a secondary reinforcing stimulus.

The distinctive characteristics of this type of experimental procedure are as follows: (1) the secondary reinforcing stimulus is discrete and not some fixed characteristic of the experimental situation which persists through time, thus paralleling a typical primary reinforcing event such as the appearance and disappearance of a bit of food and water; (2) during training, primary reinforcement never appears without being preceded by the secondary reinforcing stimulus; however, the appearance of such a stimulus does not guarantee primary reinforcement; (3) the intermittent reinforcement ratios are relatively high.

The Role of Discrimination

In his conceptualization of secondary reinforcement, Hull (1943) indicated that stimuli could become secondary reinforcers by close and consistent occurrences with primary reinforcement. Although Saltzman (1949), in his early study, and, more recently, Wike and McNamara (1957) have indicated that neutral stimuli could acquire secondary reinforcing characteristics by being consistently associated with reward, studies by Schoenfeld, Antonitis, and Bersh (1950); Dinsmoor (1950), Webb and Nolan (1953), and McGuigan and Crockett (1958) have tended to support the position that some type of discrimination training is a necessary condition for a stimulus to acquire secondary reinforcing properties. In the Schoenfeld et al. study, two groups of rats were provided with food for a bar-pressing response. With the experimental group, a light of one second duration went on at the onset of eating while no light was presented to the control group. (It should be noted that typical secondary reinforcing procedures involve the presentation of the secondary reinforcing stimulus prior to the organism making the consummatory response.) Rate of bar pressing during the extinction trials when light alone was presented revealed no significant differences between the two groups. As a result, the authors have concluded that selective reinforcement or discrimination training is required in order to yield a measurable effect of secondary reinforcing stimuli. These experimental findings have indicated the necessity for neutral stimuli, if they are to become secondary reinforcers, to be discriminative stimuli as well.[9] The suggestion is that we must consider secondary reinforcing stimuli as having at least two independent functions; a cue function as well as a reinforcing function.

Wyckoff, Sidowski, and Chambliss (1958) have carried this point a step further by arguing that in order to establish that a stimulus is a secondary reinforcer it is necessary to show an ef-

[9] McGuigan and Crockett (1958) have indicated that what constitutes a discriminative stimulus as well as the specifications of the methods for its development become important questions to answer. It is possible that when they are answered, conflicting findings in the area may be reconciled.

fect on behavior which cannot be attributed to the action of that stimulus as a cue. They point out that if the strength of a response increases, or remains high, when a stimulus is introduced and if this is to be taken as evidence of secondary reinforcement, then one must show that the increase was not due to a cue effect. Their experiment was an attempt to demonstrate secondary reinforcement while attempting to differentiate the reinforcing function from the cue function of a stimulus. They trained rats to approach and lick a water dipper in response to a buzzer. Such training was followed by a test period during which time the lever pressing produced a buzz but no water. Control subjects were given identical training. During the test period, each control animal was "yoked" to an experimental animal so that whenever the experimental animal pressed the bar and received the buzz, the control animal also received the buzz (unless it had responded during the preceding 10 seconds). This type of "yoked" control was necessary, Wyckoff et al. argued, in order to control for the cue action of the buzzer. (A typical control group would have been one in which the buzzer was eliminated during the lever-pressing session. The authors have pointed out that the buzzer would result in the subject running vigorously to the water dipper, and such activity, tending to keep the animal awake and active, would increase the probability of additional lever pressing responses.) The experimental findings provided no indication of secondary reinforcing effects, and as a result, the secondary reinforcing data gathered in the Skinner-box studies have been questioned.[10]

One last consideration should be noted relative to secondary reinforcement and the concept of discrimination. Many studies which have purportedly demonstrated secondary reinforcement have utilized an extinction situation in order to do so. One problem with this type of design is related to a discrimination hypothesis that Mowrer and Jones (1945) formulated and which Bitterman and his associates (Crum, Brown, and Bitterman 1951, Longenecker, Krauskopf, and Bitterman 1952, and Bitterman, Fedder-

---

[10] A series of studies by Crowder and his associates (Crowder, Morris, and McDaniel 1959, Crowder, Gill, Hodge, and Nash 1959, Crowder, Gay, Bright, and Lee 1959, and Crowder, Gay, Fleming, and Hurst 1959) are also relevant. A variety of situations (extinction, acquisition, reconditioning, and retention) were employed to measure secondary reinforcing effects. In all instances "yoked" animals were used which served to control for the facilitation effects of the secondary reinforcing stimulus. Results, contrary to those found by Wyckoff et al. (1958) revealed secondary reinforcing effects in each of the situations employed.

sen, and Tyler 1953) have further expanded. Briefly, the notion is that the rate of extinction is inversely related to the similarity between conditions of training and extinction. In some studies, (Bugelski 1938, McClelland and McGown 1953), in which the experimenter has been interested in investigating secondary reinforcement, a secondary reinforcing stimulus has been presented during training and then the group has been divided in half and extinguished, one with the secondary reinforcing stimulus present and the other with it absent. Typically, the experimental group takes longer to extinguish and therefore indicates the efficiency of the secondary reinforcing stimulus in prolonging resistance to extinction. Another explanation for the finding, however, can be made simply in terms of the aforementioned hypothesis. That is, since training and extinction trials for the experimental group are more similar than for those of the control group, the experimental group will have greater difficulty in discriminating between training and extinction and will thus require a longer time to reach the extinction criterion.

6 • OTHER MOTIVATIONAL
       ANTECEDENTS

As we have previously noted, some psychologists in the late twenties hypothesized that physiological needs provided the basic structure from which all other types of motivation were derived. This point of view has been extremely persistent and has had considerable acceptance over the past thirty years.

In recent years, other writers have hypothesized the existence of other antecedents which they believe are as basic to behavior as are the physiological needs. Harlow (1953a), for example, has consistently reiterated the thesis that external stimulation (other than tissue injury) is as significant a source of behavior elicitation as internal stimulation. He writes: "I wish to emphasize that on purely theoretical grounds external stimulation is at least as basic and important a source of behavior elicitation as internal stimulation, and that there is no justification on phylogenetic, ontogenetic, or physiological grounds for assuming that motives aroused by one source are more basic or important than motives aroused by the other."

This chapter will examine the various types of motivational antecedents which investigators believe are as fundamental as an organism's physiological needs.

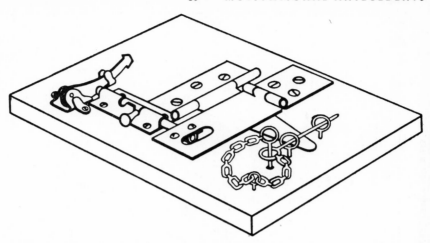

FIG. 6–1. SIX-DEVICE MECHANICAL PUZZLE. (Adapted from Harlow and McClearn, 1954)

THE ROLE OF EXTERNAL STIMULATION

"Manipulative" Stimuli

A series of studies by Harlow and his associates have provided the experimental basis upon which Harlow has attacked the position that physiological needs constitute the prime motivational antecedents for most organisms. In the first of these, Harlow, Harlow, and Meyer (1950) provided four rhesus monkeys with 12 days' experience in manipulating an assembled mechanical puzzle whose solution did not lead to any special incentive such as food or water. Four other monkeys had disassembled puzzles placed in their cages for the same period of time. The performance of the two groups was then compared by noting the responses to the assembled puzzles for five-minute periods on the next two days of the experiment. The results indicated that the experimental monkeys were significantly more efficient than their controls when measured by total number of solutions, solutions obtained in 60 seconds, and ratio of correct to incorrect responses.

A second study by Harlow (1950) with a more complex puzzle and a third by Harlow and McClearn (1954) with a discrimination type learning situation revealed findings which were consistent with those previously obtained. Figure 6.1 illustrates the complex type puzzle, and Figure 6.2 indicates how correct manipulatory responses increased as a function of days of training.

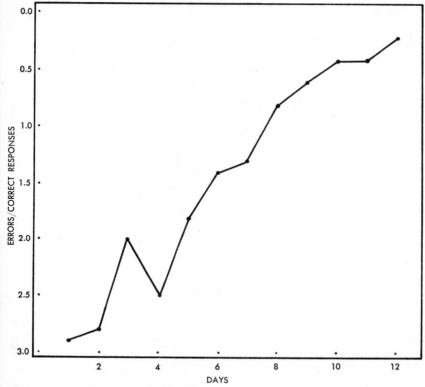

FIG. 6–2. LEARNING CURVE ON FIVE-RESTRAINING-DEVICE PUZZLE FOR TWO SUBJECTS. (Adapted from Harlow and McClearn, 1954)

Harlow has rejected any explanation based on physiological needs and their subsequent satisfaction which might be used to account for the learning of his animals in these experimental situations. He has explained his findings by positing a manipulation drive. In the Harlow, Harlow, and Meyer (1950) study, the authors state, "It is the opinion of the experimenters that a manipulation drive can best account for the behavior obtained in this investigation. The stimuli to the drive are external and, in conjunction with the animals' capacities, set the pattern of behavior. The manipulation is conceived of as having reinforcing properties that account for the precision and speed the subjects acquire in carrying out the solution, and the persistence they show in repeated performances."

Harlow, Blazek, and McClearn (1956) and Mason, Harlow, and Rueping (1959) have shown that by 20 to 30 days of age, the infant monkey exhibits strong manipulation tendencies and that such behavior tends to increase with age and experience during at least the next 15- to 30-day period. The early onset of such manipulatory behavior, and the absence of clear-cut satiation effects, has strengthened Harlow's belief that such behavior cannot be dependent upon physiological needs or any of their derivatives.

That the manipulation of objects is reinforcing to species other than the monkey has been experimentally demonstrated by Thackray and Michels (1958) using the raccoon, Miles (1958) the kitten, and Terrell (1959) the human child.

Novel Stimulation

Dashiell (1925) in an early study found that the stimulation of a checkerboard maze seemed to elicit exploratory behavior in the satiated rat. In order to "explain" such behavior, he posited a curiosity drive. Nissen (1930) a few years later also observed behavior from which he inferred the presence of curiosity. There was little general enthusiasm for the acceptance of curiosity as a motive, however, because this was the beginning of a period in which emphasis was placed upon physiological needs as the primary antecedents for motivational states.

This state of affairs changed in 1950 when Berlyne (1950) again considered curiosity as a motive, with its mode of operation based upon two postulates. The first of these stated that when a novel stimulus impinges upon an organism's receptors there will occur drive-stimulus-producing responses called curiosity. The second stated that as a curiosity-arousing stimulus continues to impinge upon an organism's receptors, curiosity will diminish. In addition, these postulates had three corollaries derived from Hull's (1943) two-factor theory of inhibition: (1) The behavior that increases such stimulation will be reinforced, (2) after a time exploration will cease, and (3) after a further lapse of time there will be a second stage of exploration but less than the first.

Berlyne's experimental apparatus designed to measure curiosity was a small box in which at one end there was a small alcove to which an object could be fastened. A beam of infra-red light passed through the box just in front of the alcove. Whenever the beam was broken by the subject investigating the object, a counter registered the approach. Berlyne's experimental findings, using rats as subjects, provided support for his postulates and corollaries.

A year later, Montgomery (1951) published the first of a series of studies in which he posited the presence of an exploratory drive in order to account for behavior similar to that found by Berlyne. Such a drive, Montgomery hypothesized, was aroused by novel stimulation which elicited exploratory behavior. Such behavior decreases with time of continuous exposure to a given stimulus situation and recovers during a period of nonexposure. Montgomery's subjects have almost invariably been white rats, and his experimental apparatus has been a Y maze divided into sections, with the number of sections traversed representing a measure of the exploratory drive.

The similarity of Montgomery's position to that of Berlyne is apparent. One primary difference between the two points of view relates to the recovery of the exploratory response as a function of an intervening interval of time. Berlyne posited that after such an interval, the second amount of exploratory behavior will be less than the first. Montgomery, however, has found complete spontaneous recovery of the exploratory behavior over a 24-hour rest period.

Montgomery was interested not only in how the presence of an exploratory drive operated to produce a systematic exploration of an apparatus, but also in determining if organisms could learn a maze habit when reinforcement consisted of a short period of *exploration* in a novel environment. Two studies (Montgomery 1954, Montgomery and Segall 1955) using T mazes examined such an interest. The first required the animal to learn a position habit while the second involved learning of a discrimination task. In this latter study, rats were given 70 trials on a black-white discrimination problem. Correct responses were followed by permitting a one-minute period of exploration in a large Dashiell-type maze; incorrect responses resulted in the animal's being confined in a small empty goal box.[1] The apparatus is illustrated in Figure 6.3.

[1] Berlyne and Slater (1957) and Chapman and Levy (1957) have called attention to the fact that frequently, so-called novel stimuli are also more spacious and complex than control stimuli. In the Montgomery and Segall study (1955), the Dashiell maze differed from the empty goal box in terms of spaciousness as well as complexity. Moreover, the spaciousness dimension could be an important one inasmuch as rats appear to learn to avoid blind alleys. Berlyne and Slater (1957) have demonstrated the importance of spaciousness by finding that rats prefer the arm of a maze which leads to a spacious goal box in contrast to an arm leading to a blind alley. In the Chapman and Levy study (1957), spaciousness was controlled by using similarly sized end boxes; novelty was produced in

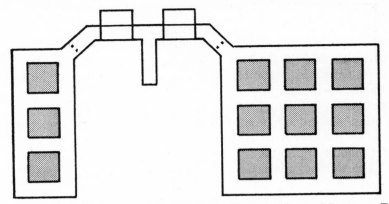

FIG. 6–3. T Maze Using Dashiell Type Checkerboard Mazes as End Boxes. Only part of the Dashiell maze on the left side of the T maze is shown. (Adapted from Montgomery and Segall, 1955)

Figure 6.4 indicates the average number of correct choices as a function of trials. It is to be noted that the mean number of correct choices increased significantly over the 70-trial period. Novel stimulation, in addition to eliciting certain types of responses, may reinforce them as well.

Inasmuch as the exploratory drive has been posited by Montgomery to be a primary source of motivation for the organism, he has been anxious to show its independence of physiological as well as other hypothesized need states. He has found that exploratory behavior is *reduced* by 24 hours of food and water deprivation (Montgomery 1953). Figure 6.5 shows the average amount of exploratory behavior as a function of time available for exploration for the deprived and control groups. A second experiment, in which 48- and 72-hour food deprivation periods were used, did not, however, result in further reductions in the amount of exploratory behavior (Montgomery 1953). Thompson (1953) has been unable to replicate these results, finding no difference in exploration be-

one of them by changing the color and texture of the goal box walls. Their findings indicated that novel goal boxes (with spaciousness controlled) resulted in more rapid running to them than nonnovel goal boxes. Finally, Berlyne and Slater (1957) in a second experiment found that rats prefer an arm which leads to complex stimuli to one which is empty. Inasmuch as their complex stimuli consisted of a number of stimulus objects not found in the empty goal box, it appears difficult, however, to differentiate their definition of complexity from one of novelty.

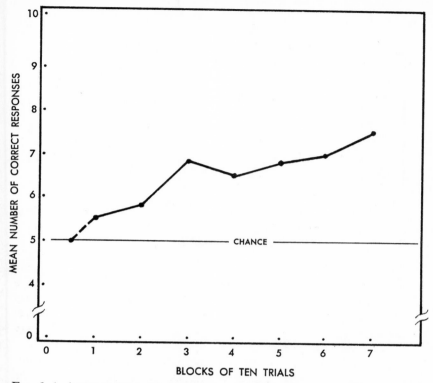

Fig. 6–4. Average Number of Correct Choices as a Function of Ten-Trial Blocks. (Adapted from Montgomery and Segall, 1955)

tween satiated animals and those under 24 and 48 hours of food deprivation. Montgomery's (1953) findings, however, have been confirmed by Zimbardo and Montgomery (1957). In this latter study, animals were placed under food as well as water deprivation for periods of 0, 24, 48, and 72 hours, with exploratory activity measured in a modified Dashiell checkerboard maze. Results indicated that food and water deprivation reduced the amount of exploration. One finding which differed from that obtained in the early study (Montgomery 1953) was that food deprivation periods of 48 and 72 hours produced greater decrements in exploratory activity than a 24-hour deprivation period. Water deprivation, however, did not show this trend.

It is impossible to differentiate the exploratory behavior which Montgomery is measuring from the way some investigators have

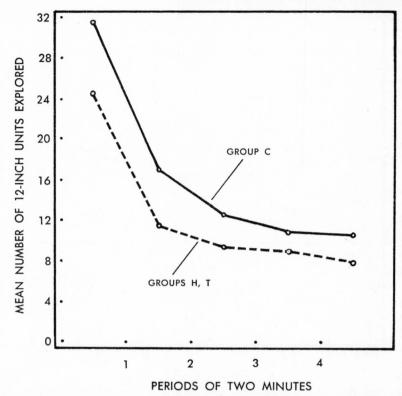

FIG. 6–5. AVERAGE AMOUNT OF EXPLORATORY BEHAVIOR AS A FUNCTION OF TIME FOR THE DEPRIVED AND CONTROL GROUPS. (Adapted from Montgomery, 1953)

measured spontaneous activity, and many of the experimental findings examining the relationship between spontaneous activity and a need for food and water, are in conflict with Montgomery's data. Dashiell (1925), Adlerstein and Fehrer (1955), and Fehrer (1956) have found that deprived animals explore more and show greater activity than satiated ones. There is some question, however, as to whether the increased activity is a function of the operation of a need state operating alone and independently of any other variable. Zimbardo and Montgomery (1957) have "explained" Adlerstein and Fehrer's findings by pointing out that Adlerstein and Fehrer's procedure for producing their food deprivation period involved placing the animals on a feeding cycle at the same time each day and in the room in which the experiment was conducted. Zimbardo and Montgomery believe that the hungry rats were particularly active because they were run at about their meal time. Internal and external cues correlated with the time of day could have produced the increased activity because of conditioned stimulation of the consummatory response.[2]

Zimbardo and Miller (1958) have also noted the conflicting findings in this area and have called attention to the possibility that the type of apparatus usually employed in these studies may set up a conflict between tendencies to continue to explore the immediate environment more thoroughly and to move on to explore the next unit. The apparatus they have employed was the familiar two-compartment-Miller-acquired-drive apparatus (See Figure 4–2). Their experimental procedure consisted of giving hungry and satiated animals either immediate or delayed access to the second compartment. Results indicated that if access to the second compartment was provided immediately, satiated animals would move to explore it more rapidly than those which were hungry. On the other hand, if the animals were delayed in the first compartment for a period of time (two minutes), the food-deprived animals would respond more rapidly than the satiated animals.

Some investigators have hypothesized that exploratory behavior is but one expression of the general activity of the organism. Montgomery (1953a), however, has shown that moderate activity deprivation over an eight-day period has no effect upon the amount of exploratory behavior.

Myers and Miller (1954) have attempted to account for findings in this general area by suggesting that monotony arouses a boredom drive which is reduced by exploratory behavior, thus attempting to integrate these studies within a drive reduction framework. Studies by Charlesworth and Thompson (1957) as well as Montgomery and Zimbardo (1957) have explored the possibility of the existence of such a drive. Charlesworth and Thompson (1957) confined rats for 3, 6, or 9 days in either a homogeneous light or dark environment (and presumably boredom producing), while a control group was permitted the normal laboratory environment. The animals were permitted to explore a box which was adjacent to their home cage following these experimental periods. Although Myers and Miller (1954) would be likely to predict that increased

[2] A further discussion of spontaneous activity and variables related to this kind of behavior will be found in Chapter 7.

boredom should result in increased exploration, Charlesworth and Thompson (1957) found no differences in such behavior among any of the groups. And in a similar but somewhat more extensive study, Montgomery and Zimbardo (1957) provided rats with either (1) a normal environment, (2) an environment in which there was both sensory and activity restriction, or (3) an environment in which activity was restricted. These environmental conditions lasted for either 25, 50, or 100 days. Each of the groups was then given the usual exploratory-behavior tests in the standard Y maze. No differences were obtained in units explored among the varying groups.

Myers and Miller (1954) did not specify those conditions which would produce boredom, and a basic problem exists in providing an adequate definition of it. Nonetheless, the experimental findings of Charlesworth and Thompson (1957) and Montgomery and Zimbardo (1957) are suggestive in indicating that sensory and/or behavioral deprivation, which one might guess would produce boredom, does not result in increased exploratory behavior in the rat. These findings make it mandatory that Myers and Miller (1954) "spell out" their hypothesis in somewhat greater detail if a "boredom drive" is to be given serious attention by future experimenters.

Welker (1956, 1956a, 1956b), using chimpanzees as his experimental subjects, has confirmed the findings of other investigators not only in demonstrating the existence of exploratory or curiosity behavior but also in demonstrating a decreasing responsiveness with repeated exposure to the novel stimuli. His experimental work has suggested that (1) young animals (one to two years of age) are much more timid about exploring and manipulating objects than are three- or four- or seven- or eight-year-olds. Seven- or eight-year-old chimps show less interest in the type of object used in the studies and this has suggested to Welker that there is an optimum period of play and exploration at about four years of age. It further appears that a novelty or strangeness factor in objects or persons elicits a fear or an initial caution on the part of the infant chimpanzees. Such behavior seems to be closely aligned to the "irrational fear" of strangers which has been discussed by Hebb and Riesen (1943).[3] It has its counterpart in rats, as Mont-

[3] In this study, the authors found that infant chimpanzees fear and avoid strange individuals, and that even with repeated presentation there is very slow adaptation.

gomery (1955) and Montgomery and Monkman (1955) have demonstrated. Montgomery's (1955) experimental work indicated that novel stimuli evoked not only exploratory behavior, but fear as well, which resulted in an approach-avoidance conflict.[4]

Welker (1957, 1959) has also been interested in this problem. He has suggested that different behaviors might result if the animal were given a choice in its exploration of the novel situation. In one study Welker (1957), investigating the animal's free versus forced choice into a novel situation, has noted that rats which were placed directly in the situation (forced) showed a high level of exploration which decreased throughout sessions, while the behavior of animals which were "free" to explore did not show such a trend. In a second study Welker (1959) found that a rat's activity was reduced if it was permitted to pass freely from the open-field situation to an adjoining enclosed, dark box. He has suggested that the activity of rats which are forced to occupy a novel situation may represent escape rather than exploratory behavior. The best test of whether or not an animal is adapted and exploring a stimulus situation for novelty can be achieved only if it is allowed access to the novel stimuli from familiar, and especially darkened places. He has concluded that "since most studies of exploration or curiosity in rats have not provided for this important control . . . the internal mechanisms which have been inferred to prompt such behavior may be other than those proposed."

An interesting aspect of the general characteristics of exploratory behavior has been indicated by Havelka (1956). Havelka provided hungry rats with a choice of securing food from either of two equally familiar situations. In one situation food was always found in the same location, whereas in the other situation, food was not only at a greater distance from the starting point but was varied

[4] Some stimuli result in the organism, approaching them, thus giving rise to inferences concerning the organism's exploratory or curiosity drive, while other stimuli result in their avoidance, from which investigators have inferred the presence of fear. Functional relationships existing between the particular characteristics of such stimulation and approach or avoidance behavior have not been examined, although Berlyne (1951) has stated that change or novelty may signify either (1) the stimulus is new in relation to the organism's whole life history or (2) the stimulus is new in relation to what has been previously experienced. He has suggested that the first situation elicits approach behavior, while the second results in fear and avoidance. Barnett (1958) has supported such a suggestion by reporting observations of wild rats. For these animals, investigatory behavior dominates in a totally new environment, while avoidance results from a relatively minor change in a familiar constellation.

from trial to trial so that the animal had to search for it. Havelka found that some animals consistently preferred the complex variable-goal situation to the simple fixed-goal situation. As a result he has argued that the behavior of his animals was an expression of something more than exploratory behavior. He has considered the behavior of his animals to be problem seeking rather than merely exploratory.

SENSORY AND BEHAVIOR DEPRIVATION

What has been posited to be another aspect of exploration, originally suggested by Harlow's work on externally elicited behavior, has been investigated by Butler and his associates in a series of experiments. In these experiments, a monkey is placed in a wire cage, and the sides are covered with opaque material which prevents the subject from looking out. This apparatus is illustrated in Figure 6.6. A trial is begun by raising an opaque screen and exposing the test stimuli to the animal. If the subject pushes against the correct stimulus, the door opens, and the animal is permitted to view the surroundings for 30 seconds. The screen is then lowered, ending the trial. If the subject pushes against the incorrect stimulus, the door does not open, but the screen is immediately lowered. In his first study, Butler (1953) has demonstrated that monkeys can learn object discriminations, and maintain their performance at relatively high levels of efficiency, with only the opportunity to explore the environment serving as a reward. Furthermore, he and Harlow (Butler and Harlow 1954) have demonstrated that such behavior extinguishes very, very slowly. A dimensional analysis of incentive conditions has not been made, although experimental evidence has demonstrated that the strength of the animal's response is a function of the type of viewing conditions. Butler (1954) has shown that frequency of response is highest when the incentive is another monkey, and lowest with an empty chamber. Rabedeau and Miles (1959) have found a marked decrease in response frequency when conditions are changed from viewing normal laboratory paraphernalia to a darkened room.

Butler considers his experimental work as demonstrating the importance of external stimulation, but unlike those studies positing a manipulation drive, it is possible to specify an appropriate motivational antecedent. The monkey in the opaque box is effectively

FIG. 6–6. VISUAL EXPLORATION APPARATUS. (Harlow, 1953)

restricted from receiving external stimulation, and thus a type of sensory deprivation appears to be such an antecedent for the instrumental behavior of the subject.

That such behavior is related to deprivation effects is indicated in a study by Butler (1957), who deprived monkeys of varied visual experience for either zero, two, four, or eight hours. Following such deprivation, the subjects were tested to determine whether their responses to visual incentives would be increased as a result of such deprivation. Reinforcement consisted of a 12-second view of the monkey colony outside the test cage, Results indicated that the number of responses to the visual incentive during the test period increased up until a 4-hour deprivation period and then leveled off. Figure 6.7 shows the relationship between the frequency of the response and the number of hours of visual exploratory deprivation.[5]

Some of the most interesting studies in the sensory deprivation area are those which have been done with humans. Bexton, Heron, and Scott (1954) studied the effects of depriving male college students of visual, auditory and many kinesthetic stimuli. The subjects were

[5] The reader will recognize that these findings are not in agreement with those of Montgomery and Zimbardo (1957), who found no increase in the exploratory behavior of the rat as a function of previous sensory restriction.

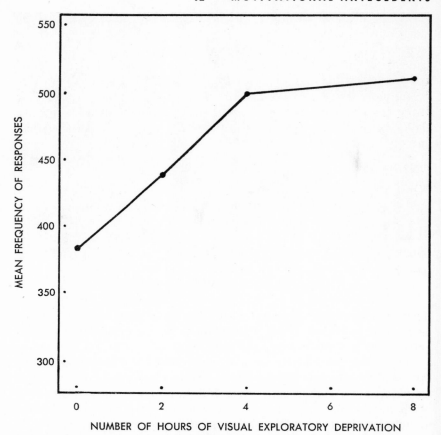

FIG. 6–7. MEAN FREQUENCY OF RESPONSES AS A FUNCTION OF DURATION OF DEPRIVATION. (Adapted from Butler, 1957)

paid twenty dollars per day to rest in a quiet room with their hands and feet encased in cardboard cylinders, diffusing goggles over their eyes, and foam rubber pads over their ears. Such conditions were relaxed only to permit the subject to eat or perform eliminative functions. During the early part of the study the students slept, but then became restless and irritable and began to have disturbing visual hallucinations. Few of them could endure the conditions for more then three days.[6] Heron, Doane, and Scott (1956) subjected themselves to six days of sensory deprivation

[6] It should be reported that Vernon and Hoffman (1956) have not been able to verify all of the Bexton, Heron and Scott findings.

under conditions paralleling the previous study, and reported similar findings. Finally, Lilly (1956) floated individuals in tanks of tepid water. The subjects, who were equipped with masks, received no visual stimulation and only limited aural stimulation. He reported that three hours was the longest that any subject was able to continue under the conditions. Furthermore, the need for stimulation was so intense that after even brief periods of deprivation, the subjects rubbed their fingers together and twitched muscles in order to obtain it.

Restriction of Spontaneous Activity

Observing a satiated rat in an activity wheel, a well-fed monkey in his cage, or a recently fed infant in its crib, reveals some activity on the part of each organism. In short, it is unusual to find organisms, even those with all of their physiological needs satisfied, in a completely quiescent state. Although some of the early investigators believed that such activity was merely an expression of the metabolic functioning of the organism, others have not been willing to accept such behavior as a "given." As a result, activity has been frequently explained by some in terms of a number of weak physiological needs which combine to provide the organism with an energy level that is capable of producing such behavior.

Still other investigators have accounted for such behavior by postulating a "need to be active." The physiological basis for such a need, however, has not been indicated. Behaviorally, evidence for such a postulation would be a positive correlation between the amount of inactivity that was imposed and the organism's subsequent activity level. Thus, restriction of activity becomes an important motivational antecedent for the postulation of any activity motive.

One of the early studies in this area was done by Shirley (1928a), who, after obtaining activity records for rats living under "normal" conditions, had them live in extremely small cages for periods of one, two, three, or five days. Following such restricted activity, the animals were placed in an activity wheel. Results indicated that a period of enforced inactivity for one or two days increased activity over normal by about 25 per cent, although this increase was not statistically significant. The longer periods of restriction, however, led to a decrease in activity-wheel behavior.

Siegel (1946), also using rats, measured activity by using a rectangular cage with a beam from a photoelectric cell dividing the

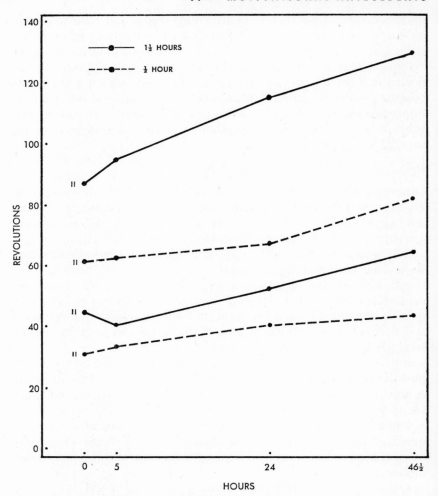

FIG. 6–8. MEAN ACTIVITY OF GROUPS I AND II FOR ENTIRE ONE AND ONE-HALF HOUR TEST SESSION AND FOR INITIAL HALF-HOUR TEST SESSION AFTER 0, 5, 24, AND 46½ HOUR OF CONFINEMENT. (Adapted from Hill, 1956)

cage in two. Locomotion from one half of the cage to the other by the rat could thus be measured. Animals were first placed in confinement chambers which were so small that it was barely possible for the animal to turn around. The length of confinement period was varied (0, 6, and 24 hours). The subjects were then placed in the rectangular cage and their activity was recorded for a half-hour period. Results indicated that six hours of confinement resulted in a significant *decrease* in activity; 12 and 24 hours of confinement resulted in a nonsignificant decrease and increase respectively.

A second study by Siegel and Alexander (1948) was undertaken to confirm the earlier findings that six hours of enforced inactivity depressed subsequent activity. The effect of such enforced inactivity was observed over two different times of day. The results indicated that when the animal was confined from late morning to early evening (11 A.M. to 8:30 P.M.) such confinement was followed by a significant diminution in general activity, thus confirming the earlier study; however, when confinement was provided during the early morning to middle afternoon (5 A.M. to 2:30 P.M.), activity remained about the same as under zero hours of confinement. These findings support the conclusion that the time of day exerts an important influence on activity. As Siegel and Alexander point out, inactivity introduced during a "natural period" of relatively high activity depresses subsequent activity.

The lack of clear evidence to support the existence of a motive based on activity deprivation in rats led Hill (1956) to measure activity-wheel behavior after 0, 5, 24 and 46½ hours of confinement. Two groups of 20 rats per group were run under such conditions, with the amount of activity measured over a ½ and 1½ hour periods. Both groups indicated that activity was an increasing function of hours of confinement, although one group did show slightly less running after five hours of confinement than after zero hours. Hill's findings are presented in Figure 6.8.

Subsequent experiments by Hill (1958) have demonstrated that increased activity following confinement (two or four days) was not specific to wheel running but also appeared when activity was measured in the stabilimeter or tilt cage. A second experiment (1958a) revealed that experimental animals confined for much longer periods (40 days) also showed greater activity in a stabilimeter than their controls immediately following release from their confined quarters, but decreased activity for several days thereafter.[7]

---

[7] The increase in activity following a long confinement period is in contrast to the findings of Shirley (1928a). Hill (1958a) has stated that the type of apparatus appears to be responsible for the divergent findings. Using the activity wheel, he also found activity decrement following long periods of confinement. The type of apparatus used also plays an important role, as indicated by Montgomery and Zimbardo's study (1957). These investigators found that activity deprivation for either 25, 50, or 100 days did not result in any increase in number of units travelled in a Y maze.

Thompson and Heron (1954) were interested in examining somewhat similar effects with dogs, although the restriction of activity continued for a much longer time than in the previously cited studies. Their experiment consisted of imposing three degrees of severity of restriction on 12 Scottish terriers for the first seven to ten months of life. Eight litter mates, reared as pets, served as control animals. The severe restriction situation consisted of placing the animal in complete isolation in a small wooden box which was lighted only on alternate days. Moderately restricted dogs were raised in groups of two or three in ordinary living cages with the front of each cage being covered with cardboard to prevent them from seeing out, but the top was left uncovered in order to allow light to enter. Slightly restricted animals, reared in living cages, had neither the fronts nor the tops of the cages covered. Furthermore, these animals were occasionally handled and taken out periodically for clipping and medication. Following one of these restrictive experiences for seven to ten months, each animal was taken to a small room and permitted to move about and explore freely for four daily one-half-hour sessions. The results, verifying the findings of the earlier and preliminary studies of Clarke, Heron, Fetherstonhaugh, Forgays, and Hebb (1951), indicated that dogs restricted in early life were more active than the control animals. In examining the effects of severity of restriction, there was some tendency for severely restricted dogs to be more active than slightly restricted dogs, but the difference was not very large. Inasmuch as all of the moderately restricted animals were in two older age groups, it was not possible to compare their behavior with either of the other two restricted groups.

Some General Considerations

At this point, it seems appropriate to examine somewhat critically some of the material which we have just presented. One problem has been the tendency of investigators to postulate the existence of different drives or motives, although the same type of behavior has been used from which to infer their presence.[8] In many of the

[8] To further confuse the issue, a number of investigators have accounted for some of these behavior patterns by recourse to nonmotivational concepts. For example, the tendency of a rat to alternate its selection of arms in a T maze has been attributed by Montgomery (1952) to the operation of an exploratory drive. Such alternation behavior has also been explained, however, by using the concepts of reactive inhibition (Hull 1943) or stimulus satiation (Glanzer 1953, 1953a). Dember and Earl (1957) have proposed that behavior which has been labeled

experiments we have cited, the investigator has had a choice of positing either a curiosity, an exploratory, or an activity drive. Montgomery, for example, could have used the behavior of his animals as indicating a curiosity drive rather than an exploratory one. Inasmuch as one appears to be a synonym for the other, the use of the two drive states seems superfluous. Moreover, the running behavior measured by Montgomery has been used by a number of investigators as merely a measure of general activity.

A related problem is that frequently the kind of behavior observed indicates the kind of drive state that will be inferred. It is noted that a monkey will manipulate a puzzle, and that manipulative efficiency increases as a function of trials. Since the monkey does not have any need reduced, and there is no specified reinforcement in the situation, a manipulation drive is posited to account for the learning. Such a drive presumably "explains" such behavior. There is serious difficulty in using only the behavior pattern to indicate the existence of a motive. Such a point of view will lead us to essentially the same position psychologists held when instincts were in vogue some years ago.

A second general problem has been the difficulty of fitting many of the experimental findings into the motivational framework which most investigators have found convenient to use. Up to this chapter, it has been possible to draw a distinction between those studies which have manipulated a certain class of motivational antecedents which were present *prior* to the organism's making some instrumental response (i.e.: need states or stimuli associated with need states) and those antecedents which followed the response and presumably increased the probability of responding (rewards and stimuli associated with rewards). In other words, in most experimental studies, it has been possible to relate a certain class of motivational antecedents to the energizing or arousal function of a motive, and another class of antecedents to the selective or reinforcing function.

A number of the studies which we have just considered can, of course, be fitted into such a framework. Some of Butler's work appears to indicate that sensory deprivation produces some *need* for

---

as exploration, manipulation, or curiosity belongs to the general class of behavior described as attention. By attention they consider any behavior pattern which has as its end state contact between the organism and selected portions of its environment. The variables which they have examined in this regard have not been usually conceived as motivational ones.

the organism to obtain stimulation; moreover, the receiving of certain types of stimulation will reinforce the response which is instrumental in securing it. Montgomery and Segall (1955) have shown that it is possible to *reinforce* a right-or left-turning response by permitting the rat to locomote in a Dashiell checkerboard maze, and similarly, Miles (1958) has found it possible to reinforce certain instrumental responses in the kitten if the animal is given opportunity to manipulate objects in a goal box. An examination of the studies of Montgomery and Segall (1955) and Miles (1958), although one might question what need is operating, clearly indicate the reinforcing state of affairs.

In a number of other studies, however, the distinction between the need or drive and the reinforcement is not clear. The motivational antecedents for producing a manipulation drive appear to be undefined, or at least, we do not have any defining operations in the same sense that food and water deprivation results in the hunger or thirst drive. Thus, when a monkey manipulates a puzzle, to what do we attribute the arousal or energizing function? Harlow has stated that external stimulation is as basic as internal stimulation in behavior elicitation. Presumably the arousal or eliciting function is a product of the varied stimulation which arises from the puzzle. The problem, however, is attempting to define those external stimulus situations which will elicit this type of behavior.

A second consideration relates to the nature of reinforcement in such studies. If manipulation behavior increases as a function of trials, what is reinforcing such behavior? Here there is some confusion. Myers and Miller (1954) have stated that Harlow's position is that stimuli not only elicit the drive, but also serve as a reward. Harlow, however, has stated that it is the manipulation itself which is conceived of as having reinforcing properties. In the Harlow, Harlow, and Meyer study (1950), it is stated: "The manipulation is conceived of as having reinforcing properties that account for the precision and speed the subjects acquire in carrying out the solution, and the persistence they show in repeated performances." In other words, the manipulation response is its own reinforcement. Since reinforcement is usually conceived of as some stimulus which follows and strengthens the response, it becomes difficult to think in terms of the response reinforcing itself.[9]

[9] It is possible that the proprioceptive stimulation arising from the manipulation response may be considered to be the reinforcement. Why, however, should proprioceptive stimulation act as a reward in this kind of situation but not in others?

Perhaps much of the behavior which we have considered might be classified as a reflection of an inherent motive which Woodworth (1947) some time ago called the will to perceive. Woodworth states: "The present thesis . . . is that perception is always driven by a direct, inherent motive which might be called the will to perceive. Whatever ulterior motives may be present from time to time, this direct perceptual motive is always present in any use of the senses . . . To see, to hear—to see clearly, to hear distinctly—to make out what it is one is seeing or hearing—moment by moment, such concrete, immediate motives dominate the life of relation with the environment."

In his elaboration of the Woodworth thesis, Nissen (1954) believes that the requirement of all tissues is that they perform their normal function. He believes that "the sense organs 'want to' see and hear and feel just as much as the mouth or stomach or bloodstream 'want to' eat or contract or maintain a certain nutrient balance." Stated more broadly: "Capacity is its own motivation."

Restriction of Instrumental or Consummatory Activity

The restriction or blocking of an instrumental or consummatory response has given rise to what many investigators have posited to be frustration. Before considering the motivational aspects of frustration, it is appropriate to discuss the term itself. An examination of the many ways it has been used indicates that there is much of what semanticists call "process-product confusion." That is, some individuals who use frustration have in mind primarily a process, while others have thought primarily in terms of its product. A somewhat similar point of view has been expressed by Marx (1956), who has called attention to four independent usages of the term. Marx writes that frustration has been used as (1) an independent variable—the frustration operation involves the blocking of some aspect of the instrumental response or the consummatory response itself, (2) as a dependent variable—here frustration is conceived of as a type of emotional response, (3) as a phenomenon or feeling on the part of the organism, and (4) as an intervening construct—here frustration is considered as a type of internal state which may be initiated or produced by some type of blocking operation. Such a state is frequently assumed to be motivating and has led some to posit a specific motivational state called frustration.

In an early theoretical article, Brown and Farber (1951)

pointed out that although frustration should differ from other types of motivation with regard to those conditions appropriate for its arousal as well as reduction, a frustration drive should have similar functional characteristics. Presumably, then, it should have an energizing as well as directive and selective function. With regard to the energizing function, these authors have postulated that a frustration drive should have the functional status of an irrelevant drive which should combine with other drive states to increase an organism's effective drive level. As for its directive function, they believe that the frustration drive should result in producing discriminable internal stimuli to which the organism could attach some response. Finally, the reduction of frustration should act as reinforcement in the establishment of learned responses.

Experimental Evidence

Although the contribution of Freud in the area must be acknowledged, the work of Dollard, Doob, Miller, Mowrer, and Sears (1939) in their *Frustration and Aggression* text was of major importance in placing the concept of frustration in an experimental setting. These authors postulated that if an organism was blocked in the making of a goal response, a state of affairs occurred which they termed frustration. Frustration was thus an instigator (or motivator) of other responses. Their primary purpose, however, was not to examine the motivational characteristics of frustration but to demonstrate that its product was invariably aggression. We shall return to the Dollard, *et al.* point of view in Chapter 11.

Some years later, Rohrer (1949) posited a frustration drive in order to account for his experimental findings. In his study, two groups of rats, after being trained in a modified Skinner box, were given extinction trials. One group received the nonrewarded trials at ten-second intervals, the other group at 90-second intervals. The 90-second–interval group showed significantly greater resistance to extinction. In explaining the superiority of the distributed extinction group, Rohrer assumed that an internal inhibition state builds up within the organism as a function of its making a response. This internal inhibition state, which Pavlov has called internal inhibition, but which Rohrer has termed a frustration drive, results in varied responses which interfere with the previously learned response, and thus results in extinction. The massing of trials does not permit the dissipation of this internal inhibition state, which, of course, then results in a speeding up of the extinction process.[10]

As many individuals have pointed out, it is not necessary to posit a frustration drive in order to handle Rohrer's experimental findings. The slower rates of extinction under distributed (as contrasted to massed) extinction trials have been successfully handled by existing inhibition theory. As a result, Amsel and Roussel (1952) employed a different experimental situation in order to demonstrate the motivational properties of frustration. Rats were deprived of food and trained to run along an alley into goal box "1," and from there along another alley into goal box "2." The running speeds between goal box "1" and goal box "2" were recorded. Then on half of the subsequent trials, the subjects were not given a reward in the first goal box—the omission of reward presumably producing frustration. The experimental findings revealed a significant decrease in running speed for the frustration trials, thus supporting the authors' basic premise that frustration resulted in a motivational state.[11] Figure 6.9 summarizes these findings. Their experiment indicated, however, no significant differences among 5-, 10-, and 30-second periods of delay in the empty goal box, with the result that

[10] In contrast to the findings of Rohrer (1949), a study by Sheffield (1950), who used rats trained to run down an alley for food, indicated that a 15-second interval between extinction trials resulted in resistance to extinction which was superior to a 15-minute interval. Sheffield has accounted for her findings by hypothesizing that the frustration which is generated in the nonreward situation does not have an opportunity to dissipate during the massed extinction trials, and thus maintains the vigor of the response. On the other hand, with spaced extinction trials, the frustration drive has an opportunity to dissipate. As she further points out, if the increase in the motivational complex is channeled into the response being measured, it results in slower extinction with massed trials. However, if, as Rohrer states, the frustration drive results in responses which are antagonistic to the response being measured, distributed practice will result in a slower extinction rate. Unfortunately, there appears to be no easy way to determine whether or not the frustration drive will be channeled into the response being measured.

[11] Seward, Pereboom, Butler, and Jones (1957) have objected to Amsel's interpretation, and have posited that the feeding operation provided in the first goal box slows down the performance of the control animals, thus providing the experimental animals with apparently more rapid running times. Their interpretation of Amsel's findings was supported by an experiment in which, in order to control equivalent amounts of food consumed, they prefed the experimental group .5 or 1 gram of food in a special chamber prior to being placed in the starting box.

In his reply, Amsel (1958) has agreed that prefeeding in the amounts provided by Seward, et al., does result in slower running times, but points out that the amounts which he has used in his studies were considerably less than this.

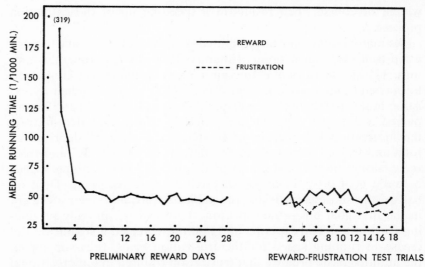

FIG. 6–9. COMPARISON OF TEST-TRIAL PERFORMANCE UNDER REWARD AND FRUSTRATION CONDITIONS. (Adapted from Amsel and Roussel, 1952)

a second assumption made by the authors that "strength of frustration varies with the time in the frustration situation" was not confirmed.

With the energizing function of the frustration drive demonstrated, Amsel and Ward (1954) attempted to demonstrate its directive function.[12] If unique and distinctive internal stimuli are produced by the antecedent operations, the organism should be able to discriminate these from other internal stimuli and learn to attach to each set of stimuli different responses.

The basic idea, then, was to have the subjects make one response following frustration and an alternative response following nonfrustration in the same situation. The difficulty with this technique is that the operations which define the frustration and the nonfrustration conditions may also give rise to differential stimula-

[12] An energizing function presumably arising from frustration has also been indicated in the studies of Skinner (1938), Finch (1942), and Sheffield and Campbell (1954). Both Skinner (1938) and Finch (1942) have called attention to increased vigor or rate of responding of animals immediately following those operations which have been posited to produce a frustration drive. Finch found that chimpanzees which were trained to press the handle of a spigot in order to obtain water would press with much more than usual energy if the water supply was shut off. Sheffield and Campbell (1954) have reported increased stabilimeter activity arising from the presentation of a cue which had previously been associated with food.

tion of a more peripheral sort. For example, if food deprivation and the securing of food were the need and reward conditions, differential stimulation might arise from food-in-mouth as against no-food-in-mouth, apart from any frustration drive.

A series of experiments by Amsel and Ward (1954) have seemingly controlled for this factor by employing water as a reinforcing agent and delaying the choice-point responses to reduce the effectiveness of the stimulus trace of water-in-mouth. The findings have confirmed the earlier study that frustration has energizing properties, as well as providing evidence that frustration provides stimulus cues to which the organism may attach a response.

We note then that the basic experimental support for the existence of a frustration motive is that the amplitude of a response which follows frustration shows some momentary increase. As Brown and Farber (1951) and, more recently, Marx (1956) have written, an alternative explanation might be that the organism has simply learned to make a more vigorous response when frustrated. Thus, Marx states: "This hypothesis is that the animal learns in previous situations to make more vigorous responses when frustrated. When the animal is frustrated in the experimental situation, he transfers, via frustration-produced cues, this earlier learning to the new situation, and we observe an increased vigor in responding." A pilot study, reported by Marx, which has tentatively supported this kind of explanation, was as follows: One group of rats was maintained in individual cages for 90 days prior to the experimental situation. There was an attempt to keep frustration at a minimum for these subjects. Another group of rats was placed in overcrowded social cages for a similar period of time. The hypothesis was that the individually raised rats had little opportunity to learn any specific response to frustration and that they could be taught with about equal ease to respond with either increased or decreased vigor following frustration. The animals raised in overcrowded cages, on the other hand, were expected to have considerably more difficulty in learning the weak response since they had lived in a competitive environment where presumably responding with more vigor was more frequently rewarded than weak responding. Following the 90-day period, all animals were given ten reinforcements in a Skinner box. The bar was so weighted that the animals had to respond with an immediately strong push in order to secure food. Following 80 reinforcements, the "frustration training" was initiated. Half of each group was rewarded only if the response was of a lesser intensity than the first five bar presses which were given each day, but which were not rewarded. In the "strong" groups, only responses stronger than the just preceding response in the nonreward series were rewarded. Training continued until the majority of responses for all subjects fell within the rewarded range. The results indicated that individually raised subjects reached a higher level of performance on the weak response than did the socially raised subjects. For the strong response, the relationship was reversed. The results were quite consistent with the point of view that increased vigor is in part a result of transfer from earlier situations in which the stronger response was learned.

Ego-Involved Antecedents and the Role of Affective States

In the examination of the experimental literature which has been concerned primarily with the motivation of human organisms, one can note a number of hypothesized motivational antecedents which, although frequently regarded as separate and distinct, nonetheless seem to have much in common. Some of these antecedents have been described as stress, frustration, threat, failure, anxiety, and fear. Iverson and Reuder (1956) have subsumed many of these concepts under the rubric of ego involvement, a term which we have also used to describe them. Before proceeding, let us briefly consider some of the characteristics of these concepts as viewed by workers in the field.

Ego Involvement

Although the concept of the ego or the self can be found in the writings of our earliest psychologists, the concept was essentially lost until 1943, when Allport (1943) again called it to attention in his paper, *The Ego in Contemporary Psychology*. Even so, references to the concept in contemporary experimental literature are few.

What is the nature of ego involvement? Although no definition would find universal acceptance, Bertocci's (1945) examination of the concept merits discussion. He has pointed out that the ego is the core or cluster of values with which the individual identifies its security or success at the time. As for ego involvement, he has stated that: "When the ego is involved, the self's value-citadel is in question, its investment in life is at stake. That is why what is relevant to the ego produces tensions in the self . . ." In somewhat different terms, Sherif and Cantril (1947) state that: "When any stimulus or situation is consciously or unconsciously related to

them by the individual, we can say there is ego involvement."
Finally, Iverson and Reuder (1956) have defined ego involvement
". . . in terms of the relationship between an individual and a
situation which is characterized by the possibility of interference
with or deprivation of the need to enhance or to maintain one's
feelings of self-esteem."

Frustration

We have noted that frustration was considered primarily within the
framework of animal experimental studies. It was viewed as a distinct motivational antecedent, and defined as a state arising from
the restriction of instrumental or consummatory activity. Such a
definition when applied to human behavior as Dollard, *et al.*
(1939) have done has led to considerable criticism.

In a series of articles, Pastore (1950, 1952) called attention
to the need for a kind of arbitrariness in producing an obstacle
which would produce frustration. Maslow (1943) indicated that
the presence of barriers which produced a deprivation condition
which threatens the personality of the individual are those which
are typically conceived to be frustrating, while those barriers
which result in a deprivation condition which is unimportant to the
organism do not. Zander (1944) maintained a similar position
when he stated that frustration occurs only when there is interference with a goal that is believed to be important and attainable.
In these criticisms we note that the individual must be "involved"
in the situation for frustration to occur—thus, the concept of ego
involvement appears to be a component part of the definition of
frustration.

A second criticism was made by Sargent (1948), who hypothesized that the frustration must produce an emotional response in
the organism, and if emotion is not aroused, frustration is not forthcoming. Emotion therefore becomes the core to any frustration response. A major point which Sargent (1948) has made has been
to protest against the description of frustration chiefly in terms of
antecedent operations and the subsequent responses to the neglect
of organismic variables.

Stress

At times, stress and frustration are considered to be synonymous;
frequently they are considered to be separate and distinct concepts.
Bindra (1959) has recently stated that stress is one of the vaguest
terms in psychology. The similarity between stress and frustration

is noted in an early definition of stress provided by Lazarus, Deese, and Osler (1952), who defined stress in terms of an intervening variable which occurs when a particular situation threatens the attainment of a goal. More recently, Lazarus and Baker (1957) have considered stress as a situation which involves a number of components. They have defined stress as occurring when "a situation is perceived as thwarting or as potentially thwarting to some motive state, thus resulting in affective arousal and in the elicitation of regulative processes aimed at the management of the affect."

Anxiety and Fear

In Chapter 4, in which fear was considered to be an acquired drive, we pointed out that many investigators consider the affective states of fear and anxiety to be synonymous. Many others, of course, do not. Freud, Goldstein, Horney, and May as well as a number of others have distinguished between the two states. May's (1950) summary of this distinction seems to be a well-accepted one. May states that the capacity of the organism to react to a threat to its values and/or existence is, in its general and original form, anxiety. Anxiety, then, is a basic underlying affective response of the organism.[13] As the organism becomes more mature, threatening objects can be differentiated within the environment, and, consequently, protective reactions can be similarly specific. Fear, then, is an expression of the same capacity of the organism to react to threat, except in a specific objectivated form. Anxiety thus becomes a primary response by the organism, while fear is a later development.[14]

[13] There are other points of view, of course. Cattell and Scheier (1958), using factor analysis in attacking the problem of adequately defining anxiety, have been able to isolate a single factor which they have found to be well replicated over thirteen studies examined. A description of this variable conforms "to the common core of semantically sanctioned use of the term 'anxiety' in such variables as tension, emotionality, and self-rated presence of clinically-accepted symptoms of anxiety." Eysenck (1958), however, has called attention to the fact that factor analytic studies are well adapted only to rectilinear regression (rather than curvilinear); furthermore, that a curvilinear relationship has relevance in this area is attested to by a large amount of experimental evidence, an area which Cattell and Scheier have ignored.

[14] A contrary point of view is that fear is the original affective state and that of anxiety, secondary. Some individuals believe that fear reactions are present from the first day of birth. Jersild (1940), for example, has referred to "unlearned" fears such as of noises, loss of support, or any intense, unexpected, or novel stimulus for which the child was unprepared. Symonds (1946) speaks of anxiety as being derived from "primitive fear states."

More specifically stated, a primary distinction between the two affective states lies in the specificity of the stimulus situation as well as that of the response. When the stimulus situation is well differentiated and the organism can make a specific and usually protective response, we have the presence of fear. On the other hand, if the organism perceives threat but cannot differentiate threatening stimuli from other stimuli in its environment, anxiety results.

There is some evidence that a physiological distinction can be made between the two states. Wolf and Wolff (1943) report their observation of a subject, Tom, a 57-year-old man, who suffered injury to his esophagus as a child and had an aperture made surgically through his abdomen and into his stomach. The relationship between Tom's affective state and his gastric functions could be observed through this aperture. During periods of fear, gastric activity sharply decreased, but in periods of anxiety, there was an increase in gastric activity.

The Relationship Among Ego Involved Variables

In an attempt to indicate some of the relationships that exist among the concepts which we have just considered, let us set up in brief outline a hypothetical experiment which involves some of these concepts.[15]

Two groups of subjects working independently are given a test which they are told measures their intelligence. After working for a period of time they are stopped. One group is told it has done poorly; the second group is told nothing. The groups are then asked to perform some other task and their performance on this task is measured, with differences among the groups being noted, such differences presumably reflecting the operation of the failure instructions given to the one group.

Now in examining the elements which comprise this experiment, the following are important. The first is that the task which is required of the subject is one which he views as important. A second

[15] Most investigators have been content to define the concept in which they are interested only in terms of the operations which they have used in their particular experiment. References to other material in the area, however, are usually limited to the particular term they have used to define their independent variable rather than to similarity of operations. Thus, an individual investigating "threat" will rarely refer to studies investigating "anxiety" or "frustration," although there may be marked similarity among the operations used to produce the concept in question.

element is that there is some thwarting of the subject's performance, so that the impression is obtained by the subject that he has not been successful. In the experiment cited, it arises from the experimenter's instructions indicating that the subject has done poorly. Finally, the last element appears to be one in which some affective state arises from the poor performance exhibited by the subject.[16]

With such an outline, our experiment now provides us the opportunity to note the relationships existing among some of the seemingly diverse and yet similar terms which we have included under ego involvement. The relationship between the individual and the test situation has been construed by some investigators as one of ego involvement, with such a designation describing their experimental procedure.[17]

Another investigator, however, might ignore the "ego-involved" aspects of the task and concentrate on the type of thwarting which was used. Under the circumstances, he might label his results as a function of failure, threat, or frustration.

Finally, some experimenters might concern themselves primarily with the individual's affective state produced by the experimental situation. Accordingly, they would indicate that their experimental variable was one of fear or anxiety. Like the proverbial blind men who described the elephant, investigators have used just one element of the experimental procedure to describe what they believe to be the important motivational antecedent, when in reality their findings have been a function of all of them.

We believe, however, that it is the affective state of the organism which represents the basic motivational antecedent, and that these other conditions are important only in that they are responsible for its arousal. A logical continuation of this point of view would be to regard what are commonly conceived to be the motivational antecedents of praise and success as conditions which arouse positive affective states just as threat and failure produce negative ones. Praise and success might be classified as ego-enhancing variables in contrast to the ego-threatening ones which we have just considered.

The position that positive affective states have motivational functions is well established. For a number of years, Young (1955,

---

[16] It should be noted that this experimental situation contains the necessary elements to be included in the Lazarus and Baker (1957) definition of stress.

[17] It is interesting to note that if instructions had been given to another group of subjects which indicated that the experimenter was interested only in establishing a set of norms, we would have a design used by many which presumably measures the influence of ego involvement.

1959) has argued that affective processes are motivational in that they arouse, sustain, regulate and direct behavior. More specifically, Young believes that an organism responds so as to maximize positive affective arousal (delight, enjoyment) and to minimize negative arousal (distress). In the previous chapter we reviewed some of the experimental evidence which he has used to support the role of affective states as motivational antecedents.

McClelland's reservations with contemporary motivational theory have also emphasized affective states as important conditions which help to define a motive. *A motive is the redintegration by a cue of a change in an affective situation* . . . The basic idea is simply this:

Certain stimuli or situations involving discrepancies between expectation (adaptation level) and perception are sources of primary, unlearned affect, either positive or negative in nature. Cues which are paired with these affective states, changes in these affective states, and the conditions producing them become capable of redintegrating a state (A') derived from the original affective situation (A), but not identical with it. . . . This means that if a buzzer is associated with eating saccharine the buzzer will in time attain the power to evoke a motive or redintegrate a state involving positive affective change. Likewise, the buzzer if associated with shock will achieve the power to redintegrate a negative affective state. (McClelland, Atkinson, Clark and Lowell 1953).

BEHAVIORAL CONSEQUENTS

7 • SPONTANEOUS ACTIVITY

Spontaneous activity has been a response measure often used to infer (1) the presence of a drive as well as (2) its energizing function. From our organizational point of view, spontaneous activity becomes an important behavioral consequent which anchors the drive or motive concepts. The present chapter is a review of much of the experimental evidence in this area. One of the first considerations, however, is to examine how activity has been measured.

MEASUREMENT

The spontaneous or random activity of organisms has been measured in a variety of ways, and it is appropriate to consider first the techniques of measurement as well as problems involved in such measurement before proceeding to our major task—the relating of primary needs to such measurement.

The activity wheel, or revolving drum, first used by Stewart (1898) and described by Slonaker (1908), has been used probably more frequently in the investigation of the relationship between need states and activity than any other type of apparatus. Figure 7.1 illustrates a type of wheel that is commonly used.

Fig. 7–1. A Revolving Drum Apparatus for Studying Activity. (Courtesy Geo. Wahmann Manufacturing Company)

The second general type of apparatus for measuring activity has been a stationary cage mounted on tambours or microswitches or perhaps suspended from a spring. These have been frequently described as stabilimeters or stabilimetric cages. Figure 7.2 illustrates such an apparatus. In some cases, a beam of light has divided the cage into halves or quarters, and its interruption has been recorded by a photo relay unit. Depending upon the sensitivity of the meas-

FIG. 7–2. A STABILIMETRIC CAGE.

uring device, movements of the animal within the cage are transmitted to a recorder. In contrast to the activity wheel, which has
been appropriate only for small animals, particularly rats, this
type of apparatus can be used with almost any type of organism.
Interesting variations of this general type of apparatus have been described by Backlund and Ekeroot (1950) to measure the movements of organisms small enough to live in a petri dish, by Spencer
(1929) to measure the activity of fish, and by Ratner and Ringer
(1959) to measure the activity of fowl.

The measurement of activity has revealed a number of prob-
A third type of activity measurement has been to use a still more
unrestricted situation. This has been accomplished by the employment of a pedometer as used by Liddell (1925) and Curtis (1937)
or simply by observing the distance traveled by the animal in an
open field (Hall, 1936; Beach, 1941) or a maze situation (Dashiell, 1925).

The measurement of activity has revealed a number of problems. The first of these is related to the instrument employed.
Particularly with the activity wheel and the stationary cage, similar
amounts of recorded activity may not reflect similar amounts of actual activity. The animal may set the wheel in motion and then
jump into its living cage or, perhaps, after the wheel has been set in

motion, stop running but continue to ride with it. An animal near the middle of the stationary cage, in contrast to the one near the perimeter, needs to engage in very little activity in order to tilt the cage, or to interrupt the beam of light dividing the cage. Furthermore, the equipment may not be equally sensitive with respect to the recording of activity. With the activity wheel, there is no guarantee that the amount of inertia and the amount of frictional torque is the same for all wheels. Lacey (1944) has demonstrated experimentally that differences in the amount of frictional torque may result in significant differences in the amount of activity. When stationary cages are in use, the same problem exists with respect to the sensitivity of the springs, microswitches, tambours, or photo relay units.

The problem has been at least partially solved by using each animal as its own control. The activity level of each animal is first obtained under normal living or ad lib conditions. The animal's activity under the experimental condition is then expressed in terms of a percentage of its normal activity. Finger (1951), Finger and Reid (1952), and Hall and his associates (Hall, Smith, Schnitzer, and Hanford, 1953; Hall, 1955) have frequently used this technique in their experiments. If this is not feasible, the equipment must be calibrated so that each wheel will reflect equivalent amounts of energy output. Lacey (1944), for example, has devised a technique by which it is possible to measure both frictional torque and moment of inertia of the activity wheel.

A second instrumental problem is related to the adaptation of the animal to the apparatus, because measurement of an animal's activity before it has been completely adapted may confound the experimental findings. Although Shirley (1928) has felt that young rats (36 days of age) require just nine days to become adapted to the activity wheel and older animals (100 days of age) require 15 days, the experimental work of Eayrs (1954) has indicated that these adaptation periods may be too short, and that 21 days represents a more adequate period.[1] An important but neglected variable in the adaptability of the animal to the activity wheel is its emotionality. Billingslea (1940) has shown that "emotional" rats require a longer time for habituation than do "unemotional" rats. Adaptation to the stationary cage seems to be much more readily obtained. Both Campbell (1954) and Eayrs (1954)

[1] Eayrs (1954) used female animals, and their oestrus cycle may have been responsible for the necessity of using this lengthy adaptation period.

report that adaptation to the stationary cages is virtually complete by 24 hours.

The second general problem relates to whether or not the activity that is measured is "spontaneous." There is some indication that activity-wheel running is not only an expression of the spontaneous activity of the animal but may be regarded as a type of instrumental response which can be strengthened by reinforcement. That is, if the experimental situation is so arranged that the animals are fed only at a given time, the activity exhibited may also reflect a "learning to run" component. A conjecture by Shirley (1928) that activity seemed to be conditioned by the feeding hour and later theorizing by Seward and Pereboom (1955) lends credence to such a point of view. Experimental evidence has also been provided by Seward and Pereboom (1955a), who have found that hungry rats acquire a readiness to turn the wheel when doing so leads to food. Finger, Reid, and Weasner (1957) and Hall (1958) have reported similar findings.

In this latter study, two groups of rats were placed on 19 hours of deprivation, and their activity was measured during the last deprivation hour. For one group, reinforcement immediately followed the activity exhibited during the last deprivation hour; for the other, the last deprivation hour was followed by being locked out of the activity wheel. The activity of the group which was fed following the last deprivation hour was significantly higher than that of the group which was locked out of the wheel. A day-by-day analysis of the 18-day experimental period is illustrated in Figure 7.3.

There is some experimental evidence that activity-wheel behavior may act as a type of reinforcement for the rat. Kagan and Berkun (1954) have found that the opportunity to run in an activity wheel is adequate reinforcement for the instrumental response of pressing a bar.

Finally, if the activity apparatus measures locomotor activity in an unrestricted situation, it is possible that such behavior is a reflection of the operation of a particular motive. As we have noted in Chapter 6, both Dashiell (1925) and Montgomery (1953, 1953a) have used maze behavior to infer the presence of an exploratory or curiosity drive.

Some of these problems are related, at least in part, to the reliability of the measured response. Under the circumstances, it is perhaps surprising that the reliability of activity-wheel behavior has been consistently high, with correlations of .90 and higher being

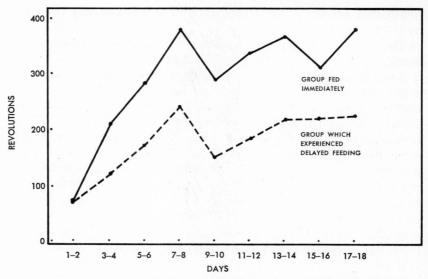

FIG. 7–3. ACTIVITY AS A FUNCTION OF WHETHER OR NOT FEEDING FOL-
LOWED THE LAST DEPRIVATION HOUR. (Adapted from Hall, 1958)

frequently reported (Shirley 1928, Anderson 1938). Siegel
(1946b), working with rats, and Isaac and Ruch (1956), with
monkeys, have also reported high reliability coefficients when activity is measured in the stationary cage. It is important to remember
that the size of the correlation is increased by the utilization of heterogeneous material, and major differences in the measuring operations of the instrument, or among the animals used, may provide
high correlations even though behavior is quite variable from day to
day. In view of the difficulties encountered in the evaluation of the
reliability coefficients, it is perhaps more meaningful, as Campbell
(1954) has suggested, to assess the reliability of the activity measuring devices by breaking down the scores into variance attributed
to: (1) consistent instrumental differences, (2) consistent individual differences in subjects, and (3) quotidian fluctuations.

An important question after reviewing the various measures of
activity is: Do the varying instruments measure the same thing? It
would appear that they do not. Reed (1947), after examining more
than 100 activity studies, has concluded that ". . . where comparable measures of activity are available from different devices, running drum and diffuse-activity cage, the results are not the same."

Treichler (1960), comparing the activity of deprived rats placed in stabilimetric cages and activity wheels, has arrived at the same conclusion. Eayrs (1954) has reported only a small correlation (.18) between activity as measured in the activity wheel and in a gallery —a type of stationary cage. Hunt and Schlosberg (1939) have suggested that the stationary cage or stabilimeter techniques measure a general restlessness of the organism in contrast to the specific running behavior as measured by the drum. In a somewhat similar vein, Strong (1957) has posited that the activity wheel measures gross locomotor activity; stationary cages, however, depending upon their sensitivity, more frequently measure fine and essentially nonlocomotor activity.

ACTIVITY AS A FUNCTION OF PRIMARY NEEDS

With the problems of measurement behind us, it is now appropriate to undertake our first major consideration—the investigation of the relationship between the varying primary need states and activity. As we have indicated earlier, this relationship has been frequently used to infer the presence of a drive state as well as to indicate its energizing function.

The Need for Food and Water as Inferred from Deprivation Periods

Although the activity in the drive-activity relationship refers to overt activity, it is interesting to note that the deprivation of food usually results in internal activity, particularly in the stomach. The experimental work of a number of investigators has indicated that food deprivation results in increased stomach contractions in a variety of living organisms (King and Connet, 1915; Rogers, 1914; Patterson, 1915; Carlson, 1916).

The effect of deprivation on overt activity, however, becomes another problem; the evidence seems controversial and contradictory.

Richter's (1922) study has provided early experimental evidence for the existence of a food deprivation–activity relationship. Using the stationary cage technique (a cage mounted on tambours), he found that the activity of the rat increased steadily until the third day of deprivation, at which time continued deprivation resulted in a decrease of activity. Siegel and Steinberg (1949) and Teitelbaum (1957), using the stationary cage, have also reported increases in activity as a function of lengthening deprivation periods. In the

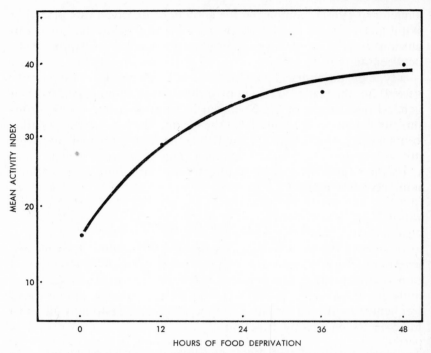

FIG. 7–4. THE RELATIONSHIP BETWEEN GROSS BODILY ACTIVITY AND THE NUMBER OF HOURS OF FOOD DEPRIVATION. (Adapted from Siegel and Steinberg, 1949)

Siegel and Steinberg study, 60 rats were divided into four matched groups and activity measured under 0, 12, 24, and 48 hours of food deprivation. Their findings are indicated in Figure 7.4. A somewhat similar finding with the human infant has been reported by Irwin (1932). The activity of 73 full-term infants, aged 8 hours to 32 days was measured through use of a two-dimensional stabilimeter. The infants were fed at 2:00 P.M., and activity was continuously recorded until 6:00 P.M., at which time they were again fed. Results indicated a constant increase in activity from the first 15 minutes of the experimental period to the last 15-minute period.

These positive findings with the stationary-cage technique have been supported by Dashiell (1925), Adlerstein and Fehrer (1955) and Fehrer (1956), measuring activity in the open field situation. Dashiell (1925) found hungry rats entering more squares in a checkerboard maze during a 60-second test period than satiated ones. Finally, the activity wheel studies of Hitchcock (1927), Wald and Jackson (1944), Finger (1951), and Hall (1956) also have indicated progressive increases in activity with increased deprivation periods.

The effects of water deprivation have not been so extensively studied as those of food deprivation. Both Wald and Jackson (1944) and Finger and Reid (1952), however, have reported that rats placed on water deprivation, with access to dry food, show progressively increased activity as a function of the increasing deprivation interval.

In contrast to these findings, Strong (1957) using an extremely sensitive stabilimeter has reported a negatively accelerated *decrease* in a rat's activity as a function of 2, 24, and 48 hours of food deprivation. Other stabilimeter studies by Nicholls (1922), using guinea pigs deprived from 0 to 72 hours, and DeVito and Smith (1959), using monkeys deprived from 6 to 54 hours, have indicated no differences in activity level as a function of hours of deprivation.

A study by Hall, Hanford, and Low (1960) investigated the activity of (a) animals placed under 22 hours of food deprivation, (b) animals placed under 22 hours of water deprivation, and (c) satiated animals in a Dashiell checkerboard maze. The testing period consisted of five consecutive two-minute periods per day for five consecutive days. Results indicated that the activity level of either group of deprived animals was never higher than that of the controls.

Finally, if the operant level of bar pressing is also regarded as a measure of spontaneous activity (a type of activity measure we did not consider), Segal (1959) has shown that food and food and water deprivation states, although increasing the stability of the bar-pressing response, decrease its response frequency.

The Need for Food and Water as Inferred from Measures of Body Weight

In the studies which we have previously examined, it has been assumed that the strength of an organism's needs, as measured by various activity measures, bears a relationship to the length of the deprivation period which is imposed. This behavioral effect of deprivation time is usually assumed to be dependent upon actual physiological changes. Time, however, is only a conceptual framework within which events take place, and it is possible that the physiological changes which are primarily responsible for hunger and thirst, are neither always nor adequately reflected by deprivation intervals. As a result, need states have been induced by manipulating body weight, and some investigators have attempted to observe the relationship between this variable and activity.

The studies of Finger (1951) and Finger and Reid (1952) to which we have previously referred are also relevant here. Finger's study indicated that weight losses of 7.1, 12.1, and 18.1 per cent of normal (produced by 24, 48, and 72 hours of food deprivation) resulted in increases of 3.2, 52.3, and 94.2 per cent over normal (ad lib) activity. Similar findings were obtained when weight loss was manipulated by depriving the animals of water for 24 or 72 hours (Finger and Reid 1952). The activity wheel was used in both studies.

In a very extensive study in this area, Moskowitz (1959) reduced the body weight of his rats in stages from 100 per cent to 60 per cent of *estimated* normal weight.[2] This reduction took place over a period of 41 days. Activity, as measured in the activity wheel, was recorded for one hour per day, with the daily food ration (adjusted to provide continuing weight loss) given 30 minutes after the animals were removed from the wheels. Figure 7.5 shows activity as a function of body weight deficit. An important conclusion which Moskowitz has drawn from this study has been that activity does not increase until body weight has decreased to between 85 and 90 per cent of normal weight.

Moskowitz's general conclusions have been confirmed as well as extended in a recent study by Treichler (1960). Treichler examined the activity of rats, confined in both wheels and stabilimetric cages, as a function of decreases in body weight produced by either food, water, or food and water deprivation periods. In each instance, the deprivation period continued until the animal reached at least 60 per cent of its estimated or adjusted body weight. Results indicated that the type of deprivation played no role in producing differences in the animal's activity pattern. How activity was measured, however, did make a difference. Stabilimetric cage activity showed little change with decreasing body weights; wheel activ-

[2] Since animals normally gain weight during the experimental period, the use of a predeprivation measure as a basis for computing body weight loss may lead to an incorrect estimate of this variable. Consider the case of a 100-gram animal who is to be reduced to 80 per cent body weight. Using the initial weight of 100 grams, body weight must be reduced to 80 grams. If the animal normally gained 10 grams during the experimental period, the normal weight should be taken as 110 grams, and 80 per cent of this figure is 88 grams.

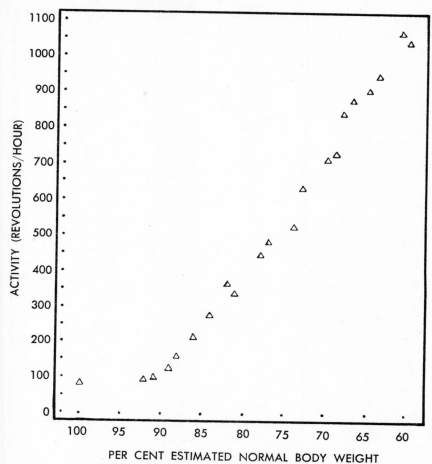

FIG. 7–5. ACTIVITY AS A FUNCTION OF BODY-WEIGHT DEFICIT. (Adapted from Moskowitz, 1959)

ity, on the other hand, demonstrated a progressive increase with increases in deprivation as expressed by the animals' weight losses. Figure 7.6 illustrates these findings.

Satiation Effects

One interesting aspect of food and water deprivation is the tendency for the activity of rats to be depressed below normal ad lib activity when the animals are returned to an ad lib diet. Hitchcock

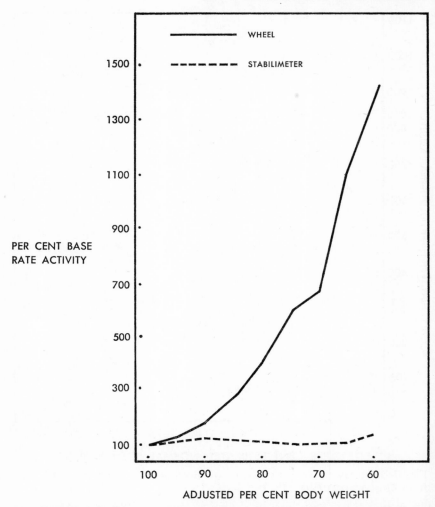

FIG. 7–6. MEDIAN INTERPOLATED ACTIVITY SCORES OF ANIMALS AT VARIOUS WEIGHT LEVELS IN ACTIVITY WHEELS AND STABILIMETERS. (Adapted from Treichler, 1960)

(1928) had noted this tendency in an early study, as had Anderson (1941, 1941a), but it remained for Finger (1951), who has called the phenomenon the "satiation syndrome," to investigate such behavior more extensively. Finger reported that the activity-wheel behavior of rats returned to an ad lib diet after having been

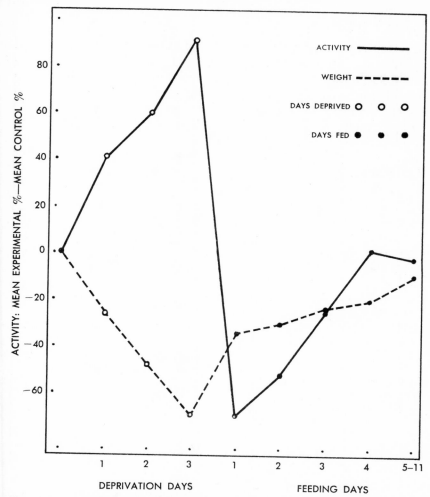

FIG. 7–7. COMPARISON OF WEIGHT AND ACTIVITY TRENDS OF RATS DURING SEVENTY-TWO HOURS OF FOOD DEPRIVATION AND SUBSEQUENT UNRESTRICTED FEEDING. (Adapted from Finger, 1951)

placed on 24 hours of food deprivation was 57 per cent of normal, while those animals placed on 72 hours of food deprivation when returned to an ad lib diet revealed only 17.6 per cent of their normal (ad lib) activity. Finger's findings are indicated in Figure 7.7. Similar findings have been reported for water deprivation (Finger and Reid, 1952).

Need for Specific Foods

It is well recognized not only that organisms need a given amount of bulk food, but that the bulk must contain specific nutrients in order to sustain life. Some investigators have studied the effect of depriving animals of certain of these constituents, and then determining their effect on activity.

The studies of Hitchcock (1928) and Anderson and Smith (1926) have indicated that a protein deficiency results in increased activity over the early part of the deprivation period, but that prolonged deprivation results in a decline in the general health of the animal and a corresponding decrease in activity. Bloomfield and Tainter (1943) found that the limitation of Vitamin B intake was promptly followed by increased running, although after five or ten days, activity decreased. This finding has been substantially supported by Wald and Jackson (1944), who have reported that when rats are deprived of Vitamin B, increases in activity takes place as an increasing function of food or water deprivation. In an extended study of such deprivation, Guerrant and Dutcher (1940) found that very young animals deprived of Vitamin B_1 were more active during the first four weeks of their test period than their controls, but after this test period the animals grew less active.

In contrast to protein and Vitamin B deficiencies, there seems to be some tendency for Vitamin A and D deficiencies to produce an almost immediate reduction in activity (Richter and Rice, 1942; Richter and Rice, 1943).

Need for Sexual Activity

Although it is recognized that the expression of sexual activity is not a biological requirement of the organism, it is necessary for the survival of the species, and so it is usually included in the list of primary needs. Presumably, deprivation operations should result in increased activity. Most studies, however, have not been concerned with deprivation states as appropriate antecedent conditions, but have been concerned with the manipulation of some physiological factor.

The early studies of Wang (1923) and Slonaker (1924) revealed that activity of the female rat was at a low level until puberty, at which time the animal's activity began to increase as well as to display a characteristic cycle. This was the oestrus cycle, and for the rat, it is four to five days in length. It will be noted that when the rat is in heat, activity increases to two or three times its normal level. Inasmuch as (1) this high level of activity is correlated with the female's being sexually receptive, (2) such activity does not appear until puberty, and (3) it disappears during pregnancy and after menopause, it would appear that this cycle is governed by ovarian secretion. Wang (1923), Richter (1927), and Young and Fish (1945) have obtained a 60 to 95 per cent decrease in activity, as well as a disappearance of the cycle, by removing the ovaries. These latter investigators found, however, that injection or implantation of estrone will raise the activity level of spayed females to that point which existed before ovariectomy. Increased amounts, however, do not result in an increased level of activity over that normally obtained. Carpenter (1942) has reported that hyperactivity also exists during most of the oestrus cycle of the female monkey.

Male rats do not show any characteristic cycle, and most investigators agree that the male rat is much less active than the female. A number of studies have shown that castration results in a reduction in the male's normal activity level. When such activity is measured with the activity wheel, the decrement in activity appears large. Thus, Slonaker (1930) found a 98 per cent, and Gans (1927) a 79 per cent reduction in activity for castrated animals; Hunt and Schlosberg (1939a) report only a 9 per cent reduction in activity for castrated animals when the stabilimeter is used to measure activity.

Other Primary Needs

The primary needs other than food, water, and sex and their relation to activity have not been extensively studied.

The maintenance of an optimum temperature is an obvious need, since all biological processes are affected by temperature. However, its relation to activity is a complex matter. Schwitalla (1924) found that the temperature of a water bath which surrounded the observation well across which an amoeba moved was an important determinant of its speed of locomotion. At 0° C. the amoeba was virtually immobile; however, as the temperature increased to 30° C., its speed of movement also increased. Falconer (1945) has reported a somewhat similar relationship for the wireworm. In this experiment he found an almost linear relationship between the organism's speed of crawling and a temperature range of 8° C. to 25° C. Stier (1930) has shown that the two-day-old mouse increases its activity as temperature increases from 17° C. to 30° C. However, Nicholls

(1922), using the guinea pig, and Browman (1943) the rat, investigating another range of temperatures, have shown that activity increases as temperature decreases. Nicholls found that at temperatures from 84° to 87° F. his animals were quite inactive, but at 65° F. they were almost continuously active. Browman (1943) found that rats were also more active under low temperatures than high.

DeVito and Smith's (1959) study, on the other hand, with monkeys as subjects, found little difference in activity between 0° and 25° C., but when temperature was increased to 35° C., there was a significant increase in activity.

Although tissue injury or pain has been frequently used in many psychological experiments, its relationship to activity has not been studied. One difficulty is that the activity of the organism to aversive stimulation is usually instrumental in removing the organism from the painful stimulus. Under the circumstances, such activity is classified as instrumental rather than spontaneous.

Acquired Needs

Fear has been one stimulus condition which has been shown to have motivational functions. Brown, Kalish, and Farber (1951) hypothesized that fear should result in the energizing of other responses during the period of its evocation. In their experimental procedure, rats were placed in a stabilimeter and given a series of trials, each of which consisted of the presentation of a conditioned stimulus (buzzer and light) with shock. Although no overt response was systematically reinforced, it was assumed that such a procedure would lead to the arousal of fear by the CS. The CS was then presented along with a loud sound which was substituted for the shock. The startle response measured in the stabilimeter and produced by the loud sound was compared with the control group, in which the CS had not been paired with shock. The results indicated that the magnitude of the startle response was significantly greater for the experimental group than for the controls, thus supporting the hypothesis.

THE ENERGIZING FUNCTION

To the question, "Why is a man active?" the answer commonly given is in terms of the energizing function of the motive. Such an answer has frequently implied that without a motive, the organism would be inactive or completely quiescent. Certainly from the point of view of Carr (1925) and Dashiell (1928), who in their introductory texts were responsible for delineating and emphasizing the energizing function, such a statement is unnecessarily restrictive. Since electrophysiological functions of the central nervous system have indicated that the brain is continuously active in all of its parts, any stimulation arising from the organism's environment is superimposed on an already existent excitatory level. If an energizing function *is* postulated, it seems more appropriate to think of it as representing an increase in an already existing level of activity.

Behavioral support for the energizing function is found in the early studies of Richter (1922, 1927) and Dashiell (1925) as well as more recent ones, many of which we have reviewed. This function has been readily acknowledged in current texts and contemporary theory. Hilgard (1957), for example, in his introductory text states that "a drive makes the organism active," while in Hull's (1943) theoretical system, a drive, or D, is regarded as a general energizing factor which combines multiplicatively with reaction tendencies of an innate or learned variety to produce overt behavior.

Some investigators have attempted to find physiological correlates for the energizing function. Brobeck (1955) has posited that the brain, probably within the hypothalamus, contains a mechanism which impels the animal to move about from place to place. Feeding tends to inhibit the operation of this mechanism. As the food is disposed through conversion to heat, etc., the inhibition produced by the feeding tends to disappear and the animal's locomotor activity begins to increase.

A more general position has been taken by Hebb (1955), who, reversing an earlier point of view (Hebb 1949), has proposed that the energizing aspect of drive is primarily related to the nonspecific or diffuse projection system of the brain stem which has been shown by Moruzzi and Magoun (1949) to be an arousal system whose activity makes organized activity possible. This system is conceived of as representing a second major pathway by which all sensory excitations reach the cortex. Excitation over this pathway is slow and inefficient and is delivered to wide cortical areas. Its primary function is to tone up the cortex, with a background supporting action that is necessary if the sensory event is to have an effect. Without such an arousal system, the sensory impulses would reach the sensory cortex by their direct route, but would go no farther.

Any sensory event, therefore, has not only its normal cue function, which results in guiding behavior, but an arousal or vigilance function as well. Without an arousal function, the cue function could not exist. Hebb states, ". . . arousal in this sense is synonymous with a general drive state, and the conception of drive therefore assumes anatomical and physiological identity."

In contrast to these points of view, a number of investigators have remained skeptical, and some have proposed other explanations for many of the empirical findings which have been taken as evidence for the presence of an energizing function. One such proposal has been that of Estes (1958). It is not appropriate to present in detail the general theoretical system which he and his associates have developed, but briefly, he has assumed that the stimulus complex consists of a finite population of stimulus events, with only a sample of these being conditioned to a response on a given trial. The probability of the occurrence of the response is determined by all cues which are present at the time of testing. Or, more specifically, probability is assumed equal to the weight of all cues connected to the response divided by the weight of all cues present.

As applied to present considerations, deprivation and satiation states, rather than giving rise to any energizing function, produce characteristic stimuli which represent one of a number of different sources or sets of stimulation present in the experimental situation. Other sources of stimulation arise from experimentally controlled signals and from the apparatus in use, as well as from extraneous sources. Each source of stimulation is represented by a weight which is determined by the number of stimulus elements within the set, and the average sampling probability of the elements. With high deprivation states, drive stimuli assume greater weight (in relation to the extraneous sources of stimulation present), which increases the probability of the response being made. At low deprivation states, extraneous cues have greater relative weight, which decreases the probability of a response.

Estes writes: "To the extent that behaviors which are tapped by a given measure of activity have become conditioned to drive stimuli, either during or previous to an experiment, a positive correlation between activity and deprivation is predictable."

A second theoretical position has been taken by Campbell and Sheffield (1953), who have posited that drives involve lowered thresholds to external stimulation. As they state: "Starvation does not instigate activity; it only lowers the threshold for normal stimuli

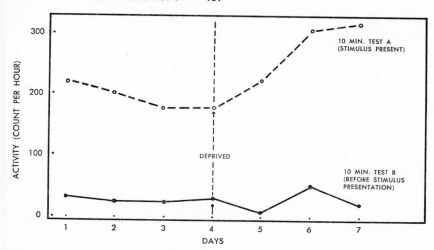

FIG. 7–8. THE EFFECT OF DEPRIVATION ON THE ACTIVITY RESPONSE TO AN ENVIRONMENTAL CHANGE. (Adapted from Campbell and Sheffield, 1953)

to activity." Therefore, an increase in an animal's drive level does not result in increased activity, but merely makes the organism more responsive to environmental changes. They would predict little change in the activity of an animal in a drive state unless there were some external stimulation.

In an effort to demonstrate their hypothesis, the activity of rats was recorded before and after an environmental change, during which time the animals were first on an ad lib diet and then completely deprived of food. Activity was recorded by using a cage so mounted on microswitches that any shift in the animals' location would be recorded. Figure 7.8 indicates their findings for ten-minute periods during which there was the presence and absence of environmental change under satiated and deprived conditions and thus supports their position.

One difficulty is that their animals' 24-hour activity records indicated a statistically significant increase in activity during the deprivation period, even though 23 hours and 50 minutes of this period consisted of no environmentally produced changes.

In a test of the Campbell-Sheffield hypothesis, Hall (1956), using 30-minute testing periods before and after environmental change, and both before and after periods of food deprivation, found significant increases in activity as a function of the environmental change,

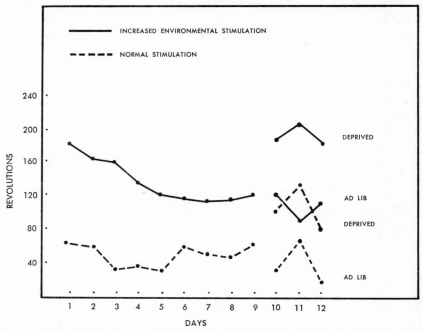

FIG. 7–9. THE EFFECT OF INCREASED ENVIRONMENTAL STIMULATION, AND FOOD DEPRIVATION ON ACTIVITY. (Adapted from Hall, 1956)

but also found that the addition of a food-deprived state increased it significantly more. Figure 7.9 presents these findings.

There is neither an easy nor obvious reconciliation of the experimental findings in this area, although a few general conclusions may be drawn from the studies which we have presented.

First, the findings from a number of the experiments appear to be dependent upon the establishment of a relationship between an organism's need and *its securing of reinforcement*. In one case, the experimental situation provides a period of deprivation followed by reward which results in strengthening those behavior patterns which are followed by reinforcement. We touched upon this problem earlier in this chapter in our discussion of whether or not the activity which was measured by activity measuring devices was "spontaneous."

An experiment which illustrates the role of a need-reward relationship is illustrated in a study by Sheffield and Campbell

(1954). These investigators found that the presentation of a stimulus which on previous occasions had been associated with food resulted in an increase in activity although no food was forthcoming. Control animals, under a similar deprivation state, who had not learned to associate the stimulus with food, did not show such an increase. Sheffield and Campbell have interpreted their findings as reflecting the conditioning of a consummatory response to the external cues which were associated with feeding. The increase in activity was posited as coming about as a product of frustration produced when a consummatory response was aroused by a conditioned stimulus but the goal object was not available. It is quite likely that the activity which has been attached to the blocking of the consummatory response has been learned, although there is little evidence to support or refute this position. Marx's (1956) experimental findings on frustration, however, which we have presented in Chapter 6, seem relevant.

Perhaps an even more basic conclusion is that whether or not activity occurs depends upon the measuring instrument. An overwhelming amount of experimental evidence supports the position that a need for food or water, as reflected by a loss in body weight of at least ten to fifteen per cent, does result in increased activity when such behavior is measured with the *activity wheel*.

Recent evidence suggests, however, that deprivation states do not produce similar increases in activity when such activity is measured with stabilimetric cages or maze-type situations. The different amounts of activity obtained by Campbell and Sheffield (1953) on the one hand, and Hall (1956) on the other, may merely reflect the use of different types of activity measuring devices. In any event, proponents for or against an energizing function must consider the role of the measuring device.

8 • CONSUMMATORY BEHAVIOR

Consummatory behavior is defined as a response which results in a reduction or a relief of a need state of the organism. Eating, drinking, and copulation are examples of this kind of behavior. These responses have been frequently used as another behavioral index from which experimenters have inferred the presence of a need or drive; for our organization, they represent consequents of a motive.

Eating and drinking as a function of some of the motivational antecedents which we have considered have been most extensively studied, and it is these two responses that we shall discuss in this chapter.

THE EATING RESPONSE

Measurement

The actual eating response has not usually been measured, but measures of the consummatory activity have frequently been inferred from the amount of food ingested or the time required to consume a given amount of food.[1] If the amount of food is meas-

[1] An exception is the work of Duckworth and Shirlaw (1955), who have designed an apparatus that will record the jaw movements of cattle. Total number of bites, time spent eating, cudding, and miscellaneous jaw movements can all be recorded.

ured, usually the food is weighed before and after the eating period. Skinner (1932), however, devised an apparatus for automatically measuring the amount of food eaten. The apparatus was so arranged that the animal had to push a light door hanging in front of a pocket that contained food. Since the food was below the level of the floor, the animal usually withdrew its head before eating. The opening of the door was recorded on a kymograph. A variation of this technique has been reported by Anliker and Mayer (1956), and used by a number of investigators. Here, animals are trained to press a lever for each pellet of food that is received, with the amount of food consumed inferred from the number of lever depressions recorded. Bousfield and Elliot (1934) devised a method in which pellets of food were placed in a glass tube, and as each pellet was removed from the space at the end of it, the movement of the descending column of food, as well as the removal of the pellet, was recorded. Finally, Fregley (1960) has recently described a feeding device in which food is placed at the end of an inclined and enclosed runway. The particular design demands that the animal consume the food where it is found.

Food Deprivation and Consummatory Activity

With the emphasis upon need states as an important component of an organism's motivational system, it seemed logical for many to assume that when an organism was permitted to satisfy a given need, some measure of consummatory activity should bear a close relationship to the intensity of the need. Therefore, one should be able to use the amount of food consumed, for example, to infer the number of hours of food deprivation.

One of the early studies investigating this relationship was done by Bousfield and Elliot (1934). After establishing a feeding rhythm by allowing the animals to eat for one hour per day for a three-week period, deprivation periods of 3½, 12, 24, and 48 hours were introduced in a random order. The investigators tried to make sure that no deprivation period was introduced until the amount of food consumed by the animal had been maintained at a normal level for at least a week. In a second experiment, in which they used their automatic device for measuring the amount of food consumed, they introduced delays of one, two, and three days. In both experiments, it was observed that the amount of food eaten *decreased* with increased periods of deprivation. Along with the smaller amount of food consumed, there was a correspondent slower rate of eating.

Baker's (1955) experimental findings are also in line with the findings of Bousfield and Elliot (1934). Rats were placed on deprivation periods of either 12, 24, or 36 hours and then given feeding periods of either 40, 80, or 120 minutes—the length of the feeding period varying with the length of the deprivation period. The experiment was carried on for 40 days. When food consumed *per day* was measured, Baker found a negative correlation between the length of the deprivation period and the amount of food consumed —the 36-hour group consuming the smallest amount, and the 12-hour group consuming most. Baker has concluded that his findings suggest that any direct relationship between the length of the deprivation interval and feeding behavior is largely the result of the organism's previously establishing a definite feeding rhythm. One difficulty with such an interpretation is that although the amount of feeding time was equated, the number of feeding sessions was not. The 12-hour deprivation group had two feedings, the 24-hour group just one, and the 36-hour group would average out to just two thirds for every 24-hour period. If the amount eaten during a single feeding period was used as the appropriate measure (thus allowing time to eat to vary from 40 minutes, depending upon the deprivation period), Baker's results indicated that the group deprived for 24 hours consumed the largest amount and the 12-hour deprivation group the least.

In contrast to the findings of Bousfield and Elliot (1934) and Baker (1955), the studies of Horenstein (1951) and Lawrence and Mason (1955a) have supported a relationship between how hungry an organism is and how much it eats. In the Horenstein study, nine rats were placed on a 23½-hour feeding cycle. Following this, they were satiated, and then deprived of food for 0, 1, 2, 6, 12, or 23.5 hours. After one of these deprivation intervals, they were permitted to eat for 20 minutes. Food intake as a function of the number of hours of deprivation is indicated in Figure 8.1.

Lawrence and Mason (1955a) first established a feeding rhythm in one group of rats (periodic) which consisted of feeding them for three hours at the same time each day. A second group (aperiodic) was also given three-hour feedings, but the deprivation interval between feedings varied from 4 to 48 hours in irregular succession. This regimen continued for 27 days. Both groups were then tested by measuring food intake after varying deprivation periods ranging from 4 to 48 hours. Both groups showed an increase in the amount

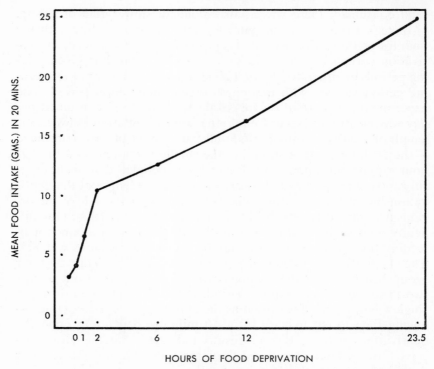

FIG. 8–1. FOOD INTAKE IN TWENTY MINUTES AS A FUNCTION OF NUMBER OF HOURS OF FOOD DEPRIVATION (Adapted from Horenstein, 1951)

eaten as a function of increasing intervals of deprivation up to 24 hours. With longer periods than this, the periodic group showed a decline in food consumption, but the aperiodic group showed no change. Figure 8.2 illustrates these findings.

Weight Loss and Consummatory Activity

As we have noted in Chapter 7, it is possible that the physiological changes which are primarily responsible for hunger and thirst are not adequately reflected by deprivation intervals. Under the circumstances, some investigators have been interested in examining the relationship between weight loss and consummatory activity.

It will be recalled that Baker (1955) found an inverse relationship between the length of the deprivation period and the amount of food consumed. He obtained a similar relationship when body

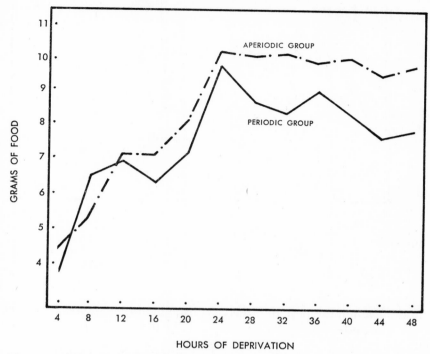

FIG. 8–2. FOOD CONSUMPTION FOR THE PERIODIC AND APERIODIC GROUPS AS A FUNCTION OF HOURS OF DEPRIVATION. (Adapted from Lawrence and Mason, 1955a)

weight was related to consummatory behavior. Animals which lost the largest amount of weight consumed the smallest amount of food.

Moll (1959) obtained similar findings. Two groups of rats were deprived so that their body weight was either 80 or 90 per cent of normal, and three response measures were obtained: (1) the amount of time elapsing between the placement of food in a feeding box and the moment the animal began to eat,[2] (2) the length of time required to eat a 2-gram pellet of food, and (3) the amount of food consumed in a five-minute period. Results indicated that although the 80 per cent group had significantly shorter response latencies than the 90 per cent group, this latter group took significantly shorter time to eat a 2-gram pellet of food, and ate more food

[2] The time or latency measure is an instrumental response, not a consummatory one.

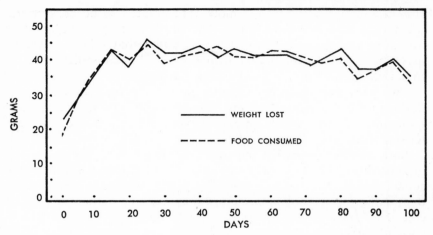

FIG. 8–3. COMPARISON OF MEAN WEIGHT LOST DURING TWENTY-THREE HOURS OF DEPRIVATION AND AMOUNT OF FOOD CONSUMED DURING THE FIRST HOUR OF FEEDING. (Adapted from Ehrenfreund, 1959)

in the five-minute period. Greater consummatory-response strength was thus indicated by the animals having the smaller loss of body weight.

Ehrenfreund (1959) has suggested that the failure to find a relationship between weight measures and food consumption for animals placed on a deprivation schedule can be attributed to the use of an inappropriate weight measure. Typically, the measure which is used is the animal's weight obtained just prior to the animal's being given its daily ration. Ehrenfreund has found that if the amount of weight loss during each preceding deprivation interval is used as the weight measure, the relationship between consummatory behavior and weight loss is quite high. Figure 8.3 shows a comparison of mean weight lost during 23 hours of deprivation and amount of food consumed during one hour of feeding for a 100-day experimental period. The relationship which was obtained between food consumption and prefeeding weight, however, was quite low and in keeping with the experimental findings of Baker (1955) and Moll (1959).

The Role of Other Variables and Consummatory Behavior

The relationship between deprivation and/or weight loss and consummatory behavior has not been completely resolved, although

Ehrenfreund's suggestion of a more appropriate weight measure to use should help in its resolution. The reconciliation of findings in this area also depends upon the recognition that other variables may affect the consummatory response and thus obscure or confound the action of the independent variable.

Two variables which have been experimentally demonstrated to interact with the consummatory response are: (1) the day-night cycle and, (2) the animal's previous experience in the deprivation-feeding situation.

Bare (1959) examined the relationship between varying levels of deprivation (2, 4, 8, 12, or 24 hours) and amount of food consumed during a typical day-night cycle. His results indicated that the number of hours of deprivation had little effect on the amount consumed and that the controlling variable appeared to be the presence of darkness.[3]

A number of other studies, (Ghent 1951, 1957, Lawrence and Mason 1955, Baker 1955, Mandler 1958, Moll 1959) have indicated the importance of the animal's experience in the deprivation-feeding situation.

Ghent (1951) deprived rats of food for 23-hour periods and noted the time the animals spent in eating as well as the amount of food consumed. During the first eating period, the animals did not compensate for their physiological need inasmuch as body weight was not maintained. The feeding period following the sixth day of deprivation revealed that the animals had doubled their intake relative to the first day, although they were still not eating enough to maintain normal body weight. A second study (1957) has provided confirming evidence. Animals deprived of food did not eat immediately or continuously when first offered food, but their latency of eating as well as the amount eaten increased with practice.

Lawrence and Mason (1955) noted that when rats were shifted from ad lib feeding to a 22-hour deprivation schedule, with a two-hour feeding period following each deprivation period, there was a 7- to 10-day period during which their food intake increased. When the animals were returned to an ad lib diet, there was another period of readjustment during which, at first, they overate, but again a 7- to 10-day period resulted in a gradual decrease to a new level.

[3] Some years before, Siegel and Stuckey (1947) had demonstrated that rats on an ad lib feeding schedule consumed significantly more food during the dark portion of the cycle (6 P.M. to 6 A.M.) than they did during the light portion (6 A.M. to 6 P.M.).

When the deprivation and ad lib schedule was repeated, there was some tendency for the first adjustment in both situations to be slower than the later ones, but there was no clear evidence that this increase in rate of adjustment continued with repeated experiences.

Finally, Mandler (1958) has found that eating behavior in the adult rat is related to deprivation schedules imposed during infancy. In general, animals placed on deprivation schedules early in infancy exhibit accelerated and more frequent consummatory behavior than control subjects raised on an ad libitum schedule. Presumably, the experimental animals, under the stress of deprivation, learn these characteristic ways of responding when food is available.

THE DRINKING RESPONSE

Measurement

The measurement of the drinking response is obtained by measuring the amount of water consumed and/or by measuring some aspect of the actual drinking process. In measuring the amount of water consumed by rats or other small animals, a calibrated drinking tube is frequently used. More complex pieces of equipment for the measurement operation, however, are sometimes employed. Adolph (1939), working with dogs, has placed a float in a water receptacle from which the animal drinks, and attached to the float is a lever which makes a continuous record of the water level. A similar type of apparatus had been previously used by Gregersen (1932), but some investigators have found such an apparatus to be rather insensitive when quantities of water less than 25 cc. were removed from the receptacle.

A somewhat similar device has been devised by Young and Richey (1952) for use with rats. Based on a partial-vacuum principle, the level of water in a glass tube falls as the animal drinks from a small cup at its base. A cork float, which rides on top of the water, is attached to a filament which passes down through the water and out to a recording pen. Inasmuch as the level of fluid in the cup is not constant, a discontinuous record is secured. If continuous records are desired, Duffy and Price's (1956) apparatus may be used utilizing a photoelectric cell to follow the fluid meniscus in a Stoppert vertical tube. Young and Richey's apparatus has been modified by Young (1957) to provide continuous drinking records for rats or other small mammals.

Some experimenters have measured the actual drinking response. Smith (1951) reports that Kappauf devised an apparatus such that every time the animal's tongue contacted the liquid a circuit was closed and a record made of the contact. A similar device has been described by Hill and Stellar (1951), who have called their apparatus a drinkometer. Although this type of apparatus is useful for recording the drinking response for a short period of time, prolonged periods of use result in the arduous task of translating the records into fluid volume. (See Smith and Duffy 1957.) If the recording paper speed is reduced to produce a more compact record, the error in translation is large.

Finally, and in less exact fashion than some of the techniques which we have discussed, some investigators have simply counted the number of gulps made by the animal in given length of time (i.e., one minute).

WATER DEPRIVATION AND CONSUMMATORY ACTIVITY

The early physiological studies of Adolph (1939) and Bellows (1939) indicated that the rate of voluntary water intake is approximately proportional to the water deficit when water deficit is defined in terms of body weight loss. Inasmuch as body weight loss is usually a function of some deprivation schedule, one can infer a relationship between amount of water intake and deprivation. Siegel (1947) deprived rats of water for 6, 12, 24, and 48 hours and noted the amount of water intake during a five-minute interval following the deprivation period. The relationship between voluntary water intake and the deprivation interval was found to be slightly sigmoid.[4] Figure 8.4 shows this relationship. This study also revealed a curvilinear relationship between hours of water deprivation and body weight loss.

Using the drinkometer, Stellar and Hill (1952) extended the findings of Siegel. Rats were deprived of water for 6, 12, 18, 24, 36, 48, 72, 96, 120, 144, and 168 hours; the rate and the amount of water consumed was measured during a two-hour period following these deprivation intervals. The results indicated that the water intake of an animal increased as a negatively accelerated function of the hours of deprivation. Furthermore, the rat drank at a constant rate; when the rate is constant, the amount of water an animal drinks is a function of the amount of time it spends drinking. With

[4] The positively accelerated portion of the curve appears to be a function of the fact that the 0 hour deprivation group actually consumed some water.

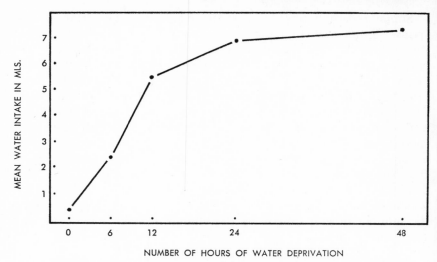

FIG. 8–4. RELATIONSHIP BETWEEN VOLUNTARY WATER INTAKE AND PERIOD
OF WATER DEPRIVATION. (Adapted from Siegel, 1947)

mild deprivation states, animals tend to drink for shorter periods of
time than under severe deprivation states.

Some investigators have been interested in producing a need for
water, not by depriving the animal, but by injecting hypertonic
saline. A series of studies by Heyer (1951, 1951a) and O'Kelly and
Heyer (1951) have demonstrated that subcutaneous injections of
saline could be used as a motivational antecedent for instrumental
behavior. Holmes and Gregersen (1950) and Wayner and Reimanis (1958) have used this technique in order to study its effects
on the consummatory response. In this latter study, 90 rats were
divided into nine equal groups, with the control group being injected
with 2.00 cc. of buffered mammalian Ringer's solution. The other
eight groups received different volumes of a 15 per cent solution
of NaCl. The mean quantities of NaCl injected were as follows:
0.3, 0.6, 1.1, 1.6, 2.2, 3.4, 5.4 and 7.5 milliequivalent. Following
the injection, the amount of water consumed over the next three-
hour period was measured. Results indicated that water intake increased proportionally to the amount of NaCl injected. Figure 8.5
reveals this function.

As with eating, learning plays a role in the drinking process.
Ghent (1957) has found that rats deprived of water and then per-

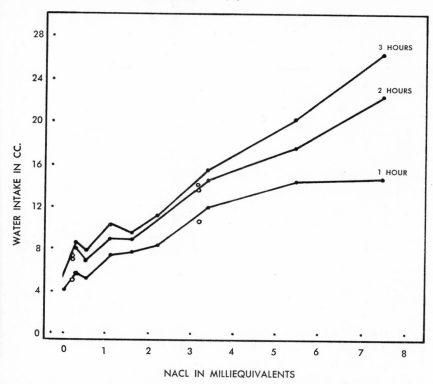

FIG. 8–5. ACCUMULATIVE ONE-, TWO-, AND THREE-HOUR WATER INTAKES FOLLOWING SUBCUTANEOUS INJECTIONS OF VARYING AMOUNTS OF NACL. (Adapted from Wayner and Reimanis, 1958)

mitted to drink do not drink immediately; but with successive testings, the animals approached water more quickly and increased their time spent in drinking as well as the amount drunk.

PREFERENCE BEHAVIOR AND THE NEED FOR SPECIFIC FOODS

Free-Feeding Experiments

We have noted in Chapter 7 that when an animal is deprived of an important part of its normal diet its activity increases only in the case of protein or vitamin B deficiency. A basic question to be considered here, however, is: if animals are deprived of a needed substance, what will be the effect on their consummatory behavior?

It is appropriate to determine whether or not an organism will select a balanced diet from an array of food which contains all the necessary components of such a diet. We know that human adults, in many instances, do not. In China, for example, there is a strong preference for polished rice, which is deficient in vitamin B and thus contributes to beriberi. One difficulty with adult humans is that learning may play an important role in overriding "natural" preferences.

An early study by Evvard (1916) indicated that pigs which were allowed to select their own diets under a free-choice system grew as well as animals fed on a diet selected by man. This experiment was later followed and supported by Pearl and Fairchild (1921), working with chickens; by Mitchell and Mendel (1921) on rats and mice; by Nevins (1927), on dairy cattle and by Davis (1928), on human infants. In this latter study, an oft-reported one, three infants, eight to ten months of age, were allowed to select their own diet for a six- to twelve-month period. Davis reports that from the beginning of the experiment the children were able to select their own foods from a list of simple natural ones, and in quantities sufficient to provide optimal health and growth. One child who had rickets at the start of the experiment selected cod-liver oil until cured, and then no longer took it.[5]

These findings suggest that both animals and infant humans can select adequate diets, thus demonstrating some relationship between food preferences and nutritional needs. One major difficulty, however, is that the experiments are usually so arranged so that only nutritional foods are available. Perhaps chance selection of them would produce the same result.

Natural foodstuffs invariably contain a number of different components; as a result, a number of studies have been undertaken to examine the ability of rats to select adequate diets when such diets were composed of purified foods. Richter, Holt, and Barelare (1938) presented the following foods to rats: olive oil, sucrose,

[5] An interesting variation of this is reported by Wilkins and Richter (1940). The authors report that a 3½-year-old boy who suffered from degeneration of the adrenal cortex was able to keep himself alive for more than two years by devouring large quantities of table salt. By such consumption, the child supplied his system with sufficient sodium to compensate for the metabolic dysfunction. When the boy was hospitalized and placed under the regular institutional diet, he developed sodium deficiency and died.

yeast, calcium, lactate, sodium phosphate, potassium chloride, wheat-germ oil, and sodium chloride. The diet selection of eight experimental animals was found to be adequate to maintain normal growth and reproduction, although the average caloric intake was 18.7 per cent less than that of their controls—the controls having been raised on a standard diet.

The studies of Scott (1946) and Pilgrim and Patton (1947), however, have not provided complete confirmation of the Richter, Holt, and Barelare (1938) study. In the Pilgrim and Patton study, which had findings similar to those of Scott, 96 normal young rats were offered casein, salts, sucrose, and fat. The patterns of selection were variable, and about one third of the rats grew at a subnormal rate.

Specific Deprivation States and Preference Behavior

One extension of the inquiries arising from the free-feeding experiments is related to the preferences that organisms have when presented, not with a whole array of foodstuffs, but with just two or three. A related question and one which we have posed earlier, is concerned with preference or choice behavior which arises from specific deprivation states. If an organism is prevented from receiving a certain nutrient which is basic to its health, will it choose that substance when given the opportunity to do so? Investigators have not only been interested in examining the behavior of organisms in these situations, but have been concerned with the examination of those factors which are related to such behavior.

Measurement

A variety of methods has been used to investigate such behavior. Perhaps the most frequently used method has been to simultaneously present two or more concentrations (or foodstuffs), with the animal having the opportunity to make a choice between or among them. Young (Young and Chaplin 1945) has termed this procedure a "foods together" technique. An example of this method is found in Bare (1949). This investigator in examining the specific hunger for sodium chloride in the rat employed two containers, one of which always contained tap water while the other contained successively increasing concentrations of salt solution. The presentation of just two foods obviously restricts the animal's choice among the stimuli, and Carpenter (1958), in order to provide a greater freedom of choice, has utilized a multiple-choice situation in which the animal is given a simultaneous choice of a number (eight) of different concentrations.

The use of two or more stimuli demands, of course, that their position in the experimental situation be randomized. Furthermore, as Beebe-Center, Black, Hoffman, and Wade (1948) have pointed out, this type of experimental situation, and the behavior of animals in it, is much the same as a discrimination study employing differential reinforcement.

A single-stimulus method has also been used. Here, the organism is presented with only a single food (or concentration) at one time, but different foods are presented on successive days, with the time spent in eating or the amount consumed providing appropriate response measures. This method is illustrated by Weiner and Stellar (1951), who placed rats on 15 hours of deprivation, and then measured the amount of salt solution consumed in the hour following the deprivation period. On different days, different concentrations of salt were used. By plotting the amount consumed as a function of the concentration of the solution, they were able to plot a preference-aversion function.

A last method involves a situation in which the animal is given a choice of responses, with each response leading to a different incentive. Young (Young and Chaplin 1945) has termed this the "foods apart" technique. A T maze might be used in which one incentive is placed on the right arm and a second incentive on the left. The animal's choice of arms over a series of trials reflects its preference behavior. In contrast to the other methods which we have described, it is obvious that this technique is one which involves the measurement of an instrumental response rather than a consummatory one.

As one might anticipate, some caution should be exercised when comparing studies which have used different methods of measurement. Stellar and McCleary (1952) compared the rat's preference for both glucose and sodium chloride with three different methods of measurement: (1) the single-stimulus method, (2) a two-stimulus method in which one of the stimuli was water, and (3) a two-stimulus method which consisted of pairing different concentrations of materials. Their findings with sodium chloride indicated that an animal's maximal salt preference was approximately 8 per cent, regardless of the method of measurement, thus confirming an earlier study by Weiner and Stellar (1951). On the other hand, the maximal preference for glucose shifted from 5 per cent to 10 per cent to 20 per cent when tested by methods 1, 2, and 3, respectively.

A second measurement consideration involves the amount of time the animal is permitted to make the consummatory response. Weiner and Stellar (1951) contrasted a five-minute test period with that of an hour, and found similar preference-aversion functions for salt. On the other hand, Young (1945) has reported that rats, permitted to eat for just 100 seconds, preferred sugar, wheat, and dried milk, in that order. If the animals were permitted to eat for ten minutes, however, dried milk was most preferred and sugar least preferred. In this situation, the amount of time that the animal spent in eating was used as the measure of preference behavior.

Specific Deprivation States and Consummatory Behavior

One of the early investigators, interested in the problem of relating specific deprivation states to consummatory behavior, was Richter (1939), who found that adrenalectomized rats had a lower preference threshold for a sodium chloride solution than normal animals. This study was later confirmed by Richter and Eckert (1941), Clark and Clausen (1943), and Bare (1949).

Other investigators, utilizing other deprivation states, have also reported positive need-preference findings. Richter, Holt, and Barelare (1937) found that rats deficient in vitamin B_1 indicated great avidity for it in their initial contact, sought it out from a variety of foods presented, and consumed large quantities of it at the first opportunity. Scott and Quint (1946) have also reported experimental findings which indicated that thiamine-deficient rats, when given an opportunity to choose a diet containing thiamine, did so almost immediately.

A number of investigators, however, have obtained negative results. Wilder (1937) has shown that rats deprived of vitamins A and D show no inclination to select foods which contain these elements, and Jukes (1938) has reported similar findings for chicks deficient in vitamins A and G. Harris, Clay, Hargreaves, and Ward (1933), in contrast to Scott and Quint (1946), were unable to find thiamine-deficient animals able to discriminate between a diet containing the vitamin from one lacking it. Luria's study (1953) is one of the most extensive in the area of thiamine deficiency. Four concentrations of thiamine (.25, .025, .0025, .00025 per cent) were presented along with tap water in a four-day test period which followed a 19-day thiamine, free diet supplemented by oxythiamine injections—an antivitamin which replaces thiamine in the tissue. Results indicated no simple relationship between the deficiency and thiamine intake, although significant increases in thiamine intake occurred at the two highest levels of concentration. The failure of Luria's rats to avail themselves of lower thiamine concentrations might appear to indicate that some complex relationship exists between thiamine deficiency and intake. There is a possibility, however, that the animals were simply unable to discriminate the low-level concentrations from tap water.

Finally, Meyer (1952), using humans, has reported no relationship between hours of deprivation (1 through 34) and the individual's threshold for sweet, salt, and bitter.

Although the generality of need-related preferences may be questioned, there is ample experimental evidence to indicate that rats which need salt will modify their consummatory behavior so as to ingest larger than normal quantities of this substance when it is made available. As a result, a number of investigators have been interested in determining the mechanisms involved in such a specific preference; others have extended their inquiry to preference behavior in general.

It appears to be well accepted that at least some of our preferences are determined by learning or habit, and Snapper (1955) has provided extensive anecdotal evidence supporting such a position. That preferences can develop without a learning component is supported by the comparative evidence presented by Frings (1947), who has written of the ready acceptance of sugar solutions in a large variety of animals, and the experimental evidence of Weiner and Stellar (1951) and Epstein and Stellar (1955). These latter investigators examined the role of learning in the normal and the adrenalectomized rat's preference for salt.

Weiner and Stellar (1951) have shown that normal, naive rats tested with (a) tap water, (b) 0.6 per cent salt solution, and (c) tap water again on three successive days, show the same elevated rate of drinking the salt solution as experienced rats. Moreover, within the first five minutes of drinking the salt solution for the first time, the naive animals ingested more than they did in similar periods when drinking tap water.

In the Epstein and Stellar (1955) study, one group of rats was permitted to ingest salt immediately and continuously following an adrenalectomy. A second adrenalectomized group, however, was not given salt until a severe salt deficiency had developed. Results indicated that the first group gradually increased their salt preference, presumably in accordance with their increasing physiological need for it. On the other hand, the second group's intake reached the exaggerated level immediately following their being given access to salt. The authors have indicated that the major point that can be made from these findings is "that postoperative experience with salt solutions is not a necessary condition for the development of the exaggerated specific hunger for salt in the adrenalectomized rat."

Richter's (1939) early work emphasized the importance of the taste mechanism in accounting for the salt preference behavior of his adrenalectomized animals. He stated, "rats ingest more salt, not because they learn that salt relieves their deficiency discomforts, but because of chemical changes in the taste mechanism in the oral cavity, giving rise to an enhanced salt discrimination." Such a position, of course, was based on the assumption that the animal's preference threshold was identical with its sensory threshold. Considerable evidence has accumulated, however, to make Richter's hypothesis untenable.

Pfaffman and Bare (1950) examined the gustatory sensory threshold of the rat [6] by measuring the afferent nerve discharges in the chorda tympani nerve. Figure 8.6 indicates where the recording electrodes were placed with regard to the peripheral nerve supply to the tongue, and Figure 8.7 indicates a diagram of the recording methods (Pfaffman 1957). Results indicated no differences in the characteristics of the nerve discharge between normal and adrenalectomized animals.

Carr (1952) and Harriman and MacLeod (1953) have presented behavioral evidence which indicates that although the adrenalectomized animal's *preference* threshold is lower than the normal animal's, its sensory threshold is not. Carr's study (1952) involved the use of a learning situation in which, if the animal selected a salt solution, the concentration of which varied from .5 per cent to .0003 per cent, it was permitted to drink for 15 seconds. The selection of only water resulted in drinking for ten seconds and one second of shock. Using this technique, Carr found no differences in threshold between normal and adrenalectomized animals. Thus, a need for salt on the part of the adrenalectomized animals did not

[6] Sensory threshold was defined as the weakest concentration of sodium chloride required to produce the discharge of taste impulses.

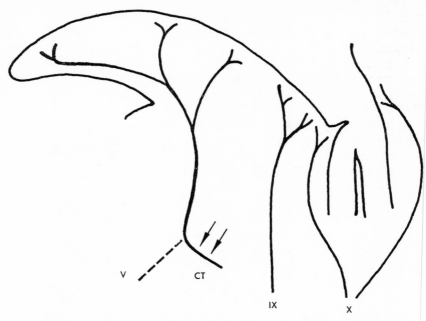

FIG. 8–6. DIAGRAM OF PERIPHERAL NERVE SUPPLY TO THE TONGUE. V, tri-geminal nerve; IX, glossopharyngeal nerve; X, vagus nerve; C.T., chorda timpani nerve; Arrows show the placement of recording electrodes. (Adapted from Pfaffman, 1957)

result in their being able to discriminate it from tap water with any greater success than those normal animals who did not have such a need.

Some investigators, although recognizing that the organism's taste threshold has not been lowered by the need, have simply as-sumed that a needed food tastes better to the deprived organism. Possibly, the lowered level of the needed substance in the body sensitizes the nervous system, which in turn enhances the accept-ability of the stimuli arising from the need-related substance.

In one study examining the role of taste, Epstein and Stellar (1955) provided adrenalectomized rats with a 3 per cent concen-tration of salt, but also gave the animal an ion exchange resin, so that the animal was able to absorb only about 50 per cent of the salt ingested. Under the circumstances, the animals doubled their in-take. As the authors state:

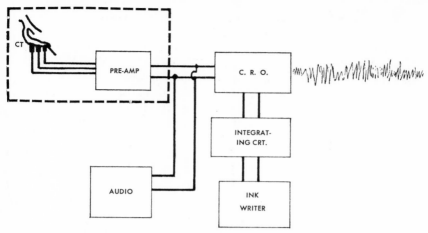

FIG. 8–7. DIAGRAM OF RECORDING METHOD. The tracings on the right are sample records. C.R.O., cathode ray oscillograph. (Adapted from Pfaffman, 1957)

. . . when the animal is drinking and tasting a 3 per cent solution, but absorbing a solution of approximately 1.5 per cent salt concentration, its intake is much closer to what would be dictated by a 1.5 per cent solution than by a 3 per cent solution. Therefore it appears that the amount of salt that is supplied to the adrenalectomized rat's internal environment is a much more important determinant of its motivation to drink 3 per cent salt solutions than is the taste stimulation provided by that solution.

The role of taste has also been examined in a study by Smith, Pool, and Weinberg (1958), who investigated sham drinking in salt-deficient rats. Their findings indicated that it was necessary for the animals to actually ingest a salt solution in order for the exaggerated preference for salt to appear. Sham drinking, in which the animals could taste the solution but not ingest it, did not result in such a preference.

As we shall note in Chapter 13, the experimental evidence appears to indicate that the regulation of food intake in general is under multi-factor control. The condition of the stomach, the blood, and the central nervous system, each make their respective contribution in determining how intake shall be regulated. It also appears that such regulation is related to the organism's previous experiences, so that associative factors play a role in this seemingly simple but actually complex type of behavior.

When we ask why an organism eats a specific type of food, rather than simply why he eats, our question is even more complex. But it does seem reasonable to assume that specific food intake or preference behavior must be also under control of many variables. We have indicated some of these variables; the presence of others, as well as how they interact, poses questions yet to be answered.

9 • INSTRUMENTAL RESPONSES, I

Since learning has been one of the basic areas in psychology, it is not surprising that considerable attention has been given to the instrumental response as a behavioral consequent arising from the manipulation of motivational antecedents. This, then, is the primary purpose of a number of chapters to follow—to investigate instrumental behavior as a function of the operation of varying motivational antecedents. The organization which many investigators have used in examining these relationships, and the one which we shall primarily follow, has been to ignore the *kind* of motivational antecedent (food deprivation, water deprivation, etc.) and place emphasis upon general operating principles.[1] Such an approach has been largely a product of Hull's theoretical system, in which he in-

---

[1] There are, of course, many noteworthy exceptions to this kind of organization. A large amount of motivational material has been organized around stress and frustration, in which these antecedents have been posited to produce specific response patterns. And in an early study, Petrinovich and Bolles (1954) posited that hunger and thirst had different behavioral attributes. Food deprivation presumably facilitated variability of response while water deprivation facilitated stereotypy. A later study (Bolles and Petrinovich 1956), however, indicated that variations in body weight, rather than the type of deprivation, were responsible for these findings.

troduced the construct of generalized drive strength or D. Here, Hull assumed that all of the organism's specific need states contributed to D, and that D could energize or facilitate the action of all effectors, regardless of the particular need state under which they had been acquired. Before proceeding, however, our first consideration is to examine the characteristics of instrumental response measurement.

MEASUREMENT

Types

It would be impossible to discuss in detail all of the varying types of instrumental activity which have been used to examine the operation of motivational antecedents. It is of some interest, however, to look at some of the early developments in the area.

A study by Moss (1924) illustrates one technique that was used quite early. Morgan (1923), in a discussion of instinct, stated that "the amount of inhibition necessary to overcome any tendency may be used as a measure of the strength of that tendency." Moss applied the principle to the measurement of drive by making a deprived animal cross a grid and receive shock in order to obtain food. The number of times that the animal would make the crossing could be used to infer the strength of the drive. Warden (1931), doing similar work in the Columbia laboratory, used the term "obstruction method" to describe this method of measuring motivation. His work resulted in the development of the Columbia Obstruction Box—the floor plan of which is illustrated in Figure 9.1.

The reliability of this apparatus has been good (Warden and Nissen 1928; Stone, Tomilin, and Barker 1935; and Graves 1936).

The validity of the apparatus is adequate for measuring variations in the strength of a *single* deprivation state. With food as an incentive, the number of instrumental responses (the number of times the animal will cross the grid) increases as a function of the hours of food deprivation. With a receptive female as an incentive, the number of times the rat crosses the grid increases as a function of the number of hours since the last mating (Warden 1931). A frequently quoted finding, using the obstruction technique, has been that the strongest need, using the experimentally determined maxima as a basis for comparison, is maternal, followed by thirst, hunger, sex, and exploration (Warden 1931). The validity of the

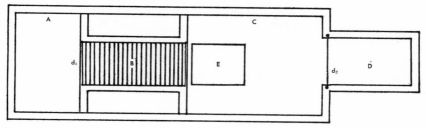

FIG. 9–1. DIAGRAM OF THE COLUMBIA OBSTRUCTION BOX. A, entrance compartment; B, obstruction compartment; C,D, divided incentive compartment; E, release plate; d_1, manually operated door of entrance compartment; d_2, automatic door (operated by the animal stepping on the release plate between the two divisions of the incentive chamber). (Adapted from Jenkins, Warner, and Warden, 1926)

apparatus for reaching this type of conclusion is questionable. Leuba (1931) has found that the results cited by Warden are a function of the length of the experimental period. Leuba has shown that the number of crossings during each five-minute period was not even approximately constant, and if a 10-minute experimental period had been used rather than a 20-minute period, the relative strength of the varying motives would have been changed. In part, such variability may be a function of the animal's adaptation to shock. A second difficulty is that, inasmuch as the strength of a motive is a function of the incentive as well as the deprivation period, a change in the amount or characteristic of the incentive provided might change the animal's behavior, and thus, the relative strength of the motive. Finally, as Maier and Schneirla (1935) have mentioned, certain deprivation states can be satisfied more effectively with a few crossings than other deprivation states. Water may alleviate thirst more quickly, for example, than food alleviates hunger.

An obstruction apparatus utilizing a barrier of paper and sand, rather than shock, has been devised by Stone (1937, 1937a). Stone believed that the use of paper or sand did not set up the undesirable fear or avoidance reactions which were frequently produced by the use of shock. Other obstruction-type apparatuses have been reported by Dorcus (1934), Freeman (1939), and Stolurow (1948).

Moss' (1924) early study revealed a second way of utilizing instrumental behavior from which to infer motive strength. He was interested in the *choice* behavior of a rat when the animal was placed under the deprivation states of both sex and food. The subject was placed in a central compartment, with food placed on one side and an animal of the opposite sex on the other. The strength of the need was measured in terms of the number of choices that the animal made to each incentive. Later, Tsai (1925) employed a similar method to investigate the same needs under somewhat better controlled experimental conditions.

A fundamental defect of using choice behavior lies in the interdependence of the motivational states which are manipulated. An animal placed under food deprivation is also thirsty, while the sex drive is weakened by the presence of the need for food.

In recent years, other and more general learning tasks have been used. Some motivational antecedent is manipulated, and the subject's performance in the learning situation is measured. Learning tasks ranging from the straight runway to multiple-T mazes, and from simple conditioned responses to complex problem-solving situations, have been used, with the strength or contribution of the motivational antecedent being inferred from the organism's performance.

General Considerations

One important consideration has to do with an examination of the interrelationships existing among the varying response measures which may be obtained from the same learning task. In the classical conditioning of the eyeblink, for example, the investigator may measure the conditioned response's latency, amplitude, frequency of occurrence, or resistance to extinction. With a rat running down a straight runway, one can measure the animal's latency in entering the runway from the starting box, its speed in running down the alley, or its resistance to experimental extinction. These measures, of course, represent but a few of the many which investigators have used in their examination of the effect of some particular motivational antecedent upon behavior.

Hull (1943), in the formulation of his theoretical system, assumed that four response measures (amplitude, latency, probability, and resistance to extinction) had functional equivalence. Many other investigators have made similar assumptions regarding the interrelationships that exist among response measures.

The results of a number of experimental studies (Campbell and Hilgard 1936, Campbell 1938, Brogden 1949, Hall and Kobrick

1952, Campbell and Kraeling 1954, Kobrick 1956), however, have been only partially successful in finding significant relationships among the variety of response measures obtained from the same task. Kobrick's study illustrates the problem. In this experiment, rats were trained to run a 12-foot runway. Eight groups of animals were used, with each group receiving either 4, 7, 10, 15, 20, 30, 40, or 50 reinforcements. Response measures were obtained from each group for latency, speed of running, and resistance to extinction. The results of correlational analysis revealed that only the relationship between latency and running time was statistically significant.

With the failure to find significant relationships among the varying measures within the same learning task, it is not surprising that the relationships existing among instrumental responses in different tasks are also usually quite low. One of the most extensive studies dealing with this problem was done by Anderson (1938). He used five instrumental response tasks: (1) a jump test in which the animals had to jump a 7-to 8½-inch gap in order to secure an appropriate goal object, (2) a sand test in which the animals had to dig through a tube of sand in order to obtain the appropriate goal object, (3) the speed of running a 27-foot runway leading to a goal object, and, finally, (4 and 5) two tasks both of which involved use of an obstruction box. With water deprivation as the manipulated need state, and water as the goal object, Anderson found few significant correlations among the test situations. The performance of the two obstruction tasks correlated .63, and the speed of the running test correlated .54 with the digging-through-sand test. Other than these, the interrelationships among the varying tasks were quite low. When food deprivation was used as the appropriate need state and food as the incentive, the intercorrelations among these test situations were likewise poor. The use of sexual stimulation, manipulated by first permitting the male to copulate with a receptive female and then using the female as an appropriate incentive, resulted in intercorrelations among the varying learning tasks higher than those with either food or water deprivation.

The examination of recently published material reveals a tendency on the part of some investigators either to concern themselves with the examination of a single response measure or to differentiate among response measures. Estes (1950), for example, has been interested only in a probability-of-response measure. Meyer (1953) and Pubols (1960), on the other hand, have made a distinction between measures which involve time (e.g., latency, running time, rate of responding), and those which are time independent (e.g., errors). A somewhat similar point of view has been expressed by Gilbert (1958) who has concluded that the fundamental dimensional properties of the operant response are those which yield quantities in time (latency, tempo, perseveration, duration) and space (amount of movement, direction).

Meyer (1953) and Pubols (1960) have considered time measures to be indices of performance, and time-independent measures to reveal associative or learning factors. The concepts of performance and learning, however, have psychological connotations other than those which have been proposed by Meyer and Pubols. Consequently, we would propose to classify instrumental responses simply in terms of: (1) rate or time of response measures and (2) probability of response measures. We would contend, moreover, that we should further categorize these responses in terms of whether or not they were obtained during acquisition or during extinction.

THE ROLE OF RELEVANT MOTIVATIONAL ANTECEDENTS

In this section, we are interested in examining how relevant motivational antecedents (i.e., antecedents which bear a direct relationship to the reward obtained by the instrumental response) are related to the acquisition and extinction of instrumental responses.

The Relationship Between the Intensity of the Motivational Antecedent and Response Acquisition

What is the relationship between the level or intensity of the motivational antecedent and the acquisition of some learned response? A straightforward approach to this question would be to provide subjects with some learning task and note their acquisition responses as a function of various intensities of the motivational antecedent.

When rate of response is used as the learning measure, almost all of the experimental evidence supports the position that learning increases as a function of the intensity of the motivational antecedent. The early studies of Wever (1932) and Hack (1933) have demonstrated that water temperature was related to a rat's speed of swimming, while the more recent studies of Deese and Carpenter (1951), Cotton (1953), Lewis and Cotton (1957), Davis (1957), and Barry (1958) have shown that an increase in

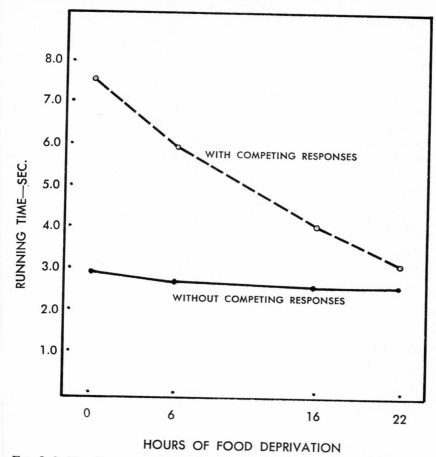

FIG. 9–2. THE RELATIONSHIP BETWEEN AVERAGED MEAN DAILY RUNNING TIME AND AMOUNT OF FOOD DEPRIVATION. (Adapted from Cotton, 1953)

food or water deprivation results in decreasing running time on the runway. Hillman, Hunter, and Kimble (1953) have obtained similar findings measuring running speed in the multiple T maze.

Cotton's study suggests that high deprivation states result in the elimination of responses which compete with the running response. In his experiment, he analyzed the animal's actual running responses as well as competing responses which were made on the runway. Results indicated that the influence of varying hours of deprivation (0, 6, 16, and 22) on running time was virtually nonexistent when trials in which competing responses were present were eliminated from the analysis. Figure 9.2 compares running time with and without competing responses as a function of varying hours of deprivation.

There is some question as to whether or not pain or fear operates in a fashion similar to the motivational antecedents which we have just discussed. Kimble (1955) investigated four intensities of shock (.2, .5, 1.0, and 2.0 ma) on the latency of a wheel turning response. Although he found latency apparently decreasing as a function of shock intensity, careful examination of his data indicates that the relationship obtained was primarily a function of the performance of the .2 ma group. The responses making up this group were primarily escape responses; responses in the other groups were of an avoidance variety. If the .2 ma group is excluded, there are no significant differences among the remaining groups' performances.

Brush (1957), making a more extensive investigation of shock intensity on the acquisition of an avoidance response in dogs, has also reported largely negative findings. Five groups of subjects were trained with shock intensities of .70, 2.06, 3.10, 4.82, and 5.59 ma. Although the percentage of animals learning was found to increase with shock intensity up to 4.82 ma, and then to decrease at the one intensity which was higher, the intensity of the shock had little effect on the latency of acquisition responses.

When probability of response is used as a response measure, the experimental findings are equivocal. Neither Hillman, Hunter, and Kimble (1953), Teel (1952), nor Armus (1958) were able to find differences in the number of errors made by their experimental animals (rats) in learning a maze as a function of varying intensities of food deprivation.

Meyer (1951) and Warren and Hall (1956), using monkeys as their subjects, have obtained findings similar to those which we have just cited. Meyer (1951) found no differences among sophisticated monkeys, placed under either 1, 23, or 47 hours of food deprivation, which had the task of learning a discrimination-reversal problem. Meyer's experimental situation (as well as Warren and Hall's) contained three conditions, however, which might have contributed to his results: (1) his subjects were sophisticated, (2) the problems were quite easy, and (3) highly desirable rewards were used. In an effort to determine the influence of these variables, Miles (1959) used naive monkeys as his subjects, employed both

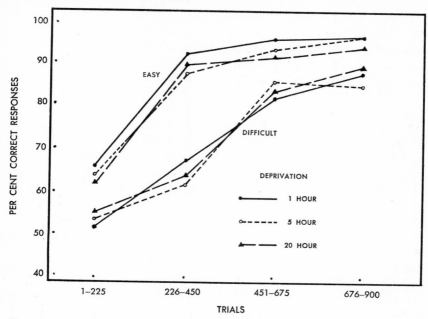

FIG. 9–3. MEAN PERCENTAGE CORRECT RESPONSES AS A FUNCTION OF TRIALS AND DEPRIVATION CONDITIONS. (Adapted from Miles, 1959)

easy and difficult problems, and used a reward which was normally found in the animal's diet. His results confirmed Meyer's general conclusion. Hours of deprivation (1, 5, or 20) played no role in determining the correctness of the animals' responses. Figure 9.3 indicates Miles' results.

In contrast to these negative findings, the early studies of Yerkes and Dodson (1908) with mice, Cole (1911) with chicks, and Dodson (1917) with rats, as well as the more recent studies of Hammes (1956) and Broadhurst (1957) also employing rats, have demonstrated that the strength of the motivational antecedent does influence the probability of response. Dodson's (1917) early study, for example, revealed that rats which were deprived of food for 41 hours learned a visual-discrimination habit more rapidly than animals deprived for 24, 31, or 48 hours.[2]

[2] If frequency of occurrence in crossing a grid in an obstruction box is conceived as a probability-of-response measure, the work of Holden (1926) and Warden (1931) has indicated that increases in food, water, and sex deprivation, at least up to some level, results in increasing the number of crossings in order to obtain the appropriate incentive.

Some of the studies in this group, in addition to investigating the effect of the intensity of the motivational antecedent, have also manipulated the difficulty of the task employed. One of the first studies in the area was done by Yerkes and Dodson (1908). Their subjects were dancing mice, and three degrees of difficulty in a visual-discrimination task were used. In addition, they used different amounts of electric shock as the motivational antecedent. Although they used relatively few subjects, their results indicated that with the easy discrimination problem, correct responses increased as a function of the strength of shock. With the medium and difficult discriminations, however, increases in the intensity of the shock resulted in first increasing but then decreasing the number of correct responses. Their findings indicated an optimum intensity of a motivational antecedent for a given degree of difficulty of task; if intensity was increased beyond the optimum, the speed of learning decreased. These findings provided the experimental base for what has become known as the Yerkes-Dodson law: "As the difficultness of discrimination is increased the strength of that stimulus which is most favorable to habit-formation approaches the threshold."

Studies by Cole (1911), Dodson (1915), and, more recently, studies by Hammes (1956) and Broadhurst (1957) have confirmed this relationship. In the Broadhurst study, three levels of difficulty of an underwater brightness discrimination, and four levels of air deprivation were used. Air deprivation was manipulated by delaying the rat either 0, 2, 4, or 8 seconds under water before releasing the animal into the learning situation. Figure 9.4 presents these findings.

In classical conditioning studies, frequently regarded as distinct from the types of learning situations which we have just been considering, the unconditioned stimulus must be considered as the motivational antecedent. When the intensity of the unconditioned stimulus is manipulated, and the frequency of the conditioned response used as the response measure, the experimental studies of Passey (1948) and Prokasy, Grant, and Myers (1958) support the position that probability of response does vary as a function of the intensity of the unconditioned stimulus.

A number of investigators have not been satisfied with the experimental design of the type of study which we have just considered. Their point of view, largely influenced by Hull's theoretical system, has been that the finding of differences in performance un-

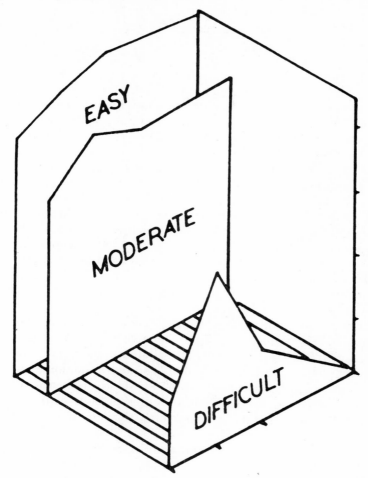

FIG. 9–4. A THREE-DIMENSIONAL SURFACE. Showing the relationship between learning scores in a discrimination task and (*a*) the intensity of the
imposed motivation (air deprivation) measured by the number of seconds'
delay underwater before release and (*b*) the level of difficulty of the task.
(Adapted from Broadhurst, 1957)

der different intensities of a motivational antecedent does not
indicate whether such performance differences can be attributed
solely to the operation of the motivational antecedent, or whether
such differences reflect the operation of some additional variable,
i.e., habit strength. Accordingly, they have asked, what is the ef-

fect of motivation intensity on (1) performance, when habit strength has been experimentally held constant, and (2) habit strength itself?

The experimental design employed to answer the first question has been to have subjects, all under the same intensity of motivation, learn some task in which a fixed number of reinforcements are provided. Following such training, the intensity of the motivational antecedent is varied, and the organism's resistance to extinction is measured. Inasmuch as it is hypothesized that habit strength does not increase during extinction, differences in resistance to extinction must reflect the operation of only the motivational antecedent.

In one of the early studies using this type of design, Perin (1942) placed 40 rats under 23 hours of food deprivation and gave them 16 reinforcements in a Skinner box. The animals were then divided into four groups, with each group given extinction trials under either 1, 3, 16, or 23 hours of food deprivation. Perin found that the mean number of extinction responses increased as a function of hours of deprivation.

An *extrapolation* of Perin's findings indicated that bar-pressing behavior could continue to be elicited in some strength even though the animals had no need for food. The experimental work of Koch and Daniel (1945) indicated that satiated animals, in spite of a large amount of previous training, showed little inclination to press the bar in the extinction situation.

Saltzman and Koch (1948) also provided rats with a large amount of previous training in learning to press a bar, and then placed the animals under ½, 1, or 2 hours of food deprivation. They found that low deprivation periods, in contrast to satiation, exerted a substantial influence on the rate of the response obtained in the extinction situation.

Yamaguchi (1951) examined the effects of 48 and 72 hours of deprivation, in addition to 3, 12, and 24 hours of deprivation, and found increases in response strength for the 48-hour deprivation group over that of the 24, but the findings for the 72-hour deprivation group were ambiguous. When the *mean* number of responses to extinction was examined, the 72-hour group was superior to all other groups (3, 12, 24 and 48 hours). The *median* response for the 72-hour group, however, was slightly below that of the 48-hour group.

Combining the Koch and Daniels (1945), Saltzman and Koch

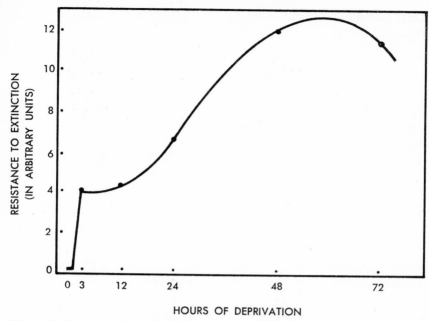

FIG. 9–5. PROPOSED REPRESENTATION OF THE RELATIONSHIP OF RESISTANCE TO EXTINCTION (IN ARBITRARY UNITS) TO HOURS OF FOOD DEPRIVATION. (Major portion of the figure was adapted from Yamaguchi, 1951.)

(1948), and Yamaguchi (1951) studies, resistance to extinction as a function of hours of deprivation is approximated by Figure 9.5.[3]

The superior performance of animals under a deprivation state of more than 24 hours as found by Yamaguchi has not been confirmed by Cautela (1956) who, in contrast to previous investigators, employed a discrimination task. A black-white discrimination habit was acquired by rats under 23 hours of food deprivation. The animals were then extinguished under either 0, 6, 12, 23, 47, or 71 hours of deprivation. Cautela's results indicated that the number of responses to extinction (defined as refusal to run within

[3] Although Kimble (1951) did not use a resistance-to-extinction measure, his study has relevance in this section. Rats were first taught a panel-pushing response under 24 hours of deprivation. Response latencies for five trials were then obtained under deprivation periods of 10, 30, 50, and 60 minutes, as well as 2, 8, 15, and 24 hours. His results were quite similar to those obtained by Salzman and Koch (1948) and Yamaguchi (1951).

three minutes) increased up to 23 hours of deprivation but then declined for the 47- and 71-hour periods.

THE RELATIONSHIP BETWEEN THE INTENSITY OF THE MOTIVATIONAL ANTECEDENT AND HABIT STRENGTH

It will be recalled that the second question arising from the theoretical system of Hull was, what is the influence of the intensity of the motivational antecedent on habit strength? Hull (1943) posited that motivation did not make any direct contribution to the formation of habit, and it has been the testing of this postulation which has been responsible for a number of the experimental studies in the area.

The experimental operations designed to enable the investigator to make inferences about the relationship between motivation and habit are similar to those which we have just encountered. Animals are placed under varying levels of deprivation and given training in which a fixed number of reinforcements is provided. Following such training, all animals are then placed under the same level of deprivation and their resistance to extinction is measured. If the data indicate no differences among the groups during extinction, such a finding indicates that the accrual of habit strength during acquisition has been similar for all groups *in spite of the varying levels of deprivation employed.* Presumably, the level of deprivation does not contribute to the growth of habit. On the other hand, if the extinction data reveal differences among the groups, such data are used to indicate that habit strength has been affected by the intensity of the motivational antecedent. Since extinction data provide the basic findings, the rate of response becomes the primary response measure.

One of the first studies in this area was made by Finan (1940), who deprived rats of food for 1, 12, 24, and 48 hours and then gave each group 30 reinforcements in learning to depress a bar to obtain food. All subjects were then extinguished under 24 hours of deprivation. Results indicated that habit strength (as inferred from the animal's resistance to extinction) increased from a relatively low level produced by conditioning under one hour of deprivation to a maximum of 12 hours of deprivation. It then declined at a negatively accelerated rate through the 24 hours and 48 hours of the deprivation period.

Later studies by Strassburger (1950) and Carper (1953), also

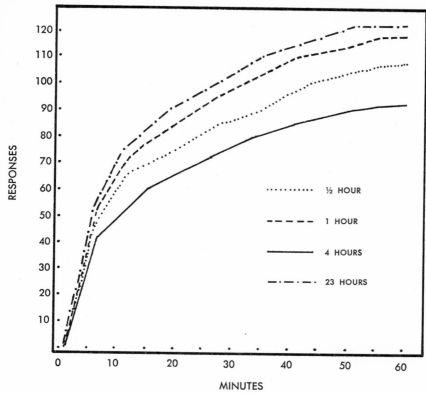

FIG. 9–6. AVERAGE EXTINCTION CURVES FOLLOWING TEN REINFORCEMENTS UNDER DIFFERENT DEGREES OF HUNGER. (Adapted from Strassburger, 1950)

using number of extinction responses in a Skinner box, have not confirmed Finan's findings. In the Strassburger study, three groups of rats learned a bar-pressing response. In experimental group A, animals were deprived of food for either 4, 11, 23, or 47 hours, with each group receiving 30 reinforcements. Experimental group B consisted of animals deprived for ½, 1, 4, and 23 hours and allowed to receive ten reinforcements. Experimental group C consisted of animals deprived for either 1, 11, 13, or 47 hours and provided only a single reinforcement. All animals in all groups were extinguished under 23 hours of deprivation. Although it was evident that resistance to extinction was a function of the number of reinforcements that the animals received, it was not related to the amount of deprivation during the original training situation. Figure 9.6 shows the extinction curves following ten reinforcements under the varying levels of food deprivation.

Factorial Studies Investigating Performance and Habit Strength

One frequent problem with an experimental design which uses an extinction measure has been the inability of the experimenter to control for stimulus-generalization effects incurred when changing from one deprivation state during the training period to another deprivation state during extinction. An investigator may be interested in examining the effect of the level of deprivation on habit, and to this end place his subjects under 2, 12, and 22 hours of food deprivation during the training period. Extinction is then carried out under 22 hours of deprivation. The difficulty in any interpretation of the findings which attempts to relate amount of deprivation to resistance to extinction, is that proper allowance is not made for the fact that the 2- and 12-hour deprivation groups, in contrast to the 22-hour group, are performing under different stimulus conditions during extinction. Or similarly, if the investigator is interested in examining the effect of level of deprivation on performance, and desires to keep habit strength constant, the subjects may be placed on 22 hours of deprivation and given n training trials. The response is extinguished with the animals under either 2, 12, or 22 hours of deprivation. Again no allowance is made for the fact that the 2- and 12-hour deprivation groups are responding under different conditions during extinction. Both Yamaguchi (1952) and Barry (1958) have shown that the changed stimulus condition under such circumstances does have an effect, in addition to any effect that the actual deprivation level may have.

A more appropriate experimental design is a factorial one in which the deprivation level is manipulated during acquisition as well as during extinction. Such a design enables one to examine the effect of deprivation level on both habit strength and performance simultaneously.[4]

[4] Although factorial designs represent a superior type of design for evaluating the influence of need level of habit strength and performance, attention should be called to one additional problem. This is known as drive-reversal effect. Deese and Carpenter (1951) divided 30 rats into two groups, with one group being placed under zero hours of deprivation, and the other group under 24 hours of deprivation. The latency of their running response in a straightaway was measured. Subjects which were trained under zero deprivation showed little change in latency during a 24-trial session; subjects under 24 hours of deprivation, how-

In the following table, the acquisition series is conducted with the subjects either under 12 or 60 hours of deprivation. Each group is then divided into subgroups, and extinction is carried on under 12 or 60 hours of deprivation.

TABLE 1

Hours of Deprivation / Hours of Deprivation	ACQUISITION	
	12	60
EXTINCTION		
12	a	b
60	c	d

Examination of the differences between the 12- vs. 60-hour acquisition group, extinguished under (1) 12 hours (a vs. b) and (2) 60 hours (c vs. d) provides information concerning the effect of the level of deprivation on the acquisition of a habit. Examination of the 12- vs. 60-hour extinction group trained under (1) 12 hours (a vs. c) and (2) 60 hours (b vs. d) provides information concerning the effect of hours of deprivation on performance level.

The reasonably stable conclusions concerning the intensity of the motivational antecedent as measured by deprivation level, and its relation to habit and performance obtained in nonfactorial designed studies have, however, given way to equivocality when the findings of factorial studies are considered. Teel (1952), using a probability of response measure, and Campbell and Kraeling (1954), using rate of response, have reported findings which indicate that deprivation level affects neither habit strength nor performance. Teel, one of the first to use a factorial design, placed rats on 1, 7, 15, or 22 hours of food deprivation and gave them 56 training trials on a T maze. Each group was then subdivided into four groups and placed on 1, 7, 15, or 22 hours and given extinction trials. The extinction criterion was defined as two or more *incorrect* trials on any daily series of four. Teel's findings indicated

---

ever, indicated great initial improvement, which leveled off after ten trials. The deprivation conditions were then reversed, the zero deprivation group being placed under 24 hours of deprivation and the 24-hour group being placed under zero hours. Training trials were then continued. The 0–24 group immediately reached the previous level of the high drive group. The 24–0 group continued at about the same level of performance even though satiated. Similar findings are reported in a study by Davis (1957), who found a tendency for animals shifting from a high to a low deprivation state to continue performing at the level which was attained prior to the shift. Animals shifting from the low to the high deprivation state, on the other hand, indicated marked improvement in their performance.

that neither the level of deprivation during acquisition nor during extinction had any effect on the animal's resistance to extinction. Both habit and performance were unaffected by the strength of the deprivation period.

Campbell and Kraeling have obtained somewhat similar findings with a rate-of-response measure obtained during extinction.

In contrast to these findings, Hillman, Hunter and Kimble (1953) found some support for the intensity of motivation affecting performance, but not habit. One group of rats was placed under 22 hours of deprivation, while a second group was placed under just 2 hours. Both groups received ten trials on a ten-unit T maze. After trial 10, each group was subdivided into 2 and 22 hours of deprivation and given five additional trials. Results indicated that the deprivation level during trials 1 through 10 had no effect on the animal's time and error scores for trials 11 through 15. Thus, deprivation level had no effect on habit. On the other hand, differing levels of deprivation during trials 11 through 15 did significantly affect performance as reflected by the time required to traverse the maze. Error scores, however, remained unaffected.

Finally, a recent study by Lewis and Cotton (1957), and confirmed by Barry (1958), has indicated that the level of motivation not only affects performance, but also has some effect on habit as well. In the Lewis and Cotton (1957) study, animals were placed on 1, 6, or 22 hours of food deprivation, and then given 30 training trials along a runway. Each acquisition group was then divided into thirds, with each third extinguished under either 1, 6, or 22 hours of food deprivation. Results indicated that speed of running during acquisition was related to hours of deprivation, the 22-hour group being the most rapid, and the 1-hour group the slowest. Holding hours of deprivation constant during acquisition but varying them during extinction indicated that the group deprived for just one hour during extinction had the slowest running times, but there was no difference in running time between the 6- and the 22-hour group. Thus, this measure of performance supported a motivational effect upon performance only in part. Finally, varying the hours of deprivation during acquisition but holding them constant during extinction produced some effect upon early extinction trials, but not upon later trials. Habit appeared to be related to motivational level only when early extinction trials were considered.

Let us attempt to summarize the experimental data which we have just reviewed. First, our firmest conclusion appears to be that an increase in the intensity of a motivational antecedent operates to increase an organism's rate of responding when it is acquiring a response, or during the extinction of that response.[5]

There is some question, however, that the probability of a response is similarly influenced. No simple reconciliation of the findings in this area, at least at this time, seems possible. The question of whether habit strength is influenced by the intensity of a motivational antecedent must be answered largely in the negative. If effects are found, they appear to be related only to the rate of response, and are of a transient nature.

These findings obtained from instrumental learning situations are in contrast to the results obtained by Spence (1953), who, using a classical conditioning situation, found that both habit *and* performance were influenced by the intensity of a UCS. This factorial-type designed study employing the conditioned eyeblink response was conducted over two sessions.[6] In the first session, the subjects were divided into two groups. One group was given 30

[5] The interpretation of these findings from a Hullian point of view would be that the increased drive results in an increased energizing function which, in turn, raises the performance level of the organism. Other interpretations, however, have been offered. Estes' (1950) position, which we described earlier, would be that high deprivation states, in contrast to low, provide a greater weight for drive stimuli. Under the circumstances, the conditioning of drive stimuli will proceed most rapidly with high deprivation states. Performance during extinction trials is related to the change in drive stimulus conditions taking place as the organism goes from one drive state during acquisition to another during extinction. Since the organism is usually trained on 22 to 24 hours of deprivation, and this most frequently represents the highest deprivation condition used in the extinction trials, groups trained and extinguished under these conditions would be expected to show greater resistance to extinction than groups trained under 22 to 24 hours of deprivation but extinguished at a deprivation level less than this.

Birch, Burnstein, and Clark (1958) have also proposed that drive stimuli make a contribution to these findings, but in a somewhat different manner than that proposed by Estes. Their point of view is that an important consideration in the general drive concept is the strength of anticipatory goal reactions, which in turn are controlled by sources of external as well as internal stimulation. One implication which follows is that performance is not a monotonically increasing function of hours of deprivation, but that the function rises to a maximum at or beyond the time of deprivation employed in the maintenance schedule and then decreases with increased deprivation. This would follow inasmuch as the fractional anticipatory goal reactions are most strongly conditioned to drive stimuli occurring just prior to feeding time as determined by the maintenance schedule. In a test of this position, rats were kept on 22 hours of food deprivation for five weeks. They were then divided into four subgroups and placed on 15, 22, 25, or 37 hours of deprivation. Results indicated that maximum running speed occurred with the 22- and 25-hour groups with the 37-hour group (as well as the 15) resulting in relatively slow running times.

[6] It is to be noted that an extinction procedure (omission of the UCS) cannot be used since this technique would not provide the necessary differential drive conditions which must be employed in the factorial type study.

conditioning trials with a weak UCS (air puff of .25 pounds per square inch) while the second group was given a similar number of trials with a strong UCS (air puff of 5 pounds per square inch). During Session II, each group was divided into half, with half of the subjects continuing to be given the same UCS while the other half was switched to the other intensity. The frequency of the conditioned responses for the first 20 trials of Session II is revealed in Table 2.

TABLE 2   MEAN NUMBER OF CONDITIONED RESPONSES
ON THE FIRST 20 TRIALS OF SESSION II

UCS (lbs./sq. in.)	SESSION I	
UCS (lbs./sq. in.)	.25	5.00
SESSION II		
.25	5.65 (a)	7.45 (b)
5.00	8.80 (c)	13.00 (d)

Significant differences in response strength during Session II were obtained as a function of: (1) the intensity of the UCS employed in the first session (a vs. b, and c vs. d), and which presumably reflected the operation of an associative or habit factor, and (2) the intensity of the UCS employed in the second session (a vs. c, and b vs. d), which reflected the operation of the motivational antecedent.

THE ROLE OF IRRELEVANT MOTIVATIONAL ANTECEDENTS

The interest in this area has stemmed largely from Hull (1943), who, in his *Principles of Behavior,* hypothesized that the additional, although irrelevant needs present, combine with those which are relevant to increase the organism's motivational level, and thus facilitate performance. The distinction between a relevant and an irrelevant need was related to the nature of the reward obtained by the organism in the experimental situation. If a rat, both hungry and thirsty, learned to run right in a T maze in order to secure food, the need for food would be classed as relevant while the need for water would be considered irrelevant.

Kendler (1945), in one of his early studies, compared the learning of one group of rats, motivated by 22 hours of food deprivation, with a second group which was motivated by 22 hours of food *and* water deprivation. Since the animals were reinforced only with food, the 22 hours of water deprivation was an irrelevant need.

Kendler's findings, which did not support Hull, indicated that the addition of the irrelevant need retarded the learning of a spatial-discrimination habit in a T maze.

As we shall note in greater detail, there is some difficulty in employing either food or water deprivation as an irrelevant need when the other is used as the relevant one. As a result, a number of investigators have used other combinations of needs. Amsel (1950) found that the addition of an irrelevant need for food did not have any effect on a rat's response which was motivated by either weak or strong shock. When the shock was eliminated, and the response was motivated by fear, the presence of the irrelevant need for food was found to result in decreased running time. Amsel believed that the strength of the shock was so great (in spite of the fact that weak shock was used as well as strong) that the addition of a need for food could not make a sufficiently large contribution to the organism's drive level to have any effect, hence the nonsignificant findings with shock. A later study by Braun, Wedekind, and Smudski (1957) investigated the learning of the rat in a modified Lashley maze as a function of the combination of a relevant need to escape from water, and an irrelevant need for food. Two levels of the relevant need were produced by using water temperatures of either 15° C. or 35° C. The irrelevant need for food was induced by 0 and 22 hours of deprivation. Results indicated that the addition of 22 hours of food deprivation resulted in significant decreases in swimming time and number of errors.

Finally, in a somewhat similar study, Levine, Staats, and Frommer (1959) combined a relevant need to escape from water with shock, which produced emotionality and was hypothesized to be an irrelevant motivational antecedent. Rats were trained to swim a single-choice water maze. Half of the animals were given a shock just prior to the first trial of each day. Each animal was given five trials per day. Although there was no difference between groups in number of errors, the swimming time for the shocked group was significantly more rapid than for the nonshocked group.

The evidence, although certainly not conclusive, would indicate that an irrelevant motivational antecedent may operate to aid in the acquisition of an instrumental response, certainly when such acquisition is measured by a rate-of-response measure.[7]

[7] Dinsmoor's (1958) study is one of the few in this general area to report negative findings. Dinsmoor trained rats to depress and release a bar in order to es-

A number of studies have examined the contribution of irrelevant motivational antecedents upon the extinction of a response.

Webb (1949) placed rats under 22 hours of food deprivation and trained them to open a door in order to secure food. After four days of training, the animals were satiated with food, but deprived of water for either 0, 3, 12, or 22 hours, and extinction trials were provided. Webb's findings indicated increasing resistance to extinction with increases in the irrelevant need. Figure 9.7 indicates this relationship. Webb's findings have been confirmed by Brandauer (1953).

On the other hand, Siegel (1946a), manipulating the action of an irrelevant need in a little different fashion, has not confirmed the findings of these investigators. Siegel placed animals under 22 hours of food deprivation and gave them either 5 or 40 reinforcements in a Skinner box. The extinction situation consisted of continuing the animals under 22 hours of food deprivation, but half of each experimental group was also placed under 22 hours of water deprivation. Siegel's results indicated that resistance to extinction was greater for the 22-hour food-deprived group than for the 22-hour food- and water-deprived groups.

The divergence of experimental findings in this area leads one to look for confounding variables, and a major one relates to the interaction existing between food and water deprivation. A number of investigators have demonstrated that for a variety of organisms, there is a decrease in food intake when access to water is prevented; similarly, a decrease in water intake takes place with food deprivation. Verplanck and Hayes (1953), for example, have found that rats which were deprived of water would eat only about 60 per cent as much food as rats not so deprived. If they were permitted to drink, they would then eat almost as much as they previously had during the deprivation period. When the animals were placed under food deprivation, water intake decreased in a similar fashion. This indicates that animals placed under food deprivation but presumably satiated with water nonetheless continue to have some need for water. In the Webb (1949) and Brandauer (1953) studies, although the animals were presumably satiated

---

cape shock. He has reported that the addition of 23 hours of food deprivation had little effect in facilitating such training. One possible explanation is that if the shock used was of such an intensity to produce an optimum level of performance, it is difficult to see how the addition of a need for food could result in any increase in response strength.

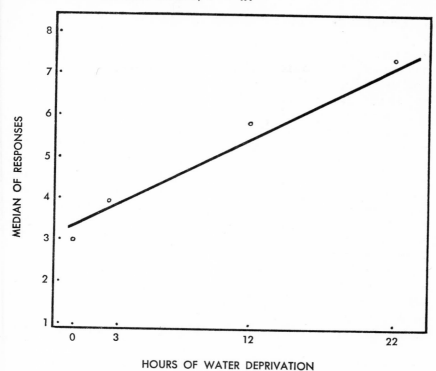

FIG. 9–7. A PLOT OF THE NUMBER OF RESPONSES MADE BY FOUR GROUPS WHICH WERE EXTINGUISHED UNDER VARYING DEGREES OF WATER DEPRIVATION. (Adapted from Webb, 1949)

with food during the extinction trials, the presence of a need for water made such satiation impossible. Webb's extinction data may be interpreted to indicate that such a need for food increased as the organism's need for water increased.

Support for this point of view is found in a study by Grice and Davis (1957). These investigators provided four groups of animals, all under approximately 23½ hours of food deprivation, with 45 reinforced trials in pushing a panel to obtain a food pellet. Thirty extinction trials were then given. One group was tested under the same food-deprivation conditions which prevailed during training, while a second group was completely satiated for both food and water prior to the extinction trials. A third group was satiated with food but the water bottle was removed 22 hours before the extinction trials. A fourth group was given treatment identical to that provided for the third group except that the animals were permitted to drink for 30 minutes just prior to being given extinction trials. The results indicated that the hungry group (group 1) showed the greatest resistance to extinction, followed by the thirsty–permitted-to-drink group (group 4). The satiated and thirsty groups followed in the number of extinction responses, with no significant differences between them. It is revealing that the satiation of the need for water in the thirsty-drink group did not lower their resistance to extinction, but actually increased it as indicated by this group's significant superiority over the thirsty group. The lack of a significant difference between the satiated and thirsty groups failed to confirm the findings of Webb (1949) and Brandauer (1953), and supported the premise that the operation of the irrelevant need was merely a reflection of the previously relevant need state.

The inappropriateness of using food and water to examine the operation of irrelevant needs has resulted in a number of investigators using other combinations of need states. Ellis (1957) first trained rats to run a 17½-foot alley under 23 hours of food deprivation. Following such training, each animal was assigned to one of nine treatment groups given varying combinations of 0, 12, and 23 hours of food deprivation operating as the relevant need, combined with zero, weak, and strong electric shock. The shock, which was administered just prior to the animal's being given a single extinction trial, resulted in emotionality and was viewed as the irrelevant need. Latencies and running times on the single extinction trial revealed that the varying levels of food deprivation (relevant need) produced differences among the groups, but the addition of shock did not.

Miles (1958a) has reported similar nonsignificant findings. Rats were first trained to press a bar in order to receive food. Following such training, the animals were satiated, injected with cocaine, and returned to the box, in which the floor had been made cold. Miles reasoned that these latter two conditions should increase the activity level of the animals, which, in turn, should energize the bar-pressing response. Results indicated that the number of bar pressing responses for the experimental animals was not significantly greater than the number obtained with control subjects. Miles concluded that irrelevant activation cannot facilitate a learned habit. Unfortunately, there were no reported data confirming the hypothesized increased activity level of Miles' experimental animals.

In contrast to the negative findings of Miles (1958a) and Ellis (1957), Webb and Goodman (1958) have reported positive findings. Hungry rats were trained to push one of two bars in order to obtain food. Following a number of training trials, they were satiated and returned to the box for a five-minute test session in which the number of times they pushed the correct bar was recorded. Following this, the apparatus was flooded with half an inch of water and a second five-minute test session was recorded. The animals' performance under conditions of satiation without flooding acted as a control for their bar-pressing performance with flooding. Results indicated that the irrelevant need to escape water, significantly increased the number of correct bar-pressing responses.

The controversial findings make it difficult to reach some stable conclusions concerning the role of irrelevant needs on the extinction of simple, learned responses. Spence (1956) and Webb and Goodman (1958), however, have called attention to one problem which investigators must consider before definite conclusions can be drawn. It is possible that, as a result of previous learning, irrelevant needs may have become attached to responses which are incompatible with the response that the investigator is measuring. The use of noxious stimulation, such as shock, may elicit response patterns of freezing, startle, etc., which are in conflict with the criterion response. To the extent that they are, irrelevant needs should not produce an increment but rather a decrement in response strength.

Irrelevant Motivational Antecedents and Task Difficulty

In analyzing the relationship between the intensity or strength of a motivational antecedent and performance, Spence has hypothesized that in situations in which there is but a single response tendency, or where correct response tendencies predominate over incorrect ones (presumably an easy task), an increase in drive strength may result in facilitation of performance;[8] on the other hand, if the

[8] Spence has also indicated that an increase in drive may increase the number of erroneous responses (and presumably impair performance). In such a case, the raising of the drive level increases the number of responses with superthreshold excitatory tendencies which increase the number of possible competing erroneous responses. Although the new superthreshold responses are weaker in habit strength than the correct responses, the operation of an oscillation factor may lead to their

habit strength of the correct response is considerably weaker than that of the competing responses (presumably a difficult task), an increase in drive will result in a decrement in performance.[9] This latter position follows from the basic Hullian assumption that drive will multiply the strengths of all response tendencies, both correct as well as incorrect. This increases the amount by which the excitatory strength of the incorrect response exceeds that of the correct response.

In summary, increases in the intensity of a motivational antecedent should generally result in easy tasks being more rapidly learned; on the other hand, motivational antecedents of low intensity should produce the most rapid learning of difficult tasks.

A large number of studies, many of which have come from the Iowa Laboratory, have been conducted within this theoretical framework. An important aspect of many of these studies has been that motivational strength has been controlled by using subjects who differ with regard to the amount of their emotional responsiveness, or manifest anxiety. This motivational antecedent is regarded as an irrelevant drive but one which, of course, contributes to the organism's generalized drive level, or total motivational strength. The measurement of manifest anxiety has been inferred from a subject's responses as expressed on a manifest anxiety scale (MAS). The scale was devised by first obtaining 200 items from the Minnesota Multiphasic Personality Inventory and submitting them to clinical staff members with instructions to designate those items that they judged to indicate manifest anxiety. The 65 items on which there was 80 per cent agreement or higher were selected for the final anxiety scale. As Taylor (1956) has indicated, the Iowa group has been interested in investigating anxiety not as a phenomenon, but only as a means by which the intensity of an individual's irrelevant motivation can be measured.

In the original study in this area by Taylor (1951), two groups

---

being stronger on some occasions. Thus, "even in instances in which the habit strength of the correct response is stronger than any of the alternative super-threshold responses, the effect of increasing the drive, and hence the number of superthreshold responses would be to increase the number of errors." (Taylor and Spence, 1952).

[9] Saltz and Hoehn (1957) have stated that the assumption of equating task difficulty with amount of competition between responses is a tenuous one. They have found it possible to construct lists of words which are equal in difficulty but unequal in the amount of competition among responses. Their findings indicated that anxious subjects perform no worse on competing than on noncompeting material.

of subjects, differing with respect to manifest anxiety level, were run in a conditioned eyelid experiment. Results indicated that the high-anxious group was consistently and significantly superior in the frequency of conditioned responses provided throughout the learning period, thus confirming Spence's prediction that high-motivation groups should have superior performance when an easy task is employed. Extinction measures, although indicating superior resistance to extinction for the anxious group, were not statistically significant. Subsequent studies coming from the Iowa laboratory, utilizing the same classical conditioning situation, have not only confirmed Taylor's findings but have extended them to the differential conditioning situation as well (Spence and Farber, 1953; Spence and Beecroft, 1954; Spence and Farber, 1954).

More recently, emotional responsiveness has been measured by pulse rate, skin conductance, and muscle action potential (MAP). Runquist and Ross (1959) selected subjects on the basis of either large pulse rate increases or skin conductance increases in response to an air puff to the eye. When the performance of these emotional subjects in an eyelid-conditioning task was compared with that of a nonemotional group, the results indicated that the emotional group was significantly superior. Runquist and Spence (1959) obtained similar findings when muscle action potential was used to measure emotional responsiveness. Four groups of subjects, selected on the basis of the magnitude of their MAP response to an air puff, were given conditioning trials. The mean number of conditioned eyelid responses for each group was found to be an increasing function of the MAP response, the rank order correlation being .52.

Hilgard, Jones, and Kaplan (1951), Prokasy and Truax (1959), and Caldwell and Cromwell (1959), all using an anxiety scale to measure emotional responsiveness, have not been able to completely confirm the findings of the Iowa investigators.[10]

[10] In studies coming from the Iowa laboratory, subjects in conditioned-eyeblink studies are given a "ready, blink" signal 2–4 seconds prior to the time the CS is presented. Prokasy and Truax (1959), not employing such a signal, have suggested that the high-anxiety groups (as defined by the Taylor scale) are more reactive to an instrumental signal, and that this manifests itself in superior conditioning scores. Caldwell and Cromwell (1959), on the other hand, have suggested that the use of a warning signal may have provided the subjects with an excellent cue regarding the onset of the CS, and thus increased the likelihood of the subjects' voluntarily responding to the CS. Protocols obtained from some of their subjects supported such an interpretation. Not all findings in this area, however, can be so accounted for. Welch and Kubis (1947, 1747a) and Bitterman

It will be recalled that the second part of Spence's formulation was one in which the role of drive was investigated in complex or difficult learning tasks. According to Spence, a low drive, in contrast to a high one, should result in the more rapid learning of a difficult task. In one of the early studies, Taylor and Spence (1952) ran high- and low-anxious groups in a serial learning situation. This situation involved the presentation of a series of 20 choices between two verbal responses. At each choice point, the subject was required to say either "right" or "left." Results were in agreement with the theoretical expectation that the highly anxious subjects would make a significantly greater number of errors, and would require a larger number of trials to reach the learning criterion. These general findings were confirmed in a stylus maze learning situation by Farber and Spence (1953), who found that the performance of anxious subjects was significantly poorer than that of the nonanxious groups. Maltzman, Fox, and Morrisett (1953), in a study involving problem-solving situations and establishment of mental sets upon their successful solution, have also reported findings in agreement with Spence's theoretical formulation.

Hughes, Sprague, and Bendig (1954), however, have been unable to replicate the Taylor and Spence findings (1952), while Axelrod, Cowen, and Heilizer (1956) were not able to obtain the stylus maze learning results obtained by Farber and Spence (1953).

The studies by Castaneda and Palermo are noteworthy in that these investigators (1) attempted to *manipulate* emotional responsiveness and (2) used a task which contained both difficult and easy components. In the first study (Castaneda and Palermo, 1955), the emotional responsiveness of elementary students was elevated by using instructions emphasizing the need for speed on a perceptual motor task. These instructions were interpreted by the authors as inducing stress. Either weak or strong training was provided on the task which consisted of the subject's responding to colored lights by pushing appropriate buttons. Following such training, the groups were given relearning trials in which some of the light-button relationships continued to be the same as before (simple task), while other light-button relationships were changed (difficult task). Half of both weak and strong training

---

and Holtzman (1952) have demonstrated that the galvanic skin response is conditioned more rapidly in anxious subjects than in nonanxious subjects. Moreover, the selection of anxious subjects in both studies was not determined by the Taylor scale.

groups were given the stress instructions, while the other halves were given normal instructions and remained as controls. Results indicated that stress operated to increase the number of errors made on the difficult part of the task, with this increase being more pronounced with increased training. On the other hand, there was a tendency for the stress group to show better performance on the simple phase of the task. Later studies by Castaneda (1956) and Palermo (1957), in which stressful instructions were also used, have confirmed these earlier findings.

Although differing emotional response levels have been most frequently used to infer motivational strength, investigators have used other types of motivational antecedents to explore this general area.[11]

Franks (1957) found that increasing the motivation of undergraduates by depriving them of food, drink, and tobacco for a day did not result in their acquiring a conditioned eyeblink (simple task) any more rapidly than subjects who were permitted to eat, drink and smoke in the usual manner.

In an interesting counterpart to the human studies, Buchwald and Yamaguchi (1955) trained two groups of rats to learn a position habit on a T maze to a criterion of ten out of twelve correct responses. One group ran under 20 hours of water deprivation, the other group under 1½ hours. They were then trained to reverse the direction of their response. At the start of the reversal learning, however, each group was divided into half, with one group continuing on the previous level of deprivation, while the other group was changed to the opposite level. A comparison of high vs. low levels of motivation, regardless of whether the original learning took place under high or low levels of motivation, indicated that the high-level groups learned the reversal significantly faster

---

[11] It seems appropriate to point out that a number of early investigators, although not working within the Hull-Spence theoretical framework, have used induced muscle tension as a type of irrelevant motivational antecedent. Some investigators (i.e., Bills 1927) have found that induced tension facilitated learning, while others (i.e., Russell 1932) have reported that induced tension produced detrimental effects. In attempting to account for both facilitating and inhibiting effects of tension, Stauffacher (1937) proposed that for any given activity, there is an amount of tension which provides optimum efficiency. Freeman (1938) and Courts (1942, 1942a), on the other hand, have proposed that the influence of induced tension will vary with the complexity or difficulty of the task, with tension facilitating performance on easy tasks more readily than difficult ones. More recently, Meyer (1953), with his efferent neural interaction theory, has attempted to integrate much of the early experimental work as well as relate his theory to some of the more recent irrelevant-drive literature.

than the low-level ones. From the original theoretical point of view, incorrect-response tendencies should have been quite strong, and a high level of motivation, in contrast to low, should have resulted in the reversal response's being learned more slowly.

Armus (1958), in a similarly designed study, was also unable to obtain findings which supported Spence, but then neither did his results confirm the findings of Buchwald and Yamaguchi (1955). Armus found that the amount of food deprivation (21½ vs. 3½ hours) was not related to the number of correct responses found in either the original or the reversal learning situation.

Child (1954), in reviewing many of these studies, has suggested an interpretation which differs from that proposed by Spence. Child states:

. . . that in simple conditioning, where a stable relationship is established between a single stimulus and a single response, what internal responses the subject is making at the time do not have any great effect, whereas the presence of high drive level does make for heightened performance; but that in complex situations, where the subject is already in conflict between various response tendencies relevant to the task, the presence of irrelevant responses made to anxiety heightens the conflict and interferes with performance to a greater extent than the increased drive improves it.[12]

A second point which Child (1954) has made is that the Iowa studies have paid no attention to possible differences among subjects in their previously learned response tendencies to the cues provided by anxiety. In this regard, the studies of Mandler and Sarason (1952) and Sarason, Mandler, and Craighill (1952) are relevant. In the Mandler and Sarason (1952) study, two groups of subjects were selected on the basis of a questionnaire designed to measure anxiety in the situation of being tested. Each group was then divided into three subgroups in which either success, failure, or neutral instructions were given to them following their performance on one form of the Kohs Block Design test. A second form of the test was then administered. Results of this second test indicated that the effect of failure produced a decrement in performance in the high-anxiety test group, but produced an increment in performance for the low-anxiety group. The interpre-

[12] Spence (1958) has acknowledged the role of competing responses in this area by stating: "We think of these interfering responses as being elicited by drive stimuli (S_D), and hence they would be incorporated in a more complete motivational theory of learned behavior."

tation of these findings which Mandler and Sarason have proposed is that the high-anxious subjects had a strong previously acquired tendency to respond to anxiety with responses which were not relevant to the task; the reference to failure by the examiner in the test situation served to elicit such responses more strongly than before, and thus interfered with adequate performance. The low-anxiety group, on the other hand, had little tendency to make task-irrelevant responses; when some degree of anxiety was evoked by the mention of failure, it was assumed that anxiety contributed to the total drive strength and motivated task-irrelevant responses which resulted in improved performance.

Spence (1958), in a more recent position, has elaborated upon the relationship existing between the level of drive and complex learning tasks. Spence has pointed out that in complex tasks, although a high-level drive should result in poor performance during the early stages of learning, as training proceeds, habit strength of the correct reinforced response should eventually overtake that of the wrong nonreinforced response. From this point on, the high drive group should be superior to the low-drive group. Thus, the performance curves of the two groups should be expected to cross. He has further indicated that serial learning tasks, for a variety of reasons, are unsatisfactory, and that the type of situation most appropriate to investigate this phenomenon is paired-associate learning. This type of learning task has been conceived of as consisting of the formation of a set of more or less isolated stimulus-response associations or habit tendencies. With such a task, it is possible to manipulate the stimulus-response units so that competition among such units can either be minimized or maximized, depending upon the nature of the investigation. When there is little competition among units, one would expect subjects under high drive to perform at higher levels than subjects under low drive, while greater competition among units should produce the reverse early in the learning trials.

In one of the early studies utilizing this type of learning situation, Taylor and Chapman (1955) made up two lists of paired nonsense syllables in which formal intralist similarity was low. A comparison of anxious and nonanxious groups indicated the anxious group to be superior both in terms of errors and trials to criterion. Using paired adjectives, again in which there was a minimum of competition among the paired words, and in which the associative connection between words was initially high, Spence,

Farber, and McFann (1956) reported findings (Experiment 1) which supported the Taylor and Chapman (1955) study.

Rather than use lists composed entirely of paired associates which provide either a maximum or minimum of competition among responses, a common technique has been to employ both types of material in the same list, thus making it possible to test both aspects of Spence's position with the same experiment.

Ramond (1953), employing this type of design, used paired associates in which half of the pairs found in the list were easy for the subject to learn, while the remaining pairs were quite difficult. Results indicated that nonanxious subjects learned the difficult part of the list significantly more rapidly than the high-anxious group. There were, however, no significant differences between groups in learning the easy material.[13]

Subsequent studies by Spence, Farber, and McFann (1956) and Spence, Taylor, and Ketchel (1956) have added to the weight of evidence supporting the Spence position. In both studies, results indicated that highly anxious groups were superior to the low when easy-paired associates were used. Although the difference was not significant, the difference was in the direction predicted by the theory.

STIMULI ARISING FROM MOTIVATIONAL ANTECEDENTS AS CUES FOR BEHAVIOR

Inasmuch as many motivational antecedents are accompanied by physiological states, it is reasonable to expect that such states may provide cues which the organism can use to which to attach appropriate responses. With Hullian behavior theory, this point is recognized by noting that drives have a stimulus or cue function (S_D) as well as an energizing function. The importance of stimuli arising from drive states has also been evident in the theorizing of Estes (1950) as well as others.

Almost all of the work investigating the role of drive stimuli in learning has been limited to the rat as the experimental subject,

[13] Chiles (1958) has recently replicated Ramond's experiment, except that motivational level was manipulated by using shock or nonshock condition rather than manifest anxiety score. His findings were more in keeping with the theoretical position of Spence in that the shock group performed significantly better on the easy part of the task, and after an initial inferiority, also performed better on the difficult part.

and to need or deprivation states as the appropriate motivational antecedents.

One of the earliest studies in this area was performed by Hull (1933), who used a modified T maze, with one alley leading to food and one to water. On certain days (randomly determined), the animals were made thirsty, while on other days they were made hungry. The object was to determine whether the subjects could learn to turn left when hungry and right when thirsty. Although learning was slow, the animals reached an acceptable level of accuracy in selecting the correct alley on the first trial of each day. A later study by Leeper (1935) confirmed Hull's findings. Wickens, Hall, and Reid (1949) have extended these findings by showing that proactive and retroactive inhibition effects can be obtained by manipulating food and water deprivation states in a manner analogous to the way in which external stimuli have been manipulated.[14]

Since the rat is able to distinguish between these different needs, the next logical step was to determine whether or not it could differentiate between two levels of the same need. That is, could the animal learn to turn left under one level of food deprivation and right under another level? Jenkins and Hanratty (1949) found that rats could discriminate between 11½ hours and 47½ hours of food deprivation; Bloomberg and Webb (1949) reported that 10 out of 12 animals used in their experiment were capable of discriminating between 3 and 22 hours of food deprivation. There would appear to be no doubt that discrimination can be obtained when the relevant cues are either the kind or intensity of the organism's need.

The mechanism underlying such discrimination, however, has been in dispute. Heron (1949) has questioned whether the Hull and Leeper animals were discriminating on the basis of the stimuli arising from the organic conditions of hunger and thirst, or whether food deprivation resulted in an empty stomach, and water deprivation resulted in a full one. On the basis of his own experimental work, Heron (1949) has hypothesized that the empty vs. full stomach cues were the relevant ones. Although most studies have not controlled for this possibility, Bailey and Porter (1955)

[14] Although Bolles (1958) has confirmed these results, he has accounted for them in terms of specific behavior patterns that hunger and thirst produce, rather than in terms of similarity or differences of the manipulated stimuli.

have done so, and their findings have not supported Heron's hypothesis.

In accounting for the ability of an animal to discriminate between hunger and thirst, Hull (1943) made the assumption that the stimulation arising from the need state was incorporated into the total stimulus pattern. Thus, differing needs produced different stimulus complexes, and to these different patterns of stimulation were attached appropriate responses. It appeared to Hull that the relationship between the stimulus arising from the need and the reinforcing state of affairs was *not* important in determining whether or not such stimuli acquired associative strength.

In an experimental test of this hypothesis, Kendler (1946) placed rats on food *and* water deprivation and then gave them a series of training trials on a T maze in which water was found on one arm and food on the other. The animals were then placed under *either* food or water deprivation, and, with the goal objects remaining in the same place, were given one test trial a day for four days. Results indicated that the animals chose the correct side (the side containing the goal object consistent with their need) 85 per cent of the time.

Hull's explanation could not account for Kendler's findings since the stimuli arising from both need states during training should have become associated with the right- as well as the left-turning response. Since both food and water needs were present during training, the Hullian explanation would predict chance behavior during the test trials—a finding which obviously did not take place. Kendler (1946) proposed two possible explanations for his findings. One is what he has termed the selective association hypothesis. This hypothesis simply stated that only those stimuli arising from need states which are themselves reduced become connected to a rewarded response. In the experiment just cited, when the animal which was both hungry and thirsty turned right to obtain food, only stimuli arising from the need state of hunger would become connected to the right-turning response.

Kendler's second explanation involved the role of fractional anticipatory goal responses. According to this interpretation, the stimuli in the food box and in the alley leading to the food box became associated with fractional anticipatory eating responses (salivation, etc.). In turn, the proprioceptive stimulus components resulting from these anticipatory goal responses became themselves conditioned to the response of entering and continuing to run down the alley to the food box. In a similar manner, the anticipatory drinking responses which were conditioned to the alley leading to water provided cues which tended to elicit the responses of approaching and continuing locomotion in that alley. Thus, when a test trial was presented with only a single need present, i.e., food, the fractional anticipatory goal responses related to that need were elicited. These goal responses provided the cues which were conditioned to evoking the responses of approaching and entering the food alley.

It was the selective association hypothesis, however, which Kendler first tended to favor, and two studies (Kendler 1949, and Kendler and Law 1950) were subsequently run which provided support for this interpretation. Amsel (1949), Levine (1953), and Sterling and Cooper (1957), in contrast, have reported experimental findings which have cast considerable doubt upon the validity of this hypothesis. Both Amsel (1949) and Levine (1953) have reported that the learning of a discrimination problem could take place on the basis of the animal's making a discrimination between two irrelevant needs. Levine (1953), for example, found that rats could learn to press a right panel if hungry and a left panel if thirsty, even though both responses resulted in the avoidance of a bright light—a reward obviously not related to the satisfaction of either the food or the water need.

The decline of the selective association hypothesis has been accompanied by an increase of interest in the fractional anticipatory goal response hypothesis. Although this interpretation had early support from Amsel (1949), Kendler and his associates (Kendler and Levine 1951; Kendler, Levine, Alchek, and Peters 1952; Kendler, Karasik, and Schrier 1954) have systematically explored its implications, particularly with reference to earlier experimental findings which had indicated that when hungry animals were trained to choose one side of a T maze leading to dry food, a shift to water deprivation resulted in the animals' switching their choice and running to the other side. From Kendler's point of view, such switching behavior was dependent upon fractional anticipatory goal responses. When an animal which had been trained to go right under food deprivation was made thirsty, the fractional anticipatory eating responses conflicted with the water deprivation condition. The conflict was reduced by the animal's turning away from the alley leading to food. This would follow inasmuch as cues in the incorrect path of the maze had not been directly conditioned to the anticipatory eating response, and, as a result, the greater the penetration into this path, the greater would be the relief from the conflict state which was postulated to exist.

As Kendler, Karasik, and Schrier (1954) have written, the implication of this point of view is that the tendency to switch is related to the strength of the anticipatory eating response at the choice point, the intensity of the need for water, and whether or not the switch is from food to water deprivation or vice versa. More specifically, the prediction would be that switching behavior would be less if: (1) the anticipatory eating response was a product of only a few training trials, (2) the thirst drive was weak, or (3) the switch was from water to food rather than food to water. These three hypotheses have been experimentally confirmed (Kendler and Levine 1951; Kendler, Levine, Alchek, and Peters 1952; Kendler, Karasik, and Schrier 1954); the net result being that an anticipatory goal response explanation appears to be assuming an important role in accounting for the Hull-Leeper type of experimental findings. One specific difficulty for such an explanation would appear to be in accounting for the ability of an animal to discriminate between two levels of the same need. In such a situation, it would have to be assumed that the fractional anticipatory goal response of eating (or drinking) under a low level of deprivation would be different than that found under a high level. Such an assumption appears to be, at least with respect to water deprivation, inconsistent with the findings of Stellar and Hill (1952), who have reported that regardless of the level of deprivation, the rat's rate of drinking remains constant. Perhaps more important, as Webb (1955) has pointed out, the fractional anticipatory response explanation changes the role of stimuli arising from the need state as an associative cue for learning and replaces it with other types of cues. More specifically, it assigns to the need the property of activating anticipatory responses which in turn become cues for learning, in contrast to the need stimuli themselves.

10 • INSTRUMENTAL RESPONSES, II

A second major motivational antecedent is the reward received by the organism in the instrumental response situation. In our last chapter, our primary task was to examine the relationship of motivational antecedents, primarily those of the physiological need variety, to instrumental behavior. The purpose of this chapter is to examine the role of rewards.

In our discussion of the nature of rewards (Chapter 5), we reviewed some of the experimental and theoretical evidence which was related to that which characterized a rewarding or reinforcing situation. It seems, at least at this time, that a reward cannot be defined by referring to any specific set of conditions or operations which are independent of the selective function of a motive. A reward must be defined as a stimulus which increases the probability of the reoccurrence of the response.

A number of individuals have pointed to the circularity of such a definition. Postman (1947) writes: "The satisfying or annoying nature of a state of affairs can usually be determined fully only in the course of a learning experiment and cannot then be invoked as a causal condition of learning without circularity." Meehl (1950), in commenting upon this same problem, has stated that such circularity may be circumvented by using one learning situation to define the nature of reward; subsequent learning tasks can be explained by reference to the reward variable. "But once having found that a certain state of affairs *is* reinforcing for a given species, there is no reason why a given case of learning cannot be explained by invoking the occurrence of this state of affairs as a causal condition."

In the Hullian system, three reward or reinforcement conditions have played an important role in influencing instrumental behavior. These have been: (1) the number of reinforcements, (2) the quantity and quality of the reinforcing agent, and, finally, (3) the delay of reinforcement. Most of the experimental studies examining the role of rewards have taken as their point of departure one or more of these conditions. Under the circumstances, these variables provide a framework around which we have organized much of the material in this chapter.

Number of Rewards

If we consider at the present time, the problem of a *continuously* rewarded series, a common finding has been that the acquisition and extinction of a response is related to the number of rewards given the organism. Such a generalization appears to hold regardless of whether the response measure is in terms of rate or probability.

Illustrative of this generalization is the study of Felsinger, Gladstone, Yamaguchi, and Hull (1947), who trained rats to make a simple bar-pressing response. The learning trials consisted of a single reinforced response each 24 hours throughout the entire training of each animal. Figure 10.1 indicates how latency decreased as a function of the number of reinforced trials.

Amount of Reward

If the number of rewards plays an important role in the acquisition of an instrumental response, it seems reasonable to assume that the amount or quantity of the reward would play a similar role. Before we proceed to an examination of the experimental evidence which can be related to this assumption, an important methodological problem of method merits consideration.

When the amount of reward is varied, conditions other than the actual amount may also vary, thus precluding any direct approach to investigating amount, per se. For example, if the

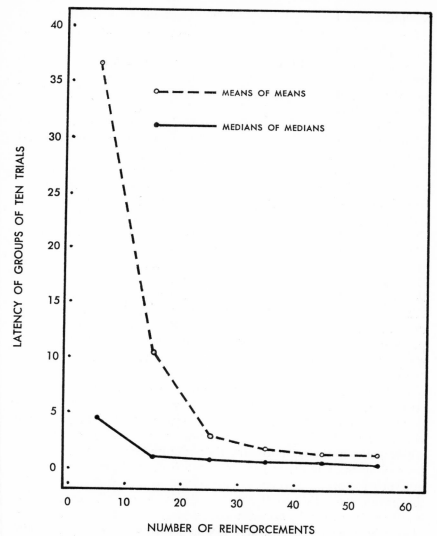

FIG. 10–1. PERFORMANCE AS A FUNCTION OF NUMBER OF REINFORCEMENTS. (Adapted from Felsinger, Gladstone, Yamaguchi, and Hull, 1947)

number of food pellets a rat receives is manipulated, there will be variation in the number of calories or amount of nutrition available to the organism, the amount of consummatory activity, and the amount of time spent in the goal box. The role of some of these variables has been indicated in the work of Wolfe and Kaplon (1941), Kling (1956), Spence (1956), Wike and Barrientos (1957), and Logan (1960).

Wolfe and Kaplon (1941) have reported increased running speeds with chickens when the same amount of food was presented in four small pieces as contrasted with one large piece. They have attributed this finding to the increased consummatory activity involved in the eating of the four pieces, although the amount of time spent in the goal box also varied. In a better controlled examination of the role of consummatory activity, Wike and Barrientos (1957) used 5 ml. of water as a reward for thirsty rats placed in a T maze. The water was contained in bottles having either a large- or small-diameter drinking tube. (Preliminary work indicated that it would take the animal almost twice as long to obtain the 5 ml. of water from the small-tube bottle than from the large). The bottle with the large-diameter tube was placed on one arm of the maze and the small-diameter tube placed on the other arm. Results indicated that the animals learned to go to the arm having the small-diameter tube. As a result, the authors have concluded that a long consummatory period was more reinforcing than a short one, although amount consumed remained constant. It must be pointed out again, however, that the amount of time that the animals spent in the goal box varied for the two groups.

In an examination of the time in goal box variable, Czeh (reported by Spence 1956) trained three groups of rats to run a straightaway. Two of the groups were rewarded with a large pellet of food while the third group was rewarded with a small pellet. One of the large-pellet groups was permitted to consume the whole pellet in the goal box, the time required being approximately four minutes. The other two groups were permitted to eat in the goal box for only 30 seconds. This period of time was sufficient for the group given the small pellet to finish eating. The 30-second–large pellet group, however, was removed from the goal box and placed in a feeding cage where it was permitted to finish eating its pellets. Results indicated that the animals' latency of response was a function of the time spent in the goal box, and not a function of the size of the pellet.

In most of the studies which we shall review in this section, investigators have paid little attention to the variables which we have just considered, and which covary with amount of reward. Rather, as Logan (1960) has done in his extensive examination of

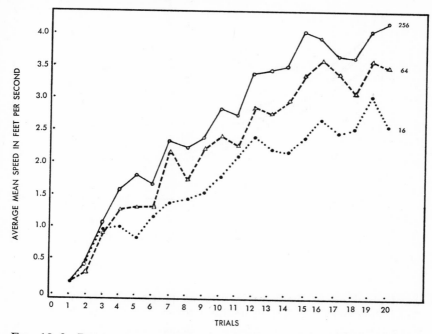

FIG. 10–2. RELATIONSHIP BETWEEN NUMBER OF REINFORCEMENTS AND LEVEL OF PERFORMANCE FOR DIFFERENT AMOUNTS OF INCENTIVE. (Adapted from Crespi, 1942)

the role of reinforcement in the rat, the focus has been on the relationship between performance and amount of reward as experimentally manipulated and not upon the possible mechanisms underlying the relationship.

What is the influence of the amount of reward upon the acquisition and extinction of a response when the response measure is that of rate? [1] Most studies have indicated that an organism's rate of responding during acquisition will reflect different amounts of re-

[1] When examining the influence of deprivation states upon instrumental behavior, a distinction between habit and performance has been frequently made. Most investigators examining the role of reward on instrumental behavior have not been concerned with this problem, and, hence, have ignored the distinction. In commenting upon this problem, Maher and Wickens (1954) state: "Examination solely of scores made during the learning trials does not allow one to determine whether obtained differences in quality of performance evidenced by two differentially rewarded groups of animals are a function of (a) greater acquisition of the habit by one group or (b) more efficient utilization of that habit."

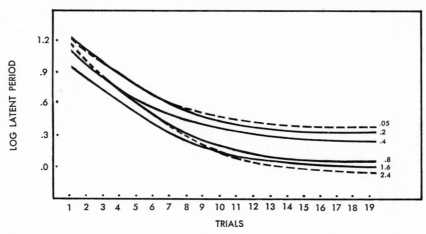

FIG. 10–3. PERFORMANCE AS A FUNCTION OF AMOUNT OF REINFORCEMENT. (Adapted from Zeaman, 1949)

ward obtained in the experimental situation. The early study of Grindley (1929), although having certain difficulties in method as Crespi (1944) pointed out, has indicated that response acquisition was a function of the amount of reward. Since this early investigation, a number of other investigators have provided confirmation.

Studies by Crespi (1942), Zeaman (1949), Young and Shuford (1955), Metzger, Cotton, and Lewis (1957), Hulse (1958), and Logan (1960), using the straight runway, have indicated that the running speed of the rat varies as a function of the amount of reward. Crespi (1942), using a 20-foot runway, provided rats with either 16, 64, or 256 grams of food as a reward. Figure 10.2 shows the relationship between the amount of reward and speed of running over the course of the experiment. Zeaman (1949), using a much shorter runway, but providing considerably more variation in the amount of food reward, obtained similar findings. As Figure 10.3 illustrates, the varying amounts of food (cheese weighing .05, .20, .40, .80, 1.60 or 2.40 grams) produced different levels of performance. It is interesting to note that in both studies, the learning curves generated by the varying amounts of reward differ with respect to the equation constants representing the asymptote of latency; however, the parameter representing the rate of approach to the limits remain unchanged. Logan (1960), combining the

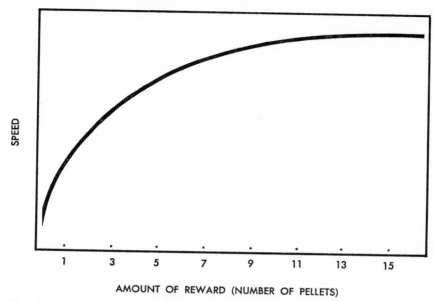

AMOUNT OF REWARD (NUMBER OF PELLETS)

Fig. 10–4. Amount of Reward (Number of Pellets). Hypothetical curve showing the relationship between performance and the amount of reinforcement. (Adapted from Logan, 1960)

findings of some six of his studies, has hypothesized that the relationship between amount of reward and performance to be as shown in Figure 10.4.

As might be expected, running speed in more complex tasks, as well as rate of responding in a Skinner box, has also been shown to reflect the presence of differing amounts of reward. This has been indicated in studies by Reynolds (1949) and Hughes (1957) using the simple T maze; Maher and Wickens (1954) and Furchtgott and Rubin (1953), using the multiple T; and Jenkins and Clayton (1949), Guttman (1953, 1954), and Hutt (1954), using the Skinner box. Guttman's (1953) study is particularly noteworthy inasmuch as by varying the concentration of a sucrose solution (4%, 8%, 16%, or 32%), he was able to control the amount of time the animal spent in the goal box and the amount of the animal's consummatory activity. Guttman's results indicated that the time required to execute 500 bar-pressing responses decreased as the concentration of sucrose increased. These general findings were confirmed in a second study, in which he (Guttman 1954) was further interested in determining if the reinforcing values of sucrose and glucose solution for rats in a bar-pressing situation were consistent with the relative sweetness of various concentrations of sucrose and glucose found by human observers. Results indicated that rate of bar pressing was an increasing function of concentration of both substances, with sucrose always producing higher rates of response than similar concentrations of glucose.

The taste of a substance is usually changed when its concentration is changed. Thus, at least one aspect of the mediating mechanism for different response rates in the Guttman (1953, 1954) studies was the taste of the solution. Hutt (1954) was interested in determining whether or not chemical modifications of a food by substances known to differ in taste would alter the effectiveness of its reward properties when the nutritive value, texture, and appearance of the food were held constant. Variations in taste were produced by adding citric acid or saccharin to a basic food mixture providing sour and sweet tastes in addition to the taste provided by the unadulterated food mixture. These three tastes were combined with three different amounts in a factorial design which resulted in nine combinations of taste and amount. These variables were examined in relation to rate of bar pressing in a Skinner box. Figure 10.5 provides the cumulative number of responses per minute for the fifth and last day of the experiment. These results show that the rate of performance of a learned response in a free responding situation was a function of the quality as well as the quantity of the reward. The fact that there was no interaction between quality and quantity suggests the additive nature of the reinforcing effects. This study confirms the results of an earlier one by Fay, Miller, and Harlow (1953), who, working with monkeys, found that quality and quantity of foods were independent determinants of food preference.

As seems to be frequently the case in areas of extensive investigation, a few investigators (Lawrence and Miller 1947, Reynolds 1950, Fehrer 1956a, and Kling 1956) have been unable to find differences in rate of responding as a function of varying amounts of reinforcement.

When rate of responding is measured during extinction, most of the findings parallel those which have been reported for acquisition. Zeaman (1949), Guttman (1953), Hutt (1954), and Young and Shuford (1955) have all reported that extinction rate is a function of the amount of reward obtained during the training

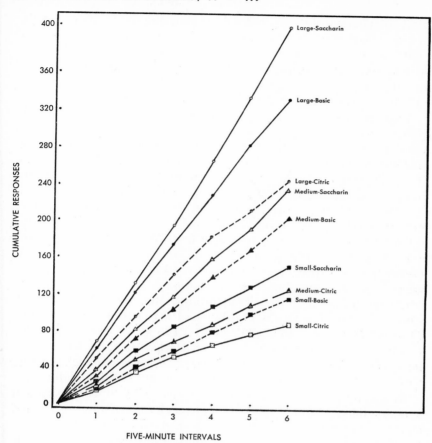

FIG. 10–5. MEAN CUMULATIVE RESPONSE CURVES FOR DAY FIVE. (Adapted from Hutt, 1954)

period. Since we have previously reported that these investigators found that rate of response during the training period varied as a function of the amount of reward, the extinction findings were undoubtedly a reflection of the fact that the larger-reward groups were responding at a higher level at the end of the acquisition period than the small-reward groups, and that this response superiority continued throughout extinction. Such an interpretation has support from a study by Metzger, Cotton, and Lewis (1957), who, after finding extinction data reflecting the operation of varying amounts of reinforcement obtained during an acquisition period, equated performance levels at the beginning of extinction trials by using analysis of covariance. These authors have concluded that the results of the analysis of covariance treatment suggest that the amount of reward affects performance on extinction through differential levels of performance just prior to extinction rather than affecting extinction performance directly.

In summary, the amount of reward appears to play an important role in determining an organism's rate of response. Interestingly enough, and as Cotton (1953) has found with deprivation states, the influence of the reward is primarily one of eliminating competing responses rather than increasing the rate of the instrumental response itself (Pereboom and Crawford, 1958).

The findings from those experimental studies in which probability of response has been used are similar to those which have used rate-of-response measures. It is true that Reynolds (1949), using a black-white discrimination problem, and Furchtgott and Rubin (1953), and Maher and Wickens (1954) using a multiple T maze, have been unable to find differences in numbers of errors made by differentially rewarded groups. But, on the other hand, studies by Reynolds (1950a), Meyer (1951a), Harlow and Meyer (1952), Greene (1953), D'Amato (1955a), Denny and King (1955), Schrier (1956), Schrier and Harlow (1956), Powell and Perkins (1957), Schrier (1958), Leary (1958), and Furchtgott and Salzberg (1959), among others, have reported positive findings.

Meyer's (1951a) positive findings led him to conclude that a major determinant in the facilitative characteristics of a given amount of reward was the range of rewards provided the organism. Until the subject had an opportunity to learn this range, the amount of reward could not function as a completely operative factor. Schrier (1956) has echoed essentially this same conclusion. He has pointed out that the organism not only has to learn the problem which has been set for it by the experimenter but that it must also learn something about the reward. He has further suggested that these two learning situations are essentially independent.

The importance of the subject's experience with the range of rewards provided by the experimenter has been experimentally demonstrated by Schrier (1958) and Leary (1958). Schrier used five groups of monkeys, four of which were designated as "non-shift" groups. These animals received either one, two, four, or eight pellets as a reward on *every* problem used in a series of dis-

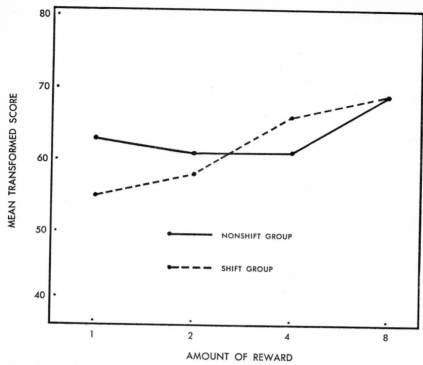

FIG. 10–6. MEAN ARCSIN-TRANSFORMED PERCENTAGE OF CORRECT RE-
SPONSES AS A FUNCTION OF THE AMOUNT OF FOOD REWARD (NUMBER OF
PELLETS). The intervals between the amounts of the abscissa are logarithmic.
Each point on the curve for the nonshift group represents a different sub-
group, whereas each point on the curve for the shift group represents the
same Ss. (Adapted from Schrier, 1958)

crimination problems. The fifth group, designated as the "shift"
group, experienced each of these reward amounts, with a *different*
amount occurring on each problem. Results indicated that for the
"non-shift" group, rewards of one, two, or four pellets produced
similar performance; the eight-pellet group's performance was,
however, significantly superior to the others'. The "shift" group, on
the other hand, revealed an increasing percentage of correct
responses following each increase in amount of reward. Figure 10.6
indicates the relationship between the two methods of investigating
the amount-of-reward variable.

Similarly, Leary (1958) has found that a group of monkeys provided with a half-peanut reward throughout a series of discrimination problems did not differ in number of errors from a group which had been given a two-peanut reward. If the monkey experienced both rewards (half a peanut on some problems and two peanuts on others), the half a peanut reward condition produced many more errors than the two-peanut reward.

The Effects of Variable Amounts of Reward

The use of shifting rewards in investigating the effect of the amount-of-reward variable calls attention to an interesting phenomenon reported by Crespi (1942). Crespi found that if an animal was shifted from one or four grams of food to sixteen grams, its performance in running a straightaway rose above the level of performance characteristic of a 16-gram group which had presumably reached its asymptote in running speed. On the other hand, if the amount of reward was reduced from 256 grams or 64 grams to just 16, running speed dropped below the level of performance characteristic of the 16-gram group at their limit of practice. Crespi has called the first performance change positive contrast or "elation" effect, while the second has been termed negative contrast or "depression" effect. Presumably these findings indicate that variations in the reward sequence produce responses which are either weaker or stronger than those which can be attributed solely to the effects of reward. Although Crespi's general findings of contrast effects have been confirmed by Zeaman (1949), subsequent experimental evidence has been controversial. Spence (1956), citing unpublished work from the Iowa laboratory, has suggested that the positive contrast effect obtained by Crespi was a function of the fact that the original high-reward subjects had not reached their asymptote of performance, and that the shift group was responding at a higher level because of additional training. Negative contrast effects, however, were obtained. O'Connor and Claridge (1958) have reported that imbeciles working at a repetitive task manifested significant elation effects in response to a sudden increase in incentive but did not show depression effects. Finally, Metzger, Cotton, and Lewis (1957) have been unable to demonstrate either effect. In this study, 50 rats were divided into five groups, differentiated by the amount of reward received per trial during the first ten and the last ten training trials on a straightaway. Group designations indicating the number of pellets received during these first ten and last ten trials were as follows: 2–2, 2–8,

5–5, 8–2, and 8–8. These 20 trials (one per day) were followed by extinction trials. Results indicated that the number of pellets received during the first ten trials had a significant effect on the speed of running. The amount of reward received on the first ten trials did not, however, have any effect on the second ten trials. Thus, contrast effects were conspicuously absent. These latter trials were affected only by the amount of reinforcement in that situation.

The conditions which have been used to investigate contrast effects are only specific instances of the more general case in which the amount of reward is varied from trial to trial according to some previously determined schedule. Logan, working with rats on the straight runway, has been particularly interested in this latter situation, and his recent book (Logan 1960) presents many of his experimental findings. He has concluded that if the amount of reward is varied between two equally likely values, as contrasted with the average of these amounts being constantly provided, differences in responding between the two conditions are dependent upon whether the average amount is small or large. If the average amount is small, then moderate degrees of variable amounts provide superior performance as contrasted with the constant amount. If the average amount is large, variable amounts provide inferior performance as contrasted with the constant amount. For example, 20 pellets is a large reward to a rat, and a constant 20-pellet reward is better than a variation of 19 and 21, which in turn is superior to a variation of 18 and 22. On the other hand, a constant 4-pellet reward results in inferior performance to a variation of 3 and 5.

Delay of Reward

The last reward variable to be considered has to do with the time interval separating the instrumental response from the securing of the reward. An early study by Watson (1917) illustrates the general problem area. Rats were trained to dig through four inches of sawdust, find a round hole giving access to a food chamber, and secure a reward which was in a shallow cup covered by a lid. One group of animals was allowed to eat as soon as they reached the food cup; a second group when reaching the cup was detained for 30 seconds before being permitted to eat.

Although Watson's findings as well as later ones (Warden and Haas 1927, Hamilton 1929, and Wolfe 1937) indicated that a relatively long delay could be interpolated between the organism's making a response and the securing of reward, most of the recent experimental evidence has indicated that if learning is to occur, the delay period must be short. The early studies did not control for the influence of stimuli in the learning situation acquiring secondary reinforcing value, and when this variable is controlled, the importance of the reward's immediately following the correct response becomes apparent.

Perin (1943) found that delays of more than 30 seconds resulted in his animals' being unable to learn a bar-pressing response. The experimental work of Perkins (1947), Grice (1948), and Smith (1951) has indicated that this temporal interval should be further reduced. In the Grice study, groups of rats were run on a black-white discrimination problem with delays of reward of 0, .5, 1.2, 2.5, and 10 seconds. The animals were run until they reached a criterion of 18 out of 20 correct, or until it appeared that they could not learn the problem. Thus, some animals were given more than 1,400 trials before being removed from the experimental situation for failure to learn. Learning curves for the varying delay groups are indicated in Figure 10.7. It will be noted that learning is a function of delay, with very little learning taking place when the delay exceeds five seconds.

Spence (1947) has hypothesized that learning with *any* delay depends upon the presence of secondary reinforcing stimuli. He has pointed out that the 30-second delay in the Perin experiment might be accounted for by assuming that the proprioceptive stimuli involved in the making of the response might have acquired secondary reinforcing properties, and that the learning taking place with even the short delay found by Grice could be attributed to secondary reinforcing attributes of the visual trace.

This hypothesis is basically untestable, since when learning does occur with a delay, unobserved physiological mechanisms can always be posited to act as secondary reinforcement. Some support for the hypothesis is found, however, in the study by Smith (1951). Smith designed his experiment so that rats were required to turn left or right at a choice point in a T maze depending upon whether they had just previously run through a black or white alley. By means of a delay chamber between the alley and the choice point of the maze, the time between the cessation of the stimulus cue and the point of choice could be varied. Delays of 0.0, 0.6, 0.75, 2.0, and 5.0 seconds were used. The gradient of the learning curve was similar to that found by Grice, and these results were interpreted by Smith

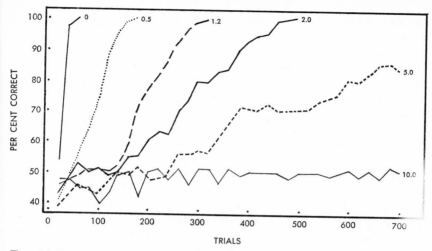

FIG. 10–7. LEARNING CURVES FOR EACH OF THE SIX DIFFERENT DELAY
GROUPS. (Adapted from Grice, 1949)

as evidence that learning can take place with the visual trace acting
as the appropriate cue for discriminative behavior. Furthermore,
the results would indicate that the visual-stimulus trace decreases
rapidly in time to become almost indiscriminate after five seconds.

In summary, the evidence is unequivocal in indicating that the
acquisition of a response, as measured by either rate or probability,
is a function of the delay introduced between the making of the response and the securing of reward.

The Effects of Variable Delays of Reward

The counterpart of Crespi's (1942) contrast effects obtained with
amount of reward is found in Logan's (1952) study manipulating
the delay period in a similar fashion. In this study, Logan (1952)
trained forty animals to respond to two bars in a Y-shaped apparatus. The depression of one bar was followed by reinforcement with
a one-second delay, and depression of a second bar was followed by
reinforcement after a five-second delay. The response measured
was the latency between the opening of a starting door and the de-
pressing of the bar. A system of forced and free trials was used in
order to give the animals equal opportunity with each bar. After 80
trials, the delay of reinforcement was reversed, with a depression
of the first bar producing reinforcement after five seconds, and de-

pression of the second bar producing the reinforcement after one. Results indicated that subjects showed a significantly greater response speed to the short-delay bar for the first 80 trials, and on free-choice trials developed a preference for it as well. When the short-delay bar was changed to the longer delay, a corresponding decrease in response speed followed. Contrast effects, however, were not found. In a somewhat similar type of study, Harker (1956) did find contrast effects when the shift in delay of reward went from a less favorable to a more favorable condition, but not in the reverse direction.

As with amount of reward, these conditions are only specific instances of the more general case in which the delay of reward is varied from trial to trial according to some experimentally determined schedule. Ferster (1953), examining the role of delay of reinforcement in pigeons, first established a stable pecking response with zero delay. Following this, he introduced a 60-second delay period which resulted in a decline in the rate of pecking to a value of zero. Very short delays were then introduced, with the length of delay being gradually increased as the animal's behavior became stable under a given delay condition. Using such a technique, it was possible to obtain a normal response rate with a 60-second delay period—a delay magnitude which had previously resulted in extinction. Ferster has pointed out that the delay in reinforcement is not a static parameter but that the effect of delay depends upon the way in which the organism is introduced to it. At least with pigeons, the gradual increase in delay permits the organism to acquire responses during the delay period which are used to bridge the temporal interval, and thus maintain the normal pecking response.

Finally, conditions have been manipulated so as to provide one delay period on some acquisition trials and a different delay period on another. In a sense, this technique is analogous to partial reinforcement situations in which reward is provided on some trials but not on others. One of the early studies investigating this type of manipulation of the delay period was by Crum, Brown, and Bitterman (1951) who found that when rats were provided with a delay of reward for 30 seconds in a goal box on half of the training trials, but received zero delay (immediate reinforcement) on the other half, their running speeds were as fast as those of a group which had received zero delay on all trials. Moreover, the variable-delay group showed superior resistance to extinction. Other investigators using different delay periods have confirmed these general conclusions. (Scott and Wike, 1956; Logan, Beier, and Ellis, 1955; Logan, Beier, and Kincaid, 1956).

The Logan, Beier, and Ellis (1955) study is interesting, for in addition to using a continuous one-second–delay group, and a group which was rewarded after a one-second delay on half of the trials and a nine-second delay on the remaining half, a third group was employed which was always rewarded after five seconds. In terms of an average delay, the second and third groups were, of course, similar. The findings confirmed those of Crum, Brown, and Bitterman (1951), in that there were no differences in acquisition between the one-second–delay group (Group I), and the varied one- and nine-second groups (Group II). The five-second–delay group, however, had significantly slower running speeds than either of the other two groups. Extinction measures, however, revealed no differences among all three groups. Recognizing that only a nine-second delay was used in the varied-delay groups in contrast to the 30-second-delay group used by Crum, et al. (1951), Logan, Beier, and Kincaid (1956) ran such a group and obtained extinction results similar to those of the Crum, et al. study.

The more recent experimental study of Peterson (1956) and the findings of Wike and McNamara (1957a) and Wike and Kintsch (1959), however, have made any general conclusion in the area tenuous. In the Peterson study, two groups of rats were given 96 acquisition trials traversing a runway. One group was given varied-delay reward periods—the delay consisting of either 0, 10, 20, or 30 seconds provided in a random order, while the second group was given zero delay. Although results indicated the varied-delay group had superior resistance to extinction, thus confirming previous experimental findings, the zero-delay group had significantly superior running speed during the acquisition trials. In the Wike and Kintsch (1959) study, five groups of rats were used for which 20-second delay periods were provided on either 2, 21, 50, 80, or 100 per cent of the acquisition trials. On all the other trials, the delay period was zero. Results, also in keeping with the early studies, revealed that the percentage of delay periods used was inversely related to runway speed at the end of the training period. Moreover, these investigators did not find any differences among groups with regard to resistance to extinction.

In summary, most of the evidence supports the conclusion that resistance to extinction is superior for a varied-delay (greater than nine seconds) group in contrast to a zero-delay group.

With regard to the acquisition of a response, the findings appear controversial. Perhaps Logan's (1960) conclusions, arrived at after extensive experimental work in the area, are as appropriate as any. He has concluded that when delay of reward is varied between two equally likely values, then among conditions having the same average delay, performance is better the wider the range of variation in delay. Thus, a constant 10-second delay produces a rate of response which is inferior to variations between 9 and 11 seconds, which in turn is inferior to variations between 8 and 12. The limiting case, and thus the best condition, is when the reward is given immediately on half of the trials.

Intermittent Rewards or Partial Reinforcement

In our discussion of the influence of number of rewards upon the acquisition and extinction of a response, we noted that the acquisition and extinction of a response was a function of the number of reinforcements. We were careful to qualify the statement, however, by modifying reinforcement with the word continuous. If continuous reinforcement is not provided, our condition becomes one of partial or intermittent reinforcement—a topic which we would like to consider at this time. Intermittent reinforcement, as Jenkins and Stanley (1950) have indicated, "refers to the reinforcement given at least once but omitted on one or more of the trials or after one or more of the responses in a series."

Although Skinner (1938) was one of the earliest investigators to give this topic serious attention, it was Humphreys' (1939) conditioned eyelid response study which aroused considerable interest. In this study, three groups of college students were given the following training: (1) 96 trials with 100 per cent reinforcement, (2) 96 trials with 50 per cent reinforcement, and (3) 48 trials with 100 per cent reinforcement. Humphreys found no significant differences among the groups during acquisition; there were, however, striking differences among the groups during extinction. The partially reinforced group extinguished much more slowly than did the groups given continuous reinforcement.

Since the early Skinner and Humphreys studies, there has been considerable interest in the phenomenon. The interested reader is referred to the fine reviews of Jenkins and Stanley (1950) and

Lewis (1960) on this topic. Much of the experimental work has been related to determining the appropriateness of certain theories which have been posited to explain the phenomenon, and it is to these theoretical orientations that we should like to direct our attention. Before proceeding, however, it seems appropriate to examine the methods involved.

Method of Presentation

In examining partial-reinforcement techniques, it is obvious that the frequency with which the reinforcement is provided is an important consideration. That is, in contrast to the 100 per cent or continuous-reinforcement situation, the experimenter may vary the percentage of reinforcement to something less than 100 per cent. Grant, Hake, and Hornseth (1951), Grant and Schipper (1952), Weinstock (1954, 1958), and Lewis and Duncan (1956, 1957, 1958) have all investigated the effect of differing percentages of reinforcement during the acquisition series on resistance to extinction.

Although the frequency of reinforcement may remain constant, the pattern of the reinforcement-nonreinforcement sequence may vary. In an early study, Grosslight and Child (1947) noted that the occurrence of a single nonrewarded response in a series of otherwise rewarded trials permitted the response of persisting after failure to occur and be rewarded. On the other hand, a pattern in which reinforcement was followed by nonreinforcement (with no other reinforcement occurring) was one which did not provide for the persisting, after, failure response to occur. These investigators noted that although percentage of reinforcement was held constant, the pattern of reinforcement-nonreinforcement responses played an important role in determining an organism's resistance to extinction. Later studies by Grosslight and his associates (Grosslight, Hall, and Murnin 1953, Grosslight and Radlow 1956, 1957) have confirmed this general finding.

Equating Trials and Reinforcements

When an investigator desires to compare a partial-reinforcement group with a continuous reinforcement one, he frequently faces the question of deciding whether to equate the groups in terms of trials or reinforcements. Thus, if a partial-reinforcement group is given 100 trials, with 50 of these reinforced, it becomes necessary to decide whether to give the continuous-reinforcement group 100 reinforced trials or just 50. A frequent procedure is to equate trials (or responses) and permit the number of reinforcements to vary. Any superiority of the partial-reinforcement group is made apparent then, in spite of the greater number of reinforcements provided the continuous group.

Measuring Response Strength

With the early Humphreys study, it was possible to compare the effects of the different reinforcing conditions on acquisition or extinction. Inasmuch as the experimental evidence indicates that the partial-reinforcement situation shows its effects primarily during the extinction situation, it has been this type of measure which most investigators have used. Some investigators (Wike, 1953; Grosslight, Hall, and Scott 1954) have felt that certain extraneous variables may play a confounding role in the extinction situation (i.e., frustration) and as a result have called attention to the possibility that wherever possible a habit reversal or transfer situation may be a more sensitive measure.

Theoretical Explanations of Partial Reinforcement

Any adequate theoretical explanation of partial reinforcement must account for the almost universal finding that partial reinforcement, in contrast to continuous, results in greater resistance to extinction or slower habit reversal.

According to the theory of expectancy, most widely associated with Humphreys' investigations, responses during acquisition are made to conditioned stimuli because these stimuli lead the subject to "expect" the unconditioned stimulus. In extinction, after continuous reinforcement, the response dies out quickly because there has been a rapid and easy shift from a regular expectancy of 100 per cent to another regular one of 0 per cent. Partial reinforcement, on the other hand, produces an irregular expectation of reinforcement, and it becomes difficult for the subject to change from an irregular expectation to the regular one needed in the extinction series.

This interpretation has been criticized for its anthropomorphic, vague, and ad hoc nature. As Sheffield (1949) has stated, subjects after experiencing continuous reinforcement during acquisition could find it harder to believe that more reinforcement was not forthcoming during the extinction series.

A recent study by Lewis and Duncan (1957), however, is pertinent to this explanation. An electronic slot machine was used which paid off money according to a prearranged schedule when buttons were pushed. Reward was provided on either 0, 11, 33, 67 or 100 per cent of 9 acquisition trials. Extinction trials followed and were continued until the subject desired to stop. Unique in this experiment was the arrangement whereby subjects had to state before each trial the confidence they held that they would win or lose on the next trial. Thus in addition to recording the number of extinction plays, a record was obtained of the subject's expectancies. Results indicated no evidence for Humphreys' hypothesis that those subjects with irregular expectancies would extinguish more slowly than those with regular expectancies. As the authors state, the findings are appropriate to trial-by-trial expectancies but not to over-all expectancies. "Insofar as Humphreys' expectancies are of the over-all variety, this study has no data bearing on the problem."

Lewis and Duncan's conclusions emphasize the fact that a working definition of expectancy which provides an opportunity for prediction and further testing has not been forthcoming. As a result, and as Lewis (1960) has recently concluded, this concept is apparently moribund as an explanation for partial-reinforcement effects.

Stimulus-response reinforcement theory has had as one of its major postulates the position that response strength was primarily related to the number of reinforcements. Under the circumstances, one would predict a weaker response with partial reinforcement than with continuous reinforcement in both acquisition and extinction situations. This view, of course, is clearly opposed to the experimental findings, which have almost universally demonstrated that partial reinforcement, in contrast to continuous, results in greater resistance to extinction.[2]

The reconciliation of these facts within the stimulus-response framework has been attempted by utilizing the concepts of (1) secondary reinforcement or (2) stimulus generalization.

The secondary-reinforcement explanation of partial reinforce-

---

[2] The facts are somewhat controversial with regard to the effect of partial reinforcement on acquisition. In their review of the partial reinforcement literature, Jenkins and Stanley (1950) have concluded that response strength is built up somewhat more rapidly under a schedule of 100 per cent reinforcement than under a partial regimen, although the differences in learning may not be large, and the level of acquisition for partially reinforced subjects may approach that for a continuously reinforced group. Studies appearing since this review have revealed other findings. Weinstock (1958), Haggard (1959), and Goodrich (1959) have found that the asymptotic running speed of partially reinforced rats was significantly higher than that of continuously reinforced animals if the latter part of the training series is examined.

ment was originally posited by Denny (1946), who hypothesized that with secondary reinforcement present on the nonrewarded trials, response strength during acquisition in a partial-reinforcement situation should be similar to that obtained with continuous reinforcement. If secondary reinforcement was absent on nonrewarded trials during acquisition, performance should be inferior. Denny's findings have supported his hypothesis. He found a significant difference in acquisition between partial (50 per cent) and continuous (100 per cent) reinforcement when the experimental conditions minimized the effects of secondary reinforcement. On the other hand, when there was no attempt to minimize secondary reinforcement, no difference between partial reinforcement and continuous reinforcement was obtained. These results suggested to Denny that secondary reinforcement was the responsible factor in determining whether or not acquisition with partial reinforcement would be as rapid as when continuous reinforcement was used. Only 12 extinction trials were provided in this experiment, and using probability of response (per cent correct) as the response measure, Denny found no difference between partial and continuous groups with secondary reinforcement either maximized or minimized. This is surprising, since it would have been expected that the partial-reinforcement group in which secondary reinforcement was maximized should show the greater resistance to extinction. Perhaps the small number of extinction trials used contributed to this finding.

Rubin's (1953) study is also relevant in examining the secondary-reinforcement hypothesis. This investigator compared the acquisition and extinction rates of a panel-pushing response acquired under conditions of continuous reinforcement and under partial reinforcement, with secondary reinforcement minimized. Using a rate-of-response measure, in contrast to Denny's probability measure, Rubin found no difference between his groups in speed of responding. This is also surprising since it meant that the partially reinforced group was able to learn to respond as rapidly in 16 trials as the continuously reinforced group given 31 trials. On the other hand, Rubin found that the continuously reinforced group was significantly superior in their resistance to extinction. Presumably, minimizing the effects of secondary reinforcement for the partially reinforced group resulted in this effect. This is one of the very few experimental studies in which such a finding has been obtained, and bears replication.

Hulse and Stanley (1956) investigated the relationship between partial and continuous reinforcement, and the presence or absence of secondary reinforcement during both acquisition and extinction trials. Like Rubin (1953) these authors used a rate-of-response measure. They found that their three conditions of training—(a) continuous reinforcement, (b) partial reinforcement with secondary reinforcement minimized, and (c) partial reinforcement with secondary reinforcement maximized—resulted in no reliable differences among the varying conditions during the acquisition trials. This finding, of course, is not consistent with that of Denny (1946) but is consistent with that of Rubin (1953). With regard to extinction, partial reinforcement resulted in greater resistance to extinction than continuous reinforcement when secondary reinforcement was maximized during training, but not when secondary reinforcement was minimized during training. Finally, partial reinforcement with secondary reinforcement maximized during training produced greater resistance to extinction than partial reinforcement with secondary reinforcement minimized during training.

Studies by Bitterman, Feddersen, and Tyler (1953) and Elam, Tyler, and Bitterman (1954) are also relevant in this area. These studies were quite similar except for the time interval used between trials. Rats were trained to run a straight runway and enter a goal box under conditions of random 50 per cent reinforcement. During training, the animals were consistently reinforced in a black (or white) goal box, and nonreinforced in white (or black). During extinction, the animals were divided into two groups, with Group I run to the goal box which was associated with previous reinforcement, while Group II was run to the goal box associated with non-reinforcement. The authors assumed that a secondary-reinforcement hypothesis would predict that resistance to extinction should be maximized when secondary reinforcement was present during extinction trials, thus favoring superior resistance to extinction for Group I. The results, however, indicated that this group extinguished more rapidly.

Freides (1957) has also manipulated the secondary reinforcing stimuli found in the goal box during extinction and has concluded that his findings strongly suggest that any simple formulation concerning the effects of secondary reinforcement (in contrast to novel stimuli or cues associated with nonreinforcement) in prolonging extinction is untenable.

In summary, although some of the studies which we have reviewed indicated that secondary reinforcement may play a role in partial-reinforcement effects, it is difficult to see how it can be used as a complete explanation for the superiority of partial reinforcement over that of continuous during extinction. In order to do so, it must be assumed that the secondary-reinforcing effects taking place during the acquisition series results in stronger habit strength than does primary reinforcement.

In contrast to the secondary-reinforcement explanation, Sheffield (1949) has attempted to account for the effects of partial reinforcement on resistance to extinction by what has frequently been called an aftereffect, or stimulus generalization hypothesis. As she states: "The basic hypothesis is that extinction necessarily involves different cues from those used during training. Omission of reinforcement alters the context and makes extinction a case of 'transfer of training' in which a certain amount of generalization decrement is expected because of the change in cues." Thus reinforcement on any trial of a continuously reinforced series produces aftereffects which become a part of a stimulus pattern on every trial after the first. In extinction of the continuously reinforced group, the stimulus pattern is changed both by the absence of the aftereffects of reinforcement and by the presence of the aftereffects of the nonreinforcement. In partial reinforcement the organism encounters cues on the nonreinforced trials taking place during acquisition which are present during extinction. Inasmuch, then, as the response has become conditioned during the training to cues which are characteristic of extinction, there is less loss through a change in the conditioned stimulus pattern when reinforcement is withheld during extinction.

Assuming that the aftereffects of reinforcement or nonreinforcement would dissipate with spaced trials during extinction, Sheffield (1949) compared the resistance to extinction of groups given (a) massed or (b) distributed training. Groups receiving massed acquisition trials were given 15 seconds between trials, while groups receiving distributed training received 15-minute intertrial intervals. Results indicated resistance to extinction following massed training was significantly greater in the 50 per cent group than in the 100 per cent group. On the other hand, following spaced training, resistance to extinction was not reliably different between the two groups. The results of this experiment substantiated her hypothesis.

A large number of subsequent studies, however, have not provided confirmation of the Sheffield results. Wilson, Weiss, and

Amsel (1955) replicated the Sheffield experiment except that in their first experiment dry food was substituted for the wet mash which Sheffield had used as reinforcement. Experiment 2 utilized water as the reinforcing agent. The authors hypothesized that the dry food used in Experiment 1 would increase the persistence of the aftereffects (stimulus trace) and enhance the Sheffield effect. On the other hand, water used as a reinforcing agent would be expected to minimize the trace and thus reduce the Sheffield effect. Their results were not in agreement with Sheffield's findings. Partial-reinforcement groups showed greater resistance to extinction than the continuous groups regardless of the intertrial interval used during acquisition or the kind of reinforcement. Lewis (1956) also duplicated the Sheffield procedure but used a spaced intertrial interval of just 2 minutes rather than 15. Analysis of his extinction data revealed a nonsignificant interaction between reinforcement (continuous vs. partial) and the intertrial interval (15 seconds vs. 2 minutes). Grant, Schipper, and Ross (1952); Fehrer (1956a); and Katz (1957) have also been unable to obtain findings supporting the aftereffect hypothesis.

Two of the most extensive studies bearing upon Sheffield's position were done by Weinstock (1954, 1958). The first, a pilot study, was replicated by a second. In this latter study, an enclosed runway was used and six groups of rats were provided with either 16.7, 33.3, 50, 66.7, 83.3, or 100 per cent reinforcement. The animals were given one trial per day under 22 hours of water deprivation. All subjects received reinforcement for the first 12 days; for the next 96 days, they were reinforced according to the group to which they had been assigned. Within every 12-day block, one group received two reinforced trials, a second group four, a third group six, etc. On reinforced trials, water was available for 30 seconds, on nonreinforced trials the subjects were left in the goal box for the same period of time. Following the acquisition trials, all animals were given sixty (one per day) extinction trials. Response measures included latency and speed of running. Since these measures yielded the same findings, Weinstock has presented just latency. Results indicated that although there was little difference among the varying groups for the first forty acquisition trials, subsequent trials revealed that the 83.3 and 100 per cent reinforcement groups had significantly slower times than the other groups. These acquisition curves are indicated in Figure 10.8. Extinction data also revealed significant differences among groups. As Figure 10.9 indicates, the animals re-

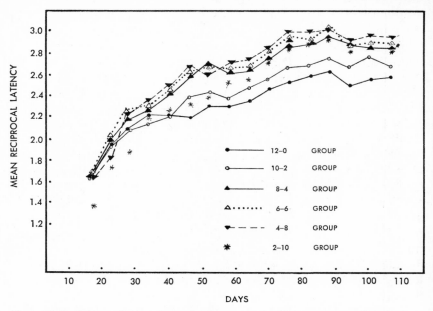

FIG. 10–8. MEAN RECIPROCAL LATENCY AS A FUNCTION OF TRIALS BY BLOCKS OF SIX FOR THE ACQUISITION PHASE. (Adapted from Weinstock, 1958)

ceiving the smallest percentages of reinforcement exhibited the greatest resistance to extinction. Inasmuch as the trials were widely spaced and provided no opportunity for the aftereffects of reinforced trials to be associated with those of nonreinforced trials, these findings represent a striking refutation of the Sheffield hypothesis.

Studies by Bitterman and his associates (Longenecker, Krauskopf, and Bitterman 1952; and Elam, Tyler, and Bitterman, Feddersen, and Tyler 1953; Tyler, Wortz, and Bitterman 1953; Bitterman (1954) have compelled them to reject partial-reinforcement theories based upon the action of either stimulus generalization or secondary reinforcement, and to propose that consideration be given to what Mowrer and Jones (1945) have termed a discrimination hypothesis. The discrimination hypothesis had its origins in a study by Mowrer and Jones (1945) in which four groups of rats were trained to make either one, two, three, or four bar depressions in a Skinner box before receiving food. Following extensive training, the animals' responses were then extinguished. Results indicated that resistance to extinction (as indicated by total number

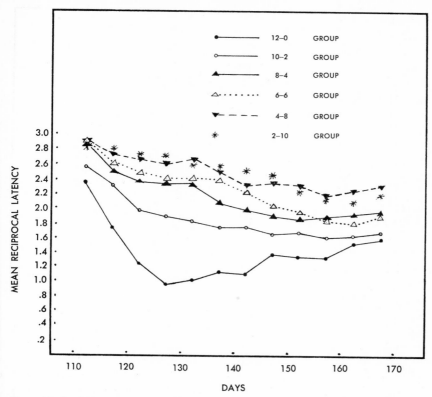

Fig. 10–9. Mean Reciprocal Latency as a Function of Trials by Blocks of Five for the Extinction Phase of the Experiment. (Adapted from Weinstock, 1958)

of bar presses) was a function of the number of bar presses in the acquisition series which was required to obtain food; thus the group required to press the bar four times prior to obtaining food took the longest to extinguish, while the group required to press only once extinguished most rapidly. As *one* explanation for these findings, Mowrer and Jones proposed that when the change from acquisition to extinction was difficult to discriminate, greater resistance to extinction should take place than when such a discrimination was easy.

In the Longenecker, Krauskopf, and Bitterman study (1952), two groups of human subjects were reinforced on 50 per cent of the training trials in the conditioning of the galvanic skin response.

With one group, reinforcement was randomly administered, while with the other, reinforced and nonreinforced trials were regularly alternated. In the Tyler, Wortz, and Bitterman (1953) study, two groups of rats were trained on a runway under similar conditions. In both studies, significantly greater resistance to extinction was found in the random group—a result which the authors believed tended to support the discrimination hypothesis, inasmuch as a random sequence should obscure the difference between acquisition and extinction more readily than an alternating sequence.[3] The stimulus-generalization hypothesis, on the other hand, would appear to predict less rapid extinction for the alternating group, inasmuch as each reinforced response was made in the absence of the aftereffects of reinforcement.

An important variable which has been hypothesized to be related to the discrimination hypothesis has been the percentage of reinforcement provided during acquisition. Here it has been posited that the smaller the percentage of reinforcement obtained by the organism in the learning trials, the more difficult it will be to discriminate between learning and extinction, which should then lead to slower extinction rates.

A number of investigators have been interested in the empirical examination of extinction as a function of the percentage of reinforced responses, and these findings can be related to the tenability of the discrimination hypothesis. In one of the early studies in this area, Grant, Hake, and Hornseth (1951) used a Humphreys type of verbal conditioning situation employing 0, 25, 50, 75, and 100 per cent reinforcement conditions. Sixty acquisition trials were followed by 30 extinction trials. Results indicated that resistance to extinction was best for the 25 per cent reinforcement group, followed by the 50, 75, and 100 per cent groups. The 0 reinforcement group extinguished most rapidly. A year later, Grant and Schipper (1952) used an eyelid conditioning situation and employed the same variety of reinforcement percentages. In this study, greatest resistance to extinction occurred for the 75 per cent reinforcement group, followed by the 50, 100, 25, and 0 per cent groups in that order.

A number of studies have also been conducted in this area by Lewis (1952) and Lewis and Duncan (1956, 1957, 1958).

[3] Longenecker, Krauskopf, and Bitterman (1952) have recognized that their findings were not in agreement with an earlier eyelid conditioning study by Grant, Riopelle, and Hake (1950). These investigators found that a single alternation group tended to extinguish less rapidly than a randomly reinforced group.

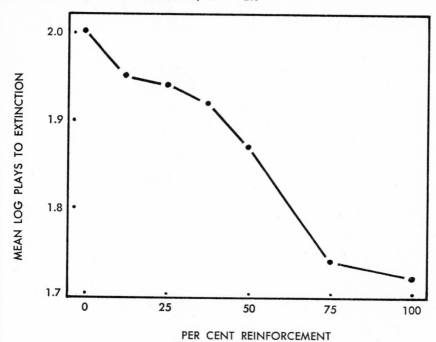

FIG. 10–10. MEAN LOG TRIALS TO EXTINCTION AS A FUNCTION OF THE PER-
CENTAGE OF TRIALS REINFORCED DURING ACQUISITION. (Adapted from Lewis
and Duncan, 1956)

Lewis (1952) employed young children in a type of gambling
game in which the obtaining of small toys served as reinforcement.
A ten-trial acquisition series was employed in which reinforcement
was provided on 0, 50, 60, or 100 per cent of the trials. Results indicated that the 50 and 60 per cent groups were most resistant to
extinction, followed by the 0 and 100 per cent groups.

In the first Lewis and Duncan (1956) study, a slot machine was
so modified that the experimenter could manipulate the reward-
nonreward sequence. Students were then run under the following
percentages of reward: 100 per cent, 75 per cent, 50 per cent,
37½ per cent, 25 per cent, 12½ per cent, and 0 per cent. The acquisition series consisted of 8 plays, followed by an extinction series. The number of plays made by each group during extinction
revealed that resistance to extinction was a function of the reinforcement percentage obtained during the acquisition trials. Figure
10.10 reveals these findings. This general finding was confirmed in

a second study (Lewis and Duncan 1958) employing a similar apparatus and design but using only three percentages of reinforcement (33, 67, and 100) combined with four lengths of acquisition trials (3, 6, 12, and 21). The general trend was for the smaller percentages of reinforcement to bring about a greater number of plays to extinction.

In another study to which we have already referred (Lewis and Duncan 1957), nine acquisition trials were provided with the following percentages of reinforcement: 0, 11, 33, 67, and 100. In addition to obtaining plays to extinction, the subjects' expectation of winning or losing on the next trial was also recorded. Results indicated that the smaller the percentage of reward, the more plays were made during extinction, except that the 0 per cent group played slightly fewer times than the 11 per cent group. Moreover, the loss of expectancies during extinction was a function of the percentage of reward with greatest extinction loss taking place with the largest percentage of reward.

Finally, attention should be called to the studies of Weinstock (1954, 1958), to which reference has already been made, as well as to those of Fattu, Auble, and Mech (1955) and Fattu, Mech, and Auble (1955). It will be recalled that Weinstock found that resistance to extinction of the running response in the rat was a function of the percentage of reinforcement provided during acquisition, and reference to Figure 10.9 reveals this relationship. The studies of Fattu and his associates have revealed a similar relationship when preschool children were used as subjects.

The results of these studies reveal that the discrimination hypothesis holds up reasonably well, although it does not provide perfect prediction of the experimental findings. In a number of the studies, the zero percentage reinforcement group did not attain maximum resistance to extinction, although the discrimination hypothesis would *appear* to make such a prediction, since it is this condition which minimizes the distinction between acquisition and extinction trials. There is some question, however, as to whether or not a zero percentage group can be properly considered as a *partial* reinforcement condition since no reinforcement is provided during acquisition.

In the Grant and Schipper (1952) study, a 75 per cent reinforcement condition resulted in greater resistance to extinction than either a 50, 25, and 0 per cent condition, a second finding which appears to be contrary to the discrimination hypothesis. The use of a conditioned-response learning situation, in contrast to some of the other types which have been used in this situation, calls attention to the nature of the response which is to be learned in the experimental situation. If the response is a part of the organism's response repertoire, the attaching of it to certain stimuli can at times be accomplished by instructions given to the subject, or within a very few trials. In other situations (conditioning, animal learning, etc.) such may not be the case, and a minimum percentage (or number) of reinforced responses must be provided in order for learning to occur. Percentages of reinforcement falling below this minimum (and presumably the Grant and Schipper findings fall in this category) result in very rapid extinction—not because of the ease or difficulty with which the organism can discriminate between acquisition and extinction, but simply because the learned response is very weak or nonexistent.

A second variable related to the discrimination hypothesis concerns the length of the acquisition series. Here it is posited that the more training of a particular type, the more readily the organism can discriminate acquisition from extinction, which should then lead to more rapid extinction. Studies by Lewis and Duncan (1958) and Capaldi (1957, 1958) have supported such a position. In Capaldi's first study, human subjects were given differing amounts of alternating partial reinforcement in a discrimination problem. Results indicated that the group given the most training extinguished most rapidly. A somewhat similar finding was obtained with rats (Capaldi 1958). In this latter study, a group of animals which had been given 14 days of training with alternating reinforcement extinguished more rapidly than a group given alternating reinforcement for just seven days. Suprisingly enough, this latter group did not extinguish more rapidly than groups given random reinforcement for either 7 or 14 days. Although Capaldi has viewed these findings as evidence for supporting the discrimination hypothesis, it raises an issue crucial to the hypothesis: the conditions which make for easy and difficult discrimination must be specified.[4]

[4] In his excellent review of recent studies in partial reinforcement, Lewis (1960) cites the Marx (1958) and Brown and Bass (1958), both of which studies revealed findings which were not consistent with a discrimination hypothesis. To the extent that a discrimination hypothesis is called upon to explain all extinction data, Lewis' citations are relevant. Our primary concern, however, is one of attempting to account for the superiority of partial reinforcement over continuous reinforcement during extinction. Inasmuch as the cited studies did not use a partial-reinforcement condition, they do not appear to be relevant.

11

- **INSTRUMENTAL RESPONSES, III**
- **FRUSTRATION, STRESS, AND OTHER**
- **EGO-INVOLVED MOTIVATIONAL**
- **ANTECEDENTS**

Our examination of the effects of varying motivational antecedents upon instrumental responses has revealed that much of it has been related to the Hullian system. Our two previous chapters have been loosely organized within this framework.

An area of interest distinct from Hullian influence has been the examination of instrumental responses as influenced by what we have previously termed ego-involved variables. Two general approaches in such an examination can be delineated. The first has been the tendency for some investigators to posit that at least some of these antecedents produce some specific type of response, with the experimental evidence being directed toward supporting (or refuting) such a position. The frustration-aggression hypothesis is an example of such an approach. The second approach has been to consider these ego-involved motivational antecedents as having the functional properties of a motive. Here, investigators have been interested in studying the influence of such antecedents on instrumental responses in much the same way as antecedents having a biological basis have been studied.[1] We shall consider this second approach first, since it represents a logical continuation of the ma-

[1] Although perception is frequently categorized as an instrumental response, we have delayed presenting material in this area until Chapter 12.

terial which we have presented in the two previous chapters. Following this, we shall then discuss the specific-response approach.

The Influence of Ego-Involved Motivational Antecedents on Instrumental Behavior

In this section, we would like to examine some of the experimental work investigating the influence of ego-involved antecedents on instrumental behavior. It will be recalled that in Chapter 6 the concepts of frustration, stress, anxiety, threat, success, and failure were types of variables that were included in this category.

What is the effect of manipulating ego-involved motivational antecedents on the learning and retention of typical laboratory tasks? In answering such a question, the type of antecedent as well as the technique involved in its manipulation must be given consideration.

One technique has been to provide the subject with some indication of the importance of the task that is to be done. "Importance" has usually been manipulated by indicating to the subject that the task is a measure of some personality or intellectual attribute.

In an early study, Alper (1946) instructed one group of subjects that the list of nonsense syllables to be learned was a test of intellectual ability; a second group was given instructions only to memorize the list. The first group Alper described as being ego oriented, while the second group was denoted as task oriented. Results indicated that immediate recall of the material revealed no difference between the groups; a test on the following day, however, revealed that the ego-oriented subjects showed no significant retention loss whereas the task-oriented subjects dropped significantly below their first recall score. A second study by Alper (1948) demonstrated that reminiscence effects were also influenced by whether the instructions given to the subjects were ego or task oriented.

A somewhat related approach has been to "ego involve" the subject by utilizing material with which he identifies or which he values socially. One of the early studies of this type was done by Zillig (1928), who used aphorisms written by prominent authors as her material. Half of them expressed opinions favorable to the female while half were unfavorable. Twenty males and twenty females were asked to read the statements and then write them from memory. Results indicated that the men recalled just 37 per cent of the favorable material, while the women recalled 63 per cent. Subsequent studies by Watson and Hartman (1939), Edwards (1941), Wallen (1942), Levine and Murphy (1943), Postman and Murphy

(1943), and Alper and Korchin (1952) have, in general, confirmed this early finding. In the Edwards study (1941), one which has been often cited, students were asked to indicate their attitudes toward the New Deal. On the basis of their scores, three groups of subjects were selected, with one group being favorable, a second group neutral, and the third group unfavorable to the program. All three groups then heard a ten-minute speech concerning the New Deal with half of the material favorable, and the other half unfavorable. Immediately following the speech, a recognition test consisting of two 23-item subtests was given. One subtest was made up from the favorable material, the other test from the unfavorable material. Twenty-one days later it was given again. Results, like those of Zillig (1928), indicated that individuals with favorable attitudes toward the New Deal tended to make more correct responses on the pro–New Deal test than they did on the anti–New Deal test. Subjects with unfavorable attitudes toward the New Deal indicated the reverse. These findings also held for the 21-day retention test.

In contrast to most studies which have used only retention tests to compare group performances, the studies of Postman and Murphy (1943) and Levine and Murphy (1943), are interesting in that these authors have also examined the *learning* of such material. In the Levine and Murphy (1943) study, an attitude scale was used to select two groups of subjects designated as either anti-Soviet or pro-Soviet. Two paragraphs, one mildly pro-Soviet and the other anti-Soviet, were then read to them. Following the reading, each subject was asked to reproduce the material. This procedure was followed for five weekly sessions, and it was thus possible to plot the learning of both sets of material for both groups. Results indicated that the pro-Soviet subjects learned significantly more pro-Soviet material than they did anti-Soviet material. Similarly, the anti-Soviet group learned significantly more anti-Soviet material than pro-Soviet material.

In the Postman and Murphy (1943) study, students' attitudes toward the United Nations and the Axis powers were obtained, and pairs of words which embodied various degrees of compatibility with these attitudes were constructed, along with an equal number of control pairs. If a subject on the attitude scale had indicated his strong agreement with the statement, "The German people are kindly," the word pair, German-kindly, was judged to have a compatibility of +2. On the other hand, if the student disagreed strongly with the statement, a value of −2 was assigned. Values of

+1, −1, and 0 were also assigned, depending upon the attitude expressed by the subject. The subjects were then required to learn pairs of words which varied in value together with the control pairs. Results indicated that pairs of words which were given a +2 rating were more rapidly learned than those rated either −1, 0, or +1. A surprising finding was that the control words were learned significantly more rapidly than the test words; it is also interesting that material which was antithetical to an individual's value system should be learned more rapidly than material which was neutral.[2] In contrast to these latter findings, Williams (1951) has found that a list of paired associates consisting of hostile or what he has termed "ego alien" words was more difficult to learn than a list of neutral words.

Although the positive findings obtained in the area are frequently explained on the basis of the material's being consistent with the individual's value system, one difficulty with such an interpretation is that in a number of these studies, one might reasonably expect subjects with a given attitude to have been exposed to material which was consistent with that attitude more frequently than material which was inconsistent.[3] In Edwards' (1941) study, one would expect that pro–New Deal subjects would be better acquainted with material favoring the New Deal than they would be with unfavorable material. Only Wallen's study (1942) dealing with attitudes toward the self and the two recently cited studies by Murphy and his colleagues, in which performance on the first learning trial was equivalent for both groups, appear to be free of this criticism.

In contrast to the facilitation of performance occurring as a function of the ego-involved antecedents which we have just discussed, the ego-involved antecedents of failure, stress, threat, and frustration have been frequently found to produce performance decrement. Seashore and Bavelas (1942) had children take the Goodenough Draw-a-Man test a number of times. Following the completion of each drawing, they insisted that their subject draw a better one. The authors, hypothesizing that this type of instruction produced stress, obtained findings which indicated that their subjects' mental age level declined as a function of such instructions. Wil-

[2] It is possible that these findings, at least in part, were a product of the differing intralist similarities of the material used.
[3] It is to be noted that this criticism, based upon the frequency with which a subject comes in contact with the experimental material, has played an important role in certain perception studies and will be discussed more fully in this context.

liams (1947), using the Wechsler Bellevue digit symbol test, has also reported performance decrement as a function of stress produced by threat of shock.

In studying the effects of frustration on discrimination, McKinney, Strother, Hines, and Allee (1951) first required subjects to make a rapid discrimination of figures enclosed in a circle. Following uninterrupted preliminary training on this task, the subjects were given the task again but "frustrated" by having the experimenter call out false norms every half minute—a level of performance they could not achieve. Results indicated that under such conditions, errors increased and, in general, efficiency was reduced.

Finally, both Smith (1954) and Chansky (1956) have reported that the learning or retention of word lists was adversely affected by the use of threat on tasks which were temporally contiguous to the experimental task.

Perhaps the most frequently found experimental design in this area has been one in which the effects of a number of different types of ego-involved antecedents have been investigated within a single experiment. These studies, frequently conducted within a school setting, have usually investigated the effects of ego-enhancing variables such as praise, success, or encouragement, as well as the ego-threatening ones of failure, blame, discouragement, threat, etc.

One of the early studies was by Hurlock (1925), who used school children as subjects and addition problems as the experimental task. She found that praise, in contrast to other antecedents (reproof, being ignored, or control), was the only one which resulted in consistent increases in performance over the five-day experimental period. The performance of the reproved group, although consistently better than that of either the ignored or the control group, showed a decrement in performance after the second experimental day. The studies of Sears (1937) and Lantz (1945) have also indicated that praise or success results in a performance increment, failure in performance decrement.

In Sears' study (1937), after having learned a list of nonsense syllables, subjects were given a card-sorting task. Following each trial, the subject was given his score and then asked to indicate how he thought he would do on the next trial. A failure group was not permitted to reach the goal they had set; a success group, on the other hand, was permitted to do so. Results indicated that the card-sorting performance for the failure group deteriorated, while the success group's performance became progressively better. Lantz (1945) examined the influence of success and failure on intelligence-test performance. Following the giving of one form of the Stanford Binet, the subjects were asked to perform on a Ball Game task, in which half of the subjects were permitted to succeed while the other half were made to fail. Immediately following this experience, the alternate form of the intelligence test was administered. Results indicated that failure significantly decreased the number of correct responses to test questions which involved the use of thought processes, while not significantly affecting responses to questions measuring visual or rote memory. Success, on the other hand, significantly increased the variability of the mean beyond the expected test-retest increase.

Other studies, however, have provided other findings. Forlano and Axelrod (1937) found blame (as indicated by the teacher's placing *Poor* on a student's paper) to be more effective in increasing a student's performance in a number cancellation test than praise (as indicated by the teacher's placing *Good* on the paper). Thompson and Hunnicutt (1944), replicating the Forlano and Axelrod (1937) study, found that both praise and blame resulted in performance increment but that there was no difference between these two variables.

The early studies of Gates and Rissland (1923) and Hurlock (1924), as well as a relatively recent one by Silberman (1957), have also indicated little difference between ego-enhancing and ego-threatening variables in increasing performance. In Silberman's (1957) study, the effects of praise and reproof (manipulated by a teacher's verbal behavior) on reading growth was investigated. The author reported no difference in their effect.

Osler's (1954) study is interesting, since she was concerned with not only success and failure, but fear as well. Her subjects were grammar school children and the task was one of solving long-division problems. Following the administration of preliminary problems, which were provided to equate groups and permit a comparison with subsequent performance, the test situation was run. The three basic treatments were as follows: (1) failure: students were notified that they had failed the preliminary test, (2) fear: students were notified that a serious complaint had been received about them and they were to report to the school official at the end of the test period, and (3) success: students were told that they had done well on the previous test. Combinations of these treatments were used to provide four experimental groups: (1) failure alone, (2) failure and fear, (3) success, and (4) success and fear, as well as a control group. Results indicated that the performance of the success group was best, followed by that of the control, success-fear, failure, and failure-fear groups.

Although the findings in this area have been controversial, almost all of the studies we have considered have indicated that some type of ego-involved variable can operate to influence performance. Some investigators, however, have been unable to find that these variables make any contribution to performance change. Russell (1952) had subjects learn a list of nonsense syllables but found no difference between subjects who were given instructions that the task was a test of scholastic aptitude and those to whom the material was described as being merely a practice list. The studies of Adams (1940), Lazarus and Eriksen (1952), and Hardison and Purcell (1959) are only a few of the many studies which have reported no differences in the mean performance of some laboratory task between subjects who have been presumably frustrated or placed under some stress condition as contrasted with control subjects. Ross, Rupel, and Grant (1952), investigating the effects of electric shock, auditory distraction, and "heckling," as well as all combinations of these, upon performance in the Wisconsin Card Sorting Test, found that only the shock conditions resulted in deterioration of performance; moreover, the effect was quite temporary. Zimny (1956), also utilizing a number of ego-involving conditions—(a) the incentive of an excused classroom assignment, (b) threat of electric shock, (c) instructions that the learning task was an indicator of intelligence—and a control group, found no differences among groups with regard to the learning of a list of nonsense syllables and only a temporary increment in card-sorting performance for the incentive group.

The reconciliation of the findings in this area appears to be, at least in part, dependent upon solving a number of problems inherent in the handling of ego-involved type variables. It is quite possible that in many instances subjects were sufficiently sophisticated to "see through" the instructions which attempted to "ego involve" them. It does not seem too farfetched to assume that many college students do not always accept at face value instructions which indicate, for example, that the learning of a list of nonsense syllables is an indication of an individual's intelligence. It is also quite possible that the task required of the subject means so little to him that indications of his performance, which the investigator construes as success, or failure, or threat, are not similarly construed by the subject. It becomes important, then, to obtain some indication that the subject is truly "ego involved."

A second problem relates to how performance is measured. In a recent study, Murphy (1959) instructed subjects to deal cards from the top of the deck, calling out certain identifying characteristics. Threat was induced in one group by attaching electrodes to their ankles and informing them that they would be shocked for each error. The time needed to complete all of the identifications and the number of errors made were used to measure performance. Results indicated that the threat of shock resulted in a performance decrement, if such performance was measured by the amount of time taken to complete the task. On the other hand, if the number of errors was used as the performance measure, the threat-of-shock group made significantly fewer errors.

A third problem noted by a number of investigators has been that ego-involved antecedents often increase the variability of performance among groups, although the groups' mean performance frequently remains the same. This finding has suggested that motivational antecedents utilized by the experimenter do not mean the same thing to each individual, or that the effects of these variables are dependent upon particular characteristics of the subject.[4]

Gates and Rissland (1923), in analyzing their data, found that discouragement appeared to affect subjects who had low initial scores to a considerably greater extent than subjects who had made high scores, while Hurlock (1924) noted that the intellectual level of the subject appeared to be an important determiner of whether praise or reproof was the more effective variable in increasing performance. And both Forlano and Axelrod (1937) and Thompson and Hunnicutt (1944) have found that the introversion or extroversion of their subjects played an important role in determining whether or not praise or blame influenced performance.

Recent studies have attempted to evaluate experimentally these

---

[4] A good example of this is indicated in a report by Mahl (1950). Mahl used stomach acidity as a measure of anxiety, and made measurements on students just prior to their taking an important examination. Although six subjects showed a significant increase in acidity, two showed a decrease. Interviews revealed that one of these students had little academic motivation and was content only to pass the course, while the other, although having high academic motivation, had already been accepted into medical school; hence, the test was of little importance to him.

interaction effects. Lazarus and Eriksen (1952), using a digit symbol test, have found that students with high grade point averages tended to show increments in performance while under stress, while students with low grade point averages indicated a decrement. Fleishman (1958), presenting instructions to Air Force personnel indicating that performance on a complex co-ordinating task would be important in determining their future assignments, has reported that subjects with high initial ability on this task improved their performance, while the performance of subjects with low initial ability deteriorated. In contrast to these findings, Willingham (1958), in examining the flight performance of naval trainees, has reported that failure on one of the important periodic "check flights" results in a performance decrement on the next flight, with superior trainees showing these effects to a greater extent than inferior ones. Bernardin and Jessor (1957) have found that negative verbal reinforcement lowered maze performance of dependent subjects significantly more than of those subjects who were judged to be independent.

The popularity of Taylor's Manifest Anxiety Scale has resulted in a number of individuals' examining the interaction of anxiety (as measured by the scale) and ego-involved motivational antecedents on varying types of tasks. Lucas (1952) has found that stress, as inferred from inducing failure on a preliminary experiment, resulted in anxious subjects' being inferior to nonanxious ones in the learning of nonsense syllables. As the amount of stress was increased, performance for the anxious group grew progressively inferior, while the nonanxious group's performance grew progressively superior. Davidson, Andrews, and Ross (1956) have also reported that stress on anxious subjects significantly reduced their performance on a color-naming test. They have suggested that anxiety appears to have a priming function—one which results in the heightening of a subject's sensitivity to stress situations.

Studies by Deese, Lazarus, and Keenan (1953) and Lazarus, Deese, and Hamilton (1954), however, have not been in keeping with these findings, although their technique of inducing stress was not comparable. Anxious and nonanxious subjects required to learn a list of nonsense syllables were: (1) never shocked, (2) shocked for making wrong responses, or (3) shocked randomly. Results indicated that the anxious–shocked-for-wrong-response group was superior to its nonanxious counterpart. In contrast to the previously reported studies, stress appeared to combine with anxiety to produce superior performance. The complexity of the general problem is indicated, however, by the Lazarus, Deese, and Hamilton (1954) study in which the experimental conditions of the Deese, Lazarus, and Keenan (1953) study were replicated, except that the material to be learned was of considerably greater difficulty. The findings here indicated no differences among any of the groups.

The search for personality variables, important in their interaction with ego-involved motivational antecedents, led Otis and McCandless (1955) to consider the role of social needs in influencing responses to frustration. Using 3½-to 5½-year-old children enrolled in laboratory preschools, and a blocking task devised by Lerner to induce frustration, they confirmed a number of their hypotheses which related the type of dominant social need found in the individual—power dominance or love affection—to the amount of aggression exhibited over a series of trials in the frustration task. They found, for example, that children who ranked high on power dominance showed more aggressive and less submissive behavior in the frustration series than children ranked low on this variable.

In contrast to studies which have attempted to examine the effects of motivational antecedents as influenced by the specific characteristics of the individual, another approach has been to assume that the responses which are made to ego-involved motivational antecedents are those which the individual has previously learned. Davitz (1954) hypothesized that subjects who were trained to respond aggressively would show more aggression after frustration than subjects who had been trained constructively. Furthermore, he hypothesized that subjects who had been trained constructively would behave more constructively after frustration than would subjects who had been trained aggressively. Children, ages seven to nine, were first observed in a free-play situation. Following this, either constructive or aggressive training was provided. The aggressive training consisted of a series of games which involved considerable physical contact among the players, while constructive training consisted of drawing murals and completing jigsaw puzzles. The frustration situation was induced after the training period by giving the children a bar of candy and showing them the first reel of a two-reel movie. At a crucial point in the second reel, the subjects were told they could not see anymore films, the candy was removed from their hands, and they were ushered into the play room. An 18-minute period of free play was then provided, with the behavior of both groups being filmed. Results indicated that although both groups were equivalent in the free-play situation prior to training, the training period produced an effect in that the constructively trained subjects behaved more constructively after frustration than the aggressively trained subjects. The aggressively trained subjects, on the other hand, behaved more aggressively after frustration than the constructively trained subjects.

Ego-Involved Antecedents and Their Relationship to Completed and Incompleted Tasks

One topic of interest in this general area has been to investigate the role of ego-involved variables on the recall of completed and incompleted tasks. It will be recalled that an hypothesis flowing from the Gestalt school was that interrupted or incompleted tasks should be better recalled than completed ones. Such an hypothesis followed from the belief that the successful completion of a task resolved all tension that was generated by it; on the other hand, the interruption of the task resulted in the tension persisting, which provided the basis for better retention. Studies by Zeigarnik (1927) and others have provided experimental verification of the phenomenon.

A number of investigators have found, however, that this finding is dependent upon ego-involved variables. In an early study by Rosenzweig (1943), jigsaw puzzles were used as the experimental materials, with instructions given to one group of subjects that the puzzles were indicators of intelligence. A second group was given the material under more informal conditions—here they were told that they were helping to classify the puzzles for further use. The subjects' performance on half of the puzzles was interrupted, while the subjects were permitted to complete the other half. Results indicated that the group under the formal conditions recalled significantly more finished tasks.[5] In "explaining" his findings, Rosenzweig postulated that the informal subjects were motivated mainly by what he called need persistence, whereas the subjects under formal conditions were motivated by ego defense.

Both Lewis and Franklin (1944) as well as Eriksen (1952), although defining the motivational variable somewhat differently from Rosenzweig, have nonetheless confirmed his findings. In the

---

[5] One confounding variable in this study was the fact that the subjects were not homogeneous. Those making up the formal condition were freshman advisees from the Harvard Psychological Clinic while subjects in the informal condition were obtained from the Student Employment Bureau.

Eriksen (1952) study, the task was one of making meaningful sentences from a number of scrambled two- and three-word phrases. Eight of the sentences were solvable, while eight were not. One group was ego oriented by being told that the task was an intelligence test and that the experimenter was interested in selecting bright subjects for another experiment. The second group was task oriented—their instructions indicated that some of the items were too difficult to solve in the time permitted. Results indicated that the ego-oriented subjects recalled more completed than incompleted problems than did the task-oriented group. Task oriented subjects, however, recalled significantly more incompleted tasks. Glixman (1949) has hypothesized that as stress increased, the recall of completed tasks should also increase; conversely, the recall of incompleted tasks should decrease. In his study, three groups of subjects were first exposed to varying amounts of stress, defined by the type of instructions given prior to the testing situation. The task consisted of 20 paper and pencil problems in which two minutes were given for the completion of each one. Unlike other studies, there was no control over which tasks the subjects completed and those which were not. Results indicated that as stress increased, the recall of incompleted tasks decreased, thus supporting part of Glixman's hypothesis. The increased recall of completed tasks as a function of increases in stress was not completely supported, rather a type of curvilinear relationship was found in which recall scores were highest for the intermediate stress condition.

Ego-Involved Antecedents and Repression

Stemming from the work of Freud, the concept of repression or what some have termed motivated forgetting has also been an area of interest which has relevance to ego-involved motivational antecedents. Briefly, repression refers to the hypothesis that material which is threatening or produces anxiety tends to be pushed from the conscious into the unconscious. Thus, an individual is unable to recall material which he has at some previous time known. In the interim, the material has become unacceptable; removal of the reason for its "unacceptableness" should presumably result in the individual's again remembering it.

In some of the studies which we have already discussed, although certain ego-involved antecedents have produced poorer retention for certain types of material, the general type of experimental design does not adequately test the repression concept. As Zeller (1950) has indicated, an appropriate test of the concept demands that control and experimental subjects first show equal amounts of learning as indicated by some retention test. Following this, some incident is produced which is designed to produce repression, with a retention test so demonstrating it. Finally, removal of the incident should result in both experimental and control groups' once again being equivalent with respect to amount retained.

Zeller's review (1950) of the literature in this area revealed, to him at any rate, that no experiment had been conducted which fulfilled this criterion of a laboratory test of repression. Two studies (1950a, 1951) which he has conducted, however, have appeared to demonstrate the phenomenon. In the first of these, two groups of subjects were first required to learn a list of nonsense syllables, and then returned 72 hours later to relearn the list to a criterion of one errorless trial. Presumably, both groups had learned the material equally well. Following this, the experimental group was given a block-tapping test, in which the experimenter indicated that they had done quite poorly. The control group was given a similar task but the failure instructions were not provided. Following this treatment, a relearning test of the nonsense syllables indicated that the experimental group showed significantly poorer retention scores than the control group. Twenty-two hours later, poorer performance on the part of the experimental subjects was again indicated. Following such poorer performance, the experimental subjects were again given the block-tapping task, in which they were permitted success. A relearning of the nonsense syllables then indicated that they had reached the level of the control group.[6]

A more recent study by Aborn (1953) has provided somewhat similar findings when the material acquired was of an incidental variety. The author found that the introduction of threat significantly depressed the retention of material which was acquired incidentally. The alleviation of the threat, however, produced recovery of the loss.

FRUSTRATION-PRODUCED RESPONSES

Unlike the operation of many motivational antecedents, frustration as a motivational antecedent has been frequently approached from the point of view that it results in a specific type of

[6] Bugelski's (1956) comments on this study merit presentation. Bugelski points out that it is the block-tapping that should have been repressed and items associated with this experience rather than the list of nonsense syllables.

behavior consequent. Some writers have posited it to be aggression, while others have believed it to be regression or fixation. This is the approach which we outlined at the beginning of the chapter and is one which we would now like to consider.

Aggressive Responses

An early and major contribution in the area was made by Dollard, Doob, Miller, Mowrer, and Sears (1939) in their text *Frustration and Aggression*. These authors argued that if an organism was interfered with in its making of a goal response, a state of affairs occurred which was termed frustration. Frustration thus served as a kind of motive for the organism. The basic hypothesis of the authors, however, was that such frustration invariably results in aggressive behavior—"aggression is always a consequence of frustration." [7]

The authors recognized that other psychological factors, in addition to frustration itself, needed to be taken into account in order to obtain a better understanding of the aggressive response. As a result, a series of corollaries were formulated relating this response to other variables. More specifically, they posited that aggression was a function of: (1) the strength of the motivation for the blocked response, (2) the degree of blocking the instrumental response, (3) the frequency with which instrumental responses are blocked, as well as (4) the anticipation of punishment for the aggressive response. Finally, they proposed that the expression of any aggressive act was a catharsis which reduced the instigation to all other acts of aggression although a footnote limited the generality of this position. Aggression, it was here indicated, would continue if the original frustration persisted, or if the aggressive response became a learned one.

An impressive amount of evidence was obtained to support these corollaries, although much of it was either anecdotal or in the form of questionnaire studies in which the subjects reported what they had done, or would do when in a frustrating situation.

Workers in the area were quick to criticize many of these propositions on the grounds of ambiguity and oversimplification, as

---

[7] In 1941 Miller (1941a) revised this statement to read: "Frustration produces instigations to a number of different types of response, one of which is an instigation to some form of aggression." Although such a statement still proposes that some form of aggression is always tied to frustration, the possibility exists that other types of response may be exhibited by the organism.

well as being contrary to many experimental findings. Most attacks concentrated on the major premise that frustration *always* causes aggression. Bateson (1941), for example, provided anthropological evidence showing the existence of certain primitive cultures in which aggression was not a typical response to frustration. The Balinese, he pointed out, are infinitely willing to suffer frustration without becoming aggressive.

A whole host of both experimental and descriptive studies revealed that the aggressive response was only one of a number which might be made when a consummatory or instrumental response was blocked. Levy (1941) found that puppies whose sucking needs were not satisfied did not show aggressive behavior, but only perverted sucking. Scott (1948), working with pairs of hungry goats, induced frustration by placing grain in a bucket which would accommodate only a single animal or by placing their heads close together in order to obtain food. Presumably either situation should result in frustration. Results indicated, however, that only dominant animals became aggressive when their consummatory responses were blocked. If the animal was paired so that it was placed in a subordinate position, aggressive behavior was not in evidence. Studies by Frederiksen (1942), Sherman and Jost (1942), and Seashore and Bavelas (1942) as well as others in which humans were used as subjects resulted in the general conclusion that aggression was not an invariant response to frustration.

Similarly, descriptive studies by Zander (1944), McClelland and Apicella (1945), and Stanford and Hsu (1948) have also indicated that a number of different types of response may be made by the individual when placed in a frustrating situation.

A second line of attack was directed at the authors' description of the antecedent conditions necessary for producing frustration. Thus, in our earlier discussion of the topic, we called attention to the writings of Maslow (1941), Zander (1944), and Sargent (1948), among others, who have emphasized not so much the environmental obstruction as a condition for frustration, but the significance of the obstruction to the individual.

Finally, some objections were directed toward the catharsis principle—the tenet that the expression of any aggressive act was a catharsis which reduced the instigation to all other acts of aggression. In an early article, Morlan (1949) indicated that such an hypothesis did not square with certain obvious facts; aggression, rather than leading to a cathartic effect, frequently led to further aggression.[8]

Although many empirical investigations have been made in this area, crucial tests of the principle, as Berkowitz (1958 has indicated in his excellent review of this topic, have been exceedingly difficult to make.

Regressive Responses

In their formulation of the frustration-aggression hypothesis, the Yale group acknowledged its indebtedness to Freud, whose early writing contained many examples of this phenomenon. Similarly, it was Freud who called attention to the phenomenon of regression. Mowrer (1950) has nicely described Freud's contribution:

In a paper that appeared in 1912, Freud presented a detailed statement of his conception of regression in the etiology of neurotic illness and posited that its occurrence or nonoccurrence is primarily contingent upon two factors: (a) *fixation* and (b) *frustration*. According to the view developed at that time and subsequently held with relatively little modification, the erotic life (libido) of civilized human beings passes through several more or less discrete stages in its development from the so-called narcissism of infancy to the genital heterosexuality of normal adult life. Because of the continuing pressure of the socializing and educational forces in modern society (plus the changing needs of the child, produced by physical maturation), each of the intermediate stages is successively achieved and then abandoned for the next higher level of adjustment, until the final adult goal is reached. If, however, for any of several possible reasons, this developmental process does not go forward in the usual way and the individual never advances beyond one of the intermediate stages, there results what may be called *absolute* fixation. This is a phenomenon that actually occurs in the lives of some persons and is assumed to provide the basis for the sexual perversions. But since there is here no question of a *return* from a later to an earlier mode of adjustment, the problem of regression is not, of course, involved.

On the other hand, in the lives of persons who do make the prescribed

---

[8] It is interesting to note that Dollard (1938) made essentially this point in an earlier publication. Dollard indicated that studies of individuals have frequently demonstrated the existence of the following mechanisms: (1) wishes to injure other people or the accomplishment of such injury; (2) a fear of retaliation based on what has been done or intended; (3) the appearance of new aggression against the wronged object. This vicious circle phenomenon, Dollard further points out, can lead to apparently reasonless hostile behavior toward those who are guilty only of being the objects of hostility.

step-by-step transitions in their sexual development (however falter-ingly), the habits that are acquired and reinforced at each successive stage necessarily have a certain strength or intensity (cathexis) that is more or less enduring; and it is the varying strength of such habits that determines the extent to which *relative* fixation may be said to have oc-curred at any given point. This phenomenon, in contradistinction to absolute fixation, is of special significance for the understanding of the mechanism of regression; for it is presumably the specific nature and extent of the relative fixations in an individual's life history which de-termine the pattern of regression ("choice of neurosis") that will occur if, subsequently, a superimposed mode of adjustment or habit system meets with an insuperable obstacle (i.e., if *frustration* occurs) and if there is relatively little opportunity for further *progression* (i.e., for the development of still other new habits). In other words, the greater the strength of a relative fixation, other things equal, the greater the tendency for regression to occur to the level of that fixation when subsequently acquired habits (in the same impulse-need system) are thwarted, pun-ished, or otherwise prevented from functioning effectively and bringing the customary satisfaction.

A number of animal studies have been done with the investigator attempting to place them within this Freudian framework. The general technique has been to teach the animal one response in order to secure a goal object, and then teach the organism an al-ternative response. During this second learning situation, the ex-perimental animals are usually given some kind of noxious stimula-tion, and the change in the animal's behavior is compared with those animals not given such stimulation. An early study by Hamil-ton and Krechevsky (1933) illustrates this type of experimental design. Their apparatus consisted of a single T maze in which one arm was twice as long as the other. Although both ends of the T were reinforced, food was obtained more rapidly if the animal chose the shorter arm. In training on the first habit, the short arm was on the right so that this represented the most direct route to food. Training was given until the right turn was occurring on 90 per cent of the trials. The arms were then reversed so that the ani-mal, in order to obtain food most directly, had to make a left turn. As a result, the earlier right-turning habit was superseded by the new left turning one. The animals were then divided into a control and an experimental group; each animal of the experi-mental group received a strong shock administered at a point just before the choice point. Control animals, of course, received no shock. Results indicated that the control animals began to show left-turning behavior with increasing regularity, while the experimental animals showed a decided tendency to revert to their former right-turning behavior. The authors believed that these experimental findings supported the Freudian hypothesis and that regression occurred when the organism was placed in a strong emotional situation.[9]

Many of the subsequent studies in this area (Everall 1935, Sanders 1937, Martin 1940, and O'Kelly 1940), patterning their methods after that of Hamilton and Krechevsky (1933), have also obtained evidence for regressive behavior. Sanders' (1937) study is interesting since in one experiment the presentation of a loud noise at the *choice point* did not reveal evidence of regression. Martin (1940) was also unable to obtain regressive behavior if animals were given a shock at the starting point of a run rather than at the choice point.

There is some question, however, as to whether or not experimental findings of this type are relevant in supporting the Freudian conceptualization of regression. One problem is related to the kinds of response which the organism has available at the choice situation. Most studies have used situations in which there are only two available responses. The use of noxious stimulation may be such as to produce an avoidance of the second response, which means that the only other response available to the organism is one which must be labeled "regressive."

A test related to this general notion was provided by Kleemeier (1942), whose apparatus consisted of a runway with four alternatives at the choice point rather than the usual two. The animals were given preliminary training involving both free and forced runs. Following this they were given 50 trials in which the choice of the second alley led immediately to food. Although the animals received food at the end of the other three alleys, it was not available until after a 90-second delay period. Following this training the animals were given training in which alley number 4 was positive. After this training was completed, shock was introduced along the general pathway leading to a choice point. On the first shock trial, no animal regressed to alley number 2, and 13 of 20 subjects selected alley number 4. Seven animals went to either alley number 3 or 1. Nine subsequent trials also revealed little regression to alley number 2. Subsequent experiments were con-

[9] In this study as well as in a number of subsequent ones, it is apparently presumed that an emotional situation is also a frustrating one.

ducted in which each of the other alleys were positive for the first habit period, and the results corroborated the finding of the first study in that regression was only infrequently found.

A second consideration in the interpretation of the regression studies is related to the effect that the shock produces in the experimental situation. One possibility is that responses which have been most closely associated in time with shock should be inhibited. Using a method similar to that of Hamilton and Krechevsky (1933), Sanders (1937) found that if animals were given ten seconds of shock in an unrelated compartment and were then placed in the maze situation, regression did not occur. Although she indicated that the animals were still in an emotional state when placed in the maze, she felt that emotionality of the animals must be closely integrated with the situation in order for regression to occur.[10]

It is also possible that shock adds a stimulus increment which makes the test situation essentially a new one. Such a situation may result in the disinhibition of the effects of the extinction of the first response, or it may be related to certain transfer effects.

Some support for the analysis of regression behavior in terms of transfer effects rather than in terms of emotionality is found in the early study of O'Kelly (1940), as well as one more recently completed by Perkins and Tilton (1954). O'Kelly (1940) shifted animals from a thirst drive to satiation and found that six of seven animals regressed. Perkins and Tilton (1954) also indicated that nonstress changes in stimuli near the choice point would result in animals' shifting from a recently acquired response to a previously acquired one. In this study, rats were first trained to turn right, and, following this, were given training to turn left. After a criterion of five correct successive responses on this left-turning response, the original unpainted stem of the T maze, which also contained a hardware cloth hurdle, was replaced by a stem section painted black and without a hurdle. A control group which had not been given training on the original right-turning habit, but which

[10] Mowrer's (1950) explanation for the differing effects of shock has been that the animal, prior to its making a choice, anticipates a given response and that shock given during the anticipatory response is as effective in inhibiting the response as if punishment had been administered during or after the act. If punishment is given but there is no connection with the response, there is no specific deterring effect. He has felt that such a hypothesis ". . . serves as a tentative means of bringing the results of these experiments into line with the concept of regression which holds that the precipitating cause is a *specific frustration* (habit interference) rather than a generalized emotional disturbance."

had been given the left-turning training was also used. Results indicated that 67 per cent of the experimental animals regressed to the right-turning habit on the test trial, while just 8 per cent of the control animals indicated such behavior. The authors have pointed out that "the results suggest that regression resulting from an electric shock at the choice point . . . is not dependent upon the noxious nature of the change in the stimulus complex which is introduced."

Some animal studies, however, have been free of the difficulties which we have discussed. In an early study by Hull (1934), rats were trained to run a 20-foot straightaway in order to receive food. The length of the alley was then increased to 40 feet. Although at first the animals showed some tendency to stop at about the 20-foot mark, continued training of the animals resulted in their learning to run steadily down the entire length of the runway. When extinction trials were instituted (the extinction operation being regarded as a source of frustration), the tendency to stop at the 20-foot point again reappeared.

It was Mowrer's (1940) ingenious study with animals, however, which has provided the best analogue of human regression. In this experiment, experimental animals were placed individually into an apparatus in which shock was permitted to build up gradually from zero to a maximum intensity and remain there for 15 minutes. At such a time, the shock was turned off and the animal removed from the apparatus. Under such conditions, the animals discovered that if they sat quietly on their hind legs and held their forepaws well above the grille, they received comparatively little shock. The result was that after a few sessions, this response was immediately adopted by the animals as soon as the shock built up to an intensity which appeared to produce pain. Following such training, these animals were then placed into an apparatus in which a pedal had been placed at one end of the box, the depression of which resulted in immediate termination of the shock. Mowrer reports that although some animals showed enough random activity to result in their pressing the pedal, with some animals it was necessary to pinch their toes in order to break up the posture response so that they could learn the pedal-pressing response. A control group which had not learned the posture response was also given training in learning to depress the pedal in order to terminate shock. By the end of three days, the animals in the experimental group were as proficient in executing the second habit as were the control animals. On the day following the end of training of the pedal-pressing response, the animals in both groups were placed into the apparatus with the pedal accessible. However, the touching of the pedal resulted in the animal's receiving a slight shock from the surface. Under these circumstances, control animals continued to respond with the second response; four of the five experimental animals, however, "regressed" to the earlier posture response.

Shortly after Mowrer's paper appeared, an experimental study of regressive behavior with humans was reported by Barker, Dembo, and Lewin (1941) at the University of Iowa. The Barker, Dembo, and Lewin study of frustration and regression is, of course, a very familiar one. It will be recalled that in this experiment, 30 children, ages 2 to 5, were observed during two sessions. The experiment was conducted in a room which could be divided by a wire screen. During the first session, the child was brought into one part of the room and permitted to play with ordinarily attractive toys. Following this, the second session consisted of permitting the child to play in another part of the room in which there were much more attractive toys. When the child had become fully involved in play in this situation, he was made to withdraw to the other part of the room and play with the less attractive toys. A wire screen was lowered so that the more attractive toys could be seen, but not played with. The child was in essentially the same physical situation as he was in the original free-play situation except for the visibility of the more desirable toys. The child's play with the ordinary toys was rated on a scale of constructiveness, both during the original free-play situation and also immediately following the frustration situation. Behavior descriptions and ratings indicated a mean regression in the constructiveness of play to approximately 22 months at the 4½-year level and 5 months at the 2½-year level. In general, the amount of regression was positively related to the strength of frustration. Some children, however, who showed weak frustration actually improved in the constructiveness of their play.[11]

[11] The conditions which result in a subject's improving constructiveness of play under frustration have been described by Barker (1938–1939) as follows:

(1) When the second activity is motivated in part by the original motivation which had been motivating the frustrated activity. In essence, the second activity functions as a substitute for the first.

(2) When the frustration drive leads to an attempt to escape from reminders of the frustrated activity, and the second activity is used as the mode of escape.

(3) If the individual was unmotivated with respect to the second activity, it is possible that the quality of performance may be favorably influenced by the increased drive more than it is unfavorably influenced by interference.

Wright (1942, 1943), in examining the behavior of pairs of young children in the frustrating situation, has tended to confirm the Barker, Dembo, and Lewin study (1941).

The general theoretical position of the Iowa group was that the personality of the adult individual is "more differentiated" than that of the child. As a result of frustration, the personality of the individual becomes less completely structured and the differentiation tends to break down. As Lewin has stated (1937), a person under pressure should "regress" to a more "primitive" level at least as far as his degree of differentiation is concerned. Lewin further points out that this regression to a primitive level (or primitivization as it has been called) takes place not because of previously learned habits which were overt at an early time in the individual's life history, but merely because frustration or tension tends to destructure the personality. In contrast to Freud, Lewin's theory of regression is completely ahistorical.

The Barker, Dembo, and Lewin (1941) interpretation of their findings has been challenged by Child and Waterhouse (1952, 1953). Briefly, the hypothesis offered by these authors is that the frustration of one activity effects a lowering of the quality of performance in a second activity only to the extent that it gives rise to competing responses which interfere with the responses involved in the second activity. These competing responses may be categorized as (1) the attempt to continue the activity which was interfered with, as well as (2) responses evoked by the frustration drive itself (aggressive responses, attempts to escape, etc.). The authors have contended that the lowered constructiveness of play found in the Barker, Dembo, and Lewin study is adequately explained by the interference of responses of these two types with the responses of playing with the available toys during the frustration period.

In an experimental demonstration of their general point of view, Waterhouse and Child (1953) hypothesized that frustration would produce a decrease in quality of performance only to the extent that other responses (i.e., worry) which arose from the frustration drive would interfere with the outgoing performance. Subjects were first given a personality questionnaire in order to provide the investigators with some information concerning their subjects' habitual response to frustration. Following this, the subjects were asked to perform a variety of tasks (motor, routine, and intellectual) in which half of them were subjected to criticism, presumably producing frustration, while the other group was not so subjected. Results indicated that for those subjects for whom frustration produced a great deal of interference, performance resulted in a *decrement*. For the low-interference group, frustration produced a large *increment*.

General Considerations

The experimental findings of both animal and human studies indicate that when an organism is frustrated in a given situation, a type or kind of behavior which is different from that just previously found in the experimental situation frequently occurs. If this kind of response change is all that is meant by regression, there would be little argument, for most of the experimental evidence indicates it to be a real phenomenon. Unfortunately, the term used to describe behavior in clinical as well as experimental situations has acquired surplus meanings which have resulted in considerable confusion.

One source of controversy has to do with the characteristics of the "regressed" response. Lewin has hypothesized that such behavior has not been previously learned, but in most of the animal studies which have presumed to demonstrate regression, such behavior has been experimentally "placed" in the organism's response history.

A related difficulty has to do with the strength of the motivational antecedents which are presented following the frustration experience. Presumably, in addition to the original motivational antecedent, a second, arising from frustration, is present. How these interact will be an important determinant of the organism's behavior in the test situation. McClelland (1951), for example, has pointed out that behavior which is used as a defense against the anxiety which has arisen out of the frustration will undoubtedly be found to obey laws different from those in which behavior is a means of obtaining some form of the original frustrated goal response. A careful classification of the variables operating in the situation, as well as the varying types of responses, is needed in order to help clarify the situation.

Fixation

In sharp contrast to the consideration of aggressive and regressive responses as produced by frustration, Maier has proposed still another—that of fixation. The essence of his point of view can be found in his text *Frustration: the Study of Behavior Without a Goal,* which appeared in 1949.[12] It is Maier's basic thesis that frustration results in a stereotyping of an organism's response. Stereotypy, or fixation, as it has been more frequently termed, is used by the author to designate an extremely persistent type of response. Because such persistency seems to be much greater under the frustration situation than found in typical learning situations, Maier (1949) believes that such behavior cannot be explained by using learning principles. Therefore, a dichotomy between the operation of frustration and motivation is proposed.

The experimental operations which he has used to produce frustration and to obtain fixated responses are as follows: an animal is given training on a jumping apparatus in which it jumps from a small stand to one of two stimulus cards which have been placed about twelve inches from the stand. Preference is expressed by jumping at and striking one of the stimulus cards. If the correct card is struck, it falls over and the animal lands on a feeding platform where it may eat. If the incorrect card is struck, the card, being securely fastened, remains in place and the animal receives a bump on the nose and then falls into a net below. In contrast to a typical learning situation in which either a stimulus card or a position is regularly reinforced, Maier's technique for inducing frustration has been to have neither cue consistently rewarded or punished. After a number of such trials, the animal will refuse to jump. The resistance to jumping, however, is overcome by giving the animal either an electric shock at the jumping stand, prodding with a stick, or blowing a blast of air on it. After a short time, the animal may develop a fixation or stereotyped response to the situation. It may always choose the card on its right, despite the fact that this choice is punished on half of the trials. Most of the time Maier reports the stereotyped response is related to position, with such a response being repeated without variation for several hundred trials without the animal's once attempting an alternative.

To reiterate the point made earlier, Maier's basic position is that in frustration-instigated behavior, there is no goal orientation, and that the behavior is a terminal response rather than a means to an end. Separate and distinct from frustrations produced behavior is

---

[12] More recently, Maier (1956) has restated and extended his thesis. He has not, however, materially changed his point of view in this extension, but has concerned himself with a physiological basis for frustration mechanisms as well as certain clinical considerations.

behavior related to motivation. Motivation as used by Maier characterizes the process by which the expression of behavior is determined or its future expression is influenced by consequences to which such behavior leads.[13]

Maier points out that an examination of the behavior properties associated with frustration reveals that they are quite different from those found in motivated problem solving and learning. Some of these differences are as follows:

1. A problem situation produces stereotyped behavior in the frustrated organism whereas it produces variable behavior in the motivated.
2. Responses produced under frustration, in so far as they show fixation, are rigid and stereotyped to a degree that exceeds responses produced by rewarded learning. Thus, the motivated organism is characterized by plasticity—the frustrated organism by rigidity.
3. Responses produced during frustration are not responsive to alteration by punishment although reward-learned responses can be so altered.
4. Punishment may serve as a frustrating agent, and when this happens, a learned response may be replaced by a characteristic frustrated response.
5. Frustration-induced responses seem to be an end in themselves. Motivated responses are a means to an end.
6. The method of guidance is highly effective for altering frustration-produced responses, but it has no great value for replacing reward-learned responses.
7. Frustration-instigated responses are compulsive in nature whereas responses appearing in motivation situations are choice reactions.
8. The degree of frustration can be relieved by the expression of responses, regardless of whether or not the response is adaptive. Responses expressed by a motivated organism are satisfying only when the responses are adaptive.
9. Frustration-instigated responses are either nonconstructive or destructive in nature whereas motivated responses are constructive.

[13] Maier's definition of motivation emphasizes the selective function of a motive while ignoring other functions. He points out that the random behavior of a hungry animal cannot be regarded as motivated unless this random behavior is shown to be more than restlessness. Such a statement obviously excludes the energizing function of a motive.

10. The response expressed during frustration is influenced to a great extent by its availability to the organism, whereas the response expressed in the state of motivation is influenced more by anticipated consequences than by availability.

11. Learning takes place under motivation and permits an increase in the number of differentiations the organism can make, whereas frustration leads to dedifferentiation (regression) and in some cases convulsive or mass behavior.

An examination of these differences reveals that a number of them are essentially restatements of Maier's basic position and cannot be experimentally tested. Maier has, however, attempted to provide experimental support for some of the others. In an attempt to show the difference in persistence between responses developed through frustration and those with the use of reward, Maier refers to two studies from his laboratory. The general technique was to train animals so that a position response would be obtained by use of (1) reward or by (2) frustration. Following the practicing of these types of responses, a transfer situation was used in which the animals were required to form a symbol-reward response. In one study (Maier and Klee, 1943), it was found that just four animals out of eleven in the group that had acquired a stereotyped response were able to learn the new habit within 200 trials, while nine of ten animals that were trained by using reward were able to learn the second habit. In two other studies (Maier and Klee, 1941, 1945), similar findings were obtained. Thus, in combining the three studies, only 29 per cent of the animals which had developed stereotyped responses were able to abandon this response and learn a symbol response in 200 trials or less. This was in contrast to 74 per cent of the animals which had learned the original response with reward.

A second type of evidence used by Maier relates to the permanent nature of abnormal fixations. In a study by Maier and Klee (1941), ten animals which had fixated responses were subjected to a variety of experiences which included (1) a period of four months in which no tests were given and (2) injections of metrazol. Of the ten animals, seven completely retained their position response fixations and their specific patterns of abortive jumping during a subsequent test program involving the symbol-reward discrimination problem.

It is interesting to note that Maier has not ignored the earlier experimental findings relating aggression and regression to frustration. The integration of the frustration-aggression hypothesis with his theory of frustration is accomplished by regarding aggression as an end product of frustration and not as goal-oriented behavior. The same reasoning is applied to the experimental work done on regression. Maier (1949) states, "Regressive behavior readily lends itself to classification under nongoal-oriented behavior. Regressive responses appear spontaneously and without learning so that they do not appear to be learned techniques for gaining attention and other possible goals."

As might be anticipated in a psychology in which learning theory plays a prominent role, Maier's position has aroused considerable criticism. One explanation for Maier's findings has been proposed by McClelland (1950, 1951), who feels that Maier is describing only differences between behavior motivated by pleasure seeking and by pain avoiding. McClelland assumes that Maier's frustrated rats developed an avoidance motive in the course of attempting to satisfy an approach motive characterized by a need for food. Thus, when the problem of discriminating the correct stimulus becomes too difficult, the adaptive response of not jumping would normally be made except that the use of shock or of an air blast does not permit this response. As a result, the animals become oriented around escaping or avoiding the jumping stand rather than approaching the food boxes. Such behavior can be regarded as adaptive in that it results in momentary relief from pain and tension. In these terms, McClelland (1951) has restated Maier's results as follows: ". . . *avoidance motives produce behavior which, generally speaking, is more rigid or less variable than behavior produced by approach motives . . .*"

Studies by Farber (1948) and Wilcoxon (1952) have been attempts to deal experimentally with Maier's point of view. Farber's hypothesis was that the fixation of what might be conceived to be nonadaptive responses in shock situations comes about as a result of a learning principle—that of anxiety reduction. External cues which are present at the time of shock acquire the capacity to evoke anxiety, and the removal of the cues which reduce anxiety constitutes a reinforcing state of affairs. Farber believed that feeding in a situation in which anxiety had been developed would be adequate to remove the anxiety state. His experimental design consisted of giving two groups of rats 100 trials on a T maze with food reward. During the last sixty trials these animals were shocked immediately after the choice point in the maze. Following the completion of these trials, one group was fed for two ten-minute periods in the maze at the place where shock was administered. It was hypothesized that such feeding would reduce the anxiety produced by the shock. On the day following the learning trials, food was placed in the opposite goal box and shock was discontinued. The animals were then run to an extinction criterion consisting of two successive responses to the nonpreferred side which now led to food. In order to control for the possibility that the feeding activity affected the original response directly rather than by way of anxiety elimination, two additional groups were trained under similar conditions but were not shocked. As in the case with the shocked animals, one group was fed in the arm of the maze immediately after the choice point while the other group was not. Results indicated that the responses of the shocked–not-fed group were significantly more resistant to extinction than those of the shocked-fed group. Finally, there was no significant difference in resistance to extinction between the responses of the shocked-fed animals and those of the two control groups. Farber has concluded that these findings strongly suggest that fixation resulting from shock may be the result of anxiety reduction, and thus support a learning theory interpretation of Maier's findings.[14]

Wilcoxon (1952) called attention to the fact that the creation of an insoluble problem resulted in a type of partial reinforcement for the organism. As a result, he essentially replicated Maier's experimental technique except that he introduced a partial-reinforcement group. In addition to a continuous-reinforcement group, in which the animal secured continuous reward for the

[14] Maier and Ellen (1951) have re-examined Farber's data and have pointed out certain details which they believe cannot be accounted for by an anxiety-reduction theory, but which appear to be adequately explained by frustration theory. An examination of the shocked animals' behavior reveals that there is evidence of a bimodal distribution. Maier and Ellen point out that an anxiety-reduction theory does not postulate a break or split in the population, while the frustration theory would posit that some rats would not be frustrated by the shock and would extinguish as nonshock animals, whereas others would be frustrated and would show high extinction scores. Farber did indicate in his original study that rats were obtained from the anatomy and pharmacology departments as well as the psychology department, and his examination of the individual scores revealed great differences between animals bred in the psychology department from those obtained from the other laboratories. He has indicated that animals obtained from nonpsychology laboratories were much more emotional, and it would appear that the animals to which Maier and Ellen are referring came from this group. Farber's original article indicated that a test run between shocked and shock-fed subjects obtained only from the psychology laboratory indicated a difference which was significant at the 1 per cent level of confidence.

correct response, and an insoluble-problem group, in which the stimulus cards were locked in random fashion, a partial-reinforcement group was added. For this group, the correct side was unlocked on 50 per cent of the trials while the other side was always locked. Following the experimental training, all groups received a problem in which the response which led to food required a shift from the initial response. Thus, rats with position habits received visual discrimination problems, while rats with discrimination habits received problems in which a position habit led to food. Two hundred trials were allowed to permit the animals to switch to a new response and subjects failing to change were considered fixated. Results indicated that 92 per cent of the partial-reinforcement group had fixations, while just 58 per cent of the insoluble-problem group had fixations. Of the continuous-reinforcement group, 38 per cent had fixations. The difference between the partial-reinforcement- and insoluble-problem groups was significant at the 5 per cent level of confidence. Thus the greater persistence of response acquired under partial-reinforcement conditions was in line with a stimulus-response learning theory.

One observation made by individuals working in this area is that although the animals do not give up position (stereotyped) responses and adopt a discrimination habit in the test situation, they do behave differently when the positive and negative cards are on the fixated side. When the negative card is on the side of the fixation, the animals show resistance to jumping. If the positive card is on the fixated side, however, they jump directly. Ellen (1956) states: "These findings suggest that the persistence of the position response is not due to the absence of a learned alternative mode of behavior, but rather to the inherent strength of the fixated response which interferes with the expression of the learned discrimination." He has further hypothesized that if a situation was created in which the fixated response did not interfere with the expression of the learned discrimination response, the nature of the stimulus card should influence the choice of the response; thus choice of response in such a situation should be dependent on whatever learning has occurred.

In order to examine this phenomenon, the apparatus, which typically consists of two windows, was modified to include a third window. The left window was designated as number 1, the middle window as number 2, and the right window as number 3. The procedure was to place the jumping stand between either windows 1 and 2, or between 2 and 3. If the stand was placed between windows 1 and 2, the animal's fixated response was on the right side, there would be two windows on the animal's right. Ellen's (1956) technique was to place the positive card in one of these two right windows and the negative card in the other. The positive card could be on the near right side or the far right side. Essentially, the same technique could be used for the animal's left position habits when the jumping stand was placed between windows 2 and 3. Results indicated that the positive or negative attributes of the card on the fixated side determined the choice between the near and far windows on that side. Thus, when the animal was confronted with a near and far window on the fixated side, the near window would be chosen more frequently than the far if the near window contained the positive card. If the far window contained the positive card, that window would be chosen more frequently. Ellen believes that the results of this study refute any theory which attempts to account for the persistence of abnormal fixations by assuming that the animals are concerned primarily in reducing anxiety conditioned to the jumping platform and are not interested in avoiding the negative card. He further believes that the animals are able to express variable, adaptive behavior when the expression of such behavior is compatible with the fixated response. This means that when a response becomes fixated, the fixation refers only to the response tendency itself and is not attached to any particular place or object in space.

12 • INSTRUMENTAL RESPONSES, IV
MOTIVATIONAL ANTECEDENTS
AND THE PERCEPTUAL PROCESS

As we have indicated earlier, in this chapter we are interested in examining the role of motivational antecedents on those instrumental responses from which the operation of a perceptual process has been inferred. In contrast to a number of other investigators, we are defining perception as a process rather than as a response or product.[1] Thus, perception is a process which mediates some instrumental response.

One problem with this definition, and one with which many individuals have grappled, has been to distinguish instrumental responses mediated by the perceptual process from those mediated by other processes. Garner, Hake, and Eriksen (1956) have written of the "converging operation" to be used in making this distinction; Hochberg (1956) has posited more specific criteria. Perceptual processes, Hochberg (1956) points out, are inferred (1) from responses dealing with events which are phenomenally "here, now and real," and (2) from the ambiguity existing in certain stimulus-response relationships. The first criterion differentiates a perceptual process from a memorial one, the second dis-

[1] Allport (1955), for example, has stated that perception can be regarded as nothing more or less than a discriminatory response.

tinguishes perceptual processes from processes involved in sensation on the one hand and imagery on the other. Hochberg suggests a continuum with one extreme expressing a psychophysical correspondence in which "our knowledge of the variance of some aspect of the stimulus object is necessary and sufficient to predict completely the response variance of the subject." Here then, we have sensation. At the other end of the continuum, "the subjects' responses are completely independent of the presented stimulus, knowledge of which is neither necessary nor sufficient for prediction of response." Here we are confronted with judgment or imagery. Between these two extremes is an area in which the stimulus accounts for some but not all of the response variance. Here, Hochberg asserts, the perceptual process operates, and it may be fruitful to inquire as to how much of the residual variance may be sought in factors of motivation and habit.

Our primary task in this chapter, however, is not to set up arbitrary criteria in an attempt to distinguish perceptual processes from others, but rather to examine those studies which the investigators themselves have hypothesized to tap the perceptual process.

Interest in this general area has been recent and vigorous. Some of the impetus for such interest has been generated by the experimental work of Murphy and his colleagues, who have emphasized an autistic approach to perception—the notion that perceptual processes move in the direction of need satisfaction. The early work of Bruner and Postman (1949) is also important, inasmuch as it was these investigators who stressed the point of view that perception was an instrumental activity, with such activity related to the motivation of the organism.[2] Before proceeding to our major task, it seems appropriate to examine once again types of response measurement.

MEASUREMENT

Types

It would be impossible to discuss in detail all of the varying types of stimulus situations and their responses which have been used in

[2] This general position has been reformulated. As more recently conceived by these authors (Bruner 1951, Postman 1951), the perceptual response is now believed to be dependent upon the strength of the organism's hypothesis or set. An important determinant of hypotheses strength, however, is motivational support. In essence, then, motivation plays its role through its effects on the determination of hypotheses.

the investigation of the influence of motivational antecedents on perception. An examination of the bulk of the experimental studies in the area, however, reveals four primary types. The first relates to the use of projective measures. Murray's Thematic Apperception test or a variation thereof, for example, has been a frequently used stimulus. Although such stimuli may be tapping imaginal processes, they are more frequently conceived to be perceptual in nature. The second type of response relates to recognition thresholds obtained for either words or pictures with, typically, the employment of some psychophysical procedure. Words or pictures, often related to some motivational antecedent, may be presented with a tachistoscope at speeds or under illumination levels which make recognition impossible on early presentations of the material. The material is then presented at slower speeds or increased levels of brightness until the subject is just able to recognize it. A third type has been one in which the subject is asked to estimate the size of some object. Investigators in the area have often presented some type of disc, perhaps coins of varying denominations or similar sized slugs, to their subjects, who were then asked to estimate their size. Finally, the last type of measurement concerns the use of ambiguous figures. Subjects are given training to "see" one aspect of an ambiguous figure. After such training, the total figure is presented with the perceptual process inferred from what the subject reports.

That there is a measurement problem, related to the interrelationships among these response measures, is obvious. Postman (1953), in discussing this topic, has stated that an inference concerning the operation of a perceptual process may be made only if it was based on two classes of responses. For example, recognition threshold measures might be supplemented by measures based on size estimation. Or size estimation measures might be supplemented by the use of responses obtained by some projective technique. Although it is often tacitly assumed that the operation of one variable which produces an effect upon a response should produce similiar effects upon other response measures, studies examining such interrelationships have been almost non-existent. In this regard, we have previously noted a similar state of affairs existing in the area of learning. In general, it may be said that the basic approach in the area at the present time has been merely to demonstrate that motivational antecedents *do* play a role in the operation of the perceptual process.

MOTIVATIONAL ANTECEDENTS

Physiological Needs

One of the earliest studies which related motivational antecedents of a physiological nature to perceptual processes was that of Sanford (1936). Interestingly enough, Sanford did not conceive of his experiment as being related to perceptual processes at all, but rather to imaginal ones. Children ranging in age from seven to eleven years were given a form of the TAT and a word association test either (a) after breakfast, or (b) before lunch, or (c) after lunch. Each subject was tested under all conditions. Results indicated that all subjects examined immediately prior to the meal gave significantly more food responses than when presented with similar material after a meal. In a second study (1937), college students were tested at varying times during the normal eating cycle as well as at the end of 24 hours of deprivation. Using number of food responses as the dependent variable, and the hours of deprivation (1 through 5) as the independent variable, a rough S curve was obtained; i.e., the greater the deprivation period, the more food responses were obtained. The 24-hour-deprived group provided responses only slightly greater than those subjects who were examined near the close of the normal eating cycle.

In another early study, Levine, Chein, and Murphy (1942) used a ground glass screen to provide ambiguity to a number of chromatic and achromatic drawings. Subjects were asked to verbalize their associations to such stimuli. Control subjects were tested after eating, while subjects comprising the experimental group (five subjects rotated through the conditions) were tested after either one, three, six, or nine hours of deprivation. The findings revealed that the number of food responses to achromatic cards increased at three and six hours of deprivation, but decreased at nine hours to a point slightly below the three-hour period. Responses to chromatic cards, on the other hand, increased up to the three-hour deprivation interval but decreased after that.[3]

The studies of McClelland and Atkinson (1948) and Atkinson and McClelland (1948) have tended to support these early findings. In the McClelland and Atkinson study, candidates for

[3] It should be pointed out that when total number of responses were analyzed, the number of food responses for the experimental group was not significantly different from that of the control.

submarine training school were placed under either 1, 4, or 16 hours of food deprivation. The investigators, under the guise of investigating subliminal perception, presented 12 blank "pictures." As each blank was presented, the subjects were asked to answer a number of questions about it. In a second phase of their experiment, smudges or shadows were projected on the screen instead of the visual blanks. In the second study (Atkinson and McClelland 1948), pictures drawn mostly from Murray's TAT were substituted for the blanks. The subjects were again under 1, 4, or 16 hours of food deprivation, and given 20 seconds to observe the picture and then given five minutes to write about it. Questions designed to elicit object, instrumental, and consummatory responses were used to guide the subject's writing. The findings of both studies revealed that responses related to goal objects (i.e., apples) did not show any relationship to deprivation states; responses related to consummatory activity decreased markedly, while responses related to instrumental objects (i.e., knives) and instrumental activity, increased as a function of hours of deprivation.

A continuation of these studies has been made by Clark (1952), who, using college students, investigated the effects of sexual needs by using sexually arousing stimuli (pictures of female nudes or the presence of an attractive, perfumed female test administrator) on written stories based on TAT slides. His results, in contrast to what might be expected, indicated that control groups, which had been shown a series of slides of landscape scenes, etc., revealed *more* sexual responses in the written stories than the experimental groups. These findings were interpreted that under normal conditions the guilt evoked by sexual arousal was sufficient to inhibit the expression of sexual responses.

Lindner (1953) on the other hand, using types of projective techniques developed by himself, obtained significantly more sexual responses from sexual offenders than from prisoners who were incarcerated for other offenses.

Wispe (1954), interested in relating deprivation states to responses obtained in a word association test, deprived college students of food and water for 0, 10, or 24 hours, and then presented them with a list of neutral, food, and water-related words. Each subject was instructed to give the first word that came to mind and to continue associating for a period of time. The first 19 responses to each word for each subject were recorded. Results indicated that more food, water, and neutral word-association responses were made to food, water, and neutral words respectively. There was an increase in the number of food and water responses at 10 hours of deprivation but a decrease at 24. Analysis of the type of response revealed that responses which were concerned with behavior instrumental to need satisfaction increased, while responses related to goal objects decreased—a finding similar to that obtained by McClelland and Atkinson (1948).

The findings of Keys, Brozek, Henschel, Mickelsen, and Taylor (1950) provide the only evidence to cast doubt upon the validity of the previously cited studies. The major objective of the Keys, *et al.* study was to describe and analyze psychological changes induced by a prolonged reduced diet. The subjects, volunteer conscientious objectors, lived on such a diet for 24 weeks. Although it was observed that the overt behavior of the men was drastically changed by the need for food, (reading of cookbooks, acquiring food-related items such as hot plates, coffee pots, etc. and development of food-substitute practices), there was no tendency for projective techniques to reveal significant changes in any of the scoring categories as a function of the deprivation period.

In contrast to responses to projective techniques, recognition thresholds have also been used to investigate the influence of physiological needs.

Lazarus, Yousem, and Arenberg (1953) tachistoscopically presented ten slides containing food as well as nonfood objects to subjects who had gone without food for varying numbers of hours. This latter information was obtained from their subjects after the experiment had been terminated. When recognition thresholds for the pictures were plotted against hours of deprivation, thresholds for food objects decreased for two and four hours of deprivation, but then rose sharply at six, the longest deprivation period which was reported. Recognition of nonfood pictures on the other hand, indicated no relationship to hours of food deprivation. In a second experiment, in which a multiple-choice response situation was substituted for the free-association response, deprivation periods did not produce a similar effect.

Wispe and Drambarean (1953), using a word—rather than a picture—recognition test and actually manipulating food and water deprivation periods (0, 10, or 24 hours deprivation), also found lowered recognition thresholds to be associated with increased hours of deprivation. Taylor's (1956a) replication of this study, however, did not provide confirmation.

Finally, Gilchrist and Nesberg (1952) have conducted a series of studies investigating the influence of food and water deprivation on an individual's ability to make illuminance matches of projected pictures of food- and liquid-related objects. The experimental procedure consisted of projecting images of food objects, i.e., fried chicken, T-bone steak, etc. on a screen for 15 seconds. The projector light was then turned off for 10 seconds, following which the subjects were asked to adjust the brightness of the image to the degree of illumination which they had previously seen. Food-deprived subjects made one series of matches immediately following their noon meal, another after the time they usually would have eaten their evening meal, and a final one right after they usually would have eaten breakfast the next morning. A control group followed the same routine except that they ate each of the two meals missed by the deprived group. Results indicated that the deprived group made significantly brighter matches than the satiated group, and that this effect increased as a function of hours of deprivation. Similar findings were obtained in Experiment II when the subjects were asked to go without food or water for a period of up to eight hours, and the projected images were water-related objects. Experiments III and IV not only confirmed the results obtained in the first two studies, but also indicated the necessity for using need-related images in order to obtain the experimental findings. Images consisting of homogeneous color fields, or landscapes, did not result in the deprived group's making brighter matches.

The interaction of physiological needs with other variables has been an area which has received scant attention. In one such study, Klein (1954) investigated the relationship between thirst and interference proneness. This latter variable was measured by having the subject read aloud as quickly and as accurately as possible the colors red, green, yellow, and blue, which were printed in incongruent color names. For example, if the word "blue" appeared in red ink, the subject was to read "red." On the basis of ease or difficulty that the subjects had in performing the task, thirsty and satiated groups were further broken down into high- and low-interference groups. Perpetual tasks required of the subject involved free association, recognition thresholds, and size estimations. In the size-estimation task, the only task which indicated the interference effect, the subject adjusted a variable circle of light until it appeared equal in size to a standard disc which was at his left. The disc was slightly less in size than a half dollar and upon it appeared a symbol which was either thirst-related (i.e., coke, highball, etc.) or neutral. The discs were matched for size, brightness, and color. Results based on size errors indicated that thirst was not a significant variable independently but was when it interacted with the interference variable.

Discussion

One difficulty with many of the studies in which the physiological needs of the organism have been manipulated has to do with the problem of set. In those studies in which the subject has been instructed to refrain from eating and/or drinking for a given period of time, there is the problem of evaluating whether or not such instructions have also resulted in producing a set for stimuli related to the needs—the set, then, becoming the significant variable. Taylor's (1956a) replication of the Wispe and Drambarean (1953) study not only failed to confirm their findings but also indicated that subjects given an appropriate set exhibited significantly lower thresholds for need-related words than did a "no set" group. Similarly, Postman and Crutchfield (1952), using a type of projective technique, found that the establishment of a food set was an important variable in eliciting food-related words. In this study, the investigators provided their subjects with skeleton words—words in which two letters were missing in various positions. The task was to construct meaningful English words by filling in the blanks. All of the critical stimulus words had at least two solutions, one of which was a food word and the other a nonfood word. In addition to manipulating stimulus words, for which the probability of food responses varied from high to low, the subject's set was varied by forcing different groups of subjects to give either 0, 1, 2, 3, or 5 food responses before responding to the ambiguous words on the list. The intensity of hunger was obtained by having the subject indicate the number of hours since he had last eaten, and also by obtaining a rating from each subject regarding how hungry he was. The findings indicated that the length of the deprivation period was not a significant variable, although it did interact significantly with that of set.

Where, of course, the deprivation conditions are not manipulated, as in the Lazarus, Yousem, and Arenberg (1953) study, the problem of set does not manifest itself. Since the independent variable was not manipulated, however, it is possible that some other condition which covaried with deprivation was responsible for the effect.

In spite of these difficulties, the weight of the experimental evidence supports the view that perceptual responses, certainly as measured with projective techniques, reflect the operation of motivational variables related to an individual's physiological needs.

Ego-Involved Antecedents

Most of the studies investigating the motivation-perception area have been interested in motivational antecedents which, in contrast to physiological needs, are believed to be of considerably more importance in the motivational system of man. Attempts have been made to manipulate such variables as success, failure, threat, and anxiety in an effort to determine their influence on the perceptual process. In keeping with our previous discussion, we would group these under the more general motivational antecedent of ego involvement.

Achievement and Success Needs

McClelland and Liberman (1949), using the familiar TAT cards as well as performance on an anagram task, grouped subjects into either a high, middle, or low need for achievement (n-achievement). Some weeks after these measures were obtained, the subjects were asked to recognize 30 tachistoscopically presented words. Ten of these words were achievement related, ten were security related, and ten were neutral. Relative to the threshold for the neutral words, the high n-achievement group perceived achievement-related words at significantly lower thresholds than either the middle or low n-achievement groups. Security-related words, on the other hand, were perceived significantly more easily by the high and middle n-achievement groups than for the low. The authors' general hypothesis that an increase in n-achievement leads first to avoid failure and then to greater concentration on success, was confirmed.

A somewhat related approach but one in which the motivational antecedent was success or failure rather than a need for achievement, was taken by Postman and Brown (1952). A level of aspiration task was initially used to establish a framework of success or failure. Members of the success group were then permitted to exceed their stated goals while members of the failure group were not. Following this, four words connoting success, four connoting failure, and four connoting instrumental striving, along with equally familiar control words were presented for tachistoscopic recognition. Results indicated that the success group perceived the success-related words, and the failure group perceived the failure words, with both groups doing so at significantly lower recognition thresholds than for equally familiar control words.

That success or failure experiences do exert some influence upon the perceptual process has been further indicated in a study by Wapner, Werner, and Krus (1957), who found that the localization of a horizon in space was effected by whether or not a student had received an A (success) or F (failure) on a recent examination.

Value

Many investigators have been interested in examining the influence of value without attempting to place it within some motivational framework. In our discussion of motivational antecedents, however, we noted that ego involvement was related to the value system with which an individual identifies; hence, value can be conceived of as a motivational antecedent which has its roots in ego involvement.

In one of the pioneer studies in this area, Bruner and Goodman (1947) examined the influence of value on size estimation. This study has been referred to so frequently in the literature that it is only necessary to point out some of its significant details. Ten-year-old children, coming from either rich or poor environments, adjusted a light source to the size of a variety of coins present and also from memory. A control group adjusted a light source to the size of a grey disc which varied in size so that it fit the sizes of the coins used in the experimental-group situation. The results indicated that the coins, presumed to be socially valued objects, were judged larger than the grey discs. Results also indicated that the poor group of children overestimated the size of the coins more than did the rich group.

A second study by Bruner and Postman (1948), as well as studies by Ashley, Harper, and Runyon (1951), Dukes and Bevan (1952), and Solley and Lee (1955), have also reported findings which have supported the position that size estimation is influenced by value. In the Bruner and Postman (1948) study, the effect of symbolic value on perception was investigated. The positive symbol used was a dollar sign, the negative was a swastika, while the neutral symbol was a square with two diagonals. The varying symbols were inscribed in black ink on bright plastic circular discs which varied in diameter in quarter-inch steps from ¾ to 1½ inches. There were two experimental groups, one which made judgments of neutral and positive discs, while the other group made size judgments of neutral and negative discs. Results indicated that the discs inscribed with the dollar symbol were judged largest, while the swastika discs were judged next in size, with the neutral discs judged smallest.

The Ashley, Harper, and Runyon (1951) study is an interesting one since their subjects were hypnotized, and an artificial life history which stressed either a poor or rich economic status was induced. The subjects were then instructed to adjust the size of a spot of light until it looked to them to be the size of a penny, nickel, dime, or quarter. In one phase of the study, the subjects had to make judgments based upon the remembered size of each of the four coins, while in the second phase, the coin was present on a card and the judgment was made from this. Results indicated that the size of the light spot that the subject set as equal to the coins differed markedly between the rich and poor states in both the present and remembered size of the coins. A second part of their experiment consisted of using a grey metal slug as the experimental disc with the subjects told that it was made up either of lead, silver, white gold, or platinum. Again the task was to adjust the spot of light until it appeared to be the size of the slug. Results indicated that the size of the slug increased with the cost of the metal of which the subject was told the slug was made.

There is an obvious relationship between value and affective states; in general, objects which are of value to the organism are liked as well. As a result, Beams' (1954) investigation of the influence of an individual's affective state on size estimation has relevance in this section. Subjects were first selected on the basis of liking and disliking certain desserts. The experimental procedure consisting of then showing them these actual desserts for a period of five seconds. Following this, they were asked to adjust a Kodachrome image of the food object until in their judgment it was the same size as the actual object. Results indicated 51 of the 60 subjects used made a larger comparative image of the liked dessert than of the disliked. As Beams has concluded, it would seem to follow that a subject's like or dislike for the desserts used influenced his perception of the magnitude of the object. A somewhat similar finding, viewed within a value context, had been previously reported by Dukes and Bevan (1951) who found that children judged jars filled with candy (a valued object) to be heavier than similarly weighted jars filled with sand and sawdust.

Unfortunately, the empirical evidence has not always supported the hypothesis that value (or affective states) influences the perceptual response of size estimation. Carter and Schooler's (1949) replication of the early Bruner and Goodman study (1947) did not confirm these latter investigator's findings.[4]

Similarly, Klein, Schlesinger, and Meister (1951) were unable to confirm the Bruner and Postman (1948) findings of the role of symbolic value. Finally, Lysak and Gilchrist (1955), interested in this area, used paper currency and control rectangles with signs of varying complexity as stimulus objects. Adult subjects were used instead of children, and the authors introduced an additional condition in which the subjects were told that accurate estimation would lead to the obtaining of the stimulus object. Results indicated that the monetary value of the bills (one, five or ten dollars) did not appreciably influence size estimation nor did the "goal availability" of the stimulus object.

A second perceptual response measure—recognition threshold—has also been used to measure the influence of value. In an early study, Postman, Bruner, and McGinnies (1948) administered the Allport-Vernon Study of Values to college students. Following

---

[4] A later study by Bruner and Rodrigues (1953) attempted to explore some of the factors which might have produced divergencies in the findings of Bruner and Goodman (1947) and Carter and Schooler (1949). The variables which differed between the two experiments and those which were manipulated in the Bruner and Rodrigues study were: (1) the value of the disc, (2) attitudes of the subjects, and (3) the characteristics of the light patches. One group of subjects was presented with a penny, nickel, and quarter to judge, while a second group was presented with correspondingly sized nickel-colored metal discs. A third group judged grey cardboard discs. Half of the children in each group were given the set to think of the buying power of the money, while the other half was given the set to think about the accuracy of the size judgments which they were making. Finally, one third of the subjects used a variable six-chorded light figure for matching, a second third used a nine-chorded figure, while the last third used a circular light figure. The most crucial and significant finding of the study was, that as one increases the value of the coins, the extent of the overestimation increases more significantly than with metal or paper discs. This, the authors have called relative accentuation.

this, six sets of words, each of which represented one of the All-port-Vernon value categories, were presented tachistoscopically. Experimental findings indicated that lower recognition times were found for those words which were related to an individual's dominant value system. Haigh and Fiske (1952), using a somewhat different method for measuring value, and Vanderplas and Blake (1949) using auditory rather than visual recognition thresholds, have obtained findings confirming those reported by Postman, Bruner, and McGinnies (1948). Finally, Smith, Parker, and Robinson (1951) had groups of subjects recognize clusters of white dots flashed on a screen. Control subjects were given one point for each correct cluster reported; experimental subjects were given one point for each dot in each correct cluster. Prizes of five and ten dollars were used to motivate the subjects but an effort was made to insure honest reporting by deducting 10 per cent from a subject's score for each incorrect response. Such a technique motivated both groups toward strict accuracy but subjects in the experimental group were provided with conflicting motivation to see as many dots as possible. Results indicated that the experimental group generated significantly more overestimations.

A number of the studies which we have cited have lent support for a motivating function which Postman, Bruner, and McGinnies (1948) have called sensitization. That is, certain types of motivational antecedents (i.e., value) result in the organism becoming more sensitive to stimuli which are related to the antecedents themselves. Such sensitization is purported to be reflected in the varying response measures which presumably tap the perceptual process.

In addition to sensitization, a second motivational function—that of perceptual defense—has also been posited. Perceptual defense has been conceived to be a learned, functional response consisting of a delay in the recognition of an inimical stimulus until such a time as accurate identification was inescapable. Thus, any stimulus, the perception of which has been associated with threat, anxiety, or punishment, presumably results in an initial delay in its recognition and acceptance. Emphasis upon this function leads to a consideration of the role of these types of motivational antecedents.

Anxiety or Fear

One of the early studies investigating anxiety or fear on perception was that of Murray (1933). Children were asked to rate photographs of individuals taken from a current magazine on a nine-point scale. The judgments were made on the basis of how pleasant or malicious the faces appeared. Ratings were obtained under pleasure-producing as well as fear-producing conditions, the latter situation invoked by having the children play a game of murder. Results indicated that 73 per cent of the photographs were judged to be more malicious following the fear-producing situation.

An early study, in which the defense mechanism was hypothesized, however, was done by Bruner and Postman (1947a), who had their subjects report the first word associated with each of a series of words, among which were a number of emotionally toned ones. The six words having the slowest reaction times, the six with the fastest, and six from the middle were then selected for tachistoscopic presentation. Results indicated that increased recognition times were associated with those words which had long association reaction times; the increased recognition times were interpreted as representing a type of defense mechanism which protected the individual from anxiety-laden stimuli. Some words with lengthy associative reaction times were recognized at exposures well below the average recognition threshold, and these findings were interpreted as representing the sensitization function which we have already discussed. Presumably, such words touched relevant value systems of the individuals.

The use of the word association test to obtain words which were related to an individual's anxiety, or emotionality in general, was replaced by using taboo words. McGinnies (1949) selected a list of neutral words (apple, dance, child, etc.) and seven taboo or emotionally toned words (raped, whore, kotex, etc.), presented them tachistoscopically, and obtained recognition thresholds as well as galvanic skin responses. The perceptual defense mechanism was inferred from the findings which indicated that the subjects displayed significantly higher recognition thresholds for the taboo than for the neutral words. Moreover, during the pre-recognition period, the subjects responded to the taboo words with a significantly greater galvanic skin response magnitude than to the neutral words.

One weakness of many of the sensitization and perceptual-defense studies was identified almost immediately. In general, the experimenters did not control for differences in the familiarity or frequency of the words which they used. As a result, a number of studies were undertaken to assess the importance of this variable.

Solomon and Howes (1951) replicated the Postman, Bruner, and McGinnies (1948) study—the study which had demonstrated the influence of value on recognition thresholds. In order to control frequency, they devised new lists in which half of the words for each value area was of a high frequency, and the other half was low. Their findings indicated that when recognition thresholds for *high frequency* words were related to the subjects' value profiles, no relationship was obtained. On the other hand, the recognition thresholds for *low frequency* words did indicate a positive relationship. Rather than assigning a sensitizing function to value in order to account for these latter findings, the authors posited that people who are highly interested in a subject generally use words associated with that subject more often than people who have no special interest in that subject. Thus, high value areas increase the probability that an individual has had more familiarity with words in that value area.[5]

A second study by Howes and Solomon (1951) demonstrated that the visual duration threshold of a word, measured tachistoscopically by an ascending method of limits, had an approximately linear function of the log of the relative frequency with which the word occurs in the Thorndike-Lorge word count. Product moment correlations between the two variables ranged from $-.68$ to $-.75$.[6]

McGinnies' (1949) experimental findings, which had led to the positing of a perceptual defense mechanism, were also questioned by Howes and Solomon (1950) on the basis that the high recognition

[5] Postman and Schneider (1951), although confirming the findings of Solomon and Howes (1951), rejected frequency or response probability as a basic psychological variable and continued to maintain that directive factors such as the variable of personal values are useful in the development of a general theory of perception.

[6] A little different way of looking at the influence of frequency is to assume that the organism acquires certain response strengths or biases as a function of the frequency of his observations, and it is these biases which determine what he reports. Studies by Goldiamond and Hawkins (1958) and Newbigging (1960) have provided experimental support for such a position. In the Goldiamond and Hawkins study, subjects were given training in which they read nonsense syllables with different frequencies. Following such training, they were given the task of "recognizing" these words when they were presumably flashed on the screen. Actually blanks were projected. Results indicated that the words which were "recognized" were a function of the frequency of previous presentation. Newbigging (1960), after selecting individuals on the basis of dominant value areas on the Allport-Vernon-Lindzey Study of Values, instituted a training session in which words selected from each of the six value areas were pronounced by the subjects. The subjects were then instructed to report which of these words they saw when they were supposedly flashed on the screen. Actually, a plain white card rather than a word was exposed. Results indicated a significant tendency for subjects to report more words related to their dominant value area as compared with their nondominant value areas.

thresholds for taboo words were a function of response suppression —the tendency for a subject not to report the objectionable words, or at least to withhold them until they were absolutely certain of their content. Although this argument was rejected by McGinnies (1950), a considerable amount of evidence has been obtained to attest to its importance.

Postman, Bronson, and Gropper (1953) examined those conditions which influence a subject's readiness to give verbal reports of taboo words. Four different sets of instructions were given prior to the presentation of a stimulus list which included taboo words as well as neutral ones. An uninformed group was not given any indication that taboo words would be included among the list. A second, informed group, was explicitly warned to expect some taboo words among the stimuli. A third group, a facilitation one, was told to expect taboo words and also told that difficulties in perceiving such words were characteristic of poor adjustment. A fourth group, an inhibition one, was given to understand that difficulty in perceiving taboo words was indicative of good personal adjustment.

Results indicated that the uninformed group (Group I) had higher relative thresholds than any of the groups forewarned to expect taboo words. Remaining differences among the forewarned groups indicated that the facilitation group (Group III) had the lowest relative thresholds for the taboo words. It is also interesting to note that the thresholds for the informed group (Group II)— the group which had been neither encouraged nor discouraged to report taboo words—were essentially the same as those of the inhibition group (Group IV). The experimental findings of Lacy, Lewinger, and Adamson (1953) as well as Freeman (1954) and Cowen and Obrist (1958) have also provided support for the position that the kind of instructions provided the subject may be responsible for producing differences in the recognition of normal and taboo words.[7]

One might expect that the more commerce or reinforcement a subject has with taboo words in an experimental situation, the more willing he would be to report them. Experimental support for this point of view is found in the studies of Bitterman and Kniffin (1953) and Banks and Walters (1959). Bitterman and Kniffin

[7] Although Cowen and Obrist (1958) found that instructions which increased a subject's tendency to expect threat words decreased the discrepancy between threat- and neutral-word thresholds, they did find that threat words had a higher report threshold than neutral words. This finding was in contrast to that which was reported by Postman, Bronson, and Gropper (1953).

found a marked decline in the thresholds for taboo words as a function of the position of the words in the series. The fact that no order effect was evident for neutral words suggested that the order effect found for critical words could not be attributed to tachistoscopic practice. Banks and Walters (1959) found that a training session in which taboo words were reinforced reduced the visual recognition threshold for these words.

Finally, descriptive evidence for the operation of a response-suppression variable has also been provided by Whittaker, Gilchrist, and Fischer (1952).

As a result of the word-frequency and response-suppression criticisms, some studies have attempted to control these variables. One such technique, used by Cowen and Beier (1950, 1954), was to have subjects examine a test booklet in which decreasingly blurred visions of a single word appeared as the pages were turned. Findings from their first study indicated that the recognition of the taboo words took significantly longer than recognition of the neutral words. With regard to response suppression, they believed that their technique of reading to the subjects a long list of words, some of which they indicated they were going to use in the experiment at a later time, encouraged their subjects not to withhold their responses. Although they did not actually match the taboo words with the neutral ones for frequency, their inability to find a correlation between the number of trials required for correct identification of the test words and word frequency was interpreted as evidence that the frequency of the words did not contribute to their experimental findings.

And, Aronfreed, Messick, and Diggory (1953), in an effort to eliminate response suppression, used unpleasant rather than taboo words. Although their findings supported the perceptual defense function, Goodstein's (1954) analysis of the words used in their study revealed that the frequency variable was not controlled—the unpleasant words had a much lower frequency rating than the neutral or pleasant ones.

A study by Wiener (1955) is interesting in that frequency was controlled by using identical stimulus words; their neutrality- or anxiety-producing quality was achieved by embedding them with other words. An example of the technique would be in placing the word "fairy" among other words such as angel or fantasy. On the other hand, the threat quality was obtained by embedding "fairy" with such words as queer, male, or odd. The test booklet used by

Cowen and Beier, previously described, was used. Surprisingly enough, the threat group required significantly *fewer* trials than the "neutral" group to report the tabooed words correctly. Presumably, the anxiety situation resulted in a sensitizing rather than a defense function. The reconciliation of this finding with other experimental studies was made in a subsequent experiment by Carpenter, Wiener, and Carpenter (1956), which differentiated individuals on the basis of clinical criteria into sensitized or defense groups. Individuals who were classified as "sex sensitizers" perceived sexual words with significantly fewer trials than those classified as "sex repressors."

The Carpenter, *et al.* study points up the possibility that personality characteristics of the individual may play an important role in the operation of the perceptual functions of defense and sensitization. Mathews and Wertheimer (1958), for example, have found that subjects scoring high on the hysteria scale of the Minnesota Multiphasic Personality Inventory demonstrated a significant perceptual defense effect—an effect over and above that which could be attributed to response suppression.

Discussion

The failure of many investigators to control the word-frequency and response-suppression variables in investigating the role of motivational antecedents makes any conclusion in this general area hazardous, because the experimental findings have indicated that both of these variables are important in influencing experimental findings.

It should be pointed out, however, that there may be some overemphasis upon the role of frequency. What is meant here may be illustrated by a study by Solomon and Postman (1952), confirmed by King-Ellison and Jenkins (1954) and Sprague (1959). In the Solomon and Postman study, pronounceable syllables were presented with frequencies ranging from 1 to 25 during a training period. Subsequently, these syllables were then presented tachistoscopically and recognition thresholds obtained. Although a subject's recognition threshold was related to the frequency of presentation during training, there was little difference in the thresholds between those words which during training had been presented just 10 times as contrasted to 25 repetitions.

Sprague (1959) has obtained similar findings. He provided a

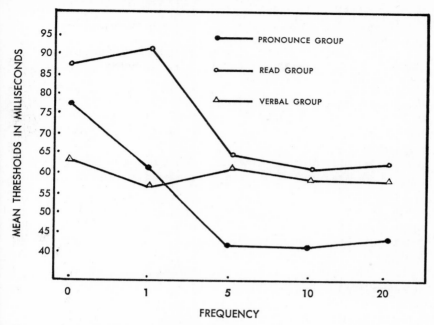

FIG. 12–1. THE EFFECT OF DIFFERENTIAL TRAINING AND FREQUENCY OF PRESENTATION ON TACHISTOSCOPIC RECOGNITION THRESHOLDS. (Adapted from Sprague, 1959)

training period which consisted of presenting nonsense words (i.e., kesqul) either 0, 1, 5, 10, or 20 times to three groups of experimental subjects. One group had to pronounce the word, a second group had to read it, while a third group pronounced it after hearing the experimenter pronounce it. Results indicated that the frequency variable was significant; an examination of Figure 12.1, however, indicates little difference among the groups after having been presented with the word five or more times.

Nonetheless, the variables of word frequency and response suppression are sufficiently pervasive in their influence that other techniques should be used to examine the role of motivational antecedents on the perceptual process. The use of rewards and punishments manipulated during the training period and then followed by a perceptual task represents one method by which the influence of these variables may be minimized.

The Influence of Rewards and Punishments

In contrast to the sensitizing and defense functions of motivational antecedents, Murphy (1947) has hypothesized that perceptual responses are learned in essentially the same way as other instrumental responses—that is, that perceptual learning develops in the direction of reward and away from punishment. In contrast to the studies which we have already discussed, the experimental technique investigating reward and punishments has involved the use of a learning situation in which certain stimuli may be rewarded and/or punished. A test situation is then used to examine the influence of the independent variable.

Early studies emphasizing the action of both reward and punishment in the experimental situation were done by Proshansky and Murphy (1942), using size estimations as an indicator of a perceptual response, and Schafer and Murphy (1943), using ambiguous figures. The material used by Proshansky and Murphy (1942) consisted of varying weights or lengths of lines. Lines drawn on white cards with black ink were either long (5, 6, or 7 inches); intermediate (2½, 3, or 3½ inches); or short (2, 3, or 4 inches). The weights were also divided into three classes: heavy, intermediate, or light. After a pretraining period for the experimental group in which the subjects were asked to estimate the materials, a training period was instituted in which the subjects perceived the lines and weights without making overt responses. Long lines and heavy weights were rewarded by having the subjects receive 15 cents; short lines and light weights were punished by removing 15 cents; intermediate lines and weights were rewarded or punished on a random schedule. In the test period, the subjects re-estimated the lines and weights. A control group was given similar training, but neither rewards nor punishments were provided. Results indicated that the experimental subjects showed a significant shift in estimates of both lines and weights in the direction of those which had been rewarded, while the control group showed no significant shifts.[8]

The stimuli used by Schafer and Murphy (1943) were ambiguous figure-ground drawings comprising two faces that fit within a circle, with each half circle being seen as a separate face. During the

[8] The results are somewhat difficult to interpret, however, since one would have predicted that reinforcement might have resulted in the individual's overestimating the length of the long lines; one would also have expected an underestimation of those lines and weights which were punished. This latter finding did not occur.

training period, the faces were cut out and separately presented along with their associated names. When one of the two faces appeared, the subject was rewarded by being given two or four cents; whenever the other appeared, the subject was punished by the loss of the same amount. Training was divided into two sets of fifty presentations. A test series was then provided, the subject being informed that there would be no rewards or punishments but that he was to demonstrate how well he had learned the faces and their names. Thirty-two presentations of the reversible figures were provided. The findings, limited to the first sixteen presentations, indicated that of a total of 67 presentations of faces, 54 of these were perceptions of those faces which had been rewarded in the training series.

A subsequent and similar study was done by Rock and Fleck (1950), however, and did not confirm the Schafer and Murphy (1943) findings. Rock and Fleck reported no reliable differences between the number of rewarded faces and the number of punished faces perceived during the test period. Jackson (1954) believed that some of the apparatus and procedure differences between the two studies might have accounted for the different findings, and in his first experiment, which essentially replicated the Schafer-Murphy (1943) study, his results confirmed the findings of these investigators. On the other hand, a second experiment, in which the phenomenal size of the figure presented was more in keeping with the Rock and Fleck study, resulted in findings which were similar to those of Rock and Fleck. As Jackson (1954) has indicated, the evidence suggests that the method of presentation may be an important variable in accounting for the differences between the two studies.

The influence of reward and punishment on recognition thresholds has been investigated by Rigby and Rigby (1956) and Snyder and Snyder (1956). In the Rigby and Rigby study, a training period was first provided in which children played a block-tossing game. Varying letters were placed on the sides of a block, and when certain letters were turned up, the children were rewarded with candy. For other letters, candy was taken away, while finally, some letters provided neither reward nor punishment. A second group of children was given similar treatment, except that the letters which resulted in reward or punishment for the first group were not exposed. Tachistoscopic thresholds for the letters presented during training to the first group were obtained for both groups. Results indicated that lower recognition thresholds were associated with those letters which were reinforced. Moreover, letters which were associated with five reinforcements had lower thresholds than those which were associated with two. No differences, however, were found among letters which were punished, neutral, or absent in the training series.

Snyder and Snyder (1956) used an auditory recognition test in order to examine the influence of reward and punishment. During a training period, money was given to the subject whenever one voice was presented, and taken away with the presentation of a second. In the test situation, the two voices were presented together and in competition, with the subject asked to report the material which was presented. Results for this test period indicated significantly more recognition of the material presented by the rewarded voice.

Reward

In an effort to better control the effects of reward and punishment, some investigators have manipulated these conditions singly. In a series of studies, Sommer and his associates (Sommer and Ayllon 1956, Solley and Sommer 1957, Solley and Santos 1958) have examined the influence of reward on the perception of ambiguous figures.

In the first study, Sommer and Ayllon (1956) used an ambiguous, tactual-kinesthetic, figure-ground situation. The experimental material consisted of two reversible profiles, formed by grooves in a plaster cast. These two casts had different backgrounds so that the subject could differentiate between them. A third cast, consisting of an open face, was used to disrupt the subject's set, while the fourth cast was used in the test situation. The first three casts were also given men's names for identification. Figure 12.2 illustrates this experimental material. The three training casts were presented in a random order with the subject asked to look at them while tracing the grooves with his finger. One of the reversible profiles was rewarded intermittently (a reward was 25 cents) while the other was not. Following 24 training trials 9 of the rewarded profile, 9 of the nonrewarded profile, and 6 of the set-breaking profile), the subjects were blindfolded and given 14 trials with the test profile. Results indicated that the test profile was identified as the rewarded one significantly more frequently than the nonrewarded profile. This difference was not in evidence on the first test trial, however,

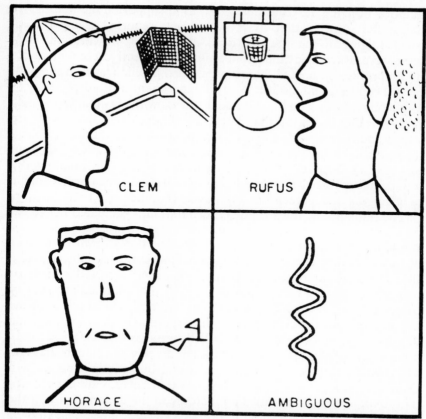

FIG. 12–2. DIAGRAMMATIC DRAWINGS OF THE PLASTIC CASTS. (Adapted from Sommer and Ayllon, 1956)

since there seemed to be a response preference for the left-pointing face.

In a second study, Solley and Sommer (1957) trained ten children, ages 5 to 7, under the typical Schafer-Murphy conditions. The child received 15 cents every time one figure appeared, but nothing when the other was presented. Results indicated that on the first test trial, nine of ten subjects reported seeing the rewarded profile. For the entire test series (20 trials) nine subjects reported seeing more rewarded profiles than nonrewarded profiles; one subject reported an equal number of each. A second experiment by these authors, utilizing 12 children, ages 6 to 9, supported the findings of the earlier study in that 11 of 12 subjects reported seeing the rewarded figure on the first test trial. An interview, in which the children were asked questions concerning the affective characteristics of the profiles, indicated that the rewarded profile was also the happiest, brightest, and closest. A third experiment utilized pleasant or unpleasant stories and associated these with reversible figures. Again results indicated that 19 of 24 children saw the test figure which had been associated with a pleasant story. Additional confirmation of the influence of reward was obtained by Solley and Santos (1958) in a study with college students. These investigators found that a verbal reinforcing stimulus (good, fine) was capable of changing the perception of a Necker cube.

The influence of reward on size estimation is indicated in the experiment by Lambert, Solomon, and Watson (1949). In their study, an experimental group of children turned a crank a number of times in order to receive a poker chip, which, when placed into a slot, led to a candy reward. A control group received candy for turning the crank without going through the intermediary step of receiving the poker chip. All children had been asked to judge the apparent size of the chip prior to the experiment and then after ten days of reward. They were also asked to judge the size of the chip after extinction trials, and again after the reward had been reinstated. Results indicated that the control group's judgments did not change significantly with the varying experiences. The experimental group, however, indicated an increase in the apparent size of the chip after ten days of using it to obtain a reward, a decrease in their estimate to the pretest level following the extinction procedure, and then a tendency in the direction of overestimation when the reward was reinstated.[9] Figure 12.3 illustrates these findings. A second study by Lambert and Lambert (1953) provided confirming evidence.

Punishment

In those studies which have employed both reward and punishment within a single experiment, punishment has been operationally defined as the removal of the reward which the subject had obtained under a reward condition. This technique of manipulating punish-

[9] Some of the experimental subjects received just ten rewards while others received fifty. The authors report no differences between these subgroups and have combined them into a single experimental group.

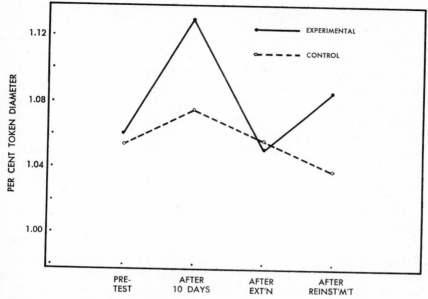

FIG. 12–3. EFFECTS OF THE EXPERIMENTAL CONDITIONS UPON CHILDREN'S ESTIMATES OF THE DIAMETER OF A TOKEN WHEN THESE ESTIMATES ARE TAKEN AS PERCENTS OF THE TRUE DIAMETER. (Adapted from Lambert, Solomon, and Watson, 1949)

ment cannot, of course, be used when the investigator is interested in examining the effects of punishment alone. In such cases, electric shock is frequently employed as the punishing agent.

At least three hypotheses have been advanced in order to account for the influence of punishment on perception. Murphy's autistic position states that perception should not only move in the direction of need satisfaction or reward, but away from punishment. In a test of this position, Smith and Hochberg (1954) manipulated shock in the perception of ambiguous figures. An experimental procedure similar to that used by Schafer and Murphy (1943) was employed except that during the training period, one figure was associated with shock (rather than reward), while the other figure was associated with no shock. Results indicated that for one set of figures, no significant differences were obtained between the perception of shocked and nonshocked faces. A second test figure, however, did indicate that the association of a profile with shock reduced its tendency to be later perceived.

In contrast to Murphy's position, Ayllon and Sommer (1956), using the Tolman, Hall, and Bretnall (1932) study as a point of departure, have argued that punishment, particularly if it was strong, should result in the subject's becoming more vigilant of the punishing characteristics of his environment. More specifically, Ayllon and Sommer hypothesized that if a subject experienced shock as moderate, or very unpleasant, the punished aspect of an ambiguous figure would be best perceived. On the other hand, if the shock was only slightly unpleasant, the reverse should be true and the nonpunished aspects of the figure should be best perceived. In a test of their hypothesis, they employed the tactual-kinesthetic, figure-ground material which consisted of men's profiles and which had been used in their previous study (Sommer and Ayllon 1956). The training and testing procedure which had been used in this earlier study was also employed, although various intensities of shock were used as the motivational antecedent. These intensities were evaluated by a rating scale which the subjects filled out and by behavioral indices provided by the subject during the experiment and noted by the experimenter. Surprisingly, there was little relation between these two measures of shock intensity. Results indicated that if the subject's rating of shock intensity was used, there was a tendency for subjects during the test situation to perceive the figure which during training had been associated with moderate or severe punishment. On the other hand, the nonpunished figure was perceived best when contrasted to the figure which had been associated with only slight punishment.

A third position concerning the effects of punishment on perception has been one which considers the perceptual response as a type of instrumental response, with its acquisition governed by learning principles. In evaluating the influence of shock on the perceptual response, such a position dictates that consideration be given to the following variables: (a) the intensity of the shock, (b) whether or not the subject can escape, and (c) the interval of time existing between the perception of the stimulus and the occurrence of the shock.

McNamara, Solley, and Long (1958), using the materials and method employed by Sommer and Ayllon (1956), ran a series of experiments designed to examine how the perceptual response is influenced by these variables, i.e., shock intensity, opportunity to escape from shock, and temporal interval between the tracing of the figure and the receiving of punishment. Results indicated that this

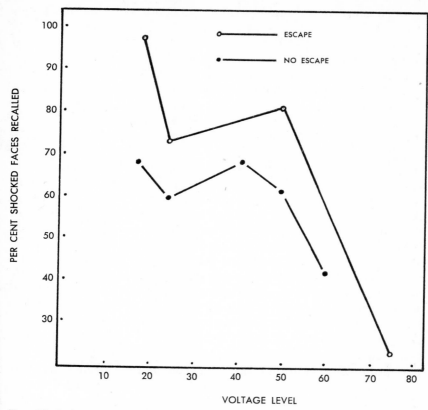

FIG. 12–4. AVERAGE NUMBER OF SHOCKED FACES REPORTED AS A FUNCTION OF VOLTAGE LEVEL AND ESCAPE CONDITION. (Adapted from McNamara, Solley, and Long, 1958)

last variable was found to be of no significance; the importance of shock intensity and opportunity to escape from shock is revealed in Figure 12.4. Here we note that the perception of the shocked face decreases as a function of the intensity of the punishment. This is true for both escape and no-escape groups, although the opportunity to escape does increase the perception of the shocked face.[10]

---

[10] The response measure used by these investigators was the average number of shocked faces reported on 14 test trials. It should be pointed out that if only the subject's first test trial response is used as the response measure, the no-escape condition does not show this relationship. Rather, the perception of the shocked face increases with a voltage level up to 50 volts, then shows a precipitous decline at the next higher intensity level.

McNamara, Solley, and Long's (1958) findings have had support from Mangan (1959) who, also using figure ground material which involved various degrees of ambiguity, has noted a tendency for his subjects to "see" that material which had been previously associated with either mild or intermediate levels of shock. Very severe shock, however, resulted in defense responses on the part of his subjects.

When recognition thresholds have been used as the response indicator of perception, the influence of punishment has been examined by Lysak (1954), Reece (1954), and Rosen (1954). All of these studies have, in general, been consistent with those which have been just reported. Lysak has shown that in the face of impending shock, recognition thresholds for shock syllables were significantly higher than for nonshock syllables. Reece was also interested in examining recognition thresholds for nonsense syllables which had been associated with shock. A paired-associate-learning situation was first used with shock administered when the response was presented. For some subjects, the pronunciation of the response syllable was followed by cessation of shock, while for others, shock was continued for the entire time the syllable was exposed in the drum. Visual recognition thresholds for all nonsense syllables were determined prior to and after the learning task. Statistical analysis indicated that the factor of escape from shock was a significant variable in the determination of lowered recognition thresholds following the learning situation. Unfortunately, the fact that the escape-shock subjects achieved a significantly higher degree of learning than the nonescape subjects resulted in some confounding of the study since this differential learning obviously resulted in differing degrees of familiarity with the stimulus material.

Discussion

A number of experimental difficulties have permeated the findings in this area. One such difficulty, particularly with some of the early studies, has been that the statistics were invariably based upon the number of responses rather than the number of subjects used. Thus the results could be generalized not to other individuals but only to other responses made by the subjects serving in the experiment.

A second, and more pervasive, difficulty has been related to the manipulation of the intensity of the motivational antecedents of reward and punishment. In the early Schafer and Murphy study (1943), for example, rewards of just two and four cents were used.

One certainly may question whether such an amount actually served as a rewarding state of affairs for the subject. In fact, Jackson (1954) has indicated that protocols obtained from subjects participating in this type of study have frequently indicated that the monetary rewards were not regarded as rewards at all. In certain instances, subjects have considered them to be distractors. Although more recent studies have increased the total amount of reward that a subject can obtain to two or three dollars, one may also question whether even these amounts act as important incentives.

Problems associated with the manipulation of punishment are even more complex. Does the removal of money that a subject has previously won act as punishment? Moreover, does this type of operation produce results similar to those obtained when an electric shock is used as the punishing agent?

When shock intensity is manipulated, what criteria are used to judge whether or not the shock is light, moderate, or severe? Should physical measures, such as voltage, be used? Or should the subjective evaluation by the subject or the experimenter be employed? The complexity of the problem is indicated in the studies of Ayllon and Sommer (1956) and McNamara, Solley, and Long (1958). Ayllon and Sommer found no relationship between the intensity of shock when judged by the subject and by the experimenter from the subject's actions in the experimental situation. McNamara, Solley, and Long (1958) have found that physical measures and subjective evaluations of shock are interchangeable when the subject can make an escape response, but if escape is not possible, there is no relationship between these two variables.

In spite of these experimental deficiencies, it is in keeping with most of the evidence to assert that motivational antecedents play some role in the modification of the perceptual process. The action of reward seems to be relatively straightforward, providing that the rewarding situation is conceived by the subject to be one of reward. The action of punishment, on the other hand, is equivocal, since one must consider not only the strength of the punishing agent itself, but whether or not the organism can escape from its effect.

We would propose, however, that so-called weak punishment is not punishment at all, but merely a stimulus which directs the organism's attention to certain stimuli and thus increases perceptual efficiency or the probability that certain stimuli will be perceived. Severe shock from which the subject cannot escape should evoke responses which are generally incompatible with the responses demanded by the experimenter and thus lead to response inefficiency. If the organism is permitted to escape from the severe shock, however, the reduction in pain should reinforce the response associated with pain reduction. If the response is compatible with the response demanded by the experimenter, one would hypothesize that perceptual efficiency should increase; if the response is incompatible, perceptual inefficiency should be the rule.

13 • PHYSIOLOGY OF MOTIVATION
• PHYSIOLOGICAL BASIS OF NEEDS
• AND REWARDS

Although need states and rewards represent just two of a number of motivational antecedents which we have considered, there is little doubt that they are two of the most important. And of the varying needs that an organism may have, hunger and thirst have been employed more frequently than any other in examining the role of motivation in behavior. Similarly, reward states have played an important role in the motivation area.

It would appear inevitable that some individuals working with these variables should be concerned with their physiological basis, and in this chapter we are going to review some of the physiological work that has been done in the area of hunger and thirst, as well as to consider recent developments in which brain stimulation appears to have at least some of the characteristics of rewards.

NEED STATES: THEIR PHYSIOLOGICAL BASIS

As we have just indicated, the primary needs, particularly those of hunger and thirst, have played an important role in the area of motivation; consequently, it is not surprising that a number of psychologists have joined the physiologists in being interested in their physiological basis. As Stellar (1954) has reminded us, the physiological model which most psychologists have used has been based upon that proposed by Cannon (1934) in his classical statement of the local theories of hunger and thirst. Although these theories represent a convenient point of departure for discussion, there is the clear recognition at the present time that Cannon had indicated only one of the many variables which contribute to the urge to eat or drink. Moreover, an equally important question, not answered by Cannon's theoretical position, was, why do we stop? Most current research regards these two questions as part of the larger and more general problem of how organisms regulate their intake so as to maintain normal health and growth.

Measurement

As we have done in previous chapters, and prior to more specific discussion, attention should first be directed to the problem of how food and water needs have been measured in a physiological setting. Although the presence of such needs may be inferred by manipulating hours of deprivation, most frequently, it is the characteristics of the organism's response which are used to infer their presence. In the examination of such response measures, we often think of subjective or introspective reports provided by the organism. Thus, the presence of hunger may be inferred by the subject's verbal report, "I feel hungry." It is obvious, however, that such a response cannot be used with organisms other than humans, and as a result, other response measures have been more frequently used.

The most frequent response measure is consummatory behavior. One variation of this response has been developed by Miller (1955), who has called it the "progressive quinine test." This measure involves the pitting of an aversion by animals for quinine against food or water deprivation periods. Miller (1956) has described this test as follows:

A series of bottle caps are counter-sunk on the periphery of a metal disc that is driven by a slipping clutch and escapement mechanism. The bottle caps appear immediately below an opening in the floor of a small cage that is arranged so that the rat can reach only one cap at a time. After a hungry rat has learned to drink a few drops of milk from each bottle cap as soon as it appears, it is presented at 30-second intervals with a series of 10 bottle caps, each cap containing three drops of milk, and each solution being adulterated with progressively increasing amounts of quinine hydrochloride ranging from concentrations of 0,

0.004 per cent, 0.008 per cent, to 1%. For each cup that he cleans up, the rat receives 2 points; for each one started without finishing, 1 point; and for cups not touched, zero. The cumulative score has been found to be a sensitive and reliable measure of hunger.

A second measure that investigators have utilized is an instrumental response. Here we frequently find that an organism that learns to make some instrumental response leading to food or water is usually considered to be hungry or thirsty.

Finally, physiological measures are sometimes used. For example, the measurement of stomach motility has been used to infer the presence of hunger.[1]

The relationship among these varying response measures has been discussed by Miller (1955), and an early study by Miller, Bailey, and Stevenson (1950) with rats indicates the nature of the problem. Using rats with hypothalamic lesions that produce obesity, they found that when these rats had relatively easy access to food in dishes with unweighted lids, they consumed much more than their normal controls. When weights were attached to these lids in order to increase the work involved without exceeding the strength limit of the animal, the experimental group ate less food than did normal controls. When the weighted lids were removed, the experimental animals returned to eating greater quantities. Use of the progressive quinine test, to which we have previously referred, also resulted in the experimental animals' eating less than their controls. And an examination of instrumental activity revealed that the experimental animals, in contrast to controls, ran more slowly down an alley to food, worked at a slower rate at pressing a bar for food, and were stopped from eating by lower levels of electric shock. These instrumental behavioral tests revealed that the experimental animals were less hungry than normal animals, even though they consumed more when fed ad lib.

Miller (1956) has also reported a comparison of four response measures obtained from normal animals which illustrates the general problem even more clearly. The amount of food consumed immediately after varying periods of deprivation increased rapidly during the first six hours, reached a maximum somewhere around thirty hours, and then fell off. Stomach contractions, on the other hand, increased rapidly during the first six hours and then leveled

[1] There is a number of difficulties in obtaining appropriate measurements of the stomach's movements. For a discussion of the problem, see Davis, Garafolo, and Gault (1957).

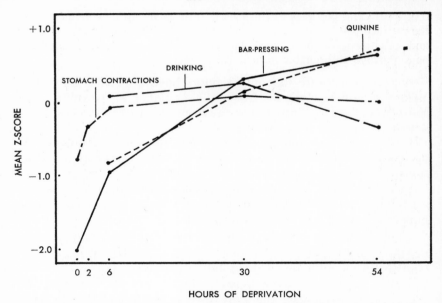

FIG. 13–1. COMPARISON OF FOUR MEASURES OF HUNGER. (1) Drinking—the volume of enriched milk required to satiate the rats; (2) the amount of adulteration with quinine required to prevent eating; (3) the rate of bar pressing reinforced by food on a variable-interval schedule; and (4) sum of excursions of the record of stomach contractions measured from a balloon permanently implanted on the end of a plastic fistula. (Adapted from Miller, 1956)

off. The rate of bar pressing and amount of quinine required to stop eating, continued to increase with food deprivation throughout the 54-hour period which was measured. Figure 13.1 indicates these findings. When animals were made thirsty, the interrelationships among these varying response measures were similar to those obtained with food deprivation.

These experimental results should not be taken to indicate that the varying response measures which have been used never agree, but attention is called to the problem to indicate that caution must be observed in interpreting certain findings in the area.

HUNGER

An examination of the physiological factors in hunger reveals that hunger has been related to (1) gastric contractions and distention as well as oropharyngeal stimulation, (2) conditions of the blood, and finally, (3) central nervous system factors.

Gastric Contractions, Distention, and Oropharyngeal Stimulation

The concept that the sensation of hunger was related to stomach contractions has been most notably associated with Cannon, although a number of men before him presented the same point of view. Early articles by Cannon (1911–1912) and Cannon and Washburn (1912) both contain the general thesis that hunger was caused by stomach contractions. In the Cannon and Washburn (1912) study, the famous "balloon in the stomach" technique was used. Here the sensation of hunger was related to gastric contractions that were measured by pressure changes in a partially inflated balloon which had been swallowed by the subject.[2,3] Carlson (1916), a few years later, reiterated the point that the ultimate cause of the hunger sensation was gastric contractions.

In his review of the role of the digestive tract in regulating food ingestion, Quigley (1955) has agreed that hunger contractions are real and occur spontaneously in man and animals. He has cited the following types of evidence by which their existence has been verified: (1) seen in an individual with a gastrostomy, or as ripples of the abdominal wall in individuals with diastasis of the recti; (2) observed fluoroscopically, following the swallowing of barium sulfate; (3) felt by the hand when placed on the abdominal wall; (4) recorded from radio-opaque clips fastened to the gastric serosa to outline the stomach; (5) recorded from an open tube introduced into the proximal end of the stomach; (6) recorded with the balloon-water manometer technique. The analysis of such contractions indicates that they occur as a peristaltic wave which sequentially involves (1) the gastric fungus, (2) the corpus, (3) the antrum, and (4) the proximal duodenum. A few hours of food deprivation results in weak waves, while with longer fasting times the period of gastro-intestinal activity becomes prolonged and activity is almost continuous. Paralleling increased motility is the sensation of hunger which humans report becomes increasingly severe.

It must be pointed out, however, that all investigators have not accepted the proposed relationship between the sensation of hunger

---

[2] Quigley and Brody (1952) as well as others have pointed out that the air-filled system, used by Cannon and Washburn (1912) and many later investigators, is difficult to standardize and the obtained recordings frequently fail to differentiate between pressure and volume changes. Under the circumstances, interpretation of the records is difficult. A better technique has been to fill the balloon tubing and tambour with water.

[3] A neat technique for using the balloon in the stomach with rats has been presented by Morrison, Ju Lin, Eckel, Van Itallie, and Mayer (1958).

arising from an empty stomach and stomach contractions. Alvarez (1948) has stated, "I have never been able to satisfy myself as to the nature of the difference, if there is one, between hunger contractions and the normal waves of the lower half of the stomach." Recently, Davis, Garafolo, and Kveim (1959) have also questioned this correlation. Using an electrical recording method in which the electrodes were placed externally on their subjects (Davis, Garafolo, and Gault 1957), they have found that the recorded activity of the stomach is at its lowest point when the stomach is *empty*. They have also found that the introduction of a balloon into the stomach increases the electrical activity of the stomach, and this increase, they have hypothesized, has been the principal factor in producing the contractions which previous investigators have reported.

Whether or not the relationship between the sensation of hunger and gastric contractions is accepted, there is considerable difficulty with any theory that makes stomach contractions a necessary condition for the sensation of hunger.

Wangensteen and Carlson (1931) report that a patient who had a total gastrectomy stated that following the operation, hunger sensations were "just the same." And if consummatory behavior is used as an index of the presence of hunger, Tsang (1938) has found that rats which had their stomachs removed and which were placed on deprivation states showed as much time in feeding activity as normal animals. Furthermore, their instrumental behavior was as efficient in providing them with food reward as that of normal rats. Similar findings are reported when the nerve pathways leading from the stomach to the brain are severed. Thus, the experimental findings of Bash (1939) as well as Morgan and Morgan (1940) have indicated that operated animals' consummatory, as well as instrumental, behavior was not different from that of normal animals.

Quigley's (1955) recent conclusions concerning the role of the digestive tract in regulating food ingestion are as appropriate a summary for this area as any. Quigley states (1955):

It is not essential that animals or humans experience sensations from the contracting empty stomach to have a desire to ingest food. We have observed, and so have many others, that food intake is not significantly decreased in dogs or man by cutting both vagi, cutting the splanchnics, by vagotomy combined with splanchnectomy and celiac-ganglionectomy, or by partial or total gastrectomy. Decorticated dogs or anencephalic infants will not seek food but will swallow what is placed in their mouths. Such observations should not be interpreted as evidence that hunger contractions play no role in regulating the ingestion of food. Food intake is an activity so essential to the maintenance of health and life that nature has provided several mechanisms which influence it. These mechanisms insure that food will be ingested reasonably well even in the absence of sensations from the contracting stomach or from taste or smell receptors.

An early study by Cowgill (1928) stressed the importance of calorie content as one of the important mechanisms which controlled the ingestion of food. Measuring the food consumption of a dozen dogs placed on diets which varied in the number of calories per unit of weight, Cowgill (1928) concluded that the healthy adult dog tends to regulate the amount of food that it eats so as to maintain a constant body weight, a constant state of nutrition, and a constant intake of energy. His basic conclusion was that calories per unit of body weight constituted a common denominator of such an adjustment. A later study by Harte, Travers, and Sarich (1948), in which the food and calorie consumption of infant rats was studied, supported Cowgill's findings. These authors concluded that the primary purpose in eating was to satisfy energy requirements.

More recent studies have also examined the role of calories on food intake. Share, Martyniuk, and Grossman (1952) examined food consumption in dogs when calorie intake was provided intragastrically in amounts of 33, 50, 66, or 133 per cent of the animal's normal requirement. The results indicated that the amount of food consumed had some relationship to the number of calories which were provided intragastrically, although the relationship was not perfect. Animals which were given 133 per cent of their calorie requirement reduced but did not abolish oral intake completely. Moreover, the change in the amount consumed took place quite slowly. On the other hand, animals which were given just 33 per cent of their calories intragastrically did not reduce their oral intake over that found during the control period.

The negligible effect of the addition of small calorie increments on food consumption has also been found by Janowitz and Grossman (1948, 1949a). In their first study, these authors found that intraperitoneal administration of glucose and hydrolysate mixtures in the rat in amounts ranging from 17 to 25 per cent of their daily calorie requirement did not result in the animals' reducing their food intake beyond that produced by an equal volume of noncaloric material. A second study by these authors (Janowitz and Grossman 1949a) also noted the same effect when food was introduced directly into the stomach. The administration of 11 to 20 per cent of the animal's average daily intake resulted in no corresponding depression of oral intake.

We have previously called attention to Share, Martyniuk, and Grossman's finding that a period of time was necessary for animals given 133 per cent of their caloric requirements to readjust their eating behavior. The importance of a learning period in such studies is further indicated by Janowitz and Hollander (1955). Although these authors found that the intragastric administration of 50, 100, or 175 per cent of the dog's calorie requirement resulted in a compensatory reduction in eating, a number of weeks of such administration was required before such an adjustment took place. Moreover, such compensation was not perfect, since the 100 per cent condition did not suppress oral intake completely.

The introduction of a substance into the stomach distends it, and some investigators have been interested in this variable as a contributor to the consumption of food. Janowitz and Grossman (1949a) found that introducing into a dog's stomach 40 to 46 per cent of the animal's average daily intake inhibited oral intake by approximately a corresponding volume; however, noncaloric bulk yielded the same findings. The authors interpreted the animal's food regulatory mechanism as being dependent upon stomach distention factors rather than caloric content. The importance of stomach distention was also noted by Share, Martyniuk, and Grossman (1952), who found that water-filled balloons, placed in the stomach and allowed to remain there for one or two weeks, resulted in a persistent reduction of oral feeding, the degree of reduction bearing some relationship to the amount of water in the balloon. When the amount of water in the balloon approximated 75 per cent of the volume of food eaten during the control period, for example, food consumption decreased by approximately 50 per cent. Finally, James and Gilbert (1957) found that food injected directly into the stomach of a dog resulted in inhibiting the eating response and have accounted for their findings in terms of stomach distention. Unfortunately, they did not control for the caloric variable.

The failure of stomach distention and caloric intake to account completely for how much the organism ingests not only indicates the complexity of the problem but demands that other variables be considered. As a result, there is some evidence that oropharyngeal factors; i.e., sight, smell, taste, and/or swallowing of food, play a role in the metering of food intake.

Janowitz and Grossman (1951) have reported that placing a portion of food directly into the stomach of a dog just prior to feeding its regular meal results in less suppression of oral intake than if the animal is permitted to eat that same portion prior to being given its meal. And Kohn (1951), using rats as subjects, found that if an instrumental response (panel pushing) was used to measure hunger, prior ingestion of 144 cc. of milk via the mouth resulted in significantly fewer instrumental responses than if milk was injected directly into the stomach. Milk injected into the stomach resulted in significantly fewer responses, however, than if a control injection of saline was used.

Since there may be some question as to whether an instrumental response adequately measures "hunger," Berkun, Kessen, and Miller (1952) performed a similar study except that the consummatory response was measured. Results confirmed those of Kohn (1951) as well as those of Janowitz and Grossman (1951). Milk injected directly into the stomach produced a prompt reduction of amount consumed, but milk taken normally by mouth produced an even greater reduction.

Smith and Duffy (1957b) have indicated that these findings do not hold universally. These authors were unable to find differences in consummatory behavior between mash which had been injected into the animal's stomach and that which was normally ingested. They have called attention to the fact that in the Berkun, *et al.* (1952) study, the food in the test situation was the same as the food which was placed in the stomach, while in their study, it was not. They also pointed out that in the Berkun, *et al.* (1952) study, milk which passed through the mouth would be expected to have somewhat greater osmotic pressure than milk introduced by fistula and that the tonicity of the latter might actually be the critical variable.[4]

Glucostatic Factors

Carlson's (1916) finding of an inverse relationship between blood sugar level and hunger contractions provided an appropriate stimulus for a host of experimental work, and the general position that

[4] A subsequent study by Schwartzbaum and Ward (1958) has confirmed the importance of the tonicity of gastronintestinal content on the short-term regulation of food intake. The authors found that the ingestion of food by the rat was a function of the tonicity of the substance placed in the stomach regardless of its caloric content.

blood sugar level was responsible for hunger. The result has been that some investigators have attributed hunger to glucostatic factors in contrast to the role of the digestive tract. In indicating what is meant by the glucostatic theory, Mayer (1955) has stated that, according to this general theory, "the mechanisms postulated for the short-term regulation of energy intake rest on the concept that somewhere, possibly in the hypothalamic centers shown to be implicated in the regulation of food intake, perhaps peripherally as well, there are glucoreceptors sensitive to blood glucose in the measure that they can utilize it." Mayer has further indicated that the glucostatic theory does not point to a specific role of glucose as a chemical messenger, but only means that it is the main source of high-energy phosphate bonds to the hypothalmic centers. The designation, glucostatic, does not exclude the possibility that other metabolites may have an action on food similar to that of glucose. It emphasizes only the special position of glucose in the regulating scheme.

The experimental work in this area has frequently involved two general techniques. The first has utilized the injection of glucose which, of course, increases blood sugar level. If hunger is dependent upon blood sugar level, injections of glucose should decrease it. The second technique involves the injection of insulin which lowers blood sugar level. Thus, injections of insulin should increase hunger.

The difficulties involved in the measurement of hunger are in particular evidence when we attempt to evaluate the glucostatic hypothesis. Consequently, it is necessary to consider the evidence in relation to a number of measures.

Blood Glucose Level and Deprivation Periods

Scott, Scott, and Luckhardt (1938) made blood sugar determinations preceding, during, and after food deprivation periods and found that within a range of ±5 per cent there was no variation in blood sugar level. This finding with humans confirmed an earlier one by Mulinos (1933) who had used dogs as subjects.[5]

---

[5] It is generally agreed that glucose utilization should be measured by arteriovenous (A-V) glucose differences rather than absolute glucose level. The "hunger state" is the state in which peripheral arteriovenous glucose differences tend toward zero. Since these investigators used absolute glucose level, this general type of finding cannot be considered as crucial evidence against a glucostatic hypothesis.

Blood Glucose Level and Gastric Contractions

Bulatao and Carlson (1924) have reported that stomach contractions in dogs could be inhibited within a few minutes as a result of an intravenous infusion of a 5 to 10 gram 50 per cent glucose solution. Control infusions of hypertonic saline or lactose, however, did not produce such an inhibition. An early study by Templeton and Quigley (1930) appeared to confirm this finding; a subsequent study by Quigley and Hallaran (1932), however, did not. The latter study was fairly extensive in that there were 71 observations on 12 dogs, with the quantity of glucose injected ranging from 1 to 25 grams. Results indicated that the hyperglycemia produced by the glucose had no immediate effect on spontaneous gastric motility. Moreover, the authors reported that each of the three or four balloons which were placed in tandem and which were located in various parts of the stomach showed similar findings.

Stunkard and Wolff (1954, 1956) have presented findings, however, supporting the early Bulatao and Carlson (1924) study. Their general procedure involved intravenous glucose administration to adult subjects on 40 different occasions, with the subsequent measurement of gastric hunger contractions as well as peripheral capillary venous glucose differences. Results indicated that on 19 of the 40 occasions, the administration of 50 ml. of a 50 per cent solution of glucose was followed in five minutes by cessation of hunger contractions. In no case, however, did the control procedures of intravenous injection of 70 ml. of isotonic saline, venipunctures, or finger punctures have any effect on gastric motility.[6] The determination of capillary venous glucose differences in the 19 cases in which hunger contractions were inhibited, revealed that they were significantly higher than those in the group in which contractions persisted. In 14 of the 19 cases, contractions returned approximately 47 minutes after they had been inhibited by the intravenous administration of glucose. Capillary venous differences obtained when the contractions returned were lower than the capillary venous differences at 10 and 20 minutes after the glucose injection. This difference, however, was not significant.

[6] A number of investigators have shown that the presentation of an extraneous stimulus (i.e., loud sounds, finger punctures, etc.) inhibits existing contractions. Under the circumstances, venipunctures, or finger punctures, are appropriate controls for this possibility.

The authors have concluded that if hunger and satiety are conceptualized as two different states, their findings are relevant to the function of satiety, inasmuch as metabolic events which accompanied increased peripheral removal of glucose had an inhibiting effect on gastric hunger contractions. These findings did not support the point of view, however, that depletion of carbohydrate stores of the order produced by overnight fasting was the sole or even sufficient condition for hunger.

Blood Glucose and the Subjective Experience of Hunger

Janowitz and Ivy (1949) have reported that an individual's hunger sensations were essentially unaltered by intravenous injections of glucose. And in a more recent study, Bernstein and Grossman (1956) have also obtained results which have supported this earlier finding. In this study, a model of good experimental design, neither the test subjects nor the interviewer who recorded the data were aware of which treatment had been administered. Hyperglycemia was produced by intravenous or intragastric glucose administration in young adult males. Saline was used as an appropriate control. Results indicated that the subjects' desire for food, as indicated on a five-point scale following glucose administration, was not significantly different from that produced by the saline solution. The suppression of appetite following glucose administration was also much less than that produced by eating a small breakfast. On the other hand, Van Itallie, Beaudoin, and Mayer (1953) have correlated A-V glucose differences with hunger feelings in normal and diabetic subjects and have concluded that a satisfactory correlation existed between A-V glucose differences and a desire for food. In the Stunkard and Wolff (1954) study which was reported earlier, these authors found that the subjective experience of hunger was removed by the intravenous injection of glucose.

Blood Sugar Level and the Consummatory Response

In a rather extensive study by Mayer and Bates (1952), rats were given two daily subcutaneous injections of glucose, fructose, or adrenaline which produced hyperglycemia of short duration. Results indicated that injections of these substances (given over a period of 14 to 23 days) resulted in a statistically significant decrease in food intake even when the calorie equivalent of the injected substance was taken into account. Injections of fat or sucrose, however, had no effect.

These findings are in sharp contrast to most other studies in the area. Janowitz and Grossman (1948), also using rats, found that 15 cc. of a 10 per cent glucose solution injected intraperitoneally twice a day did not result in any greater depression of food intake than injections of saline given control animals. Two subsequent studies by these authors (Janowitz and Grossman, 1949a, 1951), using dogs, have revealed that large infusions of glucose administered intravenously did not change food consumption any more than injections of saline. Smyth, Lasichak, and Levey (1947), and Bernstein and Grossman (1956) have reported similar findings with humans. In the Bernstein and Grossman (1956) study, the first part of which we have already reported, nine normal males were given either glucose or saline solution before a test meal. Administration of the solution was given intravenously or intragastrically, with each subject serving under each condition in a random order. During the hyperglycemic period, although A-V differences in blood glucose level showed the expected elevation, food consumption, as measured in terms of calories, was not significantly different from those times during which saline treatment was given.

Smith and Duffy (1957b) have reported that intraperitoneal injections of isotonic glucose depressed eating as compared with isotonic saline, thus presumably supporting the earlier reported study of Mayer and Bates (1952). A puzzling finding, however, was that similar injections of sorbitol and sucrose similarly depressed eating. As the authors state: "Although some absorption of all the solutions could have occurred, sucrose could not have been converted to glucose at all, and sorbitol only very slightly. If the effect was due to the activation of glucostatic receptors, they must have been very nonspecific in response."

One point of evidence which appears to support a glucostatic theory is the fact that insulin injection elevates A-V glucose differences and increases food consumption. Grossman (1955) has proposed, however, that hypoglycemia produced by the insulin is an emergency mechanism in the regulation of hunger and does not operate in the normal physiological range of blood sugar variation.

Although most of the evidence does not support a glucostatic factor in hunger, one problem with many of the studies which we have reviewed has been that hyperglycemia which is obtained by the administration of glucose may not correspond to that following the ingestion of food, or even glucose. Injected glucose is strongly hypertonic and, in this respect, dissimilar to that obtained by intestinal absorption. It is possible that this difference has been one of the factors contributing to the difficulty in securing reproducible findings.

Hormone Factors

From time to time, a few investigators have posited the existence of a hormone in order to account for hunger. In one of the very old studies, Luckhardt and Carlson (1914) found that blood which was taken from either starving animals or animals having pancreatic diabetes, and transfused into normal animals, provided a temporary stimulus for the production of gastric contractions. Contradictory evidence, however, has been presented by Siegel and Taub (1952), and Siegel and Dorman (1954), who have reported that rats injected intraperitoneally or intragastrically with blood from hungry animals consumed no more food than animals injected with blood from satiated donors.

Interest in the role of hormones has been stimulated in recent years by the discovery of glucagon. Foa, Galansino, and Pozza (1957) have suggested that glucagon is a quick-acting hormone capable of stimulating liver glycogenolysis and, hence, of raising the blood sugar concentration and depleting liver glycogen.

Studies by Stunkard, Van Itallie, and Reis (1955), Sporn and Necheles (1956), Morrison, Ju Lin, Eckel, Van Itallie, and Mayer (1958), and Schulman, Carleton, Whitney, and Whitehorn (1958) have all demonstrated the abolition of hunger contractions with glucagon administration. Stunkard, Van Itallie, and Reis have reported that the intravenous administration of glucagon to human subjects on 16 occasions resulted in the abolition of hunger contractions in all 16 cases. After injection, glucose level in the blood increased rapidly, reaching a peak in just 30 minutes. A fall in the blood glucose level with decreasing capillary venous differences was associated with a return of hunger contractions, and the subjective experience of hunger. Control injections of saline and glucagon diluting fluid, as well as venipuncture, and finger punctures, had no demonstrable effects. As the authors have remarked, this reproducibility is in sharp contrast to the inconstant effect obtained when glucose has been used. Sporn and Necheles have noted that gastric and colon motility of dogs was depressed for 30 to 45 minutes beginning soon after the injection of glucagon, while Morrison, *et al.,* obtained similar findings with rats. In the Schulman *et al.* study, ten male patients in a State Hospital served as subjects.

The strict control over the patients' daily behavior enabled the experimenters to obtain accurate records regarding their caloric intake. The experimental period consisted of five weeks. The first week was used to learn about the patients' food preferences. Two 2-week periods followed, in which during one period intramuscular injections of 1 mg. of crystalline glucagon in 1 ml. of insulin diluting fluid were given just prior to each meal. During the other period, the injections consisted of insulin diluting fluid. The study was "blind" in that those individuals responsible for administering the injections did not know which material they were using. Results indicated that in 9 of the 10 patients, the average caloric intake was significantly less after receiving glucagon than after receiving the placebo.

Central Nervous System Factors

Although Carlson's (1916) early work recognized the existence of hunger centers in the medulla diencephalon and cerebral cortex, there was for a long time little investigation of the role that the brain played in hunger. As Brobeck (1955) states, this was probably because the gastric mechanism could be studied more easily, and in addition, observations upon vagotomized subjects appeared to indicate that the origin of the contractions was independent of central nervous system control.

In 1940, Hetherington and Ranson discovered that obesity could be produced by lesions confined to the hypothalamus. And observations by Brobeck, Tepperman, and Long (1943) indicated that such obesity was the result of hyperphagia—overeating.

Hyperphagia, produced by insult to the hypothalamus, has been an area of considerable interest to a number of investigators. It has been found to consist of two phases. The first, frequently called the dynamic phase, is one in which the animal consumes great quantities of food and at the same time, shows a very rapid and steady weight gain. The second or static phase, is one in which the animal's weight levels off at a relatively high plateau, with a concomitant decrease in food intake. Figure 13.2 reveals postoperative body weight and daily food intake of a typical operated animal compared to that of a normal control animal.

The ingestion pattern for these animals, as reported by Brooks, Lockwood, and Wiggins (1946), and Teitelbaum and Campbell (1958), reveals that dynamic hyperphagic animals increase their solid food intake by increasing their meal size as well as eating

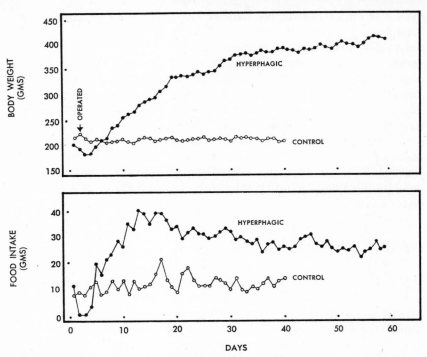

FIG. 13–2. POSTOPERATIVE BODY WEIGHT AND DAILY FOOD INTAKE OF A TYPICAL OPERATED ANIMAL COMPARED TO THAT OF A NORMAL UNOPERATED CONTROL ANIMAL. (Adapted from Teitelbaum, 1955)

more frequent meals. Static hyperphagics, on the other hand, eat larger meals but somewhat less frequently than normal animals. If a liquid diet is used, both dynamic and static hyperphagic animals do not eat any more frequently than normal animals, but simply increase their meal size.

The influence of variation of the diet on the eating behavior of hyperphagic animals has been examined by a number of investigators (Kennedy, 1953; Strominger, Brobeck, and Cort, 1953; Teitelbaum, 1955; Epstein, 1959). Teitelbaum has found that the grinding of the rat's normal diet of pellets to powder, or the addition of a .125 per cent quinine solution, results in a decrease or cessation of eating for those animals in the static phase of hyperphagia. These variations in the diet do not affect, however, the consummatory behavior of either normal animals or those in the dynamic phase of hyperphagia. If the stimulus variation is produced by adulterating the food with varying percentages of nonnutritive cellulose, normal animals maintain their intake up to approximately 50 per cent dilution. Dynamic hyperphagic animals, on the other hand, begin to decrease their intake with as little as 5 per cent dilution, and as the dilution percentage increases, the decrease in food intake accelerates. By the time the food is 75 per cent diluted, food consumption is less than that found in the normal animal. Static hyperphagic animals show a similar trend except that a dilution of only 25 per cent results in less food consumption than that found in the normal animal, and dilutions of 50 per cent or more result in almost complete cessation of eating.

In summary, Teitelbaum (1955) suggests:

After ventromedial lesions, all rats give positive exaggerated reactions to positive sensory stimuli and hence overeat. Before they get fat, it appears that they are also somewhat sensitive in a negative way to negative stimulus aspects of the diets, for they steadily decrease their intake of diets adulterated more and more with cellulose. But the positive reactions are still quite powerful, since the dynamics continue to eat more of the adulterated diet than normal rats.

Once hyperphagic rats get fat, changes in the internal environment arise which increase their negative reactions to negative stimuli to a point where they practically reject certain diets completely. . . . However, the obese hyperphagics are still quite affected by the positive qualities of the diet, for they increase their overeating in response to the taste of sugar. The nonobese dynamics, however, show little of this finickiness but rather appear to be eating heedlessly, since they do not seem to be affected by adding either quinine or dextrose to the diet.

A few years following Hetherington and Ranson's discovery that obesity could be produced by lesions confined to the hypothalaimus, Anand and Brobeck (1951), working with rats, reported that appropriate injury to the hypothalamus could also cause aphagia—undereating. Anand, Dua, and Shoenberg (1955) have extended these findings to the cat and monkey. Teitelbaum and Stellar (1954) have not only confirmed the findings of Anand and Brobeck, but found that animals which were maintained by tube feeding recovered eating and drinking functions within 6 to 65 days following the operation.

This so-called "escape" response has been noted by other investigators. Morrison and Mayer (1957) have reported that some subjects after a period of aphagia (as well as adipsia) spontaneously resume drinking and eating, and eventually regain their body weight. The daily intubation of water into operated subjects, as Teitelbaum and Stellar have noted, appears to facilitate the resumption of these responses. Williams and Teitelbaum (1959) have noted that operated animals, although refusing normal laboratory food and water, would accept a liquid diet and sustain life. Interestingly enough, these animals adjusted their volume intake of this diet according to its nutrient content in the same fashion as normal animals. Thus, when the calorie content of the diet was halved, their intake increased twofold.

Morrison and Mayer (1957) have hypothesized that the lesions which are produced affect one of the hunger or appetite controls which are normally dominant, but that alternative paths of control can take over with only little loss in efficiency.

Brobeck (1955), after reviewing much of the evidence in this area, has hypothesized that the hypothalamic mechanism is a dual one with one region having to do with feeding behavior, while the other is related to its cessation. Thus, if the region regulating feeding behavior is injured, overactivity of it will result in increased food intake, while underactivity will result in diminishing feeding. On the other hand, insult to the cessation area which results in its overactivity will produce diminished feeding, while underactivity will produce increased food consumption. The principal role of the hypothalamus in such regulation, Brobeck (1955) suggests, is in terms of facilitating or inhibiting certain reflexes which are associated with feeding behavior. More specifically, Brobeck has stated that:

. . . when food is eaten by a normal animal, there occur within the body certain changes which either directly or indirectly affect the hypothalamus. These changes serve as signals to the brain, tending to suppress the activity of the lateral hypothalamus and thus to decrease appetite, while they stimulate the medial or inhibitory portion of the mechanism and thus promote satiety. As the food is disposed of through conversion to heat, or work, or some form of stored energy, the changes produced by the feeding tend to disappear. Now the lateral hypothalamus becomes more active, while the medial hypothalamus is inhibited. At the same time, the animal's locomotor activity begins to increase. In this manner, the animal is brought into an environment where food may be found, where the facilitation of feeding reflexes and a removal of their inhibition will lead to the investigation and consequent eating of the food.

THIRST

The experimental work and theoretical orientation related to thirst parallels in many ways that which we have presented with hunger. In general, the physiological factors related to thirst reveal that investigators have been concerned with (1) dryness of the mouth, throat, and tongue, (2) conditions of the blood and tissue, and (3) central nervous system factors.

Dryness of the Mouth, Throat, and Tongue

One of the best known theories of thirst is one which has been proposed by Cannon and is frequently referred to as a "local theory," since it proposes that the sensation of thirst arises from dryness of the mucous membranes of the tongue, mouth, and throat. This theory was summarized by Cannon in his lecture before the Royal Society of London in 1918. Briefly, he stated that when the salivary glands "fail to provide sufficient fluid to moisten the mouth and throat, the local discomfort and unpleasantness which result constitute a feeling of thirst." It is important to keep in mind that Cannon has defined thirst in terms of the conscious experience or sensation of the organism.

The experimental evidence which Cannon used to support his position was largely anecdotal. He reports that Lepidi-Chioti and Fubini had observed that a child suffering from polyuria and passing from 13 to 15 liters of urine daily became very thirsty when water was withheld. The thirst sensation could be abated for from 15 to 35 minutes if the back of the mouth was cocainized. He reported two examples: the United States Cavalry lost in the desert and a missionary about to be shot by Chinese bandits all had dry throats and felt thirsty. Finally, an experiment by Bidder and Schmidt is cited in which these investigators, after having tied off the salivary glands of dogs and noting their dry mouths, observed that the desire for water was greatly increased.

Since Cannon's early work, some findings have tended to support his position. An early study by Pack (1923) indicated that although rabbits were deprived of water for a number of days, the administration of pilocarpine—a drug which induced salivation—resulted in the animal's either not drinking or drinking only about one quarter as much as control animals not under drugs in their first hour's access to water. Gregersen and Cannon (1932), after observing water consumed by dogs during one or two hours before and after the extirpation or tying off of their salivary glands, found that six of eight dogs drank more after the operation. They have concluded that "under conditions which make the mouth dry, a deficient salivary flow causes thirst and increased water intake even in the absence of bodily dehydration."

A series of studies by Holmes and Gregersen (1947, 1950, 1950a) have also been used to dispute theories of thirst based upon the condition of the blood, and thus indirectly support Cannon's local theory. In their first study, these authors found that when 250 to 300 cc. of 5 per cent sodium chloride solution was administered intravenously, the saliva flow of adult humans decreased 50 per cent or more. They also reported that the thirst sensations as reported by their subjects waxed and waned along with the decrease and subsequent increase of salivary flow. Again administering sodium chloride intravenously, they report in their second (1950) as well as third (1950a) study that the amount of water ingested following such sodium chloride administration was not determined by the amount of water required to dilute the sodium chloride solution in the plasma to isotonicity. Moreover, in their third (1950a) study, they found that the drinking response was completed in less than five minutes and that the water did not enter the blood stream and thus change the blood plasma for some 35 minutes. In support of the local theory, they state,

The suddenness with which drinking stops and the evident lack of a quantitative relation to over-all internal fluid changes leaves one with the impression that the drinking must be governed by discomfort in some local area that the water reaches immediately, that is, the region of the mouth, pharynx, esophagus, and stomach.

A considerable body of evidence has accumulated, however, to dispute the notion that thirst is solely dependent upon a dry throat. Montgomery (1931) removed the salivary glands of six dogs and measured their water intake for more than a year. Results indicated no increase in their average daily water intake and thus, she concluded, it is quite improbable that the salivary glands played a major role in the thirst sensation. And Steggerda (1939) reports that a college student's daily fluid intake of water was normal for his body weight even though he was without salivary glands. Moreover, he reports that the student was able to discriminate between a dry mouth and the sensation of thirst.

The use of fistula, through which water can be removed after being swallowed and prior to its reaching the stomach or intestines, has also been used to provide some evidence in this area. Bernard's early study, cited by Wolf (1958), was one of the early studies using such a technique. A horse with a divided esophagus, whose every swallow of water was ejected between the front legs, drank until fatigued and, following rest, it again began to drink. A fistula placed in the stomach of the dog provided similar results.[7] Here water traversed all the way to the stomach and then to the outside.

The use of the fistula in the throat or what has been known as the "sham" drinking technique was also employed by Bellows (1939) in a series of studies using dogs as subjects. In the first series, the animals were induced to sham drink by administering less than their normal requirement of water. At hourly intervals, sham drinking was permitted for a certain period of time or until the dog refused water for five minutes. Results indicated that both the number of drinks and amount of water taken at each drinking period increased. In a second series, the animal's water deficit was estimated and this was administered (with a slight excess) through the esophagus and directly into the stomach. From the time the administration was complete until the end of nine minutes, Bellows noted that the animal (which was then permitted to sham drink) drank only the amount of the deficit, and not the amount that was typically consumed in the sham drinking situation. From the tenth to fifteenth minute, the animal drank only about 20 per cent of its deficit, and from the sixteenth to thirtieth minute, the dog refused to drink. These experimental findings led Bellows to posit the presence of at least two factors involved in thirst: (a) one which appears to act immediately and is related to buccal and pharyngeal factors, and (b) one which acts after a delay and is related to organs or conditions below the fistula.

---

[7] Cannon (1918) has objected to these experiments on the grounds that the expression of "fatigued" and "rested" is an interpretation of the observer and not the testimony of the organism. That the animals stopped drinking he attributes to the fact that the animals were no longer thirsty, but started again when they became thirsty.

One interesting observation is that the time interval of 10 to 15 minutes in which the animal drastically cuts down his water intake is much shorter than water absorption time, which has been estimated at 35 minutes.

Towbin's (1949) study with sham drinking also provides some information about the thirst process. He first found the normal amount of water drunk by the dog in a sham drinking situation, and following this, placed varying percentages of that amount directly into the animal's stomach. Following an adequate time interval for absorption of the water, he permitted the animals to drink. He found that approximately 40 per cent of the amount of water which was taken in the sham drinking situation was sufficient to slake thirst completely. Thus, in the sham drinking situation the animal drank about 250 per cent of what might be thought of as its normal deficit. It appears that when water does not reach the stomach, the animal's ability to judge accurately the amount of water to drink is impaired. Stomach distention would appear to be one factor in controlling amount drunk.

Further evidence of a stomach-distention factor was indicated when Towbin (1949) placed a balloon in the stomach of a fistulated dog, and thus could fill the balloon with warm water as the animal drank water which was drained through the fistula. Here he found that the amount of water taken was reduced from the overdrinking, which is typical of sham drinking. The importance of stomach distention was also indicated when a vagotomy inhibited the effect of the balloon and the animal returned to overdrinking.

Blood and Tissue Conditions

Although Cannon's local theory of thirst has perhaps received more attention than other points of view, theories of thirst which have placed emphasis upon blood and tissue conditions have also been presented. Bernard's position (Wolf, 1958) was that thirst was the expression of only a general need of the organism. Some years later, as Wolf (1958) indicates, both Mayer and Wettendorff reported that the osmotic pressure of the blood serum rose when dogs were deprived of liquid. Mayer posited that changes in the osmotic pressure excited the walls of blood vessels and were then transmitted to bulbar centers. This resulted in drinking which reversed the osmotic pressure change. Although Wettendorff confirmed Mayer's findings, he noted that there was no rise in osmotic pressure on the first day of deprivation. He believed that the tissue ceded water to the blood, and as a result there occurred general tissue dehydration.

That cellular dehydration does play a role in thirst has been experimentally demonstrated by Gilman (1937), who administered a 20 per cent solution of sodium chloride to some dogs and a 40 per cent solution of urea to others. Both of these solutions produce the same rise in osmotic pressure in the blood, but do so at different rates. The sodium chloride diffuses into the cells slowly, while urea does so rapidly, which permits cellular equilibrium without the loss of water. When the subjects were permitted to drink for 15 minutes following the administration of the experimental liquids, those animals which were injected with sodium chloride drank large quantities of water, while those injected with urea did not drink until after more than an hour.

Central Nervous System Factors

It would be reasonable to suspect that since centers have been found for hunger, similar centers could also be found for thirst. In an early study, Andersson (1953), utilizing small tubes placed in the hypothalamic region in goats, injected small amounts (.05 to .15 cc.) of sodium chloride in various concentrations. Injections of iso- and hypotonic saline had no effect; however, hypertonic solutions resulted in the animals' drinking 500 to 2500 cc. of water almost immediately following the injection. Best results occurred when the injection was given in the middle hypothalamic region near the paraventricular nucleus.

A further study by Andersson and McCann (1955) resulted in their locating the drinking area of the hypothalamus more precisely. Here they found that injections of .003 to .01 cc. of a 2 to 3 per cent sodium chloride solution resulted in their experimental animals' (goats) drinking 30 to 60 seconds after stimulation and continuing for from two to five minutes. Drinking behavior was not always reproducible. However, reproducible drinking behavior could be obtained by using electric stimulation. Such drinking began 10 to 30 seconds after the onset of stimulation and ceased two to three seconds after the current was stopped.

In contrast to the production of the drinking response, Gilbert (1956) has reported that electrocoagulative destruction of the subcommisural area in rats resulted in death in a few days because of dehydration. Paradoxically, subcutaneous injection of aqueous extracts of rat or beef subcommisural area results in a sharp depression of water consumption with a rise in intake on the second day. Control injections failed to alter water intake. Finally, Miller, Bailey, and Richter (reported by Miller, Sampliner, and Woodrow 1957) have demonstrated that minute injections of water into the third ventricle of the hypothalamus will reduce drinking.

General Conclusions

An examination of even the limited amount of literature which we have presented indicates that the physiological factors underlying the urge to eat or drink, or the more general one related to the regulation of food and water intake are indeed complex. Food and water deprivation states, as well as the subsequent ingestion of food and water, bring about a whole host of changes within the organism, which, the experimental evidence indicates, involves mouth, throat, digestive tract, and central nervous system factors, as well as blood and tissue conditions. The early attempts to assign the "cause" of hunger or thirst, and their subsequent satiation, to a single factor have been replaced by a multiple-factor approach which, even yet, has not been able to encompass all of the experimental findings.[8]

The factor which seems to be most consistently ignored in many of the studies in this area is that of learning or experience. The response measures which are used to measure the presence (or absence) of a need in almost all instances are learned, or at least involve learned components. Ghent (1951), for example, has shown that the magnitude of the consummatory response, the response which is probably most frequently used in physiological investigations in this area, is dependent upon experience. This response has been associated with a multitude of stimuli both of an internal as well as external nature. Under the circumstances, it is quite possible that the manipulation of a particular internal variable by the investigator may result in little change in the response, particularly if all other stimuli remain the same. This may be especially true if only short-term effects are being investigated.

[8] Stellar (1954) has postulated that a multifactor approach should not only be taken with regard to investigating motivation based upon food and water needs, but to all "biological motives."

ELECTRICAL STIMULATION OF THE BRAIN [9]

Olds (1955) has reported that in an early and preliminary study electrical stimulation in the septal region of the rhinencephalon of the rat resulted in the animal's returning to the corner of the box where it had last been stimulated. The stimulation itself was a 60-cycle alternating current with voltages ranging from ½ to 5 volts. In a published study describing this phenomenon, Olds and Milner (1954) have reported that animals which had electrodes implanted at a similar location, when placed in Skinner boxes in which stimulation was correlated with pressing of the bar, would continue to make the bar-pressing response again and again. These findings have been interpreted in terms of the effects of such stimulation acting upon a reward or positive reinforcing area in the brain. Subsequent studies in which implants have been used with both cats and monkeys have indicated the generality of the phenomenon.

Recently, Glickman (1960) has pointed to the wide range of self stimulation rates obtained from within the mesencephalic portion of the activating system. He has felt that small differences in the locus of stimulation appear to offer the most promising explanation of these findings, which in turn, necessitates the postulation of a hitherto undemonstrated degree of functional localization within the mesencephalic activating system in general and the reticular formation in particular.

In contrast to the findings of rewarding effects, some investigators have reported that brain stimulation results in punishing effects as inferred by escape or avoidance behavior. One of the early studies touching upon this area was Masserman's (1941) attempt to demonstrate the inadequacy of the position that direct hypothalamic stimulation would produce not only the external manifestations of anger, but also a true experience which could be conditioned to a neutral stimulus. Although Masserman found that control animals (cats) were capable of learning to escape as well as avoid peripheral pain produced by shock, his results indicated that when hypothalamic stimulation was substituted for shock,

---

[9] In this section, we have limited our discussion primarily to the experimental work which has related electrical stimulation to the motivational functions of such stimulation. Those studies which have used electrical stimulation of varying parts of the brain to explore accompanying motor and emotional activity, as well as EEG patterns and verbal sensations, have not been included.

experimental animals were unable to acquire either an escape or an avoidance response, even though as many as 480 conditioning trials were provided. Masserman (1941) concluded that direct stimulation of the hypothalamus was not accompanied by either experiential or conative components of fear.

Two criticisms have been leveled at this conclusion. The first was that good control over the location of the implanted electrodes was lacking. Thus, there was some question that the stimulation provided Masserman's animals produced a complete affective defense response. The second criticism was that the experimental animals were given no special pretraining which would have placed, in their repertoire of responses, a response which would reduce painful stimulation. In a sense, animals which received hypothalamic stimulation had nowhere to run.

Since Masserman's early work, studies by Delgado, Roberts, and Miller (1954), as well as Cohen, Brown, and Brown (1957), have demonstrated that it is possible to motivate escape or avoidance behavior by brain stimulation.[10] In the Delgado, Roberts, and Miller (1954) study, cats were trained to turn a paddle wheel in order to terminate a peripheral shock. Electrical stimulation was then provided in the tectal area, the lateral nuclear mass of the thalamus and the hippocampus, and after a number of trials, the animals learned to rotate the wheel in order to terminate such stimulation. In a second study, essentially the same procedure was used except that a tone was used as a conditioned stimulus and paired with the central stimulation. If the wheel was turned in time, central stimulation could have been avoided. Although the tone did not elicit any response at first, after a number of avoidance conditioning trials, the cats learned to avoid the central stimulation.

In the Cohen, Brown, and Brown (1957) study, four cats were prepared with permanently implanted hypothalamic electrodes and then given 20 trials a day for ten days in learning to

---

[10] Studies by Nielson, Doty, and Rutledge (1958), Ward (1959), and Bower (1959), are relevant to an examination of the characteristics of the stimulation which is provided the organism. Nielson, et al., have demonstrated that in order for electrical stimulation to act as a motivator in the cat, the intensity of the stimulation must be considerably greater than would be needed for such stimulation to act as a conditioned stimulus. Bower (1959) has shown that the latency of an escape response in the rat is inversely related to the current intensity, pulse duration, and pulse frequency of the square-wave used in the stimulation of the brain.

respond (hurdle jumping in a shuttle box) to a tone which was sounded for 15 seconds prior to the onset of hypothalamic stimulation. Results indicated that the percentage of avoidance responses increased from 20 per cent on Day 1 to 97.5 per cent on Day 10.

In contrast to these studies, in which central stimulation is believed to produce pain, Delgado, Rosvold, and Looney (1956) have hypothesized that stimulation in certain brain areas might also be used to produce fear. In their study, monkeys were trained to overturn a left cup in response to a high tone which would prevent shock to their feet, and turn a right cup in response to a low tone, or no tone at all. The latter response resulted in their receiving a peanut reward. Brain stimulation administered during the no-tone trials resulted in the elicitation of the avoidance response which had been previously conditioned to the high tone. Since such stimulation resulted in the monkeys' behaving as if they had received the high tone, the authors advanced the hypothesis that stimulation in certain brain areas (structures primarily related to the limbic system) produced in the animal a condition similar to that which is present when it is anxious or afraid of being hurt.

Alternative hypotheses, of course, could be advanced. It is possible that the stimulation received was either in pain fibers, so that the response was one of pain escape or pain avoidance, or that the stimulation was in the auditory area which was involved in the transmission of the high tone—the conditioned fear stimulus. The authors have rejected both explanations, pointing out that the stimulation which was received was not related to either pain or sensory functions.

Finally, studies by Miller (1957a), Roberts (1958, 1958a), and Brown and Cohen (1959) have indicated that electrical stimulation of certain areas in the brain may result in both rewarding and punishing effects as inferred from both approach and escape or avoidance behavior. In his first study, Roberts (1958) found that electrical stimulation would motivate cats to learn to respond correctly in a T maze in order to terminate stimulation in the posterior hypothalamus, but would not motivate them to learn to leave the starting box in time to avoid it. Roberts hypothesized that the onset of stimulation in this particular part of the brain was rewarding, but that continued stimulation in the area resulted in pain.

In his second study (1958a) this hypothesis was apparently

confirmed when it was demonstrated that cats would not only learn to press a bar in order to receive stimulation but also learn to perform an escape response in order to terminate stimulation of the same voltage. An avoidance response, however, could not be learned. In a second experiment, a symmetrical Y maze was used in which entry into one arm turned stimulation on while entry into a second arm turned it off. The third arm was a "no-change arm" and permitted the animal to make errors (which could be recorded) in its performance. Results indicated that the animals learned to oscillate back and forth between the on and off arms. Bower and Miller (1958) have found a comparable area in the brain of a rat in which stimulation can lead to both reward and escape learning.

Finally, Brown and Cohen's (1959) study merits discussion since their experimental procedure was different from that reported by other investigators. Electrodes were implanted in the lateral hypothalamus of the cat. When stimulation was applied, only those animals which exhibited classical "hypothalamic rage," and random locomotion were selected to be included in the experiment. Each animal was required to learn an approach task consisting of a straight runway, and an avoidance task which utilized a shuttle box. With this latter task, the animal was required to run from one side of the box to the other during a 15-second presentation of a CS in order to avoid the UCS. The interesting aspect of this study was that .3 seconds of stimulation served as: (a) the reward received by the animal in the goal box after traveling the runway, and (b) the UCS which was to be avoided in the shuttle box. This quantity of stimulation was selected because preliminary work had indicated that the total expenditure of electrical energy provided in each task would be about the same.

Results indicated that an animal which would learn to run the straightaway for the .3 second electrical stimulation received in the goal box would also learn to avoid that stimulation by running to the opposite side of the shuttle box when the CS was presented. Thus the performance curves for the runway and shuttle box situations were quite similar. As the authors state, the observation of avoidance behavior would lead to the hypothesis that a section of the lateral hypothalamus was a punishment center, while observation of approach behavior would lead to the hypothesis that there was a pleasure center. Inasmuch as the same cats participated in each task, and the stimulation received in each case was identical, a separate center concept was untenable to account for the findings. As a result the authors have hypothesized a nondirectional characteristic of hypothalamic stimulation.

The Relationship of Brain Stimulation to Traditional Rewards

The findings of regions in the brain which appear to be responsible for possibly an energizing and certainly a selective function have resulted in considerable interest in the area. The direction of such interest, however, has been most generally to regard brain stimulation as a new technique with which to study old problems in the area of motivation and learning rather than to use it as a means of elucidating the physiological mechanisms which are involved.

Within this framework, one of the first considerations has been to compare the effectiveness of learning with electrical stimulation with traditional motivational antecedents.

The similarity between the two is noted in an early study by Sidman, Brady, Boren, and Conrad (1955), who demonstrated that it was possible to use fixed-ratio and variable-interval reinforcement schedules using electrical stimulation as reinforcement. Cumulative response curves were similar to those found when food reinforcement was used. And, in another study, Olds (1956) examined the runway and maze performances of animals under 18 to 24 hours of food deprivation who received food as a reward, with those animals receiving brain stimulation. Performance on the runway resulted in the stimulation group's running more rapidly than the deprived-reward group, although the difference was not significant. On the other hand, running times in the maze as well as number of errors resulted in the deprived-reward group's providing significantly superior performance. One interesting observation was the fact that the performance of the stimulation animals on the first trial of one day was inferior to that obtained on the last trial of the preceding day. This, of course, was in contrast to performance of the deprived-reward group, which exhibited superior performance on the first trial of any day in contrast to the last trial of the preceding day. Olds has hypothesized that the spontaneous decrement for the stimulation group suggests that such stimulation constitutes a strong incentive only after it has been experienced on each day.

Bursten and Delgado (1958), using monkeys, have also demonstrated the superiority of food as a reward in contrast to brain stimulation. In their study, the monkey was permitted to locomote over an entire table, being stimulated when on a given side. In order to get the monkey on the other side, a peanut was rolled across the table. Results indicated that in no instance did the monkey ever choose to remain on the side in which he was receiving stimulation to forego capturing the rolled peanut.

What of adaptation and extinction effects when brain stimulation is used as a reward? Surprisingly enough, adaptation effects seem to be small. In an examination of this phenomena by Olds (1958), rats were permitted to stimulate themselves via hypothalamic or telencephalic electrodes for one hour a day for a month, and then for 48 consecutive hours. Results indicated that all subjects gave stable response rates throughout the hour, and from day to day throughout the month. In the 48-hour test, animals with hypothalamic implants self-stimulated themselves to exhaustion, but did not indicate any intrinsic satiation tendencies. Animals with telencephalic implants, however, did reveal a marked decline of self-stimulation after four to eight hours of continuous responding.

Olds (1956) examined extinction behavior on the runway and maze situation. Deprived-reward subjects were compared with brain-stimulated subjects. Little difference was noted between the groups, although the extinction curves were rather steep. More recently, Seward, Uyeda, and Olds (1959) have confirmed the general finding that electrical stimulation does produce steep extinction curves.

Since the neurological action of traditional reinforcers is largely unknown, it is possible that electrical stimulation excites elements which are involved in the mediation of reward states. Accordingly, one might hypothesize that an animal's appetite for self-stimulation would increase with hunger and decrease with satiety. The findings of Brady, Boren, Conrad, and Sidman (1957), as well as Olds (1958a), have indicated that deprivation states do have an effect, with Olds finding such effects related to the site of the stimulation. In the Brady, et al. (1957) study, following the establishment of a stable rate of lever pressing in which electrical stimulation was the only reward, cats were placed under food and water deprivation periods of 1, 4, 24, and 48 hours. They were returned to the apparatus with electrical stimulation continuing to serve as the only reward. Rats, on the other hand, were provided a series of one-hour sessions in the apparatus in which only 0 and 48 hours of food and water deprivation states were alternated. Results indicated that with both species, lever-pressing rates were significantly higher after 48 hours of deprivation than after zero or one hour. The lever-pressing rates for cats obtained after 4- and 24-hour deprivation periods tended to fall between the values obtained at the two extremes.

In the Olds (1958a) study, electrodes were placed in different parts of the rat's hypothalamus and telencephalon; following this, a food deprivation state was manipulated as well as the animal's androgen level. Thus, subjects were either 24 hours hungry or satiated, while androgen level was manipulated by castrating the animals and providing androgen injection when appropriate. Results indicated that with the placement of some electrodes, with androgen level normal, the animal's rate of responding when hungry, as contrasted to satiation, increased. This finding was similar to that found by Brady, *et al.* (1957). On the other hand, with the electrodes in the same position and the animal satiated, an increase in androgen level resulted in either no increase or a decreased rate of responding. With other electrode sites, and with the animal satiated, an increase in the androgen level resulted in an increased rate of responding. An increase in food deprivation, however, (with androgen level normal) resulted in either no increase or a decrease in rate of responding. Thus, at the site where hunger resulted in the greatest increase in responding, an increase in androgen level resulted in no increase and at times, a decrease in rate. In those sites where an increase in androgen level resulted in the greatest rise in self-stimulation rate, food deprivation resulted in no increase and at times, a decrease in rate. Olds has interpreted these findings as having an anatomical basis, and has hypothesized that there is a hunger-reward region in the brain which is structurally differentiated from one of sexual reward.

Finally, in view of the importance of secondary reinforcement, it is not surprising that there has been some interest in determining if neutral stimuli can acquire secondary reinforcement characteristics when paired with brain stimulation. In the one published study exploring this possibility, Seward, Uyeda, and Olds (1959) have been unable to obtain such an effect.

Conclusions

Considerably more experimental work is necessary before it is possible to answer the question as to whether or not reward via brain stimulation has the same characteristics as reward via traditional

314 • PHYSIOLOGY OF MOTIVATION

techniques. The need to employ such stimulation in a greater variety of tasks and under much more varied conditions is evident. So is the need to make specific comparisons with groups reinforced in the traditional way. Perhaps, as more and more investigators become acquainted with the surgical techniques necessary to provide appropriate implantation of the electrodes, these deficiencies will be remedied.

One prominent difference in the behavior provided by the two methods is that responses learned with brain stimulation serving as a reward are of a much more temporary character than responses learned with more traditional types. Such temporariness appears to be indicated by the steep extinction curves obtained when brain stimulation is omitted as well as the response decrement noted on the first trial of each day's learning trials when the animals are run for a number of days.

REFERENCES

Aborn, M. (1953) The influence of experimentally induced failure on the retention of material acquired through set and incidental learning. *J. exp. Psychol.*, 45, 225–231.

Adams, C. R. (1940) Individual differences in behavior resulting from experimentally induced frustration. *J. Psychol.*, 10, 157–176.

Adlerstein, A. & Fehrer, E. (1955) The effect of food deprivation on exploratory behavior in a complex maze. *J. comp. physiol. Psychol.*, 48, 250–253.

Adolph, E. F. (1939) Measurements of water drinking in dogs. *Amer. J. Physiol.*, 125, 75–86.

Adolph, E. F. (1947) Urges to eat and drink in rats. *Amer. J. Physiol.*, 151, 110–125.

Allport, F. H. (1924) *Social Psychology.* New York: Houghton-Mifflin.

Allport, F. H. (1955) *Theories of perception and the concept of structure.* New York: Wiley.

Allport, G. W. (1937) *Personality, a psychological interpretation.* New York: Holt.

Allport, G. W. (1943) The ego in contemporary psychology. *Psychol. Rev.*, 50, 451–478.

Alper, T. G. (1946) Task-orientation vs. ego-orientation in learning and retention. *Amer. J. Psychol.*, 59, 236–248.

Alper, T. G. (1948) Task-orientation and ego-orientation as factors in reminiscence. *J. exp. Psychol.*, 38, 224–238.

Alper, T. G., & Korchin, S. J. (1952) Memory for socially relevant material. *J. abnorm. soc. Psychol.*, 47, 25–37.

Alvarez, W. C. (1948) *An introduction to gastro-enterology.* New York: Hoeber.

Amsel, A. (1949) Selective association and the anticipatory goal response mechanism as explanatory concepts in learning theory. *J. exp. Psychol.,* 39, 785–799.

Amsel, A. (1950) The combination of the primary appetitional need with primary and secondary emotionally derived needs. *J. exp. Psychol.,* 40, 1–14.

Amsel, A. (1958) Comment on "Role of prefeeding in an apparent frustration effect." *J. exp. Psychol.,* 56, 180–181.

Amsel, A. (1958 a) The role of frustrative nonreward in noncontinuous reward situations. *Psychol. Bull.,* 55, 102–119.

Amsel, A., & Hancock, W. (1957) Motivational properties of frustration: III. Relation of frustration effect to antedating goal factors. *J. exp. Psychol.,* 53, 126–131.

Amsel, A., & Roussel, J. (1952) Motivational properties of frustration: I. Effect on a running response of the addition of frustration to the motivational complex. *J. exp. Psychol.,* 43, 363–368.

Amsel, A., & Ward, J. S. (1954) Motivational properties of frustration: II. Frustration drive stimulus and frustration reduction in selective learning. *J. exp. Psychol.,* 48, 37–47.

Anand, B. K., & Brobeck, J. R. (1951) Hypothalamic control of food intake in rats and cats. *Yale J. Biol. and Med.,* 24, 123–140.

Anand, B. K., Dua, S. & Shoenberg, K. (1955) Hypothalamic control of food intake in cats and monkeys. *J. Physiol.,* 127, 143–152.

Anderson, E. E. (1938) The interrelationships of drives in the male albino rat. II. Intercorrelations between 47 measures of drives and of learning. *Comp. Psychol. Monogr.,* 14, No. 6.

Anderson, E. E. (1941) The externalization of drive: I. Theoretical considerations. *Psychol. Rev.,* 48, 204–224.

Anderson, E. E. (1941 a) The externalization of drive: II. The effect of satiation and removal of reward at different stages in the learning process of the rat. *J. genet. Psychol.,* 59, 359–376.

Anderson, E. E. (1941 b) The externalization of drive: III. Maze learning by nonrewarded and by satiated rats. *J. genet. Psychol.,* 59, 397–426.

Anderson, J. E., & Smith, A. H. (1926) The effect of quantitative and qualitative stunting upon maze learning in the white rat. *J. comp. Psychol.,* 6, 337–359.

Andersson, B. (1953) The effect of injections of hypertonic NaCl-solutions into different parts of the hypothalamus of goats. *Acta physiol. Scandinav.,* 28, 188–201.

Andersson, B., & Larsson, S. (1956) An attempt to condition hypothalamic polydipsia. *Acta physiol. Scandinav.,* 36, 377–382.

Andersson, B., & McCann, S. M. (1955) Drinking, anti-diuresis and milk ejection from electrical stimulation within the hypothalamus of the goat. *Acta physiol. Scandinav.,* 35, 191–201.

Angell, J. R. (1908) *Psychology.* New York: Holt.

Anliker, J., & Mayer, J. (1956) An operant conditioning technique for studying feeding-fasting patterns in normal and obese mice. *J. appl. Physiol.,* 8, 667–670.

Armus, H. L. (1958) Drive level and habit reversal. *Psychol. Repts.*, 4, 31–34.

Aronfreed, J. M., Messick, S. A., & Diggory, J. C. (1953) Re-examining emotionality and perceptual defense. *J. Pers.*, 21, 517–528.

Aronson, L. R. (1948) Problems in the behavior and physiology of a species of African mouthbreeding fish. *Trans. N. Y. Acad. Sci.*, 2, 33–42.

Ashley, W. R., Harper, R. S., & Runyon, D. L. (1951) The perceived size of coins in normal and hypnotically induced economic states. *Amer. J. Psychol.*, 64, 564–572.

Atkinson, J. W. and McClelland, D. C. (1948) The projective expression of needs: II. The effect of different intensities of the hunger drive on thematic apperception. *J. exp. Psychol.*, 38, 643–658.

Axelrod, H. S., Cowen, E. L., & Heilizer, F. (1956) The correlates of manifest anxiety in stylus maze learning. *J. exp. Psychol.*, 51, 131–138.

Ayllon, T., & Sommer, R. (1956) Autism, emphasis and figure-ground perception. *J. Psychol.*, 41, 163–176.

Ayres, C. E. (1921) Instinct and capacity. *J. Phil.*, 18, 561–565.

Backlund, H. O., & Ekeroot, S. (1950) An actograph for small terrestrial animals. *Oikos*, 2, 213–216.

Bailey, C. J., & Porter, L. W. (1955) Relevant cues in drive discrimination in cats. *J. comp. physiol. Psychol.*, 48, 180–182.

Bain, A. (1868) *The senses and the intellect.* (3d ed.) London: Longmans, Green.

Baker, R. A. (1953) Aperiodic feeding behavior in the albino rat. *J. comp. physiol. Psychol.*, 46, 422–426.

Baker, R. A. (1955) The effects of repeated deprivation experience on feeding behavior. *J. comp. physiol. Psychol.*, 48, 37–42.

Baldwin, J. M. (1906) *Mental development in the child and the race.* London: Macmillan.

Banks, R. K., & Walters, R. H. (1959) Prior reinforcement as a determinant of recognition thresholds. *Percept. Mot. Skills*, 9, 51–54.

Bare, J. K. (1949) The specific hunger for sodium chloride in normal and adrenalectomized white rats. *J. comp. physiol. Psychol.*, 42, 242–253.

Bare, J. K. (1959) Hunger, deprivation, and the day-night cycle. *J. comp. physiol. Psychol.*, 52, 129–131.

Barker, R. G. (1938–39) Frustration as an experimental problem. V. The effect of frustration upon cognitive ability. *Charact. and Pers.*, 7, 145–150.

Barker, R., Dembo, T., & Lewin, K. (1941) Frustration and regression: an experiment with young children. *Univer. Iowa Stud. Child Welf.*, 18, No. 1.

Barnett, S. A. (1958) Experiments on "neophobia" in wild and laboratory rats. *Brit. J. Psychol.*, 49, 195–201.

Barry, H., III. (1958) Effects of strength of drive on learning and on extinction. *J. exp. Psychol.*, 55, 473–481.

Bash, K. W. (1939) An investigation into a possible organic basis for the hunger drive. *J. comp. Psychol.*, 28, 109–134.

Bateson, G. (1941) The frustration-aggression hypothesis and culture. *Psychol. Rev.*, 48, 350–355.

Beach, F. A. (1940) Effects of cortical lesions upon the copulatory behavior of male rats. *J. comp. Psychol.*, 29, 193–239.

Beach, F. A. (1941) Effects of brain lesions upon running activity in the male rat. *J. comp. Psychol.*, 31, 145–179.

Beach, F. A. (1942) Analysis of the stimuli adequate to elicit mating behavior in the sexually inexperienced rat. *J. comp. Psychol.*, 33, 163–207.

Beach, F. A. (1951) Instinctive behavior; reproductive activities. In Stevens, S. S. (Ed.), *Handbook of Experimental Psychology*. New York: Wiley.

Beach, F. A. (1955) The descent of instinct. *Psychol. Rev.*, 62, 401–410.

Beams, H. L. (1954) Affectivity as a factor in the apparent size of pictured food objects. *J. exp. Psychol.*, 47, 197–200.

Beebe-Center, J. G., Black, P., Hoffman, A. C., & Wade, M. (1948) Relative per diem consumption as a measure of preference in the rat. *J. comp. physiol. Psychol.*, 41, 239–251.

Beier, E. G., & Cowen, E. L. (1953) A further investigation of the influence of "threat expectancy" on perception. *J. Pers.*, 22, 254–257.

Bellows, R. T. (1939) Time factors in water drinking in dogs. *Amer. J. Physiol.*, 125, 87–97.

Berkowitz, L. (1958) The expression and reduction of hostility. *Psychol. Bull.*, 55, 257–283.

Berkun, M. M., Kessen, M. L., & Miller, N. E. (1952) Hunger-reducing effects of food by stomach fistula versus food by mouth measured by a consummatory response. *J. comp. physiol. Psychol.*, 45, 550–554.

Berlyne, D. E. (1950) Novelty and curiosity as determinants of exploratory behavior. *Brit. J. Psychol.*, 41, 68–80.

Berlyne, D. E. (1951) Attention to change. *Brit. J. Psychol.*, 42, 269–278.

Berlyne, D. E., & Slater, J. (1957) Perceptual curiosity, exploratory behavior, and maze learning. *J. comp. physiol. Psychol.*, 50, 228–232.

Bernard, L. L. (1921) The misuse of instinct in the social sciences. *Psychol. Rev.*, 28, 96–119.

Bernard, L. L. (1924) *Instinct*. New York: Holt.

Bernardin, A. C., & Jessor, R. (1957) A construct validation of the Edwards Personal Preference Schedule with respect to dependency. *J. consult. Psychol.*, 21, 63–67.

Bernstein, L. M., & Grossman, M. I. (1956) An experimental test of the glucostatic theory of regulation of food intake. *J. clin Investig.*, 35, 627–633.

Bersh, P. J. (1951) The influence of two variables upon the establishment of a secondary reinforcer for operant responses. *J. exp. Psychol.*, 41, 62–73.

Bertocci, P. A. (1940) A critique of G. W. Allport's theory of motivation. *Psychol. Rev.*, 47, 501–532.

Bertocci, P. A. (1945) The psychological self, the ego and personality. *Psychol. Rev.*, 52, 91–99.

Bexton, W. H., Heron, W., & Scott, T. H. (1954) Effects of decreased variation in the sensory environment. *Canad. J. Psychol.*, 8, 70–76.

Billingslea, F. (1940) The relationship between emotionality, activity, curiosity, persistence and weight in the male rat. *J. comp. Psychol.*, 29, 315–325.

Bills, A. G. (1927) The influence of muscular tension on the efficiency of mental work. *Amer. J. Psychol.*, 38, 227–251.

Bills, A. G., & Stauffacher, J. C. (1937) The influence of voluntarily induced tension on rational problem solving. *J. Psychol.*, 4, 261–271.

Bindra, D. (1959) *Motivation: a systematic reinterpretation*. New York: Ronald.

Bingham, H. C. (1928) Sex development in apes. *Comp. Psychol. Monogr.,* 5.

Birch, D., Burnstein, E., & Clark, R. A. (1958) Response strength as a function of hours of food deprivation under a controlled maintenance schedule. *J. comp. physiol. Psychol.,* 51, 350–354.

Bitterman, M. E., Feddersen, W. E., & Tyler, D. W. (1953) Secondary reinforcement and the discrimination hypothesis. *Amer. J. Psychol.,* 66, 456–464.

Bitterman, M. E., & Holtzman, W. H. (1952) Conditioning and extinction of the galvanic skin response as a function of anxiety. *J. abnorm. soc. Psychol.,* 47, 615–623.

Bitterman, M. E., & Kniffin, C. W. (1953) Manifest anxiety and "perceptual defense." *J. abnorm. soc. Psychol.,* 48, 248–252.

Bitterman, M. E., Reed, P., & Krauskopf, J. (1952) The effect of the duration of the unconditioned stimulus upon conditioning and extinction. *Amer. J. Psychol.,* 65, 256–262.

Blake, R. R., & Vanderplas, J. M. (1950) The effect of prerecognition hypotheses on veridical recognition thresholds in auditory perception. *J. Pers.,* 19, 95–115.

Bloomberg, R., & Webb, W. B. (1949) Various degrees within a single drive as cues for spatial response learning in the white rat. *J. exp. Psychol.,* 39, 628–636.

Bloomfield, A., & Tainter, M. L. (1943) The effects of vitamin B deprivation on spontaneous activity in the rat. *J. lab. clin. Med.,* 28, 1680–1690.

Bolles, R. C. (1958) A replication and further analysis of a study on position reversal learning in hungry and thirsty rats. *J. comp. physiol. Psychol.,* 51, 349.

Bolles, R., & Petrinovich, L. (1956) Body-weight changes and behavioral attributes. *J. comp. physiol. Psychol.,* 49, 177–180.

Bousfield, W. A., & Elliot, M. H. (1934) The effect of fasting on the eating behavior of rats. *J. genet. Psychol.,* 45, 227–237.

Bower, G. H. (1959) Response latency as a function of brain stimulation variables. *J. comp. physiol. Psychol.,* 52, 533–535.

Bower, G. H., & Miller, N. E. (1958) Rewarding and punishing effects from stimulating the same place in the rat's brain. *J. comp. physiol. Psychol.,* 51, 669–674.

Brady, J. V., Boren, J. J., Conrad, D., & Sidman, M. (1957) The effect of food and water deprivation upon intracranial self-stimulation. *J. comp. physiol. Psychol.,* 50, 134–137.

Brandauer, C. M. (1953) A confirmation of Webb's data concerning the action of the irrelevant drives. *J. exp. Psychol.,* 45, 150–152.

Braun, H. W., Wedekind, C. E., & Smudski, J. F. (1957) The effect of an irrelevant drive on maze learning in the rat. *J. exp. Psychol.,* 54, 148–152.

Broadhurst, P. L. (1957) Emotionality and the Yerkes-Dodson law. *J. exp. Psychol.,* 54, 345–352.

Brobeck, J. R. (1955) Neural regulation of food intake. In Miner, R. W. (Ed.), *The regulation of hunger and appetite*. New York: Annals of the N. Y. Acad. Sci., 63, 44–55.

Brobeck, J. R., Tepperman, J., & Long, C. N. H. (1943) Experimental hypothalamic hyperphagia in the albino rat. *Yale J. Biol. Med.,* 15, 831–853.

Brogden, W. J. (1949) Acquisition and extinction of a conditioned avoidance response in dogs. *J. comp. physiol. Psychol.,* 42, 296–302.

Brooks, C. McC., & Lambert, E. F. (1946) A study of the effect of limitation of food intake and the method of feeding on the rate of weight gain during hypothalamic obesity in the albino rat. *Amer. J. Physiol.,* 147, 695–707.

Brooks, C. McC., Lockwood, R. A., & Wiggins, M. L. (1946) A study of the effect of hypothalamic lesions on the eating habits of the albino rat. *Amer. J. Physiol.,* 147, 735–741.

Browman, L. G. (1943) The effect of controlled temperatures upon the spontaneous activity rhythms of the albino rat. *J. exp. Zool.,* 94, 477–489.

Brown, G. W., & Cohen, B. D. (1959) Avoidance and approach learning motivated by stimulation of identical hypothalamic loci. *Amer. J. Physiol.,* 197, 153–157.

Brown, J. L. (1956) The effect of drive on learning with secondary reinforcement. *J. comp. physiol. Psychol.,* 49, 254–260.

Brown, J. S. (1953) Problems presented by the concept of acquired drives. In *Current theory and research in motivation: A symposium.* Lincoln, Nebraska: Univer. Nebraska Press.

Brown, J. S., & Bass, B. (1958) The acquisition and extinction of an instrumental response under constant and variable stimulus conditions. *J. comp. physiol. Psychol.,* 51, 499–504.

Brown, J. S., & Farber, I. E. (1951) Emotions conceptualized as intervening variables—with suggestions toward a theory of frustration. *Psychol. Bull.,* 48, 465–480.

Brown, J. S., & Jacobs, A. (1949) The role of fear in the motivation and acquisition of responses. *J. exp. Psychol.,* 39, 747–759.

Brown, J. S., Kalish, H. I., & Farber, I. E. (1951) Conditioned fear as revealed by magnitude of startle response to an auditory stimulus. *J. exp. Psychol.,* 41, 317–328.

Bruner, J. S. (1951) Personality dynamics and the process of perceiving. In Blake, R. R. and Ramsey, G. V. (Eds.), *Perception: an approach to personality.* New York: Ronald.

Bruner, J. S., & Goodman, C. C. (1947) Value and need as organizing factors in perception. *J. abnorm. soc. Psychol.,* 42, 33–44.

Bruner, J. S. and Postman, L. (1947) Tension and tension release as organizing factors in perception. *J. Pers.,* 15, 300–308.

Bruner, J. S., & Postman, L. (1947 a) Emotional selectivity in perception and reaction. *J. Pers.,* 16, 69–77.

Bruner, J. S., & Postman, L. (1948) Symbolic value as an organizing factor in perception. *J. soc. Psychol.,* 27, 203–208.

Bruner, J. S., & Postman, L. (1949) Perception, cognition and behavior. *J. Pers.,* 18, 14–31.

Bruner, J. S., & Rodrigues, J. S. (1953) Some determinants of apparent size. *J. abnorm. soc. Psychol.,* 48, 17–24.

Brush, F. R. (1957) The effects of shock intensity on the acquisition and extinction of an avoidance response in dogs. *J. comp. physiol. Psychol.*, 50, 547–552.

Buchwald, A. M., & Yamaguchi, H. G. (1955) The effect of change in drive level on habit reversal. *J. exp. Psychol.*, 50, 265–268.

Bugelski, B. R. (1938) Extinction with and without sub-goal reinforcement. *J. comp. Psychol.*, 26, 121–134.

Bugelski, B. R. (1956) *The psychology of learning.* New York: Holt.

Bulatao, E., & Carlson, A. J. (1924) Contributions to the physiology of the stomach. Influence of experimental changes in blood sugar level on gastric hunger contractions. *Amer. J. Physiol.*, 69, 107–115.

Bursten, B., & Delgado, J. M. R. (1958) Positive reinforcement induced by intracerebral stimulation in the monkey. *J. comp. physiol. Psychol.*, 51, 6–10.

Butler, R. A. (1953) Discrimination learning by rhesus monkeys to visual-exploration motivation. *J. comp. physiol. Psychol.*, 46, 95–98.

Butler, R. A. (1954) Incentive conditions which influence visual exploration. *J. exp. Psychol.*, 48, 19–23.

Butler, R. A. (1957) The effect of deprivation of visual incentives on visual exploration motivation in monkeys. *J. comp. physiol. Psychol.*, 50, 177–179.

Butler, R. A. (1957 a) Discrimination learning by rhesus monkeys to auditory incentives. *J. comp. physiol. Psychol.*, 50, 239–241.

Butler, R. A., & Harlow, H. F. (1954) Persistence of visual exploration in monkeys. *J. comp. physiol. Psychol.*, 47, 258–263.

Butter, C. M., & Thomas, D. R. (1958) Secondary reinforcement as a function of the amount of primary reinforcement. *J. comp. physiol. Psychol.*, 51, 346–348.

Caldwell, D. F., & Cromwell, R. L. (1959) Replication report: The relationship of manifest anxiety and electric shock to eyelid conditioning. *J. exp. Psychol.*, 57, 348–349.

Calvin, J. S., Bicknell, E. A., & Sperling, D. S. (1953) Establishment of a conditioned drive based on the hunger drive. *J. comp. physiol. Psychol.*, 46, 173–175.

Calvin, J. S., Bicknell, E. A., & Sperling, D. S. (1953 a) Effect of a secondary reinforcer on consummatory behavior. *J. comp. physiol. Psychol.*, 46, 176–179.

Campbell, A. A. (1938) The interrelations of two measures of conditioning in man. *J. exp. Psychol.*, 22, 225–243.

Campbell, A. A., & Hilgard, E. R. (1936) Individual differences in ease of conditioning. *J. exp. Psychol.*, 19, 561–571.

Campbell, B. A. (1954) Design and reliability of a new activity-recording device. *J. comp. physiol. Psychol.*, 47, 90–92.

Campbell, B. A., & Kraeling, D. (1954) Response strength as a function of drive level during training and extinction. *J. comp. physiol. Psychol.*, 47, 101–103.

Campbell, B. A., & Sheffield, F. D. (1953) Relation of random activity to food deprivation. *J. comp. physiol. Psychol.*, 46, 320–322.

Cannon, W. B. (1911–12) A consideration of the nature of hunger. *Harvey Lect.*, 7, 130–152.

Cannon, W. B. (1918) The physiological basis of thirst. *Proc. Roy. Soc.,* London, s.B., 90, 283–301.

Cannon, W. B. (1932) *The wisdom of the body.* New York: Norton.

Cannon, W. B. (1934) Hunger and thirst. In Murchison, C. (Ed), *A handbook of general experimental psychology.* Worcester: Clark Univ. Press.

Cannon, W. B. & Washburn, A. L. (1912) An explanation of hunger. *Amer. J. Physiol.,* 29, 441–454.

Capaldi, E. J. (1957) The effect of different amounts of alternating partial reinforcement on resistance to extinction. *Amer. J. Psychol.,* 70, 451–452.

Capaldi, E. J. (1958) The effect of different amounts of training on the resistance to extinction of different patterns of partially reinforced responses. *J. comp. physiol. Psychol.,* 51, 367–371.

Carlson, A. J. (1916) *The control of hunger in health and disease.* Chicago: Univ. Chicago Press.

Carpenter, B., Wiener, M., & Carpenter, J. T. (1956) Predictability of perceptual defense behavior. *J. abnorm. soc. Psychol.,* 52, 380–383.

Carpenter, C. R. (1942) Sexual behavior of free ranging rhesus monkeys (macaca mulatta). I. Specimens, procedures and behavioral characteristics of estrus. *J. comp. Psychol.,* 33, 113–162.

Carpenter, J. A. (1958) A comparison of stimulus-presentation procedures in taste-preference experiments. *J. comp. physiol. Psychol.,* 51, 561–564.

Carper, J. W. (1953) A comparison of the reinforcing value of a nutritive and non-nutritive substance under conditions of specific and general hunger. *Amer. J. Psychol.,* 66, 270–277.

Carr, H. A. (1925) *Psychology, a study of mental activity.* New York: Longmans, Green.

Carr, W. J. (1952) The effect of adrenalectomy upon the NaCl taste threshold in the rat. *J. comp. physiol. Psychol.,* 45, 377–380.

Carter, L. F., & Schooler, K. (1949) Value need and other factors in perception. *Psychol. Rev.,* 56, 200–207.

Castañeda, A. (1956) Effects of stress on complex learning and performance. *J. exp. Psychol.,* 52, 9–12.

Castañeda, A., & Palermo, D. S. (1955) Psychomotor performance as a function of amount of training and stress. *J. exp. Psychol.,* 50, 175–179.

Cattell, R. B. & Scheier, I. H. (1958) The nature of anxiety: a review of thirteen multivariate analyses comprising 814 variables. *Psychol. Repts.,* 4, 351–388.

Cautela, J. R. (1956) Experimental extinction and drive during extinction in a discrimination habit. *J. exp. Psychol.,* 51, 299–302.

Chansky, N. M. (1956) Threat as a factor in recall in a retroactive paradigm. *J. Psychol.,* 41, 3–10.

Chapman, R. M., & Levy, N. (1957) Hunger drive and reinforcing effect of novel stimuli. *J. comp. physiol. Psychol.,* 50, 233–238.

Charlesworth, W. R., & Thompson, W. R. (1957) Effect of lack of visual stimulus variation on exploratory behavior in the adult white rat. *Psychol. Repts.,* 3, 509–512.

Child, C. M. (1924) *Physiological foundations of behavior.* New York: Holt.

Child, I. L. (1954) Personality. In Stone, C. P. (Ed), *Ann. Rev. Psychol.,* 5, 149–170.

Child, I. L., & Waterhouse, I. K. (1952) Frustration and the quality of performance: I. A critique of the Barker, Dembo and Lewin experiment. *Psychol. Rev.,* 59, 351–362.

Child, I. L. & Waterhouse, I. K. (1953) Frustration and the quality of performance: II. A theoretical statement. *Psychol. Rev.,* 60, 127–139.

Chiles, W. D. (1958) Effects of shock-induced stress on verbal performance. *J. exp. Psychol.,* 56, 159–165.

Clark, R. A. (1952) The projective measurement of experimentally induced levels of sexual motivation. *J. exp. Psychol.,* 44, 391–399.

Clark, W. C., & Clausen, D. F. (1943) Dietary "self-selection" and appetites of untreated and treated adrenalectomized rats. *Amer. J. Physiol.,* 139, 70.

Clarke, R. S., Heron, W., Fetherstonhaugh, M. L., Forgays, D. G., & Hebb, D. O. (1951) Individual differences in dogs: preliminary report on the effects of early experience. *Canad. J. Psychol.,* 5, 150–156.

Clayton, F. L. (1958) Light reinforcement as a function of water deprivation. *Psychol. Repts.,* 4, 63–66.

Cohen, B. D., Brown, G. W., & Brown, M. L. (1957) Avoidance learning motivated by hypothalamic stimulation. *J. exp. Psychol.,* 53, 228–233.

Cole, L. W. (1911) The relation of strength of stimulus to rate of learning in the chick. *J. anim. Behav.,* 1, 111–124.

Coppock, H. W. (1950) Cited in Mowrer, O. H. *Learning theory and personality dynamics.* New York: Ronald.

Cotton, J. W. (1953) Running time as a function of amount of food deprivation. *J. exp. Psychol.,* 46, 188–198.

Courts, F. A. (1942) The influence of practice on the dynamogenetic effect of muscular tension. *J. exp. Psychol.,* 30, 504–511.

Courts, F. A. (1942 a) Relations between muscular tension and performance. *Psychol. Bull.,* 39, 347–367.

Cowen, E. L. (1952) The influence of varying degrees of psychological stress on problem-solving rigidity. *J. abnorm. soc. Psychol.,* 47, 512–519.

Cowen, E. L., & Beier, E. G. (1950) The influence of "threat-expectancy" on perception. *J. Pers.,* 19, 85–94.

Cowen, E. L., & Beier, E. G. (1954) Threat expectancy, word frequencies and perceptual prerecognition hypotheses. *J. abnorm. soc. Psychol.,* 49, 178–182.

Cowen, E. L., & Obrist, P. A. (1958) Perceptual reactivity to threat and neutral words under varying experimental conditions. *J. abnorm. soc. Psychol.,* 56, 305–310.

Cowgill, G. R. (1928) The energy factor in relation to food intake: experiments on the dog. *Amer. J. Physiol.,* 85, 45–64.

Cowles, J. T. (1937) Food tokens as incentives for learning by chimpanzees. *Comp. Psychol. Monogr.,* 14, No. 5.

Crespi, L. P. (1942) Quantitative variation of incentive and performance in the white rat. *Amer. J. Psychol.,* 55, 467–517.

Crespi, L. P. (1944) Amount of reinforcement and level of performance. *Psychol. Rev.,* 51, 341–357.

Crowder, W. F., Gay, B. R., Bright, M. G., & Lee, M. F. (1959) Secondary reinforcement or response facilitation?: III. Reconditioning. *J. Psychol.,* 48, 307–310.

Crowder, W. F., Gay, B. R., Fleming, W. C., & Hurst, R. W. (1959) Secondary reinforcement or response facilitation?: IV. The retention method. *J. Psychol.*, 48, 311–314.

Crowder, W. F., Gill, K., Jr., Hodge, C. C., & Nash, F. A., Jr. (1959) Secondary reinforcement or response facilitation?: II. Response acquisition. *J. Psychol.*, 48, 303–306.

Crowder, W. F., Morris, J. B., & McDaniel, M. H. (1959) Secondary reinforcement or response facilitation?: I. Resistance to extinction. *J. Psychol.*, 48, 299–302.

Crum, J., Brown, W. L., & Bitterman, M. E. (1951) The effect of partial and delayed reinforcement on resistance to extinction. *Amer. J. Psychol.*, 64, 228–237.

Curtis, Q. F. (1937) Diurnal variation in the free activity of sheep and pig. *Proc. soc. exp. Biol. Med.*, 35, 556–567.

D'Amato, M. R. (1955) Transfer of secondary reinforcement across the hunger and thirst drives. *J. exp. Psychol.*, 49, 352–356.

D'Amato, M. R. (1955 a) Secondary reinforcement and magnitude of primary reinforcement. *J. comp. physiol. Psychol.*, 48, 378–380.

D'Amato, M. R., Lachman, R. & Kivy, P. (1958) Secondary reinforcement as affected by reward schedule and the testing situation. *J. comp. physiol. Psychol.*, 51, 737–741.

Danziger, K. (1951) The operation of an acquired drive in satiated rats. *Quart, J. exp. Psychol.*, 3, 119–132.

Dashiell, J. F. (1925) A quantitative demonstration of animal drive. *J. comp. Psychol.*, 5, 205–208.

Dashiell, J. F. (1928) *Fundamentals of objective psychology*. Boston: Houghton-Mifflin.

Dashiell, J. F. (1937) *Fundamentals of objective psychology*. 2d ed. Boston: Houghton-Mifflin.

Datel, W. E., & Seward, J. P. (1952) On the persistence of an ear-scratching response in the rat. *J. abnorm. soc. Psychol.*, 47, 58–61.

Davidson, W. Z., Andrews, T. G., & Ross, S. (1956) Effects of stress and anxiety on continuous high-speed color naming. *J. exp. Psychol.*, 52, 13–17.

Davis, C. M. (1928) Self selection of diet by newly weaned infants. *Amer. J. Diseases of Children*, 36, 651–679.

Davis, J. D. (1958) The reinforcing effect of weak-light onset as a function of amount of food deprivation. *J. comp. physiol. Psychol.*, 51, 496–498.

Davis, R. C., Garafolo, L., and Gault, F. P. (1957) An exploration of abdominal potentials. *J. comp. physiol. Psychol.*, 50, 519–523.

Davis, R. C., Garafolo, L. and Kveim, K. (1959) Conditions associated with gastrointestinal activity. *J. comp. physiol. Psychol.*, 52, 466–475.

Davis, R. H. (1957) The effect of drive reversal on latency, amplitude and activity level. *J. exp. Psychol.*, 53, 310–315.

Davitz, J. R. (1954) The effects of previous training on post-frustration behavior. *J. abnorm. soc. Psychol.*, 47, 309–315.

Davitz, J. R. (1955) Reinforcement of fear at the beginning and at the end of shock. *J. comp. physiol. Psychol.*, 48, 152–155.

Dawson, A. B. (1941) Early estrus in the cat following increased illumination. *Endocrinology*, 28, 907–910.

Deane, G. E. and Zeaman, D. (1958) Human heart rate during anxiety. *Percept. Mot. Skills.,* 8, 103–106.

Deese, J., & Carpenter, J. A. (1951) Drive-level and reinforcement. *J. exp. Psychol.* 42, 236–238.

Deese, J., Lazarus, R. A., & Keenan, J. (1953) Anxiety, anxiety reduction and stress in learning. *J. exp. Psychol.,* 46, 55–60.

Delgado, J. M. R., Rosvold, H. E., & Looney, E. (1956) Evoking conditioned fear by electrical stimulation of subcortical structures in the monkey brain. *J. comp. physiol. Psychol.,* 49, 373–379.

Delgado, J. M. R., Roberts, W. W. & Miller, N. E. (1954) Learning motivated by electrical stimulation of the brain. *Amer. J. Physiol.,* 179, 587–593.

Dember, W. N., & Earl, R. W. (1957) Analysis of exploratory, manipulatory and curiosity behaviors. *Psychol. Rev.,* 64, 91–96.

Denny, M. R. (1946) The role of secondary reinforcement in a partial reinforcement learning situation. *J. exp. Psychol.,* 36, 373–389.

Denny, M. R., & King, G. F. (1955) Differential response learning on the basis of differential size of reward. *J. genet. Psychol.,* 87, 317–320.

DeVito, J. L., & Smith, O. A., Jr. (1959) Effects of temperature and food deprivation on the random activity of macaca mulatta. *J. comp. physiol. Psychol.,* 52, 29–32.

Dinsmoor, J. A. (1950) A quantitative comparison of the discriminative and reinforcing functions of a stimulus. *J. exp. Psychol.,* 40, 458–472.

Dinsmoor, J. A. (1958) Pulse duration and food deprivation in escape from shock training. *Psychol. Repts.,* 4, 531–534.

Dodson, J. D. (1915) The relation of strength of stimulus to rapidity of habit-formation in the kitten. *J. anim. Behav.,* 5, 330–336.

Dodson, J. D. (1917) Relative values of reward and punishment in habit formation. *Psychobiol.,* 1, 231–276.

Dollard, J. (1938) Hostility and fear in social life. *Social Forces,* 17, 15–26.

Dollard, J., Doob, L. W., Miller, N. E., Mowrer, O. H., & Sears, R. R. (1939) *Frustration and aggression.* New Haven: Yale Univ. Press.

Dollard, J. and Miller, N. E. (1950) *Personality and psychotherapy.* New York: McGraw-Hill.

Dorcus, R. M. (1934) A new device for studying motivation in rats. *J. comp. Psychol.,* 18, 149–151.

Duckworth, J. E., & Shirlaw, D. W. (1955) The development of an apparatus to record the jaw movements of cattle. *Brit. J. Anim. Behav.,* 3, 56–60.

Duffy, M. L., & Price, G. E. (1956) A continuous drinking-recorder for small animals. *Amer. J. Psychol.,* 69, 664–666.

Dukes, W. F., & Bevan, W., Jr. (1952) Accentuation and response variability in the perception of personally relevant objects. *J. Pers.,* 20, 457–465.

Dunlap, K. (1919–20) Are there any instincts? *J. abnorm. Psychol.,* 14, 307–311.

Dyal, J. A. (1958) Secondary motivation based on appetites and aversions. *Psychol. Repts.,* 4, 698.

Earl, R. W. (1957) Motivation, performance, and extinction. *J. comp. physiol. Psychol.,* 50, 248–251.

Eayrs, J. T. (1954) Spontaneous activity in the rat. *Brit. J. Anim. Behav.,* 2, 25–30.

Edwards, A. L. (1941) Political frames of reference as a factor influencing recognition. *J. abnorm. soc. Psychol.*, 36, 34–50.

Ehrenfreund, D. (1959) The relationship between weight loss during deprivation and food consumption. *J. comp. physiol. Psychol.*, 52, 123–125.

Elam, C. E., Tyler, D. W., & Bitterman, M. E. (1954) A further study of secondary reinforcement and the discrimination hypothesis. *J. comp. physiol. Psychol.*, 47, 381–384.

Ellen, P. (1956) The compulsive nature of abnormal fixations. *J. comp. physiol. Psychol.*, 49, 309–317.

Ellis, N. R. (1957) The immediate effects of emotionality upon behavior strength. *J. exp. Psychol.*, 54, 339–344.

Epstein, A. N., & Stellar, E. (1955) The control of salt preference in the adrenalectomized rat. *J. comp. physiol. Psychol.*, 48, 167–172.

Epstein, A. N. (1959) Suppression of eating and drinking by amphetamine and other drugs in normal and hyperphagic rats. *J. comp. physiol. Psychol.*, 52, 37–45.

Eriksen, C. W. (1952) Individual differences in defensive forgetting. *J. exp. Psychol.*, 44, 442–446.

Estes, W. K. (1949) Generalization of secondary reinforcement from the primary drive. *J. comp. physiol. Psychol.*, 42, 286–295.

Estes, W. K. (1949 a) A study of motivating conditions necessary for secondary reinforcement. *J. exp. Psychol.*, 39, 306–310.

Estes, W. K. (1950) Toward a statistical theory of learning. *Psychol. Rev.*, 57, 94–107.

Estes, W. K. (1958) Stimulus-response theory of drive. In Jones, M. R. (Ed), *Nebraska symposium on motivation*. Lincoln, Nebraska: Univer. Nebraska Press.

Everall, E. E. (1935) Perseveration in the rat. *J. comp. Psychol.*, 19, 343–369.

Evvard, J. M. (1916) Is the appetite of swine a reliable indication of physiological needs? *Proc. Iowa Acad. Science*, 22, 375–414.

Eysenck, H. J. (1958) The nature of anxiety and the factorial method. *Psychol. Repts.*, 4, 453–454.

Falconer, D. S. (1945) On the behavior of wireworms of the genus "Agriotes" Esch (Coleoptera, Elōteridae) in relation to temperature. *J. exp. Biol.* 21, 17–32.

Farber, I. E. (1948) Response fixation under anxiety and non-anxiety conditions. *J. exp. Psychol.*, 38, 111–131.

Farber, I. E., & Spence, K. W. (1953) Complex learning and conditioning as a function of anxiety. *J. exp. Psychol.*, 45, 120–125.

Faris, E. (1921–22) Are instincts data or hypotheses? *Amer. J. Soc.*, 27, 184–196.

Fattu, N., Auble, D., & Mech, E. V. (1955) Partial reinforcement in a bar pressing situation with pre-school children. *J. genet. Psychol.*, 87, 251–255.

Fattu, N., Mech, E. V., & Auble, D. (1955) Partial reinforcement related to "free" responding in extinction with preschool children. *J. exp. Educ.*, 23, 365–368.

Fay, J. C., Miller, J. D., & Harlow, H. F. (1953) Incentive size, food deprivation, and food preference. *J. comp. physiol. Psychol.*, 46, 13–15.

Fehrer, E. (1956) The effects of hunger and familiarity of locale on exploration. *J. comp. physiol. Psychol.,* 49, 549–552.

Fehrer, E. (1956 a) Effects of amount of reinforcement and of pre- and postreinforcement delays on learning and extinction. *J. exp. Psychol.,* 52, 167–176.

Felsinger, J. M., Gladstone, A. I., Yamaguchi, H. G., & Hull, C. L. (1947) Reaction latency (str) as a function of the number of reinforcements (N). *J. exp. Psychol.,* 37, 214–228.

Ferster, C. B. (1953) Sustained behavior under delayed reinforcement. *J. exp. Psychol.,* 45, 218–224.

Finan, J. L. (1940) Quantitative studies in motivation: I. Strength of conditioning in rats under varying degrees of hunger. *J. comp. Psychol.,* 29, 119–134.

Finch, G. (1942) Chimpanzee frustration responses. *Psychosom. Med.,* 4, 233–251.

Finger, F. W. (1951) The effect of food deprivation and subsequent satiation upon general activity in the rat. *J. comp. physiol. Psychol.,* 44, 557–564.

Finger, F. W., & Reid, L. S. (1952) The effect of water deprivation and subsequent satiation upon general activity in the rat. *J. comp. physiol. Psychol.,* 45, 368–372.

Finger, F. W., Reid, L. S., & Weasner, M. H. (1957) The effect of reinforcement upon activity during cyclic food deprivation. *J. comp. physiol. Psychol.,* 50, 495–498.

Fleishman, E. A. (1958) A relationship between incentive motivation and ability level in psychomotor performance. *J. exp. Psychol.,* 56, 78–81.

Fletcher, R. (1957) *Instinct in man.* New York: International Univer. Press.

Foa, P. P., Galansino, G., & Pozza, G. (1957) Glucagon, a second pancreatic hormone. In Pincus, G. (Ed), *Recent progress in hormone research.* New York: Academic Press.

Forgays, D. G., & Levin, H. (1958) Learning as a function of change of sensory stimulation in food-deprived and food-satiated animals. *J. comp. physiol. Psychol.,* 51, 50–54.

Forlano, G., & Axelrod, H. C. (1937) The effect of repeated praise or blame on the performance of introverts and extroverts. *J. educ. Psychol.,* 28, 92–100.

Franks, C. M. (1957) Effect of food, drink, and tobacco deprivation on the conditioning of the eyeblink response. *J. exp. Psychol.,* 53, 117–120.

Frederiksen, N. (1942) The effects of frustration on negativistic behavior of young children. *J. genet. Psychol.,* 61, 203–226.

Freeman, G. L. (1933) The facilitative and inhibitory effects of muscular tension upon performance. *Amer. J. Psychol.,* 45, 17–52.

Freeman, G. L. (1938) The optimal muscular tensions for various performances. *Amer. J. Psychol.,* 51, 146–150.

Freeman, G. L. (1939) A new obstruction box. *Amer. J. Psychol.,* 52, 629–631.

Freeman, J. T. (1954) Set or perceptual defense? *J. exp. Psychol.,* 48, 283–288.

Fregley, M. J. (1960) A simple and accurate feeding device for rats. *J. appl. Physiol.,* 15, 539.

Freides, D. (1957) Goal-box cues and pattern of reinforcement. *J. exp. Psychol.*, 53, 361–371.

Freud, S. (1905) Three essays on the theory of sexuality. In *The Basic Writings of Sigmund Freud.* New York: Random House.

Freud, S. (1927) *An autobiographical study.* New York: Brentano.

Frings, H. (1947) Biological backgrounds of the "sweet tooth." *Turtox News,* 24, 133–134.

Furchtgott, E., & Rubin, R. D. (1953) The effect of magnitude of reward on maze learning in the white rat. *J. comp. physiol. Psychol.*, 46, 9–12.

Furchtgott, E., & Salzberg, H. C. (1959) Magnitude of reward and maze learning. *Psychol. Repts.*, 5, 87–93.

Gans, H. M. (1927) Studies on vigor. XIII. Effect of early castration on voluntary activity of the male albino rat. *Endocrinology,* 11, 141–144.

Garner, W. R., Hake, H. W., & Eriksen, C. W. (1956) Operationism and the concept of perception. *Psychol. Rev.*, 63, 149–159.

Gates, G. S., & Rissland, L. Q. (1923) The effect of encouragement and of discouragement upon performance. *J. educ. Psychol.*, 14, 21–26.

Ghent, L. (1951) The relation of experience to the development of hunger. *Canad. J. Psychol.*, 5, 77–81.

Ghent, L. (1957) Some effects of deprivation on eating and drinking behavior. *J. comp. physiol. Psychol.*, 50, 172–175.

Gilbert, G. J. (1956) The subcomissural organ: A regulator of thirst. *Amer. J. Physiol.*, 191, 243–247.

Gilbert, T. F. (1958) Fundamental dimensional properties of the operant. *Psychol. Rev.*, 65, 272–282.

Gilchrist, J. C., & Nesberg, L. S. (1952) Need and perceptual change in need-related objects. *J. exp. Psychol.*, 44, 369–376.

Gilman, A. (1937) The relation between blood osmotic pressure, fluid distribution and voluntary water intake. *Amer. J. Physiol.*, 120, 323–328.

Glanzer, M. (1953) Stimulus satiation: an explanation of spontaneous alternation and related phenomena. *Psychol. Rev.*, 60, 257–268.

Glanzer, M. (1953 a) The role of stimulus satiation in spontaneous alternation. *J. exp. Psychol.*, 45, 387–393.

Glickman, S. E. (1960) Reinforcing properties of arousal. *J. comp. physiol. Psychol.*, 53, 68–71.

Glixman, A. F. (1949) Recall of completed and incompleted activities under varying degrees of stress. *J. exp. Psychol.*, 39, 281–295.

Goldiamond, I. (1958) Indicators of perception: I. Subliminal perception, subception, unconscious perception: An analysis in terms of psychophysical indicator methodology. *Psychol. Bull.*, 55, 373–411.

Goldiamond, I., & Hawkins, W. F. (1958) Vexierversuch: The log relationship between word-frequency and recognition obtained in the absence of stimulus words. *J. exp. Psychol.*, 56, 457–463.

Goodrich, K. P. (1959) Performance in different segments of an instrumental response chain as a function of reinforcement schedule. *J. exp. Psychol.*, 57, 57–63.

Goodstein, L. D. (1954) Affective tone and visual recognition thresholds. *J. abnorm. soc. Psychol.*, 49, 443–444.

Granich, L. (1932) An analysis of motivation. *Psychol. Rev.,* 39, 235–244.

Grant, D. A., Hake, H. W., & Hornseth, J. P. (1951) Acquisition and extinction of a verbal conditioned response with differing percentages of reinforcement. *J. exp. Psychol.,* 42, 1–5.

Grant, D. A., Riopelle, A. J., & Hake, H. W. (1950) Resistance to extinction and the pattern of reinforcement. I. Alternation of reinforcement and the conditioned eyelid response. *J. exp. Psychol.,* 40, 53–60.

Grant, D. A., & Schipper, L. M. (1952) The acquisition and extinction of conditioned eyelid responses as a function of the percentage of fixed-ratio random reinforcement. *J. exp. Psychol.,* 43, 313–320.

Grant, D. A., Schipper, L. M., & Ross, B. M. (1952) Effect of intertrial interval during acquisition on extinction of the conditioned eyelid response following partial reinforcement. *J. exp. Psychol.,* 44, 203–210.

Graves, E. A. (1936) The reliability of the Columbia Obstruction Apparatus. *J. comp. Psychol.,* 21, 137–143.

Greenberg, I. (1954) The acquisition of a thirst drive. Unpublished Ph.D. dissertation, Univer. Penna.

Greene, J. E. (1953) Magnitude of reward and acquisition of a black-white discrimination habit. *J. exp. Psychol.,* 46, 113–119.

Gregersen, M. I. (1932) Studies on the regulation of water intake: II. Conditions affecting the daily water intake of dogs registered continuously by a potometer. *Amer. J. Physiol.,* 102, 344–349.

Gregersen, M. I. & Cannon, W. B. (1932) Studies on the regulation of water intake. I. The effect of extirpation of the salivary glands on the water intake of dogs while panting. *Amer. J. Physiol.,* 102, 336–343.

Grice, G. R. (1948) The relation of secondary reinforcement to delayed reward in visual discrimination learning. *J. exp. Psychol.,* 38, 1–16.

Grice, G. R., & Davis, J. D. (1957) Effect of irrelevant thirst motivation on a response learned with food reward. *J. exp. Psychol.,* 53, 347–352.

Grindley, G. C. (1929) Experiments on the influence of the amount of reward on learning in young chickens. *Brit. J. Psychol.,* 20, 173–180.

Grosslight, J. H., & Child, I. L. (1947) Persistence as a function of previous experience of failure followed by success. *Amer. J. Psychol.,* 60, 378–387.

Grosslight, J. H., Hall, J. F., & Murnin, J. (1953) Patterning effect in partial reinforcement. *J. exp. Psychol.,* 46, 103–106.

Grosslight, J. H., Hall, J. F., & Scott, W. (1954) Reinforcement schedules in habit reversal—a confirmation. *J. exp. Psychol.,* 48, 173–174.

Grosslight, J. H., & Radlow, R. (1956) Patterning effect of the nonreinforcement-reinforcement sequence in a discrimination situation. *J. comp. physiol. Psychol.,* 49, 542–546.

Grosslight, J. H., & Radlow, R. (1957) Patterning effect of the nonreinforcement-reinforcement sequence involving a single non-reinforced trial. *J. comp. physiol. Psychol.,* 50, 23–25.

Grossman, M. I. (1955) Integration of current views on the regulation of hunger and appetite. In Miner, R. W. (Ed), *The regulation of hunger and appetite.* New York: Annals of the N. Y. Acad. of Sciences, 63, 76–79.

Guerrant, N. B., & Dutcher, R. A. (1940) The influence of exercise on the growing rat in the presence and absence of vitamin B₁. *J. Nutrition,* 20, 589–598.

Guttman, N. (1953) Operant conditioning, extinction, and periodic reinforcement in relation to concentration of sucrose used as reinforcing agent. *J. exp. Psychol.,* 46, 213–224.

Guttman, N. (1954) Equal-reinforcement values for sucrose and glucose solutions compared with equal sweetness values. *J. comp. physiol. Psychol.,* 47, 358–363.

Hack, E. R. (1933) Learning as a function of water temperature. *J. exp. Psychol.,* 16, 442–445.

Haggard, D. F. (1959) Acquisition of a simple running response as a function of partial and continuous schedules of reinforcement. *Psychol. Rec.,* 9, 11–18.

Haigh, G. V., & Fiske, D. W. (1952) Corroboration of personal values as selective factors in perception. *J. abnorm. soc. Psychol.,* 47, 394–398.

Hall, C. S. (1936) Emotional behavior in the rat. III. The relationship between emotionality and ambulatory activity. *J. comp. Psychol.,* 22, 345–352.

Hall, J. F. (1951) Studies in secondary reinforcement: I. Secondary reinforcement as a function of the frequency of primary reinforcement. *J. comp. physiol. Psychol.,* 44, 246–251.

Hall, J. F. (1951 a) Studies in secondary reinforcement: II. Secondary reinforcement as a function of the strength of drive during primary reinforcement. *J. comp. physiol. Psychol.,* 44, 462–466.

Hall, J. F. (1955) Activity as a function of a restricted drinking schedule. *J. comp. physiol. Psychol.,* 48, 265–266.

Hall, J. F. (1956) The relationship between external stimulation, food deprivation, and activity. *J. comp. physiol. Psychol.,* 49, 339–341.

Hall, J. F. (1958) The influence of learning in activity wheel behavior. *J. genet. Psychol.,* 92, 121–125.

Hall, J. F., Hanford, P., & Low, L. (1960) The activity of hungry, thirsty, and satiated rats in the Dashiell checkerboard maze. *J. comp. physiol. Psychol.,* 53, 155–158.

Hall, J. F., & Kobrick, J. L. (1952) The relationships among three measures of response strength. *J. comp. physiol. Psychol.,* 45, 280–282.

Hall, J. F., Smith, K., Schnitzer, S. B., & Hanford, P. V. (1953) Elevation of the activity level in the rat following transition from ad libitum to restricted feeding. *J. comp. physiol. Psychol.,* 46, 429–433.

Hamilton, E. L. (1929) The effect of delayed incentive on the hunger drive in the white rat. *Genet. Psychol. Monogr.,* 5, 131–207.

Hamilton, J. A., & Krechevsky, I. (1933) Studies in the effect of shock upon behavior plasticity in the rat. *J. comp. Psychol.,* 16, 237–253.

Hammes, J. A. (1956) Visual discrimination learning as a function of shock-fear and task difficulty. *J. comp. physiol. Psychol.,* 49, 481–484.

Hardison, J., & Purcell, K. (1959) The effects of psychological stress as a function of need and cognitive control. *J. Pers.,* 27, 250–258.

Harker, G. S. (1956) Delay of reward and performance of an instrumental response. *J. exp. Psychol.,* 51, 303–310.

Harlow, H. F. (1950) Learning and satiation of response in intrinsically motivated complex puzzle performance by monkeys. *J. comp. physiol. Psychol.*, 43, 289–294.

Harlow, H. F. (1953) Mice, monkeys, men, and motives. *Psychol. Rev.*, 60, 23–32.

Harlow, H. F. (1953 a) Motivation as a factor in the acquisition of new responses. In: *Current theory and research in motivation: A symposium.* Lincoln, Nebraska: Univer. of Nebr. Press.

Harlow, H. F., Blazek, N. C., & McClearn, G. E. (1956) Manipulatory motivation in the infant rhesus monkey. *J. comp. physiol. Psychol.*, 49, 444–448.

Harlow, H. F., Harlow, M. K., & Meyer, D. R. (1950) Learning motivated by a manipulation drive. *J. exp. Psychol.*, 40, 228–234.

Harlow, H. F., & McClearn, G. E. (1954) Object discrimination learned by monkeys on the basis of manipulation motives. *J. comp. physiol. Psychol.*, 47, 73–76.

Harlow, H. F., & Meyer, D. R. (1952) Paired-comparison scales for monkey rewards. *J. comp. physiol. Psychol.*, 45, 73–79.

Harriman, A. E., & MacLeod, R. B. (1953) Discriminative thresholds of salt for normal and adrenalectomized rats. *Amer. J. Psychol.*, 66, 465–471.

Harris, L. J., Clay, J., Hargreaves, F. J., & Ward, A. (1933) Appetite and choice of diet. The ability of the vitamin B deficient rat to discriminate between diets containing and lacking the vitamin. *Proc. Roy. Soc. London,* sB, 113, 161–190.

Harte, R. A., Travers, J. A., & Sarich, P. (1948) Voluntary caloric intake of the growing rat. *J. Nutrition,* 36, 667–679.

Havelka, J. (1956) Problem seeking behavior in rats. *Canad. J. Psych.,* 10, 91–97.

Hebb, D. O. (1949) *The organization of behavior.* New York: Wiley.

Hebb, D. O. (1953) Heredity and environment in mammalian behavior. *Brit. J. Anim. Behav.,* 1, 43–47.

Hebb, D. O. (1955) Drives and the C.N.S. (Conceptual nervous system). *Psychol. Rev.,* 62, 243–254.

Hebb, D. O., & Riesen, A. H. (1943) The genesis of irrational fears. *Bull. Canad. Psychol. Assoc.,* 3, 49–50.

Heron, W., Doane, B. K., & Scott, T. H. (1956) Visual disturbances after prolonged perceptual isolation. *Canad. J. Psychol.,* 10, 13–18.

Heron, W. T. (1949) Internal stimuli and learning. *J. comp. physiol. Psychol.,* 42, 486–492.

Hetherington, A. W., & Ranson, S. W. (1940) Hypothalamic lesions and adiposity in the rat. *Anat. Record,* 78, 149–172.

Heyer, A. W., Jr. (1951) Studies in motivation and retention. III. A methodological approach to the independent manipulation of tissue dehydration and duration of water deprivation. *Comp. Psychol. Monogr.,* 20, 251–272.

Heyer, A. W., Jr. (1951 a) Studies in motivation and retention. IV. The influence of dehydration on acquisition and retention of the maze habit. *Comp. Psychol. Monogr.,* 20, 273–286.

Hilgard, E. R. (1957) *Introduction to psychology.* (2d ed.) New York: Harcourt Brace.

Hilgard, E. R., Jones, L. V., & Kaplan, S. J. (1951) Conditioned discrimination as related to anxiety. *J. exp. Psychol.,* 42, 94–99.

Hill, J. H., & Stellar, E. (1951) An electronic drinkometer. *Science,* 114, 43–44.

Hill, W. F. (1956) Activity as an autonomous drive. *J. comp. physiol. Psychol.,* 49, 15–19.

Hill, W. F. (1958) The effect of varying periods of confinement on activity in tilt cages. *J. comp. physiol. Psychol.,* 51, 570–574.

Hill, W. F. (1958 a) The effect of long confinement on voluntary wheel-running by rats. *J. comp. physiol. Psychol.,* 51, 770–773.

Hillman, B., Hunter, W. S., & Kimble, G. A. (1953) The effect of drive level on the maze performance of the white rat. *J. comp. physiol. Psychol.,* 46, 87–89.

Hinde, R. A. (1959) Some recent trends in ethology. In Koch, S. (Ed), *Psychology: A study of science.* New York: McGraw-Hill.

Hirsch, J. (1957) Careful reporting and experimental analysis—a comment. *J. comp. physiol. Psychol.,* 50, 415.

Hirsch, J., Lindley, R. H., & Tolman, E. C. (1955) An experimental test of an alleged innate sign stimulus. *J. comp. physiol. Psychol.,* 48, 278–280.

Hitchcock, F. A. (1927) The total energy requirement of the albino rat for growth and activity. *Amer. J. Physiol.,* 83, 28–36.

Hitchcock, F. A. (1928) The effect of low protein and protein-free diets and starvation on the voluntary activity of the albino rat. *Amer. J. Physiol.,* 84, 410–416.

Hochberg, J. (1956) Perception: Toward the recovery of a definition. *Psychol. Rev.,* 63, 400–405.

Holden, F. (1926) A study of the effect of starvation upon behavior by means of the obstruction method. *Comp. Psychol. Monogr.,* 3, 17.

Holmes, J. H., & Gregersen, M. I. (1947) Relation of the salivary flow to the thirst produced in man by intravenous injection of hypertonic salt solution. *Amer. J. Physiol.,* 151, 252–257.

Holmes, J. H., & Gregersen, M. I. (1950) Observations on drinking induced by hypertonic solution. *Amer. J. Physiol.,* 162, 326–337.

Holmes, J. H., & Gregersen, M. I. (1950a) Role of sodium and chloride in thirst. *Amer. J. Physiol.,* 162, 338–347.

Holt, E. B. (1931) *Animal drive and the learning process, an essay toward radical empiricism.* New York: Holt, Rinehart and Winston.

Hopkins, C. O. (1955) Effectiveness of secondary reinforcing stimuli as a function of the quantity and quality of food reinforcement. *J. exp. Psychol.,* 50, 339–342.

Horenstein, B. R. (1951) Performance of conditioned responses as a function of strength of hunger drive. *J. comp. physiol. Psychol.,* 44, 210–224.

Hoskins, H. G. (1925) Studies on vigor. II. The effect of castration on voluntary activity. *Amer. J. Physiol.,* 72, 324–330.

Howes, D. H. & Solomon, R. L. (1950) A note on McGinnies' "Emotionality and perceptual defense." *Psychol. Rev.,* 57, 229–234.

Howes, D. H., & Solomon, R. L. (1951) Visual duration threshold as a function of word probability. *J. exp. Psychol.*, 41, 401–410.

Hughes, J. B., II, Sprague, J. L., & Bendig, A. W. (1954) Anxiety level response alternation, and performance in serial learning. *J. Psychol.*, 38, 421–426.

Hughes L. H. (1957) Saccharine reinforcement in a T maze. *J. comp. physiol. Psychol.*, 50, 431–435.

Hull, C. L. (1933) Differential habituation to internal stimuli in the albino rat. *J. comp. Psychol.*, 16, 255–273.

Hull, C. L. (1934) The rat's speed of locomotion gradient in the approach to food. *J. comp. Psychol.*, 17, 393–422.

Hull, C. L. (1943) *Principles of behavior.* New York: Appleton-Century-Crofts.

Hull, C. L. (1951) *Essentials of behavior.* New Haven: Yale Univer. Press.

Hulse, S. H., Jr., (1958) Amount and percentage of reinforcement and duration of goal confinement in conditioning and extinction. *J. exp. Psychol.*, 56, 48–57.

Hulse, S. H., Jr. & Stanley, W. C. (1956) Extinction by omission of food as related to partial and secondary reinforcement. *J. exp. Psychol.*, 52, 221–227.

Humphreys, L. G. (1939) The effect of random alternation of reinforcement on the acquisition and extinction of conditioned eyelid reactions. *J. exp. Psychol.*, 25, 141–158.

Hunt, J. McV. & Schlosberg, H. (1939) General activity in the male white rat. *J. comp. Psychol.*, 28, 23–38.

Hunt, J. McV. & Schlosberg, H. (1939 a) The influence of illumination upon general activity in normal, blinded, and castrated male white rates. *J. comp. Psychol.*, 28, 285–298.

Hurlock, E. B. (1924) The value of praise and reproof as incentives for children. *Arch. Psychol.*, 11, No. 71.

Hurlock, E. B. (1925) An evaluation of certain incentives used in school work. *J. educ. Psychol.*, 16, 145–159.

Hurwitz, H. M. B. (1956) Conditioned responses in rats reinforced by light. *Brit. J. Anim. Behav.*, 4, 31–33.

Hurwitz, H. M. B., & De, S. C. (1958) Studies in light reinforced behavior: II. Effect of food deprivation and stress. *Psychol. Repts.*, 4, 71–77.

Hutt, P. J. (1954) Rate of bar pressing as a function of quality and quantity of food reward. *J. comp. physiol. Psychol.*, 47, 235–239.

Irwin, F. W. (1958) An analysis of the concepts of discrimination and preference. *Amer. J. Psychol.*, 71, 152–163.

Irwin, O. C. (1932) The distribution of the amount of mobility in young infants between two nursing periods. *J. comp. Psychol.*, 14, 429–445.

Isaac, W., & Ruch, T. C. (1956) Evaluation of four activity techniques for monkeys, *Science,* 123, 1170.

Iverson, M. A., & Reuder, M. E. (1956) Ego involvement as an experimental variable. *Psychol. Repts.*, 2, 147–181.

Jackson, D. N. (1954) A further examination of the role of autism in a visual figure-ground relationship. *J. Psychol.*, 38, 339–357.

James, W. (1890) *The principles of psychology.* New York: Holt.

James, W. T., & Gilbert, T. F. (1957) Elimination of eating behavior by food injection in weaned puppies. *Psychol. Repts.*, 3, 167–168.

Janowitz, H. D., & Grossman, M. I. (1948) Effect of parenteral administration of glucose and protein hydrolysate on food intake in the rat. *Amer. J. Physiol.*, 155, 28–32.

Janowitz, H. D., & Grossman, M. I. (1949) Effect of variations in nutritive density on intake of food of dogs and rats. *Amer. J. Physiol.*, 158, 184–193.

Janowitz, H. D., & Grossman, M. I. (1949 a) Some factors affecting the food intake of normal dogs and dogs with esophagostomy and gastric fistula. *Amer. J. Physiol.*, 159, 143–148.

Janowitz, H. D., & Grossman, M. I. (1951) Effect of prefeeding, alcohol and bitters on food intake of dogs. *Amer. J. Physiol.*, 164, 182–186.

Janowitz, H. D., & Hollander, F. (1955) The time factor in the adjustment of food intake to varied caloric requirement in the dog: A study of the precision of appetite regulation. In Miner, R. W. (Ed), *The regulation of hunger and appetite.* New York: Annals of the N. Y. Acad. of Sciences, 63, 56–67.

Janowitz, H. D., & Ivy, A. C. (1949) Role of blood sugar legvels in spontaneous and insulin-induced hunger in man. *J. applied Physiol.*, 1, 643–645.

Jenkins, J. J., & Hanratty, J. A. (1949) Drive intensity discrimination in the albino rat. *J. comp. physiol. Psychol.*, 42, 228–232.

Jenkins, T. N., Warner, L. H., & Warden, C. J. (1926) Standard apparatus for the study of animal motivation. *J. comp. Psychol.*, 6, 361–382.

Jenkins, W. O. (1950) A temporal gradient of derived reinforcement. *Amer. J. Psychol.*, 63, 237–243.

Jenkins, W. O. & Clayton, F. L. (1949) Rate of responding and amount of reinforcement. *J. comp. physiol. Psychol.*, 42, 174–181.

Jenkins, W. O., & Stanley, J. C., Jr. (1950) Partial reinforcement: A review and critique. *Psychol. Bull.*, 47, 193–234.

Jennings, H. S. (1906) Behavior of the lower organisms. New York: Columbia Univer. Press.

Jersild, A. T. (1940) *Child psychology.* New York: Prentice-Hall.

Jukes, C. L. (1938) Selection of diet in chicks as influenced by vitamins and other factors. *J. comp. Psychol.*, 26, 135–156.

Kagan, J., & Berkun, M. (1954) The reward value of running activity. *J. comp. physiol. Psychol.*, 47, 108.

Katz, S. (1957) Stimulus aftereffects and the partial reinforcement extinction effect. *J. exp. Psychol.*, 53, 167–172.

Kendler, H. H. (1945) Drive interaction: I. Learning as a function of the simultaneous presence of the hunger and thirst drives. *J. exp. Psychol.*, 35, 96–109.

Kendler, H. H. (1946) The influence of simultaneous hunger and thirst drives upon the learning of two opposed spatial responses of the white rat. *J. exp. Psychol.*, 36, 212–220.

Kendler, H. H. (1949) An experimental examination of the non-selective principle of association of drive stimuli. *Amer. J. Psychol.*, 62, 382–391.

Kendler, H. H., Karasik, A. D., & Schrier, A. M. (1954) Studies of the effect of change of drive: III. Amounts of switching produced by shifting drive from thirst to hunger and from hunger to thirst. *J. exp. Psychol.*, 47, 179–182.

Kendler, H. H., & Law, F. E. (1950) An experimental test of the selective principle of association of drive stimuli. *J. exp. Psychol.*, 40, 299–304.

Kendler, H. H., & Levine, S. (1951) Studies of the effect of change of drive: I. From hunger to thirst in a T-maze. *J. exp. Psychol.*, 41, 429–436.

Kendler, H. H., Levine, S., Alchek, E., & Peters, H. (1952) Studies of the effect of change of drive: II. From hunger to different intensities of a thirst drive in a T-maze. *J. exp. Psychol.*, 44, 1–3.

Kennedy, G. C. (1953) The hypothalamic control of food intake in rats. *Proc. Roy. Soc.*, London, s.B, 137, 535–549.

Keys, A., Brozek, J., Henschel, A., Mickelsen, O., & Taylor, H. (1950) *The biology of human starvation*. Vol. II. Minneapolis: Univer. of Minnesota Press.

Kimble, G. A. (1951) Behavior strength as a function of the intensity of the hunger drive. *J. exp. Psychol.*, 41, 341–348.

Kimble, G. A. (1955) Shock intensity and avoidance learning. *J. comp. physiol. Psychol.*, 48, 281–284.

King, J. L., & Connet, H. (1915) The gastric hunger contractions of the normal and decerebrated guinea-pig. *Amer. J. Physiol.*, 39, 123–130.

King-Ellison, P., & Jenkins, J. J. (1954) The durational threshold of visual recognition as a function of word frequency. *Amer. J. Psychol.*, 67, 700–703.

Kish, G. B. (1955) Learning when the onset of illumination is used as reinforcing stimulus. *J. comp. physiol. Psychol.*, 48, 261–264.

Kleemeier, R. W. (1942) Fixation and regression in the rat. *Psychol. Monogr.* 54, No. 4.

Klein, G. S. (1954) Need and regulation. In Jones, M. R. (Ed), *Current theory and research in motivation*. Lincoln, Nebraska: Univer. of Nebraska Press.

Klein, G. S., Schlesinger, H. J., & Meister, D. E. (1951) The effect of personal values on perception: an experimental critique. *Psychol. Rev.*, 58, 96–112.

Kling, J. W. (1956) Speed of running as a function of goal-box behavior. *J. comp. physiol. Psychol.*, 49, 474–476.

Kling, J. W., Horowitz, L., & Delhagen, J. E. (1956) Light as a positive reinforcer for rat responding. *Psychol. Repts.*, 2, 337–340.

Kobrick, J. L. (1956) The relationships among three measures of response strength as a function of the numbers of reinforcements. *J. comp. physiol. Psychol.*, 49, 582–585.

Koch, S., & Daniel, W. J. (1945) The effect of satiation on the behavior mediated by a habit of maximum strength. *J. exp. Psychol.*, 35, 167–187.

Kohn, M. (1951) Satiation of hunger from food injected directly into the stomach versus food ingested by mouth. *J. comp. physiol. Psychol.*, 44, 412–422.

Kuo, Z. Y. (1921) Giving up instincts in psychology. *J. Phil.*, 18, 645–664.

Kuo, Z. Y. (1922) How are our instincts acquired? *Psychol. Rev.*, 29, 344–365.

Kuo, Z. Y. (1924) A psychology without heredity. *Psychol. Rev.*, 31, 427–448.

Lacey, O. L. (1944) A revised procedure for the calibration of the activity wheel. *Amer. J. Psychol.*, 57, 412–420.

Lacy, O. W., Lewinger, N., & Adamson, J. F. (1953) Foreknowledge as a factor affecting perceptual defense and alertness. *J. exp. Psychol.*, 45, 169–174.

Lambert, W. W., & Lambert, E. C. (1953) Some indirect effects of reward on children's size estimations. *J. abnorm. soc. Psychol.*, 48, 507–510.

Lambert, W. W., Solomon, R. L., & Watson, P. D. (1949) Reinforcement and extinction as factors in size estimation. *J. exp. Psychol.*, 39, 637–641.

Lantz, B. (1945) Some dynamic aspects of success and failure. *Psychol. Monogr.*, 59, No. 1.

Lashley, K. S. (1938) Experimental analysis of instinctive behavior. *Psychol. Rev.*, 45, 445–471.

Lawrence, D. H., & Mason, W. A. (1955) Intake and weight adjustments in rats to changes in feeding schedule. *J. comp. physiol. Psychol.*, 48, 43–46.

Lawrence, D. H., & Mason, W. A. (1955 a) Food intake in the rat as a function of deprivation intervals and feeding rhythms. *J. comp. physiol. Psychol.*, 48, 267–271.

Lawrence, D. H., & Miller, N. E. (1947) A positive relationship between reinforcement and resistance to extinction produced by removing a source of confusion from a technique that had produced opposite results. *J. exp. Psychol.*, 37, 494–509.

Lawson, R. (1953) Amount of primary reward and strength of secondary reward. *J. exp. Psychol.*, 46, 183–187.

Lawson, R. (1957) Brightness discrimination performance and secondary reward strength as a function of primary reward amount. *J. comp. physiol. Psychol.*, 50, 35–39.

Lawson, R., & Marx, M. H. (1958) Frustration: theory and experiment. *Genet. Psychol. Monogr.*, 57, 393–464.

Lazarus, R. S., & Baker, R. W. (1957) Motivation and personality in psychological stress. *Psychol. Newsltr.*, 8, 159–193.

Lazarus, R. S., Deese, J., & Hamilton, R. (1954) Anxiety and stress in learning: The role of intraserial duplication. *J. exp. Psychol.*, 47, 111–114.

Lazarus, R. S., Deese, J., & Osler, S. F. (1952) The effects of psychological stress upon performance. *Psychol. Bull.*, 49, 293–317.

Lazarus, R. S., & Eriksen, C. W. (1952) The effects of failure stress upon skilled performance. *J. exp. Psychol.*, 43, 100–105.

Lazarus, R. S., Yousem, H., & Arenberg, D. (1953) Hunger and perception. *J. Pers.*, 21, 312–328.

Leary, R. W. (1958) Homogeneous and heterogeneous reward of monkeys. *J. comp. physiol. Psychol.*, 51, 706–710.

Leeper, R. (1935) The role of motivation in learning: A study of the phenomenon of differential motivational control of the utilization of habits. *J. genet. Psychol.*, 46, 3–40.

Lehrman, D. S. (1953) A critique of Konrad Lorenz's theory of instinctive behavior. *Quart. Rev. Biol.*, 28, 337–363.

Leuba, C. J. (1931) Some comments on the first reports of the Columbia study of animal drives. *J. comp. Psychol.*, 11, 275–279.

Levine, M. M., & Murphy, G. (1943) The learning and forgetting of controversial material. *J. abnorm. soc. Psychol.*, 38, 507–517.

Levine, R., Chein, I., & Murphy, G. (1942) The relation of the intensity of a need to the amount of perceptual distortion: a preliminary report. *J. Psychol.*, 13, 283–293.

Levine, S. (1953) The role of irrelevant drive stimuli in learning. *J. exp. Psychol.*, 45, 410–416.

Levine, S., Staats, S. R., & Frommer, G. (1959) Drive summation in a water maze. *Psychol. Repts.*, 5, 301–304.

Levy, D. M. (1941) The hostile act. *Psychol. Rev.*, 48, 356–361.

Lewin, K. (1937) Psychoanalytic and topological psychology. *Bull. Menninger Clinic*, No. 1, 202–211.

Lewis, D. J. (1952) Partial reinforcement in a gambling situation. *J. exp. Psychol.* 43, 447–450.

Lewis, D. J. (1956) Acquisition, extinction and spontaneous recovery as a function of percentage of reinforcement and inter-trial intervals. *J. exp. Psychol.*, 51, 45–53.

Lewis, D. J. (1960) Partial reinforcement: A selective review of the literature since 1950. *Psychol. Bull.*, 57, 1–28.

Lewis, D. J., & Cotton, J. W. (1957) Learning and performance as a function of drive strength during acquisition and extinction. *J. comp. physiol. Psychol.*, 50, 189–194.

Lewis, D. J., & Duncan, C. P. (1956) Effect of different percentages of money reward on extinction of a lever pulling response. *J. exp. Psychol.*, 52, 23–27.

Lewis, D. J., & Duncan, C. P. (1957) Expectation and resistance to extinction of a lever-pulling response as functions of percentage of reinforcement and amount of reward. *J. exp. Psychol.*, 54, 115–120.

Lewis, D. J., & Duncan, C. P. (1958) Expectation and resistance to extinction of a lever-pulling response as a function of percentage of reinforcement and number of acquisition trials. *J. exp. Psychol.*, 55, 121–128.

Lewis, H. B., & Franklin, M. (1944) An experimental study of the role of the ego in work. II. The significance of task orientation in work. *J. exp. Psychol.*, 34, 195–215.

Licklider, L. C., & Licklider, J. C. R. (1950) Observations on the hoarding behavior of rats. *J. comp. physiol. Psychol.*, 43, 129–134.

Liddell, H. S. (1925) The relation between maze learning and spontaneous activity in the sheep. *J. comp. Psychol.*, 5, 475–483.

Lilly, J. C. (1956) Mental effects of reduction of ordinary levels of physical stimuli on intact healthy persons. *Psychiat. Res. Repts.*, 5, 1–9.

Lindner, H. (1953) Sexual responsiveness to perceptual tests in a group of sexual offenders. *J. Pers.*, 21, 364–374.

Lindsley, D. B. (1957) Psychophysiology and motivation. In Jones, M. R. (Ed), *Nebraska Symposium on Motivation*. Lincoln, Nebraska: Univ. of Nebraska Press.

Loeb, J. (1918) *Forced movements, tropisms, and animal conduct*. Philadelphia: Lippincott.

Logan, F. A. (1952) The role of delay of reinforcement in determining reaction potential. *J. exp. Psychol.*, 43, 393–399.

Logan, F. A. (1960) *Incentive*. New Haven: Yale Univ. Press.

Logan, F. A., Beier, E. M., & Ellis, R. A. (1955) Effect of varied reinforcement on speed of locomotion. *J. exp. Psychol.*, 49, 260–266.

Logan, F. A., Beier, E. M., & Kincaid, W. D. (1956) Extinction following partial and varied reinforcement. *J. exp. Psychol.*, 52, 65–70.

Longenecker, E. D., Krauskopf, J., & Bitterman, M. E. (1952) Extinction following alternating and random partial reinforcement. *Amer. J. Psychol.*, 65, 580–587.

Lorenz, K. Z. (1937) Über die Bildung des Instinktbegriffs. *Die Naturwissenschaften*, 25, 289–300, 307–318, 324–331.

Low, L. (1958) An experimental study of an attempt to obtain an acquired drive based upon a hunger drive. Unpublished Ph.D. dissertation, The Penna. State Univer.

Lucas, J. D. (1952) The interactive effects of anxiety, failure and intraserial duplication. *Amer. J. Psychol.*, 65, 59–66.

Luckhardt, A. B., & Carlson, A. J. (1914) Contributions to the physiology of the stomach. XVII. On the chemical control of the gastric hunger mechanism. *Amer. J. Physiol.*, 36, 37–46.

Luria, Z. (1953) Behavioral adjustment to thiamine deficiency in albino rat. *J. comp. physiol. Psychol.*, 46, 358–362.

Lysak, W. (1954) The effects of punishment upon syllable recognition thresholds. *J. exp. Psychol.*, 47, 343–350.

Lysak, W., & Gilchrist, J. C. (1955) Value, equivocality, and goal availability as determinants of size judgments. *J. Pers.*, 23, 500–501.

Maher, W. B., & Wickens, D. D. (1954) Effect of differential quantity of reward on acquisition and performance of a maze habit. *J. comp. physiol. Psychol.*, 47, 44–46.

Mahl, G. F. (1950) Anxiety, HCl secretion, and peptic ulcer etiology. *Psychosom. Med.*, 12, 158–169.

Maier, N. R. F. (1949) *Frustration: the study of behavior without a goal*. New York: McGraw-Hill.

Maier, N. R. F. (1956) Frustration theory: restatement and extension. *Psychol. Rev.*, 63, 370–388.

Maier, N. R. F., & Ellen, P. (1951) Can the anxiety-reduction theory explain abnormal fixations? *Psychol. Rev.*, 58, 435–445.

Maier, N. R. F., & Klee, J. B. (1941) Studies of abnormal behavior in the rat: VII. The permanent nature of abnormal fixations and their relation to convulsive tendencies. *J. exp. Psychol.*, 29, 380–389.

Maier, N. R. F., & Klee, J. B. (1943) Studies of abnormal behavior in the rat. XII. The pattern of punishment and its relation to abnormal fixations. *J. exp. Psychol.*, 32, 377–398.

Maier, N. R. F., & Klee, J. B. (1945) Studies of abnormal behavior in the rat: XVIII. Guidance versus trial and error in the alteration of habits and fixations. *J. Psychol.*, 19, 133–163.

Maier, N. R. F., & Schneirla, T. C. (1935) *Principles of animal psychology.* New York: McGraw-Hill.

Maltzman, I., Fox, J., & Morrisett, L., Jr. (1953) Some effects of manifest anxiety on mental set. *J. exp. Psychol.*, 46, 50–54.

Mandler, G., & Sarason, S. B. (1952) A study of anxiety and learning. *J. abnorm. soc. Psychol.*, 47, 166–173.

Mandler, J. M. (1958) Effect of early food deprivation on adult behavior in the rat. *J. comp. physiol. Psychol.*, 51, 513–517.

Mangan, G. L. (1959) The role of punishment in figure-ground reorganization. *J. exp. Psychol.*, 58, 369–375.

Martin, R. F. (1940) "Native" traits and regression in rats. *J. comp. Psychol.*, 30, 1–16.

Marx, M. H. (1956) Some relations between frustration and drive. In Jones, M. R. (Ed), *Nebraska Symposium on Motivation.* Lincoln, Nebraska: Univ. of Nebraska Press.

Marx, M. H. (1958) Resistance to extinction as a function of continuous or intermittent presentation of a training cue. *J. exp. Psychol.*, 56, 251–255.

Marx, M. H., Henderson, R. L., & Roberts, C. L. (1955) Positive reinforcement of the bar-pressing response by a light stimulus following dark operant pretests with no aftereffect. *J. comp. physiol. Psychol.*, 48, 73–76.

Maslow, A. H. (1941) Deprivation, threat and frustration. *Psychol. Rev.*, 48, 364–366.

Maslow, A. H. (1943) Conflict, frustration and the theory of threat. *J. abnorm. soc. Psychol.*, 38, 81–86.

Mason, D. J. (1957) The relation of secondary reinforcement to partial reinforcement. *J. comp. physiol. Psychol.*, 50, 264–268.

Mason, W. A., Harlow, H. F., & Rueping, R. R. (1959) The development of manipulatory responsiveness in the infant rhesus monkey. *J. comp. physiol. Psychol.*, 52, 555–558.

Masserman, J. H. (1941) Is the hypothalamus a center for emotions? *Psychosom. Med.*, 3, 3–25.

Mathews, A., & Wertheimer, M. (1958) A "pure" measure of perceptual defense uncontaminated by response suppression. *J. abnorm. soc. Psychol.*, 57, 373–376.

May, M. A. (1948) Experimentally acquired drives. *J. exp. Psychol.*, 38, 66–77.

May, R. (1950) *The meaning of anxiety.* New York: Ronald.

Mayer, J. (1955) Regulation of energy intake and the body weight: the glucostatic theory and the lipostatic hypothesis. In Miner, R. W. (Ed), *The regulation of hunger and appetite.* New York: Annals of the N. Y. Acad. of Sciences, 63, 15–43.

Mayer, J., & Bates, M. W. (1952) Blood glucose and food intake in normal and hypophysectomized, alloxan treated rats. *Amer. J. Physiol.*, 168, 812–819.

McClelland, D. C. (1942) Functional autonomy of motives as an extinction phenomenon. *Psychol. Rev.*, 49, 272–283.

McClelland, D. C. (1950) Review of Maier's Frustration. *J. abnorm. soc. Psychol.*, 45, 564–566.

McClelland, D. C. (1951) *Personality*. New York: Dryden.

McClelland, D. C., & Apicella, F. S. (1945) A functional classification of verbal reactions to experimentally induced failure. *J. abnorm. soc. Psychol.*, 40, 376–390.

McClelland, D. C., & Atkinson, J. W. (1948) The projective expression of needs: I. The effect of different intensities of the hunger drive on perception. *J. Psychol.*, 25, 205–222.

McClelland, D. C., Atkinson, J. W., Clark, R. A., & Lowell, E. L. (1953) *The achievement motive*. New York: Appleton-Century-Crofts.

McClelland, D. C., & Liberman, A. M. (1949) The effect of need for achievement on recognition of need-related words. *J. Pers.*, 18, 236–251.

McClelland, D. C., & McGown, D. R. (1953) The effect of variable food reinforcement on the strength of a secondary reward. *J. comp. physiol. Psychol.*, 46, 80–86.

McDougall, W. (1908) *Primer of physiological psychology*. London: J. H. Dent.

McDougall, W. (1923) *Outline of psychology*. New York: Scribner.

McDougall, W. (1926) *An introduction to social psychology*. Boston: J. W. Luce.

McGinnies, E. (1949) Emotionality and perceptual defense. *Psychol. Rev.*, 56, 244–251.

McGinnies, E. (1950) Discussion of Howes' and Solomon's note on "Emotionality and perceptual defense." *Psychol. Rev.*, 57, 235–240.

McGuigan, F. J., & Crockett, F. (1958) Evidence that the secondary reinforcing stimulus must be discriminated. *J. exp. Psychol.*, 55, 184–187.

McKinney, F., Strother, G. B., Hines, R. R., & Allee, R. A. (1951) Experimental frustration in a group test situation. *J. abnorm. soc. Psychol.*, 46, 316–323.

McNamara, H. J., Solley, C. M., & Long, J. (1958) The effects of punishment (electric shock) on perceptual learning. *J. abnorm. soc. Psychol.*, 57, 91–98.

Meehl, P. E. (1950) On the circularity of the law of effect. *Psychol. Bull.*, 47, 52–75.

Melton, A. W. (1950) Learning. In Monroe, W. S. (Ed), *Encyclopedia of educational research*. New York: Macmillan.

Metzger, R., Cotton, J. W., & Lewis, D. J. (1957) Effect of reinforcement magnitude and of order of presentation of different magnitudes on runway behavior. *J. comp. physiol. Psychol.*, 50, 184–188.

Meyer, D. R. (1951) Food deprivation and discrimination reversal learning by monkeys. *J. exp. Psychol.*, 41, 10–16.

Meyer, D. R. (1951 a) The effects of differential rewards on discrimination reversal learning by monkeys. *J. exp. Psychol.*, 41, 268–274.

Meyer, D. R. (1952) The stability of human gustatory sensitivity during changes in time of food deprivation. *J. comp. physiol. Psychol.*, 45, 373–376.

Meyer, D. R. (1953) On the interaction of simultaneous responses. *Psychol. Bull.*, 50, 204–220.

Miles, R. C. (1956) The relative effectiveness of secondary reinforcers throughout deprivation and habit-strength parameters. *J. comp. physiol. Psychol.*, 49, 126–130.

Miles, R. C. (1958) Learning in kittens with manipulatory, exploratory, and food incentives. *J. comp. physiol. Psychol.*, 51, 39–42.

Miles, R. C. (1958 a) The effect of an irrelevant motive on learning. *J. comp. physiol. Psychol.*, 51, 258–261.

Miles, R. C. (1959) Discrimination in the squirrel monkey as a function of deprivation and problem difficulty. *J. exp. Psychol.*, 57, 15–19.

Miller, N. E. (1941) An experimental investigation of acquired drives. *Psychol. Bull.*, 38, 534–535.

Miller, N. E. (1941 a) The frustration-aggression hypothesis. *Psychol. Rev.*, 38, 337–342.

Miller, N. E. (1948) Studies of fear as an acquirable drive: I. Fear as motivation and fear-reduction as reinforcement in learning of new responses. *J. exp. Psychol.*, 38, 89–101.

Miller, N. E. (1951) Learnable drives and rewards. In Stevens, S. S. (Ed), *Handbook of experimental psychology*. New York: Wiley.

Miller, N. E. (1955) Shortcomings of food consumption as a measure of hunger; results from other behavorial techniques. In Miner, R. W. (Ed), *The regulation of hunger and appetite*. New York: Annals of the N. Y. Acad. of Sciences, 63, 141–143.

Miller, N. E. (1956) Effects of drugs on motivation: The value of using a variety of measures. In Whitelock, O. v. St. (Ed), *Techniques for the study of behavorial effects of drugs*. New York: Annals of the N. Y. Acad. of Sciences, 65, 318–333.

Miller, N. E. (1957) Experiments on motivation: studies combining psychological, physiological and pharmacological techniques. *Science,* 126, 1271–1278.

Miller, N. E., Bailey, C. J., & Stevenson, J. A. F. (1950) Decreased "hunger" but increased food intake resulting from hypothalamic lesions. *Science,* 112, 256–259.

Miller, N. E., Sampliner, R. I., & Woodrow, P. (1957) Thirst reducing effects of water by stomach fistula vs. water by mouth measured by both a consummatory and an instrumental response. *J. comp. physiol. Psychol.*, 50, 1–5.

Mitchell, H. S., & Mendel, L. B. (1921) The choice between adequate and inadequate diet as made by rats and mice. *Amer. J. Physiol.*, 58, 211–226.

Moll, R. P. (1959) The effect of drive level on acquisition of the consummatory response. *J. comp. physiol. Psychol.*, 52, 116–119.

Montgomery, K. C. (1951) Spontaneous alternation as a function of time between trials and amount of work. *J. exp. Psychol.*, 42, 82–93.

Montgomery, K. C. (1952) A test of two explanations of spontaneous alternation. *J. comp. physiol. Psychol.*, 45, 287–293.

Montgomery, K. C. (1953) The effect of hunger and thirst drives upon exploratory behavior. *J. comp. physiol. Psychol.*, 46, 315–319.

Montgomery, K. C. (1953 a) The effect of activity deprivation upon exploratory behavior. *J. comp. physiol. Psychol.*, 46, 438–441.

Montgomery, K. C. (1954) The role of exploratory drive in learning. *J. comp. physiol. Psychol.*, 47, 60–64.

Montgomery, K. C. (1955) The relation between fear induced by novel stimulation and exploratory drive. *J. comp. physiol. Psychol.*, 48, 254–260.

Montgomery, K. C., & Monkman, J. A. (1955) The relation between fear and exploratory behavior. *J. comp. physiol. Psychol.*, 48, 132–136.

Montgomery, K. C., & Segall, M. (1955) Discrimination learning based upon exploratory drive. *J. comp. physiol. Psychol.*, 48, 225–228.

Montgomery, K. C., & Zimbardo, P. G. (1957) Effect of sensory and behavioral deprivation upon exploratory behavior in the rat. *Percept. Mot. Skills,* 7, 223–229.

Montgomery, M. F. (1931) The role of the salivary glands in the thirst mechanism. *Amer. J. Physiol.*, 96, 221–227.

Moon, L. E., & Lodahl, T. M. (1956) The reinforcing effect of changes in illumination on lever-pressing in the monkey. *Amer. J. Psychol.*, 69, 288–290.

Morgan, C. T. (1957) Physiological mechanisms of motivation. In Jones, M. R. (Ed), *Nebraska symposium on motivation.* Lincoln, Nebraska: Univer. of Nebraska Press.

Morgan, C. T., & Morgan, J. D. (1940) Studies in hunger: II. The relation of gastric denervation and dietary sugar to the effect of insulin upon food intake in the rat. *J. genet. Psychol.*, 57, 153–163.

Morgan, J. J. B. (1923) The measurement of instincts. *Psychol. Bull.*, 20, 94.

Morlan, G. K. (1949) A note on the frustration-aggression theories of Dollard and his associates. *Psychol. Rev.*, 56, 1–8.

Morrison, S. D., Ju Lin, H., Eckel, H. E., Van Itallie, T. B., & Mayer, J. (1958) Gastric contractions in the rat. *Amer. J. Physiol.*, 193, 4–8.

Morrison, S. D., & Mayer, J. (1957) Adipsis and aphagia in rats after lateral subthalamic lesions. *Amer. J. Physiol.*, 191, 248–254.

Moruzzi, G., & Magoun, H. W. (1949) Brain stem reticular formation and activation of the EEG. *EEG clin. Neurophysiol.*, 1, 455–473.

Moskowitz, M. J. (1959) Running-wheel activity in the white rat as a function of combined food and water deprivation. *J. comp. physiol. Psychol.*, 52, 621–625.

Moss, F. A. (1924) Study of animal drives. *J. exp. Psychol.*, 7, 165–185.

Mowrer, O. H. (1939) A stimulus-response analysis of anxiety and its role as a reinforcing agent. *Psychol. Rev.*, 46, 553–565.

Mowrer, O. H. (1940) An experimental analogue of "regression" with incidental observations on "reaction formation." *J. abnorm. soc. Psychol.*, 35, 56–87.

Mowrer, O. H. (1947) On the dual nature of learning—a re-interpretation of "conditioning" and "problem-solving." *Harv. educ. Rev.*, 17, 102–148.

Mowrer, O. H. (1950) *Learning theory and personality dynamics.* New York: Ronald.

Mowrer, O. H., & Aiken, E. G. (1954) Contiguity vs. drive-reduction in conditioned fear: variations in conditioned and unconditioned stimuli. *Amer. J. Psychol.*, 67, 26–38.

Mowrer, O. H., & Jones, H. (1945) Habit strength as a function of the pattern of reinforcement. *J. exp. Psychol.*, 35, 293–311.

Mowrer, O. H., & Solomon, L. N. (1954) Contiguity vs. drive-reduction in conditioned fear: the proximity and abruptness of drive-reduction. *Amer. J. Psychol.*, 67, 15–25.

Mowrer, O. H., & Suter, J. W. (1950) Further evidence for a two-factor theory of learning. In Mowrer, O. H. *Learning theory and personality dynamics.* New York: Ronald.

Mulinos, M. G. (1933) The gastric hunger mechanism. IV. The influence of experimental alteration in blood sugar concentration of the gastric hunger contractions. *Amer. J. Physiol.*, 104, 371–378.

Murphy, G. (1947) *Personality: a biosocial approach to origins and structure.* New York: Harper.

Murphy, R. E. (1959) Effects of threat of shock, distraction, and task design on performance. *J. exp. Psychol.*, 58, 134–141.

Murray, H. A., Jr. (1933) The effect of fear upon estimates of the maliciousness of other personalities. *J. soc. Psychol.*, 4, 310–329.

Myers, A. K. and Miller, N. E. (1954) Failure to find learned drive based on hunger; evidence for learning motivated by "exploration." *J. comp. physiol. Psychol.*, 47, 428–436.

Nevins, W. B. (1927) Experiments in the self-feeding of dairy cows. *Univ. Illinois Agric. Exper. Station, Bull.*, 289.

Newbigging, P. L. (1960) Personal values and response strength of value— related words as measured in a pseudo-perceptual task. *Canad. J. Psychol.*, 14, 38–44.

Nicholls, E. E. (1922) A study of the spontaneous activity of the guinea-pig. *J. comp. Psychol.*, 2, 303–330.

Nielson, H. C., Doty, R. W., & Rutledge, L. T. (1958) Motivational and perceptual aspects of subcortical stimulation in cats. *Amer. J. Physiol.*, 194, 427–432.

Nissen, H. W. (1930) A study of exploratory behavior in the white rat by means of the obstruction method. *J. genet. Psychol.*, 37, 361–376.

Nissen, H. W. (1954) The nature of the drive as innate determinant of behavioral organization. In Jones, M. R. (Ed), *Nebraska Symposium on Motivation.* Lincoln, Nebraska: Univer. of Nebraska Press.

O'Connor, N., & Claridge, G. S. (1958) A 'Crespi effect' in male imbeciles. *Brit. J. Psychol.*, 49, 42–48.

O'Kelly, L. I. (1940) An experimental study of regression. II. Some motivational determinants of regression and perseveration. *J. comp. Psychol.*, 30, 55–95.

O'Kelly, L. I., & Heyer, A. W., Jr. (1951) Studies in motivation and retention. V. The influence of need duration on retention of a maze habit. *Comp. Psychol. Monogr.*, 20, 287–301.

Olds, J. (1955) Physiological mechanisms of reward. In Jones, M. R. (Ed), *Nebraska Symposium on Motivation.* Lincoln, Nebraska: Univ. of Nebraska Press.

Olds, J. (1956) Runway and maze behavior controlled by basomedial forebrain stimulation in the rat. *J. comp. physiol. Psychol.*, 49, 507–512.

Olds, J. (1958) Satiation effects in self-stimulation of the brain. *J. comp. physiol. Psychol.*, 51, 675–678.

Olds, J. (1958 a) Effects of hunger and male sex hormones on self-stimulation of the brain. *J. comp. physiol. Psychol.*, 51, 320–324.

Olds, J., & Milner, P. (1954) Positive reinforcement produced by electrical stimulation of septal area and other regions of the rat brain. *J. comp. physiol. Psychol.*, 47, 419–427.

Olson, W. C. (1929) *The measurement of nervous habits in normal children.* Minneapolis: Univer. Minnesota Press.

Oppenheimer, O. (1947) The functional autonomy of motives. *J. soc. Psychol.*, 25, 171–179.

Osgood, C. E. (1953) *Method and theory in experimental psychology.* New York: Oxford Univer. Press.

Osler, S. F. (1954) Intellectual performance as a function of two types of psychological stress. *J. exp. Psychol.*, 47, 115–121.

Otis, N. B., & McCandless, B. (1955) Responses to repeated frustrations of young children differentiated according to need area. *J. abnorm. soc. Psychol.*, 50, 349–353.

Pack, G. T. (1923) New experiments on the nature of the sensation of thirst. *Amer. J. Physiol.*, 65, 346–349.

Palermo, D. S. (1957) Proactive interference and facilitation as a function of amount of training and stress. *J. exp. Psychol.*, 53, 293–296.

Passey, G. E. (1948) The influence of intensity of unconditioned stimulus upon acquisition of a conditioned response. *J. exp. Psychol.*, 38, 420–428.

Pastore, N. (1950) A neglected factor in the frustration-aggression hypothesis: A comment. *J. Psychol.*, 29, 271–279.

Pastore, N. (1952) The role of arbitrariness in the frustration-aggression hypothesis. *J. abnorm. soc. Psychol.*, 47, 728–731.

Patterson, T. L. (1915) Contributions to the physiology of the stomach. XXIII. The cause of the variations in the gastric hunger contractions with age. *Amer. J. Physiol.*, 37, 316–329.

Pearl, R., & Fairchild, T. E. (1921) Studies in the psychology of reproduction of domestic fowl. XIX. On the influence of free choice of food materials on winter egg production and body weight. *Amer. J. Hygiene*, 1, 253–277.

Pereboom, A. C., & Crawford, B. M. (1958) Instrumental and competing behavior as a function of trials and reward magnitude. *J. exp. Psychol.*, 56, 82–85.

Perin, C. T. (1942) Behavior potentiality as a joint function of the amount of training and the degree of hunger at the time of extinction. *J. exp. Psychol.*, 30, 93–113.

Perin, C. T. (1943) A quantitative investigation of the delay of reinforcement gradient. *J. exp. Psychol.*, 32, 37–51.

Perkins, C. C., Jr. (1947) The relation of secondary reward to gradients of reinforcement. *J. exp. Psychol.*, 37, 377–392.

Perkins, C. C., Jr., & Tilton, J. R. (1954) Change in stimulus conditions as a determiner of "regression" in the rat. *J. comp. physiol. Psychol.*, 47, 341–343.

Peterson, L. R. (1956) Variable delayed reinforcement. *J. comp. physiol. Psychol.,* 49, 232–234.

Petrinovich, L., & Bolles, R. (1954) Deprivation states and behavioral attributes. *J. comp. physiol. Psychol.,* 47, 450–453.

Pfaffman, C. (1957) Taste mechanisms in preference behavior. *Amer. J. clinical nutrition,* 5, 142–147.

Pfaffman, C., & Bare, J. K. (1950) Gustatory nerve discharges in normal and adrenalectomized rats. *J. comp. physiol. Psychol.,* 43, 320–324.

Pilgrim, F. J., & Patton, R. A. (1947) Patterns of self-selection of purified dietary components by the rat. *J. comp. physiol. Psychol.,* 40, 343–348.

Postman, L. (1947) The history and present status of the law of effect. *Psychol. Bull.,* 44, 489–563.

Postman, L. (1951) Toward a general theory of cognition. In Rohrer, J. H., and Sherif, M. (Eds), *Social psychology at the crossroads.* New York: Harper.

Postman, L. (1953) The experimental analysis of motivational factors in perception. In *Current theory and research in motivation: A symposium.* Lincoln, Nebraska: Univ. of Nebraska Press.

Postman, L., Bronson, W. C., & Gropper, G. L. (1953) Is there a mechanism of perceptual defense? *J. abnorm. soc. Psychol.,* 48, 215–224.

Postman, L., & Brown, D. R. (1952) The perceptual consequences of success and failure. *J. abnorm. soc. Psychol.,* 47, 213–221.

Postman, L., Bruner, J. S., & McGinnies, E. (1948) Personal values as selective factors in perception. *J. abnorm. soc. Psychol.,* 43, 142–154.

Postman, L., & Crutchfield, R. S. (1952) The interaction of need, set and stimulus structure in a cognitive task. *Amer. J. Psychol.,* 65, 196–217.

Postman, L., & Murphy, G. (1943) The factor of attitude in associative memory. *J. exp. Psychol.,* 33, 228–238.

Postman, L., & Schneider, B. H. (1951) Personal values, visual recognition and recall. *Psychol. Rev.,* 48, 271–284.

Powell, D. R., Jr., & Perkins, C. C., Jr. (1957) Strength of secondary reinforcement as a determiner of the effects of duration of goal response on learning. *J. exp. Psychol.,* 53, 106–112.

Prokasy, W. F., Jr., Grant, D. A., & Myers, N. A. (1958) Eyelid conditioning as a function of unconditioned stimulus intensity and intertrial interval. *J. exp. Psychol.,* 55, 242–246.

Prokasy, W. F., Jr., & Truax, C. B. (1959) Reflex and conditioned responses as a function of manifest anxiety. *Amer. J. Psychol.,* 72, 262–264.

Proshansky, H., & Murphy, G. (1942) The effects of reward and punishment on perception. *J. Psychol.,* 13, 295–305.

Pubols, B. H., Jr. (1960) Incentive magnitude, learning, and performance in animals. *Psychol. Bull.,* 57, 89–115.

Quigley, J. P. (1955) The role of the digestive tract in regulating the ingestion of food. In Miner, R. W. (Ed), *The regulation of hunger and appetite.* New York: Annals of the N. Y. Acad. of Sciences, 63, 6–14.

Quigley, J. P., & Brody, D. A. (1952) A physiologic and clinical consideration of the pressures developed in the digestive tract. *Amer. J. Med.,* 13, 73–81.

Quigley, J. P., & Hallaran, W. R. (1932) The independence of spontaneous gastrointestinal motility and blood sugar levels. *Amer. J. Physiol.,* 100, 102–110.

Rabedeau, R., & Miles, R. C. (1959) Response decrement in visual exploratory behavior. *J. comp. physiol. Psychol.,* 52, 364–367.

Ramond, C. K. (1953) Anxiety and task as determiners of verbal performance. *J. exp. Psychol.,* 46, 120–124.

Ratner, S. C., & Ringer, R. K. (1959) An activity cage and recorder for domestic fowl. *Anim. Behav.,* 7, 245–247.

Raup, R. B. (1925) *Complacency, the foundation of human behavior.* New York: Macmillan.

Reece, M. M. (1954) The effect of shock on recognition thresholds. *J. abnorm. soc. Psychol.,* 49, 165–172.

Reed, J. D. (1947) Spontaneous activity of animals. *Psychol. Bull.,* 44, 383–412.

Reid, L. S., & Slivinske, A. J. (1954) A test for generalized secondary reinforcement during extinction under a different drive. *J. comp. physiol. Psychol.,* 47, 306–310.

Rethlingshafer, D. (1943) Experimental evidence for functional autonomy of motives. *Psychol. Rev.,* 50, 397–407.

Reynolds, B. (1949) The acquisition of black-white discrimination habit under two levels of reinforcement. *J. exp. Psychol.,* 39, 760–769.

Reynolds, B. (1950) Resistance to extinction as a function of the amount of reinforcement present during acquisition. *J. exp. Psychol.,* 40, 46–52.

Reynolds, B. (1950 a) Acquisition of a simple spatial discrimination as a function of the amount of reinforcement. *J. exp. Psychol.,* 40, 152–160.

Reynolds, R. W. (1958) The relationship between stimulation voltage and rate of hypothalamic self-stimulation in the rat. *J. comp. physiol. Psychol.,* 51, 193–198.

Richter, C. P. (1922) A behavioristic study of the activity of the rat. *Comp. Psychol. Monogr.,* 1, No. 2.

Richter, C. P. (1927) Animal behavior and internal drives. *Quart. Rev. Biol.,* 2, 307–343, 23, 46.

Richter, C. P. (1936) Increased salt appetite in adrenalectomized rats. *Amer. J. Physiol.,* 115, 155–161.

Richter, C. P. (1939) Salt taste thresholds for normal and adrenalectomized rats. *Endocrinology,* 24, 367–371.

Richter, C. P., & Eckert, J. F. (1938) Mineral metabolism of adrenalectomized rats studied by the appetite method. *Endocrinology,* 22, 214–224.

Richter, C. P., Holt, L. E., Jr., & Barelare, B., Jr. (1937) Vitamin B_1 craving in rats. *Science,* 86, 354–355.

Richter, C. P., Holt, L. E., Jr., & Barelare, B., Jr. (1938) Nutritional requirements for normal growth and reproduction in rats studied by the self-selection method. *Amer. J. Physiol.,* 122, 734–744.

Richter, C. P., & Rice, K. K. (1942) The effect of thiamine hydrochloride on the energy value of dextrose studies in rats by the single food choice method. *Amer. J. Physiol.,* 137, 573–581.

Richter, C. P., & Rice, K. K. (1943) Effects produced by vitamin D on energy, appetite and oestrous cycles of rats kept on an exclusive diet of yellow corn. *Amer. J. Physiol.,* 139, 693–699.

Rigby, W. K., & Rigby, M. K. (1956) Reinforcement and frequency as factors in tachistoscopic thresholds. *Percept. Mot. Skills*, 6, 29–35.

Rignano, E. (1923) *The psychology of reasoning.* New York: Harcourt, Brace.

Roberts, C. L., Marx, M. H., & Collier, G. (1958) Light onset and light offset as reinforcers for the albino rat. *J. comp. physiol. Psychol.*, 51, 575–579.

Roberts, W. W. (1958) Rapid escape learning without avoidance learning motivated by hypothalamic stimulation in cats. *J. comp. physiol. Psychol.*, 51, 391–399.

Roberts, W. W. (1958 a) Both rewarding and punishing effects from stimulation of posterior hypothalamus of cat with same electrode at same intensity. *J. comp. physiol. Psychol.*, 51, 400–407.

Rock, I., & Fleck, F. S. (1950) A re-examination of the effect of monetary reward and punishment on figure-ground perception. *J. exp. Psychol.*, 40, 766–776.

Rockett, F. C. (1955) A note on "An experimental test of an alleged innate sign stimulus" by Hirsch, Lindley, and Tolman. *Percept. Mot. Skills*, 5, 155–156.

Rogers, F. T. (1914) The contractions of the rabbit's stomach during hunger. *Amer. J. Physiol.*, 36, 183–190.

Rohrer, J. H. (1949) A motivational state resulting from nonreward. *J. comp. physiol. Psychol.*, 42, 476–485.

Rosen, A. C. (1954) Change in perceptual threshold as a protective function of the organism. *J. Pers.*, 23, 182–194.

Rosenzweig, S. (1943) An experimental study of "repression" with special reference to need-persistive and ego-defensive reactions to frustration. *J. exp. Psychol.*, 32, 64–74.

Ross, B. M., Rupel, J. W., & Grant, D. A. (1952) Effects of personal, impersonal, and physical stress upon cognitive behavior in a card sorting problem. *J. abnorm. soc. Psychol.*, 47, 546–551.

Ross, S., Smith, W. I., & Nienstedt, C. W., Jr. (1950) The hoarding of nonrelevant material by the white rat. *J. comp. physiol. Psychol.*, 43, 217–225.

Rubin, L. S. (1953) A demonstration of superior resistance to extinction following continuous reinforcement as compared with partial reinforcement. *J. comp. physiol. Psychol.*, 46, 28–32.

Runquist, W. N., & Ross, L. E. (1959) The relation between physiological measures of emotionality and performance in eyelid conditioning. *J. exp. Psychol.*, 57, 329–332.

Runquist, W. N., & Spence, K. W. (1959) Performance in eyelid conditioning related to changes in muscular tension and physiological measures of emotionality. *J. exp. Psychol.*, 58, 417–422.

Russell, J. T. (1932) Relative efficiency of relaxation and tension in performing an act of skill. *J. gen. Psychol.*, 6, 330–343.

Russell, W. A. (1952) Retention of verbal material as a function of motivating instructions and experimentally-induced failure. *J. exp. Psychol.*, 43, 207–216.

Ryan, T. A. (1958) Drives, tasks, and the initiation of behavior. *Amer. J. Psychol.*, 71, 74–93.

Saltz, E., & Hoehn, A. J. (1957) A test of the Taylor-Spence theory of anxiety. *J. abnorm. soc. Psychol.,* 54, 114–117.

Saltzman, I. J. (1949) Maze learning in the absence of primary reinforcement: a study of secondary reinforcement. *J. comp. physiol. Psychol.,* 42, 161–173.

Saltzman, I. J., & Koch, S. (1948) The effect of low intensities of hunger on the behavior mediated by a habit of maximum strength. *J. exp. Psychol.,* 38, 347–370.

Sanders, M. J. (1937) An experimental demonstration of regression in the rat. *J. exp. Psychol.,* 21, 493–510.

Sanford, R. N. (1936) The effects of abstinence from food upon imaginal processes: A preliminary experiment. *J. Psychol.,* 2, 129–136.

Sanford, R. N. (1937) The effects of abstinence from food upon imaginal processes: A further experiment. *J. Psychol.,* 3, 145–159.

Sarason, S. B., Mandler, G., & Craighill, P. G. (1952) The effect of differential instructions on anxiety and learning. *J. abnorm. soc. Psychol.,* 47, 561–565.

Sargent, S. S. (1948) Reaction to frustration—a critique and hypothesis. *Psychol. Rev.,* 55, 108–114.

Schafer, R., & Murphy, G. (1943) The role of autism in a visual figure-ground relationship. *J. exp. Psychol.,* 32, 335–343.

Schoenfeld, W. N. (1950) An experimental approach to anxiety, escape and avoidance behavior. In Hoch, P. H. and Zubin (Eds), *Anxiety.* New York: Grune and Stratton.

Schoenfeld, W. N., Antonitis, J. J., & Bersh, P. J. (1950) A preliminary study of training conditions necessary for secondary reinforcement. *J. exp. Psychol.,* 40, 40–45.

Schreier, F. T. (1957) *Human motivation, probability and meaning.* Illinois: The Free Press.

Schrier, A. M. (1956) Amount of incentive and performance on a black-white discrimination problem. *J. comp. physiol. Psychol.,* 49, 123–125.

Schrier, A. M. (1958) Comparison of two methods of investigating the effect of amount of reward on performance. *J. comp. physiol. Psychol.,* 51, 725–731.

Schrier, A. M., & Harlow, H. F. (1956) Effect of amount of incentive on discrimination learning by monkeys. *J. comp. physiol. Psychol.,* 49, 117–125.

Schulman, J. L., Carleton, J. L., Whitney, G., & Whitehorn, J. C. (1958) Effect of clucagon on food intake and body weight in man. *J. appl. Physiol.,* 11, 419–421.

Schulz, R. W., & Lawrence, D. H. (1958) Learning of a discrimination by satiated and deprived rats with sucrose as incentive. *Amer. J. Psychol.,* 71, 563–567.

Schwartzbaum, J. S., & Ward, H. P. (1958) An osmotic factor in the regulation of food intake in the rat. *J. comp. physiol. Psychol.,* 51, 555–560.

Schwitalla, A. M. (1924) The influence of temperature on the rate of locomotion in Amoeba. I. Locomotion at diverse constant temperatures. *J. Morph.,* 39, 465–513.

Scott, E. D., & Wike, E. L. (1956) The effect of partially delayed reinforcement and trial-distribution on the extinction of an instrumental response. *Amer. J. Psychol.*, 69, 264–268.

Scott, E. M. (1946) Self selection of diet. I. Selection of purified components. *J. Nutrition*, 31, 397–406.

Scott, E. M., & Quint, E. (1946) Self selection of diet. IV. Appetite for protein. *J. Nutrition*, 32, 293–301.

Scott, J. P. (1948) Dominance and the frustration-aggression hypothesis. *Physiol. Zool.*, 21, 31–39.

Scott, W. W., Scott, C. C., & Luckhardt, A. B. (1938) Observations on the blood-sugar level before, during and after hunger periods in humans. *Amer. J. Physiol.*, 123, 243–247.

Sears, R. R. (1937) Initiation of the repression sequence by experienced failure. *J. exp. Psychol.*, 20, 570–580.

Seashore, H. G., & Bavelas, A. (1942) A study of frustration in children. *J. genet. Psychol.*, 61, 279–314.

Segal, E. F. (1959) The stability of operant level and its relation to deprivation. *J. comp. physiol. Psychol.*, 52, 713–716.

Seward, J. P. (1953) How are motives learned? *Psychol. Rev.*, 60, 99–110.

Seward, J. P., & Pereboom, A. C. (1955) Does the activity wheel measure goal striving? *J. comp. physiol. Psychol.*, 48, 272–277.

Seward, J. P., & Pereboom, A. C. (1955 a) A note on the learning of 'spontaneous' activity. *Amer. J. Psychol.*, 68, 139–142.

Seward, J. P., Pereboom, A. C., Butler, B., & Jones, R. B. (1957) The role of prefeeding in an apprent frustration effect. *J. exp. Psychol.*, 54, 445–450.

Seward, J. P., Uyeda, A., & Olds, J. (1959) Resistance to extinction following cranial self-stimulation. *J. comp. physiol. Psychol.*, 52, 294–299.

Share, I., Martyniuk, E., & Grossman, M. I. (1952) Effect of prolonged intragastric feeding on oral food intake in dogs. *Amer. J. Physiol.*, 169, 229–235.

Sheffield, F. D., & Campbell, B. A. (1954) The role of experience in the "spontaneous" activity of hungry rats. *J. comp. physiol. Psychol.*, 47, 97–100.

Sheffield, F. D., & Roby, T. B. (1950) Reward value of a non-nutritive sweet taste. *J. comp. physiol. Psychol.*, 43, 471–481.

Sheffield, F. D., Roby, T. B., & Campbell, B. A. (1954) Drive reduction versus consummatory behavior as determinants of reinforcement. *J. comp. physiol. Psychol.*, 47, 349–354.

Sheffield, F. D., Wulff, J. J., & Backer, R. (1951) Reward value of copulation without sex drive reduction. *J. comp. physiol. Psychol.*, 44, 3–8.

Sheffield, V. F. (1949) Extinction as a function of partial reinforcement and distribution of practice. *J. exp. Psychol.*, 39, 511–526.

Sheffield, V. F. (1950) Resistance to extinction as a function of the distribution of extinction trials. *J. exp. Psychol.*, 40, 305–313.

Sherif, M., & Cantril, H. (1947) *The psychology of ego involvements.* New York: Wiley.

Sherman, M., & Jost, H. (1942) Frustration reaction of normal and neurotic persons. *J. Psychol.*, 13, 3–19.

Shirley, M. (1928) Studies of activity. I. Consistence of the revolving drum method of measuring the activity of the rat. *J. comp. Psychol.,* 8, 23–38.

Shirley, M. (1928a) Studies in activity: II. Activity rhythms; age and activity; activity after rest. *J. comp. Psychol.,* 8, 159–186.

Sidman, M., Brady, J. V., Boren, J. J., Conrad, D. G., & Schulman, A. (1955) Reward schedules and behavior maintained by intracranial self-stimulation. *Science,* 122, 830–831.

Siegel, P. S. (1943) Drive shift, a conceptual and experimental analysis. *J. comp. Psychol.,* 35, 139–148.

Siegel, P. S. (1946) Activity level as a function of physically enforced inaction. *J. Psychol.,* 21, 285–291.

Siegel, P. S. (1946 a) Alien drive, habit strength and resistance to extinction. *J. comp. physiol. Psychol.,* 39, 307–317.

Siegel, P. S. (1946 b) A simple electronic device for the measurement of gross bodily activity of small animals. *J. Psychol.,* 21, 227–236.

Siegel, P. S. (1947) The relationship between voluntary water intake, body-weight loss, and number of hours of water privation in the rat. *J. comp. physiol. Psychol.,* 40, 231–238.

Siegel, P. S., & Alexander, I. E. (1948) A further observation on the effect of physically enforced inaction on the activity level of the rat. *J. genet. Psychol.,* 72, 57–62.

Siegel, P. S., & Dorman, L. B. (1954) Food intake of the rat following the intragastric administration of "hungry" and "satiated" blood. *J. comp. physiol. Psychol.,* 47, 227–229.

Siegel, P. S., & MacDonnell, M. F. (1954) A repetition of the Calvin-Bicknell-Sperling study of conditioned drive. *J. comp. physiol. Psychol.,* 47, 250–252.

Siegel, P. S., & Steinberg, M. (1949) Activity level as a function of hunger. *J. comp. physiol. Psychol.,* 42, 413–416.

Siegel, P. S., & Stuckey, H. L. (1947) The diurnal course of water and food intake in the normal mature rat. *J. comp. physiol. Psychol.,* 40, 365–370.

Siegel, P. S., & Taub, D. V. (1952) A "hunger hormone?" *J. comp. physiol. Psychol.,* 45, 250–253.

Silberman, H. F. (1957) Effects of praise and reproof on reading growth in a non-laboratory class room setting. *J. educ. Psychol.,* 48, 199–206.

Simon, C. W., Wickens, D. D., Brown, U., & Pennock, L. (1951) Effect of the secondary reinforcing agents on the primary thirst drive. *J. comp. physiol. Psychol.,* 44, 67–70.

Skinner, B. F. (1932) Drive and reflex strength, I and II. *J. gen. Psychol.,* 6, 22–48.

Skinner, B. F. (1938) *The behavior of organisms.* New York: Appleton-Century-Crofts.

Slonaker, J. R. (1908) Description of an apparatus for recording the activity of small animals. *Anat. Rec.,* 2, 116–122.

Slonaker, J. R. (1924) The effects of pubescence, oestration, and menopause on the voluntary activity of the albino rat. *Amer. J. Physiol.,* 68, 294–315.

Slonaker, J. R. (1930) The effect of the excision of different sexual organs on the development, growth and longevity of the albino rat. *Amer. J. Physiol.,* 93, 307–317.

Smith, D. E. P., & Hochberg, J. E. (1954) The effect of "punishment" (electric shock) on figure-ground perception. *J. Psychol.,* 38, 83–87.

Smith, J. G. (1954) Influence of failure, expressed hostility, and stimulus characteristics on verbal learning and recognition. *J. Pers.,* 22, 475–493.

Smith, K. R., Parker, G. B., & Robinson, G. A., Jr. (1951) An exploratory investigation of autistic perception. *J. abnorm. soc. Psychol.,* 46, 324–326.

Smith, K. U. (1951) Discriminative behavior in animals. In Stone, C. P. (Ed), *Comparative psychology.* New York: Prentice-Hall.

Smith, M., & Duffy, M. (1957) Consumption of sucrose and saccharine by hungry and satiated rats. *J. comp. physiol. Psychol.,* 50, 65–69.

Smith, M., & Duffy, M. (1957 a) Evidence for a dual reinforcing effect of sugar. *J. comp. physiol. Psychol.,* 50, 242–247.

Smith, M., & Duffy, M. (1957 b) Some physiological factors that regulate eating behavior. *J. comp. physiol. Psychol.,* 50, 601–608.

Smith, M., & Kinney, G. C. (1956) Sugar as a reward for hungry and non-hungry rats. *J. exp. Psychol.,* 51, 348–352.

Smith, M., Pool, R., & Weinberg, H. (1958) Evidence for a learning theory of specific hunger. *J. comp. physiol. Psychol.,* 51, 758–763.

Smith, M., Pool, R., & Weinberg, H. (1959) The effect of peripherally induced shifts in water balance on eating. *J. comp. physiol. Psychol.,* 52, 289–293.

Smith, M. P. (1951) The stimulus trace gradient in visual discrimination learning. *J. comp. physiol. Psychol.,* 44, 154–161.

Smith, O. A. (1956) Stimulation of lateral and medial hypothalamus and food intake in the rat. *Anat. Rec.,* 124, 363–364.

Smyth, C. J., Lasichak, A. G., & Levey, S. (1947) The effect of orally and intravenously administered amino acid mixtures on voluntary food consumption in normal men. *J. clin. Investig.,* 26, 439–445.

Snapper, I. (1955) Food preferences in man: Special cravings and aversions. In Miner, R. W. (Ed), *The regulation of hunger and appetite.* New York: Annals of the N. Y. Acad. of Sciences, 63, 92–106.

Snyder, F. W., & Synder, C. W. (1956) The effects of monetary reward and punishment on auditory perception. *J. Psychol.,* 41, 177–184.

Solley, C. M., & Lee, R. (1955) Perceived size: closure versus symbolic value. *Amer. J. Psychol.,* 68, 142–144.

Solley, C. M., & Santos, J. F. (1958) Perceptual learning with partial verbal reinforcement. *Percept. Mot. Skills,* 8, 183–193.

Solley, C. M., & Sommer, R. (1957) Perceptual autism in children. *J. gen. Psychol.,* 56, 3–11.

Solomon, R. L., & Howes, D. W. (1951) Word frequency, personal values and visual deviation thresholds. *Psychol. Rev.,* 58, 256–270.

Solomon, R. L., & Postman, L. (1952) Frequency of usage as a determinant of recognition threshold for words. *J. exp. Psychol.,* 43, 195–202.

Sommer, R., & Ayllon, T. (1956) Perception and monetary reinforcement: I. The effects of rewards in the tactual modality. *J. Psychol.,* 42, 137–141.

Spence, K. W. (1947) The role of secondary reinforcement in delayed reward learning. *Psychol. Rev.,* 54, 1–8.

Spence, K. W. (1956) *Behavior theory and conditioning.* New Haven: Yale Univ. Press.

Spence, K. W. (1958) A theory of emotionally based drive (D) and its relation to performance in simple learning situations. *Amer. Psychol.,* 13, 131–141.

Spence, K. W., & Beecroft, R. S. (1954) Differential conditioning and level of anxiety. *J. exp. Psychol.,* 48, 399–403.

Spence, K. W., & Farber, I. E. (1953) Conditioning and extinction as a function of anxiety. *J. exp. Psychol.,* 45, 116–119.

Spence, K. W., & Farber, I. E. (1954) The relation of anxiety to differential eyelid conditioning. *J. exp. Psychol.,* 47, 127–134.

Spence, K. W., Farber, I. E., & McFann, H. H. (1956) The relation of anxiety (drive) level to performance in competitional and noncompetitional paired-associates learning. *J. exp. Psychol.,* 52, 296–305.

Spence, K. W., Taylor, J., & Ketchel, R. (1956) Anxiety (drive) level and degree of competition in paired-associates learning. *J. exp. Psychol.,* 52, 306–310.

Spencer, H. (1872) *Principles of psychology.* London: Williams and Norgate.

Spencer, W. P. (1929) An ichthyometer. *Science,* 70, 557–558.

Sporn, J., & Necheles, H. (1956) Effect of glucagon on gastrointestinal motility. *Amer. J. Physiol.,* 187, 634.

Sprague, R. L. (1959) Effects of differential training on tachistoscopic recognition thresholds. *J. exp. Psychol.,* 58, 227–231.

Stanford, J. W., & Hsu, E. H. (1948) Experimental frustration in human adults. *J. clin. Psychol.,* 4, 269–276.

Stauffacher, J. C. (1937) The effect of induced muscular tension upon various phases of the learning process. *J. exp. Psychol.,* 21, 26–46.

Stebbins, W. C. (1959) Relation of amount of primary reinforcement to discrimination and to secondary reinforcement strength. *J. comp. physiol. Psychol.,* 52, 721–726.

Steggerda, F. R. (1939) The relation of dry mouth to thirst in the human. *Amer. J. Physiol.,* 126, 635.

Stellar, E. (1954) The physiology of motivation. *Psychol. Rev.,* 61, 5–22.

Stellar, E., & Hill, J. H. (1952) The rat's rate of drinking as a function of water deprivation. *J. comp. physiol. Psychol.,* 45, 96–102.

Stellar, E., Hunt, J. McV., Schlosberg, H., & Solomon, R. L. (1952) The effect of illumination on hoarding behavior. *J. comp. physiol. Psychol.,* 45, 504–507.

Stellar, E., & McCleary, R. A. (1952) Food preferences as a function of the method of measurement. *Amer. Psychol.,* 7, 256.

Sterling, T. D., & Cooper, G. P. (1957) Effects of irrelevant drive on extinction of bar-pressing. *Psychol. Repts.,* 3, 615–618.

Stewart, C. C. (1898) Variations in daily activity produced by alcohol and by changes in barometric pressure and diet, with a description of recording methods. *Amer. J. Physiol.,* 1, 40–56.

Stier, T. J. B. (1930) Spontaneous activity of mice. *J. gen. Psychol.,* 4, 67–99.

Stolurow, L. M. (1948) Rodent behavior in the presence of barriers. I. Apparatus and methods. *J. comp. Psychol.,* 41, 219–231.

Stone, C. P. (1922) The congenital sexual behavior of the young male albino rat. *J. comp. Psychol.,* 2, 95–153.

Stone, C. P. (1937) A sand tube obstruction apparatus. *J. genet. Psychol.,* 50, 203–206.

Stone, C. P. (1937 a) A paper-window obstruction apparatus. *J. genet. Psychol.*, 50, 206–209.

Stone, C. P., Tomilin, M. I., & Barker, R. G. (1935) A comparative study of sexual drive in male rats as measured by direct copulatory tests and by the Columbia Obstruction Apparatus. *J. comp. Psychol.*, 19, 215–241.

Strassburger, R. C. (1950) Resistance to extinction of a conditioned operant as related to drive level at reinforcement. *J. exp. Psychol.*, 40, 473–487.

Strominger, J. L., Brobeck, J. R., & Cort, R. L. (1953) Regulation of food intake in normal rats and in rats with hypothalamic hyperphagia. *Yale J. Biol. Med.*, 26, 55–74.

Strong, T. N., Jr. (1957) Activity in the white rat as a function of apparatus and hunger. *J. comp. physiol. Psychol.*, 50, 596–600.

Stunkard, A. J., Van Itallie, T. B., & Reis, B. B. (1955) The mechanism of satiety. Effect of glucagon on gastric hunger contractions in man. *Proc. Soc. Exper. Biol. and Med.*, 89, 258–261.

Stunkard, A. J., & Wolff, H. G. (1954) Correlation of arteriovenous glucose differences, gastric hunger contractions and the experience of hunger in man. *Federation Proc.*, 13, 147.

Stunkard, A. J., & Wolff, H. G. (1956) Studies on the physiology of hunger. I. The effect of intravenous administration of glucose on gastric hunger contractions in man. *J. clin. Investig.* 35, 954–963.

Symonds, P. M. (1946) *The dynamics of human adjustment.* New York: Appleton-Century-Crofts.

Taylor, J. A. (1951) The relationship of anxiety to the conditioned eyelid response. *J. exp. Psychol.*, 41, 81–92.

Taylor, J. A. (1956) Drive theory and manifest anxiety. *Psychol. Bull.*, 53, 303–320.

Taylor, J. A. (1956 a) Physiological need, set, and visual duration threshold. *J. abnorm. soc. Psychol.*, 52, 96–99.

Taylor, J. A., & Chapmen, J. P. (1955) Anxiety and the learning of paired-associates. *Amer. J. Psychol.*, 68, 671.

Taylor, J. A., & Spence, K. W. (1952) The relationship of anxiety level to performance in serial learning. *J. exp. Psychol.*, 44, 61–64.

Tell, K. S. (1952) Habit strength as a function of motivation during learning. *J. comp. physiol. Psychol.*, 45, 188–191.

Teel, K. S., & Webb, W. B. (1951) Response evocation in satiated trials in the T-maze. *J. exp. Psychol.*, 41, 148–152.

Teitelbaum, P. (1955) Sensory control of hypothalamic hyperphagia. *J. comp. physiol. Psychol.*, 48, 156–163.

Teitelbaum, P. (1957) Random and food-directed activity in hyperphagic and normal rats. *J. comp. physiol. Psychol.*, 50, 486–490.

Teitelbaum, P., & Campbell, B. A. (1958) Ingestion patterns in hyperphagic and normal rats. *J. comp. physiol. Psychol.*, 51, 135–141.

Teitelbaum, P., & Stellar, E. (1954) Recovery from the failure to eat produced by hypothalamic lesions. *Science,* 120, 894–895.

Templeton, R. D., & Quigley, J. P. (1930) The action of insulin on the motility of the gastro-intestinal tract. II. Action on the Heidenhain pouch. *Amer. J. Physiol.*, 91, 467–474.

Terrell, G. (1959) Manipulatory motivation in children. *J. comp. physiol. Psychol.*, 52, 705–709.

Thackray, R. I., & Michels, K. M. (1958) Externally-aroused drives in the racoon. *Anim. Behav.,* 6, 160–163.

Thistlethwaite, D. (1951) A critical review of latent learning and related experiments. *Psychol. Bull.,* 48, 97–129.

Thompson, G. G., & Hunnicutt, C. W. (1944) The effect of repeated praise or blame on the work achievement of 'introverts' and 'extroverts.' *J. educ. Psychol.,* 35, 257–266.

Thompson, W. R. (1953) Exploratory behavior as a funtcion of hunger in "bright" and "dull" rats. *J. comp. physiol. Psychol.,* 46, 323–326.

Thompson, W. R. and Heron, W. (1954) The effects of early restriction on activity in dogs. *J. comp. physiol. Psychol.,* 47, 77–82.

Thorndike, E. L. (1911) *Animal intelligence: experimental studies.* New York: Macmillan.

Tinbergen, N. (1951) *The study of instinct.* London: Oxford Univer. Press.

Tinbergen, N. (1957) On anti-predator responses in certain birds—a reply. *J. comp. physiol. Psychol.,* 50, 412–413.

Titchener, E. B. (1913) *A textbook of psychology.* New York: Macmillan.

Tolman, E. C. (1925–26) The nature of fundamental drives. *J. abnorm. soc. Psychol.,* 20, 349–358.

Tolman, E. C., Hall, C. S., & Bretnall, E. P. (1932) A disproof of the law of effect and a substitution of the laws of emphasis, motivation and disruption. *J. exp. Psychol.,* 15, 601–614.

Towbin, E. J. (1949) Gastric distention as a factor in the satiation of thirst esophagostomized dogs. *Amer. J. Physiol.,* 159, 533–541.

Treichler, F. R. (1960) The relationship between deprivation weight loss and two activity measures. Unpublished Ph.D. dissertation, The Penna. State Univer.

Tsai, C. (1925) The relative strength of sex and hunger motives in the albino rat. *J. comp. Psychol.,* 5, 407–416.

Tsang, Y. C. (1938) Hunger motivation in gastrectomized rats. *J. comp. Psychol.,* 26, 1–17.

Tyler, D. W., Wortz, E. C., & Bitterman, M. E. (1953) The effect of random and alternating partial reinforcement on resistance to extinction in the rat. *Amer. J. Psychol.,* 66, 57–65.

Vanderplas, J. M., & Blake, R. R. (1949) Selective sensitization in auditory perception. *J. Pers.,* 18, 252–266.

Van Itallie, T. B., Beaudoin, R., & Mayer, J. (1953) Arteriovenous glucose differences, metabolic hypoglycemia and food intake in man. *J. clin. Nutrition.,* 1, 208–217.

Vernon, J., & Hoffman, J. (1956) Effect of sensory deprivation on learning rate in human beings. *Science,* 123, 1074–1075.

Verplanck, W. S. (1955) Since learned behavior is innate, and vice versa, what now? *Psychol. Rev.,* 62, 139–144.

Verplanck, W. S. (1958) Comparative Psychology. In Farnsworth, P. R. (Ed), *Annual Review of Psychology.* Palo Alto, Calif.: Annual Reviews, Inc.

Verplanck, W. S., & Hayes, J. R. (1953) Eating and drinking as a function of maintenance schedule. *J. comp. physiol. Psychol.,* 46, 327–333.

Wald, G., & Jackson, B. (1944) Activity and nutritional deprivation. *Proc. Nat. Acad. Sci.,* Washington, 30, 255–263.

Wallen, D. (1942) Ego involvement as a determinant of selective forgetting. *J. abnorm. soc. Psychol.,* 37, 20–39.

Wang, G. H. (1923) The relation between "spontaneous" activity and oestrous cycle in the white rat. *Comp. Psychol. Monogr.,* 2, No. 6.

Wangensteen, O. H., & Carlson, A. J. (1931) Hunger sensations in a patient after total gastrectomy. *Proc. Soc. exp. Biol.,* N. Y., 28, 545–547.

Wapner, S., Werner, H., & Krus, D. M. (1957) The effect of success and failure on space localization. *J. Pers.,* 25, 752–756.

Ward, H. P. (1959) Stimulus factors in septal self-stimulation. *Amer. J. Physiol.,* 196, 779–782.

Warden, C. J. (1931) *Animal motivation, experimental studies on the albino rat.* New York: Columbia Univer. Press.

Warden, C. J., & Haas, E. L. (1927) The effect of short intervals of delay in feeding upon speed of maze learning. *J. comp. Psychol.,* 7, 107–116.

Warden, C. J., & Nissen, H. W. (1928) An experimental analysis of the obstruction method of measuring animal drives. *J. comp. Psychol.,* 8, 325–342.

Warren, J. M., & Hall, J. F. (1956) Discrimination of visual patterns as a function of motivation and frequency of reinforcement. *J. genet. Psychol.,* 88, 245–250.

Waterhouse, I. K., & Child, I. (1953) Frustration and the quality of performance. *J. Pers.,* 21, 298–311.

Watson, J. B. (1914) *Behavior, an introduction to comparative psychology.* New York: Holt.

Watson, J. B. (1917) Effect of delayed feeding upon learning. *Psychobiol.,* 1, 51–59.

Watson, J. B. (1919) *Psychology from the standpoint of a behaviorist.* Philadelphia: Lippincott.

Watson, J. B. (1925) *Behaviorism.* New York: Norton.

Watson, W. S., & Hartman, G. W. (1939) The rigidity of a basic attitudinal frame. *J. abnorm. soc. Psychol.,* 34, 314–335.

Wayner, M. J., Jr., & Reimanis, G. (1958) Drinking in the rat induced by hypertonic saline. *J. comp. physiol. Psychol.,* 51, 11–15.

Webb, W. B. (1949) The motivational aspect of an irrelevant drive in the behavior of the white rat. *J. exp. Psychol.,* 39, 1–14.

Webb, W. B. (1955) Drive stimuli as cues. *Psychol. Repts.,* 1, 287–298.

Webb, W. B., & Goodman, I. J. (1958) Activating role of an irrelevant drive in absence of the relevant drive. *Psychol. Repts.,* 4, 235–238.

Webb, W. B., & Nolan, C. Y. (1953) Cues for discrimination as secondary reinforcing agents: A confirmation. *J. comp. physiol. Psychol.,* 46, 180–181.

Weiner, I. H., & Stellar, E. (1951) Salt preference of the rat determined by a single-stimulus method. *J. comp. physiol. Psychol.,* 44, 394–401.

Weinstock, S. (1954) Resistance to extinction of a running response following partial reinforcement under widely spaced trials. *J. comp. physiol. Psychol.,* 47, 318–322.

Weinstock, S. (1958) Acquisition and extinction of a partially reinforced running response at a 24-hour intertrial interval. *J. exp. Psychol.,* 6, 151–158.

Welch, L., & Kubis, J. (1947) The effect of anxiety on the conditioning rate and stability of the PGR. *J. Psychol.*, 23, 83–91.

Welch, L., & Kubis, J. (1947 a) Conditioned PGR (psychogalvanic response) in states of pathological anxiety. *J. nerv. ment. Dis.*, 105, 372–381.

Welker, W. I. (1956) Some determinants of play and exploration in chimpanzees. *J. comp. physiol. Psychol.*, 49, 84–89.

Welker, W. I. (1956 a) Variability of play and exploratory behavior in chimpanzees. *J. comp. physiol. Psychol.*, 49, 181–185.

Welker, W. I. (1956 b) Effects of age and experience on play and exploration of young chimpanzees. *J. comp. physiol. Psychol.*, 49, 223–226.

Welker, W. I. (1957) "Free" versus "forced" exploration of a novel situation by rats. *Psychol. Repts.*, 3, 95–108.

Welker, W. I. (1959) Escape, exploratory, and food-seeking responses of rats in a novel situation. *J. comp. physiol. Psychol.*, 52, 106–111.

Wetzel, R. J. (1959) The effect of experience with a taste reward. *J. comp. physiol. Psychol.*, 52, 267–271.

Wever, E. G. (1932) Water temperature as an incentive to swimming activity in the rat. *J. comp. Psychol.*, 14, 219–224.

Whittaker, E. M., Gilchrist, J. C., & Fischer, J. W. (1952) Perceptual defense or response suppression? *J. abnorm. soc. Psychol.*, 47, 732–733.

Wickens, D. D., Hall, J., & Reid, L. S. (1949) Associative and retroactive inhibition as a function of the drive stimulus. *J. comp. physiol. Psychol.*, 42, 398–403.

Wiener, M. (1955) Word frequency or motivation in perceptual defense. *J. abnorm. soc. Psychol.*, 51, 214–218.

Wike, E. L. (1953) Extinction of a partially and continuously reinforced response with and without reward alternative. *J. exp. Psychol.*, 46, 255–260.

Wike, E. L., & Barrientos, G. (1957) Selective learning as a function of differential consummatory activity. *Psychol. Repts.*, 3, 255–258.

Wike, E. L., & Kintsch, W. (1959) Delayed reinforcement and runway performance. *Psychol. Rec.*, 9, 19–28.

Wike, E. L., & McNamara, H. J. (1957) Some training conditions affecting secondary reinforcement. *J. comp. physiol. Psychol.*, 50, 345–347.

Wike, E. L., & McNamara, H. J. (1957 a) The effects of percentage of partially delayed reinforcement on the acquisition and extinction of an instrumental response. *J. comp. physiol. Psychol.*, 50, 348–351.

Wilcoxon, H. C. (1952) "Abnormal fixation" and learning. *J. exp. Psychol.*, 44, 324–333.

Wilder, C. E. (1937) Selection of rachitic and anti-rachitic diets in the rat. *J. comp. Psychol.*, 24, 547–577.

Wilkins, L., & Richter, C. P. (1940) A great craving for salt by a child with cortico-adrenal insufficiency. *J. Amer. Med. Assoc.*, 114, 866–868.

Williams, D. R., & Teitelbaum, P. (1959) Some observations on the starvation resulting from lateral hypothalamic lesions. *J. comp. physiol. Psychol.*, 52, 458–465.

Williams, M. (1947) An experimental study of intellectual control under stress and associated Rorschach factors. *J. consult. Psychol.*, 11, 21–29.

Williams, M. (1951) Rate of learning as a function of ego-alien material. *J. Pers.*, 19, 324–331.

Willingham, W. W. (1958) Performance decrement following failure. *Percept. Mot. Skills*, 8, 199–202.

Wiln, E. C. (1925) *The theories of instinct, a study in the history of psychology*. New Haven: Yale Univ. Press.

Wilson, W., Weiss, E. J., & Amsel, A. (1955) Two tests of the Sheffield hypothesis concerning resistance to extinction, partial reinforcement and distribution of practice. *J. exp. Psychol.*, 50, 51–60.

Wispe, L. G. (1954) Physiological need, verbal frequency and word association. *J. abnorm. soc. Psychol.*, 49, 229–234.

Wispe, L. G., & Drambarean, N. C. (1953) Physiological need, word frequency and visual duration thresholds. *J. exp. Psychol.*, 46, 25–31.

Wolf, A. V. (1958) *Thirst: Physiology of the urge to drink and problems of water lack*. Springfield, Ill.: Charles C Thomas.

Wolf, S., & Wolff, H. G. (1943) *Human gastric function*. New York: Oxford Univer. Press.

Wolfe, J. B. (1937) The effect of delayed reward upon learning in the white rat. *J. comp. Psychol.*, 17, 1–21.

Wolfe, J. B., & Kaplon, M. D. (1941) Effect of amount of reward and consummative activity on learning in chickens. *J. comp. Psychol.*, 31, 353–361.

Woodworth, R. S. (1918) *Dynamic psychology*. New York: Columbia Univer. Press.

Woodworth, R. S. (1947) Reinforcement of perception. *Amer. J. Psychol.*, 60, 119–124.

Wright, M. E. (1942) Constructiveness of play as affected by group organization and frustration. *Charact. and Pers.*, 11, 40–49.

Wright, M. E. (1943) The influence of frustration upon the social relations of young children. *Charact. and Pers.*, 12, 111–122.

Wyckoff, L. B., Sidowski, J., & Chambliss, D. (1958) An experimental study of the relationship between secondary reinforcing and cue effects of a stimulus. *J. comp. physiol. Psychol.*, 51, 103–109.

Yamaguchi, H. G. (1951) Drive (D) as a function of the hours of hunger (R). *J. exp. Psychol.*, 42, 108–117.

Yamaguchi, H. G. (1952) Gradients of drive stimulus (S_D) intensity generalization. *J. exp. Psychol.*, 43, 298–304.

Yerkes, R. M., & Dodson, J. D. (1908) The relation of strength of stimulus to rapidity of habit-formation. *J. comp. neurol. and psychol.*, 18, 459–482.

Yerkes, R. M., & Elder, J. H. (1936) The sexual and reproductive cycles of chimpanzees. *Proc. Nat. Acad. Sci.*, Washington, 22, 276–283.

Young, P. T. (1936) *Motivation of behavior*. New York: Wiley.

Young, P. T. (1945) Studies of food preference, appetite and dietary habit. V. Techniques for testing food preference and the significance of results obtained with different methods. *Comp. Psychol. Monogr.*, 19, 1–58.

Young, P. T. (1946) Motivation. In Harriman, P. L. (Ed), *Encyclopedia of Psychology*. New York: Philosophical Library.

Young, P. T. (1955) The role of hedonic processes in motivation. In Jones,

M. R. (Ed), *Nebraska symposium on motivation.* Lincoln, Nebraska, Univer. of Nebraska Press.

Young, P. T. (1957) Continuous recording of the fluid-intake of small animals. *Amer. J. Psychol.,* 70, 295–298.

Young, P. T. (1959) The role of affective processes in learning and motivation. *Psychol. Rev.,* 66, 104–125.

Young, P. T., & Chaplin, J. P. (1945) Studies of food preference, appetite, and dietary habit. III. Palatability and appetite in relation to bodily need. *Comp. Psychol. Monogr.,* 18, 1–45.

Young, P. T., & Richey, H. W. (1952) Diurnal drinking patterns in the rat. *J. comp. physiol. Psychol.,* 45, 80–89.

Young, P. T., & Shuford, E. H., Jr. (1955) Quantitative control of motivation through sucrose solutions of different concentrations. *J. comp. physiol. Psychol.,* 48, 114–118.

Young, W. C., & Fish, W. R. (1945) The ovarian hormones and spontaneous running activity in the female rat. *Endocrinology,* 36, 181–189.

Zander, A. F. (1944) A study of experimental frustration. *Psychol. Monogr.,* 56, No. 3.

Zeaman, D. (1949) Response latency as a function of the amount of reinforcement. *J. exp. Psychol.,* 39, 466–483.

Zeaman, D., & Wegner, N. (1954) The role of drive reduction in the classical conditioning of an autonomically mediated response. *J. exp. Psychol.,* 48, 349–354.

Zeaman, D., & Wegner, N. (1957) A further test of the role of drive reduction in human cardiac conditioning. *J. Psychol.,* 43, 125–133.

Zeigarnik, B. (1927) Das Behalten erledigter und unerledigter Handlungen. *Psychol. Forsch.,* 9, 1–85.

Zeller, A. F. (1950) An experimental analogue of repression: I. Historical summary. *Psychol. Bull.,* 47, 39–51.

Zeller, A. F. (1950 a) An experimental analogue of repression: II. The effect of individual failure and success on memory measured by relearning. *J. exp. Psychol.,* 40, 411–422.

Zeller, A. F. (1951) An experimental analogue of repression: III. The effect of induced failure and success on memory measured by recall. *J. exp. Psychol.,* 42, 32–38.

Zillig, M. (1928) Einstellung und Aussage. *Z. Psychol.,* 106, 58–106.

Zimbardo, P. G., & Miller, N. E. (1958) Facilitation of exploration by hunger in rats. *J. comp. physiol. Psychol.,* 51, 43–46.

Zimbardo, P. G., & Montgomery, K. C. (1957) The relative strengths of consummatory responses in hunger, thirst, and exploratory drive. *J. comp. physiol. Psychol.,* 50, 504–508.

Zimbardo, P. G., & Montgomery, K. C. (1957 a) Effects of "free-environment" rearing upon exploratory behavior. *Psychol. Repts.,* 3, 589–594.

Zimmerman, D. W. (1957) Durable secondary reinforcement: method and theory. *Psychol. Rev.,* 64, 373–383.

Zimmerman, D. W. (1959) Sustained performance in rats based on secondary reinforcement. *J. comp. physiol. Psychol.,* 52, 353–358.

Zimny, G. H. (1956) Effect of various motivational techniques upon learning and performance tasks. *J. exp. Psychol.,* 52, 251–257.

NAME INDEX

Aborn, M., 235
Adams, C. R., 229
Adamson, J. F., 268
Adlerstein, A., 86, 120
Adolph, E. F., 142, 143
Aiken, E. G., 62, 63, 64
Alchek, E., 189, 190
Alexander, I. E., 95
Allee, R. A., 227
Allport, F. H., 13, 253
Allport, G. W., 42, 43, 45, 104
Alper, T. G., 224, 225
Alvarez, W. C., 288
Amsel, A., 101, 102, 103, 175, 189, 215
Anand, B. K., 299
Anderson, E. E., 45, 46, 49, 118, 125, 159
Anderson, J. E., 126
Andersson, B., 48, 305
Andrews, T. G., 231
Angell, J. R., 9
Anliker, J., 136
Antonitis, J. J., 76
Apicella, F. S., 237
Arenberg, D., 258, 260
Armus, H. L., 162, 184

Aronfreed, J. M., 269
Aronson, L. R., 15
Ashley, W. R., 262, 263
Atkinson, J. W., 108, 256, 257, 258
Auble, D., 220
Axelrod, H. C., 228, 230
Axelrod, H. S., 182
Ayllon, T., 274, 275, 278, 281
Ayres, C. E., 13

Backer, R., 59
Backlund, H. O., 115
Bailey, C. J., 187, 285
Bain, A., 56
Baker, R. A., 137, 138, 140, 141
Baker, R. W., 106, 108
Baldwin, J. M., 56
Banks, R. K., 268, 269
Bare, J. K., 141, 147, 149, 151
Barelare, B., Jr., 146, 147, 148
Barker, R. G., 156, 243, 244
Barnett, S. A., 89
Barrientos, G., 194
Barry, H., III, 160, 170
Bash, K. W., 288
Bass, B., 221
Bates, M. W., 294, 295

359

Fairchild, T. E., 146
Falconer, D. S., 127
Farber, I. E., 99, 103, 128, 181, 182, 186, 249, 250
Faris, E., 13
Fattu, N., 220
Fay, J. C., 198
Feddersen, W. E., 77, 213, 216
Fehrer, E., 86, 120, 198, 215
Felsinger, J. M., 192, 193
Ferster, C. B., 206
Fetherstonhaugh, M. L., 96
Finan, J. L., 168, 169
Finch, G., 102
Finger, F. W., 116, 117, 121, 122, 124, 125
Fischer, J. W., 269
Fish, W. R., 127
Fiske, D. W., 265
Fleck, F. S., 273
Fleishman, E. A., 231
Fleming, W. C., 77
Foa, P. P., 296
Forgays, D. G., 60, 96
Forlano, G., 228, 230
Fox, J., 182
Franklin, M., 233
Franks, C. M., 182
Frederiksen, N., 237
Freeman, G. L., 157, 183
Freeman, J. T., 268
Fregley, M. J., 136
Freides, D., 213
Freud, S., 11, 12, 100, 106, 234, 238
Frings, H., 150
Frommer, G., 175
Furchtgott, E., 197, 200

Galansino, G., 296
Gans, H. M., 127
Garafolo, L., 285, 288
Garner, W. R., 253
Gates, G. S., 228, 230
Gault, F. P., 285, 288
Gay, B. R., 77
Ghent, L., 141, 144, 306
Gilbert, G. J., 305
Gilbert, T. F., 160, 290
Gilchrist, J. C., 259, 264, 269
Gill, K., Jr., 77

Gilman, A., 305
Gladstone, A. I., 192, 193
Glanzer, M., 96
Glickman, S. E., 307
Glixman, A. F., 234
Goldiamond, I., 267
Goodman, C. C., 262, 264
Goodman, I. J., 179
Goodrich, K. P., 211
Goldstein, L. D., 269
Granich, L., 29
Grant, D. A., 164, 209, 215, 218, 220, 221, 229
Graves, E. A., 156
Greenberg, I., 47, 48
Greene, J. E., 200
Gregersen, M. I., 142, 144, 302
Grice, G. R., 177, 204, 205
Grindley, G. C., 196
Gropper, G. L., 268
Grosslight, J. H., 209, 210
Grossman, M. I., 289, 290, 291, 295
Guerrant, N. B., 126
Guttman, N., 197, 198

Hass, E. L., 203
Hack, E. R., 160
Haggard, D. F., 211
Haigh, G. V., 264
Hake, H. W., 209, 218, 253
Hall, C. S., 115, 278
Hall, J. F., 67, 68, 72, 116, 117, 118, 121, 131, 132, 133, 158, 162, 187, 209, 210
Hallaran, W. R., 293
Hamilton, E. L., 203
Hamilton, J. A., 239, 240, 241
Hamilton, R., 231, 232, 233
Hammes, J. A., 163, 164
Hanford, P. V., 116, 121
Hanratty, J. A., 187
Hardison, J., 229
Hargreaves, F. J., 149
Harker, G. S., 206
Harlow, H. F., 21, 79, 80, 81, 82, 90, 91, 98, 199, 200
Harlow, M. K., 80, 81, 98
Harper, R. S., 262, 263
Harriman, A. E., 151
Harris, L. J., 149